Henrietta L. Palmer

Home-Life in the Bible

Henrietta L. Palmer

Home-Life in the Bible

ISBN/EAN: 9783337175412

Printed in Europe, USA, Canada, Australia, Japan

Cover: Foto ©Lupo / pixelio.de

More available books at **www.hansebooks.com**

"HE STANDETH AT THE DOOR AND KNOCKETH."

Come In!

"*Come in, O gracious Form! I say —*
O Workman, share my house of clay!
Then I, at bench, or desk, or oar,
With last or needle, net or pen,
As Thou in Nazareth of yore,
Shall do the Father's will again."

Home-Life in the Bible

BY

HENRIETTA LEE PALMER

AUTHOR OF "THE STRATFORD GALLERY"

EDITED BY

JOHN WILLIAMSON PALMER

TWO HUNDRED AND TWENTY ILLUSTRATIONS

BOSTON
JAMES R. OSGOOD AND COMPANY
1881

Copyright, 1881,
By JAMES R. OSGOOD & CO.

All rights reserved.

*Electrotyped and Printed by Rand, Avery, & Co.,
Boston, Mass.*

Dedication.

TO

C. E. P.

WITH HIS MOTHER'S LOVE.

"My son, hearken unto me, . . . and mark my words with thy heart. I will show forth doctrine in weight, and declare His knowledge exactly."

ECCLESIASTICUS XVI. 24, 25.

A Thanksgiving for his Home

IN THE GREEN PARISH OF DEVONSHIRE.

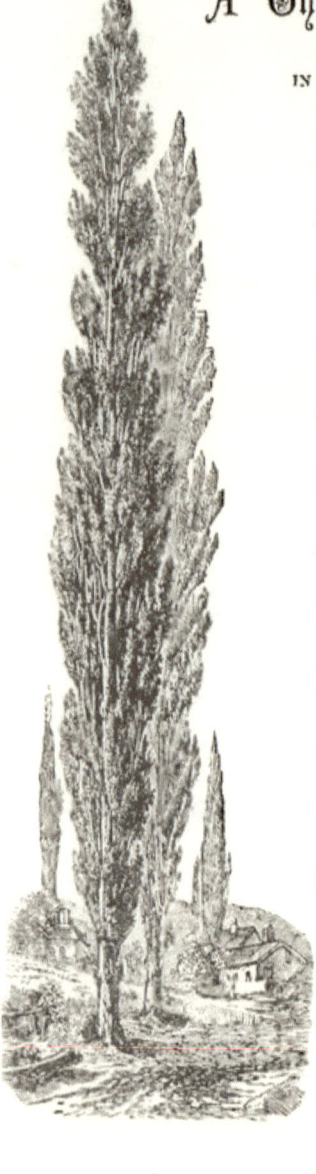

LORD! Thou hast given me a Cell
    Wherein to dwell;
A little House, whose humble Roof
    Is weather-proof,
Under the Spars of which I lie
    Both soft and dry;
Where Thou, my Chamber for to ward,
    Hast set a guard
Of harmless thoughts, to watch and keep
    Me while I sleep.
Low is my Porch, as is my fate,—
    Both void of state;
And yet the threshold of my Door
    Is worn by th' Poor,
Who thither come, and freely get
    Good words or Meat.
Like as my Parlor, so my Hall
    And Kitchin's small;
A little Buttery, and therein
    A little Bin,
Which keeps my little Loaf of bread
    Unchipt, unflead;
Some little sticks of thorn or briar
    Make me a Fire,
Close by whose living coal I sit,
    And glow like it.
Lord, I confess too, when I dine
    The Pulse is Thine;
And all those other bits that bee
    There placed by Thee:

The Worts, the Purslain, and the mess
　　Of Water-cress,—
Which of Thy kindness Thou hast sent;
　　And my Content
Makes those, and my beloved Beet,
　　To be more sweet.
'Tis Thou that crown'st my glittering Hearth
　　With guiltless Mirth,
And giv'st me Wassail-bowls to drink,
　　Spiced to the brink.
Lord, 'tis Thy plenty-dropping Hand
　　That soils my Land,
And gives me, for my Bushel sown,
　　Twice ten for one.
Thou mak'st my teeming Hen to lay
　　Her Egg each day,
Besides my healthful Ewes to bear
　　Me Twins each year.
The while the conduits of my Kine
　　Run Cream for wine.
All these, and better, Thou dost send
　　Me, to this end:
That I should render, for my part,
　　A Thankful Heart,
Which, fired with incense, I resign
　　As wholly Thine;
But the Acceptance, that must be,
　　My Christ, by Thee!

ROBERT HERRICK. [1651.]

Contents.

I.	Habitations and Homes	1
II.	Furniture and Utensils	34
III.	Marriage, Widowhood, and Divorce	53
IV.	Children: Their Training and Schooling	92
V.	The Higher Education	129
VI.	Employments and Servants	144
VII.	Larder, Kitchen, and Table	159
VIII.	Dress and Ornaments	203
IX.	The Toilet and the Bath	227
X.	Domestic and Public Worship	252
XI.	Music: Sacred and Secular	291
XII.	Alms and Hospitalities	300
XIII.	Seedtime and Harvest	312
XIV.	Flocks and Herds	332
XV.	Sickness and Death	366
XVI.	Burial and Mourning	380

List of Illustrations.

	PAGE
"He standeth at the Door, and knocketh"	Frontispiece
Vignette	i
Lombardy Poplars	vii
Dawn of Creation	1
An Ancient Stronghold	2
The Brick Mounds of Babylon	3
A Walled Town	5
A City Gate	6
Cavern at Banias: Head of the Jordan	7
Cave Dwellings	10
Tent-Life	11
An Encampment	12
Babel	13
Brick, with Name of Nebuchadnezzar	14
Masons of Ancient Egypt	15
Where Thieves break through	16
A Group of Dwellings	17
Battlemented House	18
Prayer on the House-Top	19
Roofs and Battlements	20
Conventional Ornament	21
Court of an Eastern House	22
The Court of the Garden	23
Outer Staircase	24
A Chamber on the Wall	25
Egyptian Latticed Window	26
Windows	26
Egyptian Door and Hinges	28
Egyptian Door	29
The Palm	31

LIST OF ILLUSTRATIONS.

	PAGE
EXTERIOR DECORATION	32
SCULPTURED PILLARS	33
WATER-POTS	34
DATE-PALM	36
ASSYRIAN COUCH	38
EGYPTIAN COFFERS, OR ARKS	39
SEVEN-BRANCHED CANDLESTICK	41
LAMPS	42
EGYPTIAN POTS AND PANS	43
PITCHERS	44
HAND-MILL	44
WOMEN AT THE MILL	45
EGYPTIAN EARTHEN VESSELS	46
SKIN BOTTLES	47
EGYPTIAN BASKETS	48
CONVENTIONAL ORNAMENT	50
SYMBOLICAL FIGURES	53
HAGAR AND ISHMAEL	55
FLOWER ORNAMENT	57
GROUP OF FLOWERS	60
RUTH AND BOAZ	61
CENSERS	66
THE WOOING OF REBEKAH	69
TOBIAS AND SARA	72
THE MARRIAGE FEAST AT CANA	75
THE BRIDEGROOM	77
BOUQUET OF ROSES	78
MUSICAL INSTRUMENTS	79
WEDDING PROCESSION	81
GROUP OF MUSICAL INSTRUMENTS	83
"THY WIFE SHALL BE AS A FRUITFUL VINE"	85
FLOWER ORNAMENT	87
JEALOUSY	89
VIGNETTE	91
THE STAR IN THE EAST	93
INNOCENCE	94
CHAPEL OF THE NATIVITY AT BETHLEHEM	96
SIMEON AND ANNA	97
SHRINE OF THE ANNUNCIATION AT NAZARETH	99
BETHLEHEM	100
CONVENTIONAL ORNAMENT	101
MOTHER AND CHILD	103
TURTLE DOVE	105

LIST OF ILLUSTRATIONS.

	PAGE
THE OFFERING	107
FLOWER PANEL	110
CORINTHIAN GAMES	112
WRESTLERS	113
WREATHS OF OAK AND OLIVE	115
THE PATRIARCH	117
CONVENTIONAL ORNAMENT	120
"SUFFER LITTLE CHILDREN TO COME UNTO ME"	122
"THE ANGEL, WHICH REDEEMED ME FROM ALL EVIL, BLESS THE LADS!"	123
TWO PAGES OF THE SAMARITAN PENTATEUCH	127
THE BOOK, OR ROLL IN ITS CASE	131
WRITING ON STICKS	133
THE PHARAOH OF THE NILE	135
SAMARITAN COPY OF THE LAW	137
MEDIEVAL BIBLES	138
EGYPTIAN WRITING IMPLEMENTS	140
FLOWER ORNAMENT	141
SEALS AND SIGNETS	143
BETHANY	144
A CARPENTER'S SHOP IN MODERN NAZARETH	146
CROSSING THE DESERT	148
THE SISTERS OF BETHANY	151
EASTERN LANDSCAPE	153
SIDE ORNAMENT	154
THE HEBREW NURSE	156
A HILL TOWN	158
HEAD-PIECE	159
ASSYRIANS FEASTING	160
ROMANS AT TABLE	160
EGYPTIAN TABLES	161
FLOWER PANEL	164
ASSYRIAN BRONZE KNIVES	167
EGYPTIAN COOKS	167
"HOW OFTEN WOULD I HAVE GATHERED THY CHILDREN TOGETHER"	169
ASSYRIANS HUNTING	171
HUNTING WILD BULLS	173
SEA OF GALILEE	175
JORDAN	179
OLIVE-JARS	182
SIDE ORNAMENT	183
THE GRAPES OF ESHCOL	185
CEDARS OF LEBANON	189
GREEK DRINKING-CUPS	191

LIST OF ILLUSTRATIONS.

	PAGE
ASSYRIAN ENTERTAINMENT	195
TREE OF THE "APPLES OF SODOM"	197
DATE-PALMS	199
FRUIT-PIECE	202
HEAD-PIECE	203
THE FRINGED GARMENT	204
THE PHYLACTERY	205
PALMS	208
HORNED HEAD-DRESSES	209
THE SITE OF BABYLON	210
VEILS	213
EGYPTIAN SHOES	214
THE PRODIGAL'S RETURN	215
SANDALS	218
EARRINGS AND NOSE-JEWELS	219
EGYPTIAN JEWELRY	220
EGYPTIAN BRACELET	221
MIRRORS	222
ORNAMENT	224
"THE PEARL OF THE EAST,"— DAMASCUS	226
ORIENTAL BARBER	227
EGYPTIAN HEAD-DRESSES	229
SIDE ORNAMENT	231
ALTAR OF INCENSE	233
ANTIQUE VASES	234
GREEK AND ROMAN ALABASTRA	239
THE FOUNTAIN IN THE COURT	243
BY THE NILE	245
EWER AND BASIN	246
SUPPOSED SCENE OF THE TRANSFIGURATION	247
ROMAN MIRROR AND VESSELS	248
FIG IN FLOWER AND FRUIT	250
GROUP OF FLOWERS	251
ALTAR PANEL	253
MOONLIGHT ON THE NILE	254
PRAYER IN THE GARDEN	256
CONVENTIONAL ORNAMENT	258
EARTHEN DIVINING BOWL OF BABYLON	262
ZION	264
THE FLIGHT INTO EGYPT	265
IN THE STABLE AT BETHLEHEM	269
UNLEAVENED BREAD	274
ALTAR PANEL	275

LIST OF ILLUSTRATIONS.

	PAGE
The Way of the Cross at Jerusalem	276
Dawn	281
The Mountain of the Scapegoat	283
Ecce Homo!	285
Passion-Flower	287
Gloria in Excelsis!	292
Ancient Stringed Instruments	293
"Strike the Cymbals"	294
Choir of Angels	295
Egyptian Cymbals	297
The Timbrel	298
Sunrise	299
"God loveth a Cheerful Giver"	301–
"If thine Enemy hunger, feed him"	305–
Samaritan Coins	309
The Shekel of the Sanctuary	310
The Sower	312
Egyptian Carts	314
Peacock of the Old Testament	315–
Ploughs, Yokes, and Goad	318
Threshing-Floor	321
Cedars of Lebanon	323
A Vineyard	325
Mount of Olives, and Garden of Gethsemane	329–
Sheep and Shepherd	332
Flocks and Herds reposing	334
Syrian Shepherd-Dog	335
Fat-Tailed Sheep	336
A Sheepfold	337
The Good Shepherd	339
Syrian Goat	340
Four-Horned Ram	341
Marking Cattle	343–
Camels Equipped for the Desert	346
The Desert, from the Wells of Moses	347–
Thistle	349
Lassoing Wild Asses	351–
Cactus	354
Jacob's Well	357–
Solomon's Pools	361–
"As the Hart panteth after the Water Brooks"	363
The Healed Waters of Jericho	365
Ancient Sun-Dials	367

xviii   LIST OF ILLUSTRATIONS.

	PAGE
"Go, wash in the Pool of Siloam!"	370
Panel	373
"In a Pleasant Land"	375
The Bird of the Tombs	377
"That I may die in mine own City"	378
Rock-Tombs in Syria	380
Tomb of David	381
At the Tombs	384
Released	387
Panel	390
Rachel's Tomb	393
The Wailing-Place: Wall of Jerusalem	396
Tear-Bottles	397
Repose	401

Home-Life in the Bible.

Home-Life in the Bible.

I.

HABITATIONS AND HOMES.

IN treating of Home-Life in the Bible, that first glorious home in Eden, whose "Builder and Maker was God," must be left to the sanctified imagination, to be spiritually discerned,—a vision of such supernal beauty that any attempt to depict it would be equally presumptuous and futile. It is not, then, the home of the once sinless pair whom God placed in His garden, with which we have to do, but the dwelling-places of their descendants, who, inheriting the consequences of the primal sin, inherited also, through the Divine mercy, the saving impulse of domestic love and co-habitation. It is our purpose to follow these, by the light of Scripture record and research, into the humble homes of a primitive people, whose needs were as simple as those of the beasts of the field or the fowls of the air.

The first plain assertion in the Bible suggestive of permanent habitations, clustered together for mutual convenience and security, is that Cain " builded a city, and called the name of the city after the name of his son, Enoch" (Gen. iv. 17). To reach any idea, however vague, of what is meant by a " city" in this primitive period, we must ignore all modern thought or experience. Such a settlement was certainly nothing more than a few tents or rude huts, where families were drawn together by ties of blood; or who for their agricultural or pastoral pursuits were attracted to a favorable locality; or for mutual defence against neighboring clans; or, most probably, for all these considerations combined.

AN ANCIENT STRONGHOLD.

For additional protection, a certain area around these habitations would be enclosed by a ditch and a stone hedge or wall, and so become a " fenced city." It was such a city that Cain built, for we are told that in the Oriental idiom to " build " a city means also to " fortify " or " fence " it; such the cities in which the Avims dwelt (Deut. ii. 23), — the word " Hazerim " in this text (translated " town " and " village " in others) meaning more correctly the temporary camping-grounds of wandering tribes, with a rude stone wall hastily thrown up for protection against wild beasts and marauders. So the tribes of Gad and Reuben, and the half-tribe of Manasseh, refusing to go over the river Jordan with the rest of

THE BRICK MOUNDS OF BABYLON.

Israel, said to Moses: "We will build sheepfolds here for our cattle, and cities for our little ones;" "They shall dwell in the fenced cities, because of the inhabitants of the land;" "Our little ones, our wives, our flocks, and all our cattle, shall be there in the cities of Gilead" (Num. xxxii. 16, 17, 26). It is easy to imagine what sort of "fenced cities" these husbands and fathers would build for the protection of their families and substance, while they "passed over, armed before the Lord, into the land of Canaan."

Very different, however, were the cities of the Canaanites, of which the children of Israel were going on, by Divine appointment, to take possession, — " great and goodly cities," said Moses, "which thou buildedst not, and houses full of all good things, which thou filledst not, and wells digged, which thou diggedst not, vineyards and olive-trees, which thou plantedst not" (Deut. vi. 10, 11). Even at the early period when Abraham came into Canaan, there were already many large towns, mentioned by name in the Book of Genesis: Sodom, Gomorrah, Zeboim, Admah, Hebron, and Damascus — which is almost certainly the

A WALLED TOWN.

oldest city in the world. It is probable that these towns were all walled, if not fortified; in the Book of Joshua we read of at least six hundred similar places taken by the Israelites, who drove the inhabitants before them out of the land. It is supposed that the high walls of even the fortified cities were not altogether of stone, but of some combustible materials, since the prophet Amos predicts of "Gaza," of "Tyrus," of "Teman" and "Rabbah," that the Lord "will send a fire on the wall . . . which shall devour the palaces thereof" (Amos i. 7, 10, 12, 14). The gates of a walled city were very imposing structures, rendered doubly secure by heavy plates of iron or brass, and bars: when St. Peter was delivered by an angel from the prison in Jerusalem, "they came unto the iron gate that leadeth unto the city, which opened of his own accord, and they went out" (Acts xii. 10); the Psalmist sings of the "wonderful works" of God: "For He hath broken the gates of brass, and cut the bars of iron in sunder" (cvii. 16); and Isaiah declares the word of the Lord to Cyrus: "I will go before thee, and make the crooked places straight: I will break in pieces the gates of brass, and cut in sunder the bars of iron" (xlv. 2). One of the wonderful exhibitions of Samson's miraculous gift of personal strength is recorded in this connection, of his exploit in the city of Gaza, the scene of his tragic end: he "arose at midnight, and took the doors of the gate of the city, and the two posts, and went away with them, bar and all, and put them upon his shoulders, and carried them up to the top of a hill that is before Hebron" (Judg. xvi. 3). The city gates were places of popular concourse, judgment-seats, halls of debate, and general trading exchanges; the large vaulted recesses in the gateways of ancient Assyrian cities are still used as shops for the sale of produce; and Elisha, prophesying deliverance from a prevailing famine, alludes to this custom: " To-morrow, about this time, shall a measure of fine flour be sold for a shekel, and two measures of barley for a shekel, in the gate of Samaria" (2 Kings vii. 1). Boaz went "up to the gate, and sat him down there,

A CITY GATE.

CAVERN AT BANIAS: HEAD OF THE JORDAN.

... And he took ten men of the elders of the city, and said, Sit ye down here; and they sat down," at the time he purchased the field from Naomi, and with it the young widow of Mahlon, her son, to be his wife (Ruth iv. 1, 2).

City gates were always supplied with one tower, often with two, for observation in time of war: as they were closed at sunset, there was a small, low gate in one side of the massive doors left open somewhat later for the accommodation of belated travellers. Some commentators find a reference to this little door in the words of our Saviour: " It is easier for a camel to go through the eye of a needle, than for a rich man to enter into the kingdom of God" (Matt. xix. 24); but there is, perhaps, a less obscure allusion to both of these gates of a city, in His solemn exhortation : " Enter ye in at the strait gate: for wide is the gate, and broad is the way, that leadeth to destruction, and many there be which go in thereat: because strait is the gate, and narrow is the way, which leadeth unto life, and few there be that find it" (Matt. vii. 13, 14).

The streets of these ancient towns were both crooked and narrow; in some of them — as in Alexandria, Cairo, Jerusalem, and Damascus to-day — two loaded camels could not pass each other, and the houses at a certain elevation almost touched from opposite sides.

To return to the dwellings in the primitive cities or camping-grounds of the Israelites, it is written of Jabal, the seventh generation after Adam, that " he was the father of such as dwell in tents." It seems reasonable, therefore, to suppose that caves in the earth, or frail huts made of mud or the boughs of trees, were the earliest dwellings known to the human family. We may certainly claim to discover one clan or tribe of " cave-dwellers " in the Horites (Gen. xiv. 6), whose name indicates them that dwell " in the cliffs of the valleys, in caves of the earth, and in the rocks" (Job xxx. 6): they were the aboriginal inhabitants of the sandstone and granite mountain-district of Seir, where their wonderful subterranean dwellings are still to be seen, and afford shelter to a humble race of shepherds and their flocks. But usually, it would seem that caves were used rather as places of temporary refuge or concealment, than as habitations; though they certainly offered many advantages — such as warmth and shelter from storm in winter, and coolness in summer — over the primitive hut or tent. The calcareous ranges of the Bible lands afforded such retreats in great abundance; and where Nature was less hospitable, they were artificially hewn in the rocky sides of the mountains. Thus, we are told of the conquered Israelites, that, "because of the Midianites the children of Israel made them the dens which are in the mountains, and caves, and strong holds" (Judg. vi. 2); so Lot "feared to dwell in Zoar; and he dwelt in a cave, he and his two daughters" (Gen. xix. 30); and in the later times of the apostles, those "of whom the world was not worthy: they wandered in deserts, and in mountains, and in dens and caves of the earth" (Heb. xi. 38).

CAVE DWELLINGS.

The familiar tent seems to us a much more agreeable dwelling: it was formed by setting poles in the ground, over which were stretched rude coverings, at first of skins, but after the process of weaving became common, of cloths made of camel's or goat's hair. Reference is made in the Song of Solomon to the tents covered with cloth made of black goat's hair by the descendants of the Ishmaelitish Kedar: "I am black, but comely, O ye daughters of Jerusalem, as the tents of Kedar, as the curtains of Solomon" (i. 5); and Isaiah eloquently magnifies the power of the Almighty, "that stretcheth out the heavens as a curtain, and spreadeth them out as a tent to dwell in" (xl. 22). The edges of the tent-covers were furnished with leather loops, to which were attached the cords of the tent, and these were fastened to the ground by means of iron or wooden pins. It was with one of these "nails of the tent" that Jael overcame Sisera, the great captain of king Jabin's army; and of her, Deborah and Barak sang: "Blessed above women shall Jael the wife of Heber the Kenite be; blessed shall she be above women in the tent. She put her hand to the nail, and her right hand to the workmen's hammer; and with the hammer she smote Sisera. At her feet he bowed, he fell, he lay down: at her feet he bowed, he fell: where he bowed, there he fell down dead" (Judg. v. 24–27).

TENT-LIFE.

Tents were of various shapes and sizes, requiring from one to nine poles: they could be divided into separate apartments by means of curtains, and the ground floor was covered with mats or skins; as of the Assyrian's tent, it is written that Judith's maid "went and laid soft skins on the ground for her over against Holofernes, which she had received of Bagoas for her daily use, that she might sit and eat upon them" (Jud. xii. 15). Wooden pegs driven into the poles of the tent answered all the domestic uses which are supplied to-day by wardrobes and closets; upon them were hung the wearing-apparel, the weapons for war or the chase, implements of husbandry, and the rude cooking-utensils in daily use. The door of the tent consisted of a heavy curtain of cloth, or a fold of the tent-cover, which might be raised at pleasure. Abraham "sat in the tent-door in the heat of the day," when the Lord appeared to him in the plains of Mamre, with the promise of that "seed" in which "shall all the nations of the earth be blessed" (Gen. xviii. 1); and in those days of the Exodus of Israel, "all the people rose up and worshipped, every man in his tent-door," while "the Lord spake unto Moses face to face, as a man speaketh unto his friend" (Exod. xxxiii. 10, 11). Is it any wonder, when Balaam looked from the top of Peor upon such an encampment of the hosts of the Lord,— "Israel abiding in his tents according to their tribes,"—that "the Spirit of God came upon him," and that "he took up his parable and said: How goodly are thy tents, O Jacob, and thy tabernacles, O Israel! As the valleys are they spread forth, as gardens by the river's side, as the trees of lign-aloes which the Lord hath planted, and as cedar-trees beside the waters" (Num. xxiv. 5, 6).

AN ENCAMPMENT.

This period, when the twelve tribes dwelt in tents, was of so much importance in their national history that at its expiration, on their entrance into "a peaceable habitation, and in sure dwellings, and in quiet resting-places," in the land promised to their fathers, God commanded them to keep the memorial Feast of Tabernacles forever: "Ye shall dwell in booths seven days . . . that your generations may know that I made the children of Israel to dwell in booths when I brought them out of the land of Egypt" (Lev. xxiii. 40–43).

Building materials are first described in the Bible in the account given by Moses of a journey undertaken by the descendants of Noah, when " they found a plain in the land of Shinar; and they dwelt there. And they said one to another, Go to! let

BABEL.

us make brick, and burn them thoroughly. And they had brick for stone, and slime had they for mortar. And they said, Go to! let us build us a city, and a tower, whose top may reach unto heaven" (Gen. xi. 2–4). This refers to the building of the famous Tower of Babel, of which, according to scientific travellers, there are three stupendous ruins that present equal claims to the distinction of having been the original of that presumptuous structure. One of these is described as "an oblong mass, composed chiefly of unbaked brick, rising from the plain to a height of one hundred and ten feet:" from which we may conclude that sun-dried bricks, cemented with mortar, bitumen, or simple clay, after the ancient method, were among the earliest building materials known; and frail as they appear, they are proved to be much more lasting than marble or granite. The superb palaces of the kings of Nineveh, and the Nimrood pyramid, were constructed chiefly of this crude brick; but the Babylonian edifices of importance were faced with bricks that had been burned or highly glazed. Egyptian bricks were made of clay moistened with water, with or without the admixture of straw, chopped barley, or stubble. All ordinary buildings — houses, tombs, fortresses, and even temples and pyramids — were constructed of this rude material: stone was used principally for the large public works, such as reservoirs and quays. It was customary to stamp Egyptian and Babylonian bricks with the name of the reigning sovereign. The pictorial monuments of Egypt represent the process of the manufacture of bricks, which was a royal monopoly: a shallow pit receives the mud or clay with the proper proportion of chopped straw, which is then mixed by the feet of the laborer, a very severe and fatiguing task. Nahum, foretelling the miserable straits of Nineveh, calls upon her to defend herself against her enemies: "Draw thee waters for the siege, fortify thy strong holds; go into clay, and tread the mortar, make strong the brick-kiln" (iii. 14). An ancient fresco from Thebes depicts the toil of the oppressed Hebrews in this special handicraft, in which the taskmasters with their whips are conspicuous objects of interest. Egyptian burnt brick is of a comparatively late date. In mountainous and rocky regions, where it was difficult to procure clay, hewn

BRICK, WITH NAME OF NEBUCHADNEZZAR.

or irregularly broken stone was used for public edifices, while the better class of private dwellings were built of blocks of light, porous limestone, cut with a rude saw. Amos speaks of the oppressors of the poor, the receivers of bribes, in his time, who had "built houses of hewn stone," representing them as dwellings of unusual luxury (Amos v. 11); David had prepared for the Temple "all manner of precious stones, and marble stones in abundance" (1 Chron. xxix. 2); the palace of the Persian king was upheld by "pillars of marble" (Esth. i. 6); Ahab made a "house of ivory" (1 Kings xxii. 39); David sings of "the ivory palaces" (Ps. xlv. 8); Amos speaks of "the winter house with the summer house; and the houses of ivory, and the great houses" (iii. 15); while Jeremiah describes by inference "a wide house and large chambers," with windows, "ceiled with cedar and painted with vermilion" (xxii. 14). These few allusions, taken at random, show that there were spacious and costly dwellings in ancient Palestine, other than the royal residences; but it is equally true that the homes of the lower classes were mere hovels made of mud, or rude brick, or heaps of stones, destitute of the simplest conveniences.

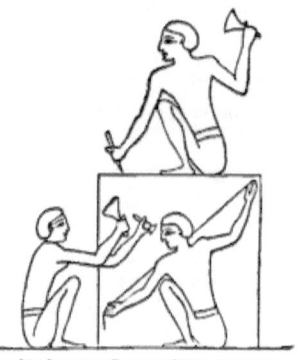

MASONS OF ANCIENT EGYPT.

There were several sorts of these clay houses, and those of the unburnt brick; others were constructed of a framework of light wood or wicker, overlaid with a thick plastering of mud; and in others the walls were made of layer upon layer of mud, which, having been rammed into moulds, was placed in position to dry as the work proceeded. Such walls cannot stand against heavy rains, and require to be thickly coated with a "tempered mortar" of lime or sand; the prophet teaches a profound moral lesson by the figurative use of these familiar processes:

"One built up a wall, and, lo! others daubed it with untempered mortar. Say unto them which daub it with untempered mortar, that it shall fall: there shall be an overflowing shower; and ye, O great hailstones, shall fall; and a stormy wind shall rend it" (Ezek. xiii. 10, 11).

It is easy to understand what a temptation these soft, penetrable walls offered to thieves: by means of any sharp instrument, or even a bit of wood, a man could make a hole in them without noise, and enlarge it to admit his body, by tearing away the clay and mortar. Job had these clay walls in mind, when he wrote of the thieves and assassins of his time: "In the dark, they dig through houses, which they had marked for themselves in the day-time" (xxiv. 16); and our Lord refers indirectly to the same houses, when He warns us of thieves that "break through (*dig*) and steal" (Matt. vi. 19).

WHERE THIEVES BREAK THROUGH.

But whatever the materials or mode of construction, there was no difference of opinion among these ancient builders as to the imperative necessity for a solid foundation. Job speaks, in a subtle figure, of "them that dwell in houses of clay, whose foundation is in the dust" (iv. 19); and it is literally true that none but the poorest would thus venture to build his house in the Holy Land. In the better class of habitations, it was usual to dig down to the solid rock for the foundation; a precautionary measure made necessary by the steep mountain heights and deep valleys of the country, and the suddenly overwhelming storms in the rainy season, whose torrents uprooted trees, overturned rocks, and carried away houses, in their angry course. In the Saviour's parable of the two house-builders, there could surely have been no "hard saying" to the natives of Palestine: "Whosoever cometh to me, and heareth my sayings, and doeth them, I will show you to whom he is like: He is like a man which built a house, and digged deep, and laid the foundation on a rock; and when the flood arose, the stream beat vehemently upon that house, and could not shake it; for it was founded upon a rock. But he that heareth, and doeth not, is

A GROUP OF DWELLINGS.

like a man that without a foundation built a house upon the earth; against which the stream did beat vehemently, and immediately it fell; and the ruin of that house was great" (Luke vi. 47–49). Not only floods, however, but the annual inundations, especially of Egypt, made the foundation of peculiar importance: in the land of the Nile, to this day, there is no security for towns, walls, structures of any sort, except by erecting them upon solid and enduring bases, natural or artificial.

A feature of the private dwellings of all ancient Oriental cities was the extreme and almost rude simplicity studiously affected for their external appearance. A succession of blank walls met the eye of the passer-by as he threaded his way along the narrow street, relieved only by the doors, some projecting windows, closely latticed, at a considerable elevation, and the wide staircases leading straight up to the flat roof, — the houses differing in size and the expensiveness of material, but all equally forbidding and plain.

We are apt to give undue prominence to the hemispherical roof in any notions we conceive of these ancient cities; whereas it is comparatively a recent invention, adopted by the Saracens for their mosques and other public buildings, and adhered to by their descendants. The only dome that can claim the precedent of antiquity is a sort of conical roof, peculiar to the rural districts, that also serves as a chimney for a rude fireplace in the middle of the hut it covers: there is an entire village of these curious little mud houses not far from Aleppo. The ancient sculptures preserve specimens of Assyrian houses with domes, built at least as early as 750 B. C. But the Orientals have, for very evident reasons, always given the preference to the flat roof for their private residences; and it must have been generally adopted at an early period by the Hebrews, since its mode of construction constituted a point of legal enactment in their eminently protective code: "When thou buildest a new house, then thou shalt make a battlement for thy roof, that thou bring not blood upon thine house, if any man fall from thence" (Deut. xxii. 8). This battlement, or parapet, was usually about breast-high, — somewhat lower, perhaps, between neighboring houses, to

BATTLEMENTED HOUSE.

divide roof from roof. One would think that few householders could be so reckless as to leave a housetop unguarded, where it was the daily resort of even the children of the family; especially as in the dry, hot summers it was also the general sleeping-place for all but the very young or the aged — the servants lying in the open court below. A certain part of the roof over the *alliyeh*, or upper chamber (of which we shall speak presently), elevated above and distinct from the main housetop, was the preferred place for private devotions — the pious Israelite, like Daniel, reviving his heart with at least a longing look toward the Holy House at Jerusalem; so, the Apostle Peter, lodging in Joppa with Simon the tanner, " went up upon the housetop to pray

PRAYER ON THE HOUSE-TOP.

about the sixth hour," and there beheld in a vision the Calling of the Gentiles (Acts x. 9). It was also a place of conference, as " Samuel communed with Saul upon the top of the house ; " and a resort after the heat of the day, for family groups to sit or walk, enjoying the cool air, as was the custom of the Psalmist, when at eventide " David arose from off his bed, and walked upon the roof of the king's house" (2 Sam. xi. 2); and so Nebuchadnezzar, the king, walked upon his palace, and boasted himself of the "great Babylon" that he had builded by the " might of *his* power, and for the honor of *his* majesty " (Dan. iv. 30). In houses where windows were sparingly introduced and seldom opened, it was natural that the housetop should be the place for sight-seeing (especially of the women and children), when something of public interest or excitement or danger was to be seen in the streets. Thus, when the Prophet laments the invasion by the Persian hosts, and eloquently apostrophizing his people under a figure, exclaims: " What aileth thee now, that thou art wholly gone up to the housetops! thou that art full of stirs, a tumultuous city!" (Isa. xxii. 1, 2), — he depicts the spirited scene of a community shaken to its centre by an impending calamity. In such crises of public peril and commotion, the housetop was not only a place of observation, but one of comparative safety, to which the family fled for refuge or escape; for where the dwellings were contiguous, as in large cities, it was practicable to traverse entire streets from roof to roof,

ROOFS AND BATTLEMENTS.

and thus reach the city walls or a locality remote from the imminent danger. Our Lord, warning His disciples of the approaching destruction of Jerusalem, admonished them: "Let him which is on the housetop not come down to take any thing out of his house" (Matt. xxiv. 17).

The housewife found the roof invaluable for various domestic purposes: here the clothes were hung to dry, cotton was bleached, wool and flax dried; while the fruits, vegetables, and grain, to be ripened or preserved for winter use, were here freely exposed to the wholesome operations of sun and air. In this connection, the reader will recall the hiding of the Hebrew spies by Rahab, in her house in the city of Jericho, when she "brought them up to the roof of the house, and hid them with the stalks of flax, which she had laid in order upon the roof" (Josh. ii. 6). Tents and booths were frequently erected on the roof, for protection from the sun by day, and the moon or heavy dews by night; or on some religious occasion, such as the Feast of Tabernacles, when the Israelites commemorated their dwelling in tents during the forty years' wandering in the wilderness; or in seasons of family mourning, as when Judith "made her a tent upon the top of her house," in which to afflict herself for the death of her husband Manasses (Jud. viii. 5).

Roofs were commonly constructed of large beams of timber — the tall poplar being preferred for this purpose; and of rude joists supporting smaller beams or brushwood, placed close together to receive a thick layer of mortar or clay, which required to be packed hard with a stone roller, — a process which needed to be repeated after every heavy rain. The light covering of clay and gravel made a leaky roof the frequent annoyance of the inmates of an Oriental house; and two allusions to this are found in the Book of Proverbs, both in a strictly domestic connection and to the same effect: "The contentions of a wife are a continual dropping;" "A continual dropping in a very rainy day and a contentious woman are alike" (xx. 13, xxvii. 15). A cement of oil and clay was sometimes employed to render the roof impervious to water, but the roller could seldom be dispensed with.

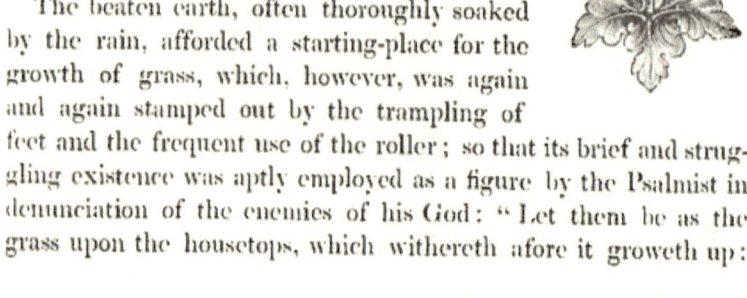

The beaten earth, often thoroughly soaked by the rain, afforded a starting-place for the growth of grass, which, however, was again and again stamped out by the trampling of feet and the frequent use of the roller; so that its brief and struggling existence was aptly employed as a figure by the Psalmist in denunciation of the enemies of his God: "Let them be as the grass upon the housetops, which withereth afore it groweth up:

wherewith the mower filleth not his hand, nor he that bindeth sheaves his bosom" (cxxix. 6, 7).

There are various opinions among interpreters of the text, as to the method employed by the four men who brought "one sick of the palsy" to Jesus: "And when they could not come nigh unto him for the press, they uncovered the roof where he was; and when they had broken it up, they let down the bed wherein the sick of the palsy lay" (Mark ii. 3, 4); but it is not difficult to discern the details of the sacred narrative when we consider that the houses of Capernaum were very low, and the flat roofs accessible by a stairway from the street or court; and that it was a matter of small moment to remove a portion of the rudely constructed roof (as is still done by the peasants in the villages of Palestine, to let down grain, straw, or other commodities into the house), and to lower the sick man by holding the corners of his "couch," or padded quilt.

The distinctive mode of constructing an Oriental house of the better class, was in the form of a cloister,—the apartments surrounding a hollow square, which was a courtyard, open to the sky. The houses of the wealthy had two or three of these courts: some in the ancient city of Damascus have seven, while the royal palaces had even more. These courts were paved with rare marbles, or laid out in gardens, with a fountain or cistern in the centre for family use, wherever the supply of water warranted a luxury so much esteemed by an Oriental. Where there was a court exclusively for the pleasure of the ladies of the house, and connected with their apartments, it was customary to provide a bathing-place in it for the use of the women and chil-

COURT OF AN EASTERN HOUSE.

dren: such a bath was in the "fair garden joining unto" the house of the wealthy Joacim, husband of the chaste Susanna (History of Susanna, i. 15); and in the court-yard of the house of Uriah the Hittite, at Jerusalem (2 Sam. xi. 2). On festive occasions of private entertainment, the court was elegantly decorated, covered with gay awnings, and furnished with carpets and mats. Mention is made in the Book of Esther of a superb royal feast given by Ahasuerus, "in the court of the garden of the king's palace, where were white, green, and blue hangings,

THE COURT OF THE GARDEN.

fastened with cords of fine linen and purple to silver rings and pillars of marble; the beds were of gold and silver, upon a pavement of red, and blue, and white, and black marble" (i. 5, 6). The Greeks and Romans erected altars to the household gods in the court-yards of their houses.

A veranda projected from the inner walls of the house, some nine or ten feet in width and surrounding the court usually on all four sides; the roof of this veranda — which, especially in Greek and Roman houses, was often paved with tiles — constituted a balcony for the apartments on the second floor, and was enclosed by a balustrade of stone or lattice work, — the whole supported by pillars, according to the Proverb: "Wisdom hath builded her house, she hath hewn out her seven pillars." All the rooms of the house opened upon this veranda, or the balcony above; in one corner of the court a staircase led up to the second story to the apartments commonly assigned to the women; and thence to the flat gravelled roof. Over the porch, or gateway of the house, there was usually a building one story higher than the main structure, the top of which was still more secluded than the roof proper: this contained one or two rooms that were set apart for guest-chambers, or, when large, for special entertainments.

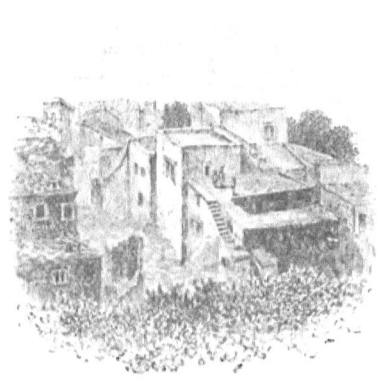

OUTER STAIRCASE.

This *alliyeh* was almost always provided with a separate staircase of wood or solid stone leading directly to the street, and which was the resort of flocks of tame pigeons or doves that built their nests under its cosey shelter: thus the mystic Song includes among the heralds of spring the familiar "voice of the turtle;" and the Bridegroom of the same sacred Pastoral addresses the Bride as one of these cherished family pets: "O my dove! that art in the clefts of the rock, in the secret places of the stairs" (ii. 12, 14).

The "little chamber" built on the wall by the "great woman" of Shunem for the prophet Elisha; the "summer-parlor" of Eglon, king of Moab, from which Ehud escaped by a private stairway (Judg. iii. 20); the "loft where abode" the prophet Elijah with the widow of Zarephath, and where, in answer to his prayer, the soul of her child returned to him again (1 Kings xvii. 19); the "chamber over the gate" of the city, to which

King David went up in his bereavement, weeping, and crying with a loud voice, "O my son Absalom! O Absalom, my son, my son!" (2 Sam. xviii. 33, xix. 4); the "upper chamber" in the house in Joppa wherein the dead body of Dorcas was laid by the widows, and restored to life by St. Peter (Acts ix. 37); the "upper chamber in Troas," where there were "many lights," and where St. Paul preached until midnight (Acts xx. 8),—all probably refer to this particular part of a well-appointed Oriental

A CHAMBER ON THE WALL.

home. Two of these apartments mentioned in the New Testament are endowed with associations of peculiar solemnity for Christians: the "large upper room furnished," in Jerusalem, in which the Lord ate the Passover with His apostles, and where He instituted the sacrament of the Holy Communion as a "perpetual memory of His death and sacrifice, until His coming again;" and that "upper room," also in the sacred city, wherein we catch the final glimpse of the august Mother of Jesus, as she continued in prayer and supplication with the "women" and "with His brethren," after the glorious ascension of her Son (Acts i. 12, 13, 14).

EGYPTIAN LATTICED WINDOW.

The "chambers over the gate" were commonly built so as to project beyond the original structure, and were supplied with windows overlooking the street. It was through the lattice of one of these windows in his upper chamber, that Ahaziah, king of Samaria, "fell down" and "died, according to the word of the Lord which Elijah had spoken" (2 Kings i. 2); and to such a one Jezebel, the proud widow of King Ahab, having "painted her face and tired her head," came and looked out "as Jehu entered in at the gate;" but out of the same window looked her two or three eunuchs. And Jehu said, "Throw her down. So they threw her down" (2 Kings ix. 30, 32, 33). In the triumphant "song of Deborah and Barak" we find another allusion to the latticed window, in the pathetic picture of the mother of the murdered warrior watching for her son, as yet unconscious of her loss, while her companions beguile her impatience: "The mother of Sisera looked out at a window, and cried through the

WINDOWS.

lattice, Why is his chariot so long in coming? why tarry the wheels of his chariots? Her wise ladies answered her; yea, she returned answer to herself, Have they not sped? have they not divided the prey: to every man a damsel or two; to Sisera a prey of divers colors, a prey of divers colors of needlework, of divers colors of needlework on both sides, meet for the necks of them that take the spoil? So let all thine enemies perish, O Lord! but let them that love him be as the sun when he goeth forth in his might" (Judg. v. 28–31).

The entrance to such houses as have just been described was by a street door of heavy wood or stone, which was kept locked and in charge of a porter. These doors were not hung on hinges, but swung in sockets that were contrived in the lintel overhead and in the threshold; a smaller gate was often cut in the door, which was easily opened, and more commonly used. The porter, usually a woman, was summoned with the "knocker," a large iron ring fastened on the outside; but admittance was by no means granted until certain questions had been satisfactorily answered by the applicant. It was not until "she knew Peter's voice" that Rhoda, the porter at the gate of Mary's house, admitted him into the presence of those who had "made prayer without ceasing" for his release (Acts xii. 13, 14). But a greater than Peter speaks while He waits outside: "Behold, I stand at the door, and knock: if any man hear my voice, and open the door, I will come in to him, and will sup with him, and he with me" (Rev. iii. 20). And so the Church sings: "It is the voice of my beloved, that knocketh" (Song of Solomon, v. 2).

This door, or "door of the gate," opened into the porch, which was provided with seats and constituted a sort of antechamber, as well as passage-way, to the court, and to the staircase that led to the upper floor. So jealous of privacy, however, were the inmates, that no view of the court could be obtained by the visitor in the act of entering, or by the casual passer-by; for the door opening from the porch into the court was never directly opposite the street door. The porch of the palace of the High Priest was the place into which St. Peter went out "and wept bitterly," at the fulfilment of the Lord's prophecy: "Before the cock crow twice, thou shalt deny me thrice."

The doors of these ancient homes were secured by a lock, frequently depicted on Egyptian sculptures, that consisted of a long hollow bar of wood, made to slide easily back and forth into

EGYPTIAN DOOR AND HINGES.

a hole made for it in the door-post. Here it was fastened in its place by small bolts of iron that fell into holes bored for them in the top of the lock. A hole was made in the door, through which, when the door was unlocked from the outside, it was necessary to pass the hand and insert the key; a custom to which allusion is made in the Song of Songs, "My beloved put in his hand by the hole of the door" (Solomon's Song, v. 4). The keys were large and clumsy, ordinarily of wood, and from six inches to two feet in length, with wire pins at the end with which to unfasten the lock; in later times they were furnished with handles of brass or even silver, ornamented with filagree work. Very ancient keys are described as shaped like a sickle and carried on the shoulder, particularly as a symbol of official authority, as referred to in the prophetic warning to Shebna, the corrupt treasurer of Hezekiah: "the key of the house of David will I lay upon his (Eliakim's) shoulder" (Isa. xxii. 22); and in Isa. ix. 6, where it is proclaimed of the coming Saviour that "the government shall be upon His shoulder;" and where our Lord says to St. Peter: "I will give unto thee the keys of the kingdom of heaven" (Matt. xvi. 19).

The doors of the inner chambers of palaces, and of the dwellings of the wealthy, were also furnished with locks to secure personal privacy: thus when "Ehud went forth through the porch" from Eglon, king of Moab, "he shut the doors of the parlor upon him, and locked them;" and the servants of the king, "having tarried till they were ashamed," "took a key, and opened them" (Judg. iii. 23, 25).

EGYPTIAN DOOR.

In the open country, where houses were exposed to the assaults of robbers, the gates were made very low, so as to prevent predatory bands of horsemen from entering through the porch into the court-yard. The doors of city houses, also, were frequently made very low and unattractive, to divert the attention of covetous men in high places from the displays of wealth within. One of the Proverbs of Solomon warned the builder of his time, that "He that exalteth his gate seeketh destruction" (Prov. xvii. 19);

by which he doubtless meant loss, not only from the professed marauders native to the country, but by the envious cupidity of high-handed men in power, who, attracted by the display of wealth, would not hesitate to enrich themselves by polite and "legal" methods, not altogether unfamiliar to later generations. Portal inscriptions were in use among the ancient Egyptians, who wrote not only the name of the resident, but some sentences of good import, upon the doors of their houses. The Jews of a very early period adopted a sort of phylactery for the house, in fulfilment of the command to keep the law of God always before their eyes, by inscribing it upon the door-posts and gates of their houses: "Therefore shall ye lay up these my words in your heart and in your soul. And thou shalt write them upon the doorposts of thine house, and upon thy gates" (Deut. xi. 18, 20). Certain passages of Scripture were written on parchment specially prepared for the purpose, having the Hebrew character representing the name of the Almighty on the outside. When rolled up and placed within a metal cylinder called the "Mesusah," and hung at the right-hand door-post of every "clean" apartment in the house, all that could be seen of the writing was the Holy Name, exposed to view through an aperture in the case. This Name was touched by the finger, and the finger kissed, as the members of the family went in and out with some words of prayer. The Mesusah was significant of the Divine protection, this promise having special reference to it: "The Lord shall preserve thy going out and thy coming in, from this time forth, and even for evermore" (Ps. cxxi. 8).

"The 'Mechilta,' an ancient Jewish commentary on the Book of Exodus, argues the efficacy of the Mesusah from the fact that since the destroying angel passed over the doors of Israel that bore the covenant-mark, a much higher value must attach to the Mesusah, which embodied the Name of the Lord no less than ten times, and was to be found in the dwellings of Israel day and night through all generations." It was believed to avert disease, and forbid the entrance of evil spirits.

HABITATIONS AND HOMES.

There is occasional mention of hearths and chimneys in the Bible, but we must not confound these domestic arrangements in primitive times with those of our own day. The first mention of a hearth is where Abraham, on the occasion of the visit of the angels, on the plains of Mamre, " hastened into the tent unto Sarah, and said, Make ready quickly three measures of fine meal, knead it, and make cakes upon the hearth" (Gen. xviii. 6); this " hearth" being the hot stones on which bread was baked. The word generally signifies the portable furnace, or stove filled with burning coals, which is in use for warming Eastern apartments to this day. Such was the hearth into which King Jehoiakim threw the leaves of Jeremiah's prophecy. " Now the king sat in the winter house in the ninth month; and there was a fire on the hearth burning before him. And it came to pass, that when Jehudi had read three or four leaves, he cut it with the penknife, and cast it into the fire that was on the hearth, until all the roll was consumed in the fire that was on the hearth" (Jer. xxxvi. 22, 23).

In the allusion to a chimney · " as the smoke out of the chimney" (Hos. xiii. 3), the same Hebrew word is employed that in other parts of Scripture is translated " window." The smoke found its way out through the windows, or in some cases through holes constructed near the ceiling for that purpose.

The " leprosy of the house," so minutely described and provided for in Lev. xiv. 34, is supposed to have been caused by the growth on the walls of two species of fungi, in reddish and greenish patches, very destructive and virulent in their effects, poisoning the air and producing disease. The admirable sanitary laws that prevailed among the ancient Israelites are specially commendable in their application to these infected buildings, which, in extreme cases, were commanded to be pulled down.

It was customary to dedicate a new dwelling, — "What man is there that hath built a new house, and hath not dedicated it?" (Deut. xx. 5), — but with what ceremonies does not appear; probably a social entertainment resembling a modern house-warming, combined with devotional exercises. A house recently obtained by inheritance or purchase might also be dedicated, as well as granaries and barns, which could in an emergency be used as dwellings; but this observance was not allowable for houses not convertible to family uses. The Thirtieth Psalm was composed, so the title runs, "at the dedication of the house of David;" and we have a record of the great public rejoicing at the completion of the wall of the holy city in the time of Nehemiah: "And at the dedication of the wall of Jerusalem they sought the Levites out of all their places, to bring them to Jerusalem, to keep the dedication with gladness, both with thanksgivings, and with singing, with cymbals, psalteries, and with harps" (Neh. xii. 27); as well as at the dedication of the Second Temple, of which it is recorded that Israel: "kept the dedication of this house of God with joy, and offered at the dedication of this house of God a hundred bullocks, two hundred rams, four hundred lambs; and for a sin offering for all Israel, twelve he goats, according to the number of the tribes of Israel" (Ezra vi. 15, 16, 17).

EXTERIOR DECORATION.

In the houses of the rich the woodwork was of olive, acacia, or cedar, and in the palaces, even the costly Indian sandalwood was introduced; the window-frames and lattices were often elaborately decorated with carving and inlaying, — a profuse veneering of ivory being the preferred extravagance in the reign of Solomon, who deprecatingly records of his own extensive architectural achievements: "I builded me houses" (Eccles. ii. 4). But however curious and elegant the carvings, no reproduction of any living creature was permitted in the Jewish house.

"So profound was the religious prejudice of the people on this point, that the palace of Herod Antipas at Tiberias was destroyed by a mob because it was decorated with representations of animals."

The expression "ceiled houses" indicates the prominence given to the decoration of the ceiling, as described in Jeremiah (xxii. 14): "ceiled with cedar, and painted with vermilion;" these were often

SCULPTURED PILLARS.

supported by rows of pillars richly ornamented. The walls and ceilings of plainer dwellings were simply washed, with whitewash or some neutral tint, the rude woodwork being usually of sycamore, without ornamentation.

II.

FURNITURE AND UTENSILS.

WATER-POTS.

HOWEVER elaborate the interior arrangements and decorations of the more costly homes of the Bible, their appointments necessarily responded to the simple needs of a primitive race, and, except in royal houses, were comparatively meagre and insignificant. In the homes of the poor in cities, consisting of two or three small rooms, all that was required for the comfort of the family was a coarse carpet, or mat of goat's hair, for the floor of the principal apartment; some thin mattresses and pillows, filled with cotton or straw, to be spread on the floor at night; a low stand, or only a sort of leather "crumb-cloth," for a dinner-table; the universal hand-mill, alluded to in Matt. xxiv. 41;— some dishes of rude pottery, wooden spoons, and a few plain cooking-utensils.

The requisite conveniences for the daily use of the wealthy scarcely surpassed this inventory, except as to intrinsic value and personal luxury; even in the houses of the better class, the principal apartment or reception room in daily use was on the ground floor, and opened to the court, as already described: it was furnished at one end with a platform, ten or twelve inches higher than the floor, and perhaps three feet in width, which usually extended around the three sides of that part of the room. This platform, or divan, was covered with carpets, or thick stuffs, sometimes of home manufacture, and was provided with cushions on which to sit or recline in Oriental fashion, — the corner being esteemed the seat of honor. Here the master of the house received and chatted with his guests; or, if a Hebrew, in the privacy of the domestic circle, sat at meat, surrounded by his family, in all the blessedness of the literal fulfilment of the promise, dear to the pious heart: "Thou shalt eat the labor of thine hands: happy shalt thou be, and it shall be well with thee. Thy wife shall be as a fruitful vine by the sides of thine house: thy children like olive plants round about thy table" (Ps. cxxviii. 2, 3).

At night, when too cool to sleep on the roof of the house, this large room was readily converted into a dormitory for the entire household, by spreading separate mattresses, with pillows and coverlets, at intervals on the cushioned platform and divans. In the light of this ancient custom we read more intelligently the parable, wherein the night-traveller would borrow bread of his friend: "And he from within shall answer and say, Trouble me not the door is now shut, and my children are with me in bed; I cannot rise and give thee" (Luke xi. 7), — the Greek expression for "in bed" implying rather in the same *room*, than in the same *bed*.

In royal palaces, the king's bed was probably made on a much more elevated platform, as we may infer from Elijah's message to the guilty Ahaziah: "Now therefore thus saith the Lord, Thou shalt not come down from that bed on which thou art gone up, but shalt surely die" (2 Kings i. 4); and from David's devout asseveration: "Surely I will not come into the tabernacle of my house, nor go up into my bed; I will not give sleep to mine eyes, or slumber to mine eyelids, until I find out a place for the Lord, a habitation for the mighty God of Jacob" (Ps. cxxxii. 3).

The beds referred to in the miracles of healing, recorded in the New Testament: the impotent man who "took up his bed and walked" (John v. 9); the "sick of the palsy," who obeyed the Divine command: "Arise, take up thy bed, and go unto thy house" (Matt. ix. 6); the paralytic, "borne of four" who "let down the bed" on which he lay "into the midst before Jesus" (Mark ii. 4; Luke v. 18); as well as the beds on which the sick were laid in the streets of Jerusalem, "that at the least the shadow of Peter, passing by, might overshadow some of them" (Acts v. 15),—all these were the simple mats or padded quilts in use among the common people, which had only to be rolled up, and carried on the shoulder by the restored invalids in question.

At one end of the large room, furnished with the divan, there was a commodious closet, built expressly for the reception and storing of the bedding used at night: in very cold weather the beds might be laid for use within this enclosure, but this was unusual. We read, that at the time of Athaliah's dreadful massacre of the seed royal, after her son Ahaziah's death: "Jehosh-eba, the daughter of king Joram, sister of Ahaziah, took Joash the son of Ahaziah, and stole him from among the king's sons which were slain; and they hid him, even him and his nurse, in the bedchamber from Athaliah, so that he was not slain" (2 Kings xi. 2). The bedchamber is literally rendered, "in the chamber of beds," and undoubtedly refers to the storeroom for bedding, which would afford every convenience for concealment. The houses of the poor had no such closet: the bedding was rolled up, and stored in a corner of the room.

The pillow in ordinary use was probably a goat's skin, stuffed with wool or other soft substance, such as David's wife made use of in her device to conceal his flight from King Saul: "And Michal took an image, and laid it in the bed, and put a pillow of goats' hair for his bolster, and covered it with a cloth" (1 Sam. xix. 13). When Saul was in camp "in the hill of Hachilah" and "lay sleeping within the trench," it is recorded that David took "the spear and the cruse of water from Saul's *bolster*" (1 Sam. xxvi. 12); and it is suggested that in this case as well as in that of the prophet Elijah under the juniper-tree, who found "a cruse of water at his head" (1 Kings xix. 6), the leather bottle filled with water was both cruse and bolster. The pillow "in the hinder part of the ship," on which Jesus lay asleep, was the rough cushion on which the rowers sat when pulling the oars (Mark iv. 38).

We find our familiar term "bedstead" only once in the Bible; and that is in Deut. iii. 11, where Moses records of Og, king of Bashan — who alone "remained of the remnant of giants" — that his "bedstead was a bedstead of iron;" "nine cubits was the length thereof, and four cubits the breadth of it, after the cubit of a man." By computing the proportions of this antique article of furniture at the ordinary measure of the cubit (sixteen or eighteen inches), we can readily perceive how it might command the attention of even the great lawgiver. But the Sacred Books afford many allusions to beds, which plainly signify bedsteads of whatever primitive sort, and which doubtless came

into general use with the Jews after their entrance into Canaan.
Bedsteads of wood and metal were common among the Egyptians, as their sculptures testify; Israel, dying in Egypt, " bowed
himself upon the bed's head;" King Solomon made himself a
"*bed*" (marginal reading) "of the wood of Lebanon; he made
the pillars thereof of silver, the bottom thereof of gold, the
covering of it of purple" (Solomon's Song iii. 9). In the profuse
and licentious time of Amos the prophet, he boldly denounces
them that "lie upon beds of ivory and stretch themselves upon
their couches," as well as those "that dwell in Samaria in the
corner of a bed, and in Damascus in a couch" (Amos vi. 4, iii.
12). Solomon, in his Proverbs, introduces us to an Oriental bed
of the utmost luxuriousness, — a bed "decked with coverings of
tapestry, with carved works, with
fine linen of Egypt;" and "perfumed with myrrh, aloes, and
cinnamon" (Prov. vii. 16); while
even in a tent in camp, Holofernes, the chief captain of the
Assyrian hosts, slept "under a
canopy which was woven with
purple and gold and emeralds
and precious stones," — a piece
of work so superb that the beautiful Jewess of the apocryphal story, who delivered her people by slaying this luxurious
warrior, thought it not unworthy to be dedicated as a gift to the
Lord (Jud. xvi. 19). We read also in the first chapter of the
Book of Esther, of "beds of gold and silver" in connection with
a royal feast; but these beds were the couches on which the
guests reclined at the banqueting tables, after the fashion of the
Persian court. They were probably frameworks of wood, inlaid
with the precious metals, on which were cushions covered with
rich silken stuffs, interwoven with gold and silver threads. The
beds themselves were (for the wealthy) stuffed with feathers and
swan's-down; but a less luxurious sort were filled with wool, seaweed, or woolly plants, or even hay and straw. Cushions and

ASSYRIAN COUCH.

pillows to correspond were furnished for the support of the left arm, on which it was usual to lean, leaving the right hand free. It was upon such a bed that Haman fell at the "banquet of wine" given to King Ahasuerus by the queen (Esth. vii. 8); and such the "stately bed, and a table prepared before it." that the prophet refers to (Ezek. xxiii. 41).

The Egyptian carpenters were very skilful in the manufacture of articles of furniture for the house: the principal woods employed for this purpose were the date or the Theban palm, acacia, and sycamore, — the fir, ebony, and cedar being reserved for the finest cabinet work. They excelled in the arts of veneering with ivory and metals; and in the imitation of rare, expensive woods imported from Ethiopia and Asia, for the benefit of those householders whose means failed to correspond with their luxurious tastes. Monumental models exhibit their ingenuity in the manufacture of cabinets or tables having secret drawers, and of curious boxes. Some of these, says Wilkinson, " had lids resembling the curved summit of a royal canopy, and were ornamented with the usual cornice; others had a simple flat cover, and some few a pointed summit, resembling the shelving roof of a house."

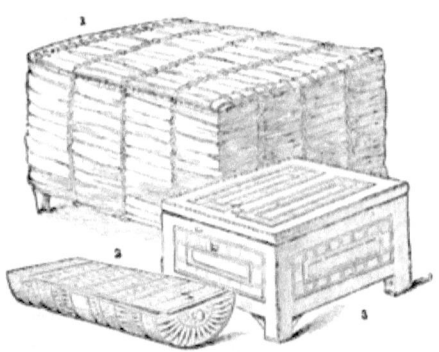

EGYPTIAN COFFERS, OR ARKS.

Every residence of any pretension was furnished with the articles now considered essential to a well-appointed establishment; many of the couches and chairs, especially, were elegant in form, made of choice woods, and covered with stamped or embossed leather or with rich stuffs; the heads, legs, and even the entire bodies of animals were favorite devices of ornamentation. In the description of Solomon's throne we observe an example of this style of ancient art which was plainly opposed to Jewish precept and prejudice: "The king made a great throne of ivory, and overlaid it with the best gold. The throne had six steps, and the top of the throne was round behind; and there were stays on either side on the place of the seat, and two lions stood beside the stays. And twelve lions stood there on the one side and on the other upon the six steps: there was not the like made in any kingdom" (1 Kings x. 18–20).

The use of chairs and stools was very general among the early Hebrews, who were slow to adopt the effeminate custom of sitting or reclining on cushions. These familiar articles are frequently mentioned in the Scriptures; we read that "Eli the priest sat upon a seat by a post of the temple of the Lord" (1 Sam. i. 9); and when, being an "old man and heavy," tidings were brought him of the death of his sons, and that the Ark of God had been taken by the Philistines, "he fell from off the seat backward by the side of the gate, and his neck brake, and he died" (1 Sam. iv. 18). Humble homes were provided with seats from eight to fourteen inches high, made of wood or wicker laced together with thongs, in the manner of our rush-bottomed chairs. The "stool" furnished by the Shunamite woman for the use of the prophet Elisha, in the "little chamber on the wall," was by no means the rude article its name suggests; the Hebrew word so translated is, in some other passages, equivalent to "throne." We may therefore conclude that this pious lady provided handsomely for the entertainment of her exalted guest. The table mentioned in the same connection (2 Kings iv. 10) was doubtless intended to hold the candlestick with its candle or lamp that burned through the night, according to the custom referred to in the delineation of a "Virtuous Woman" of that time: "her candle goeth not out by night" (Prov. xxxi. 18).

The candlestick or lamp-stand was made in varied forms, often very beautiful in design and workmanship,—of brass, silver, bronze, or even gold, and from one to four feet in height. That in use among the common people was made of wood, and in the ruder dwellings, with mud walls, it was often nothing more than a projection of clay at a convenient height, contrived in the process of building, and hollowed to receive the oil and wick.

The candlestick so familiar to us as an illustration in the Sermon on the Mount was probably one of the tall stands in use at that time, not placed on a table, but in the centre of the floor: "Neither do men light a candle, and put it under a bushel, but on a candlestick; and it giveth light unto all that are in the house" (Matt. v. 15). And so in Rev. ii. 1, our Lord represents Himself as walking "in the midst of the seven golden candlesticks."

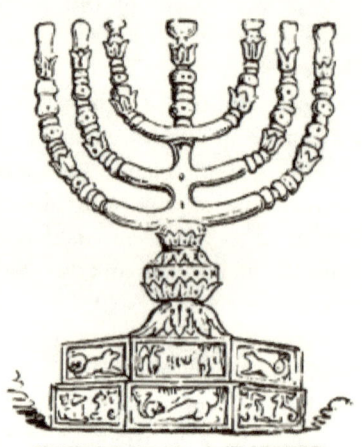

SEVEN-BRANCHED CANDLESTICK.

In lands so rich in olive-trees it was natural that the oil produced from their fruit should constitute the principal source of artificial light for the homes of God's peculiar people, as we know it did in the sacred offices of His sanctuary: "Thou shalt command the children of Israel that they bring thee pure oil olive beaten for the light, to cause the lamp to burn always" (Exod. xxvii. 20). The lamps in common use were shallow oval vessels made of baked clay, terra-cotta, bronze, and sometimes of the precious metals. We are made familiar with the shapes of ancient lamps by the innumerable specimens recovered and preserved in all important museums, or by illustrations of them: the most ancient representations are on Egyptian monuments, such as were used, no doubt, by the Hebrews during their sojourn in Egypt; and many of them date before or soon after the birth of our Lord. Small antique lamps were usually enclosed at the top, where there was a hole to receive the oil, and another for the wick: they often had handles for convenience in carrying them about the house. There were also lamps of different forms to be suspended from the ceiling, or permanently fixed upon the wall.

The "lamps within the pitchers," referred to in Judg. vii. 16, were more properly torches, whose smouldering flames were concealed until the critical moment in a small earthen pot or pitcher,—an antique dark lantern, in fact. In like manner the lamps in the beautiful Parable of the Ten Virgins were doubtless the ordinary torches common to the wedding processions of the East: these were sometimes staves having brass dishes at the top containing coarse rags, oil, and pitch, or lamps in which were rags saturated with oil, while the bearer was provided with a vessel of oil with which to feed the flame as required. Such were probably the sort of torches carried by the great multitude to the Garden of Gethsemane on the night of our Saviour's betrayal: "Judas then, having received a band of men and officers from the chief priests and Pharisees, cometh thither with lanterns and torches and weapons" (John xviii. 3). The antique lantern referred to in this text was very primitive in its construction, and probably of transparent horn or bladder, enclosed in metal rings at top and bottom. That which is still used in Oriental countries has a circular piece of perforated copper at top and bottom; while the cylindrical "sides" are made of parchment or waxed cloth, contrived to fold up into a very small compass, so that in the house it may serve as a

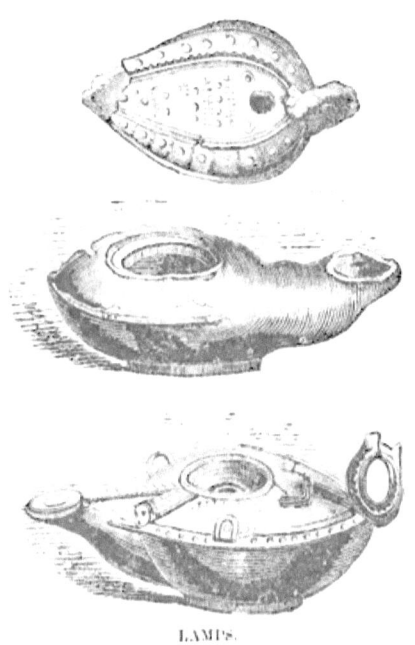

LAMPS.

FURNITURE AND UTENSILS.

candlestick, the candle within projecting above the compressed folds. Lamp-wicks were made of linen, and there is allusion to the smouldering tow dying for lack of oil in the touching promise: "A bruised reed shall he not break, and the smoking flax shall he not quench" (Isa. xlii. 3).

The kitchen appliances, whether descriptive of those in "the dwellings of Jacob," or in the "ceiled houses" of a later day, were exceedingly simple. The oven for baking bread (then, as now, the principal food of an Oriental) was, in patriarchal times, no more than a "hearth" of heated stones, or a bare spot of ground on which a fire might be kindled and the embers raked off to receive the cake of thin dough. This hearth, and the shallow pit in which the meat was buried, and a fire heaped upon the clay cover, were doubtless the earliest ovens, and are not yet altogether abandoned by travellers and wandering tribes. The "little cake" begged by Elijah from the "widow woman" of Zarephath (1 Kings xvii. 13), and the "cake baken on the coals" for the same prophet, "as he lay and slept under a juniper-tree" (1 Kings xix. 6), illustrate these methods which

EGYPTIAN POTS AND PANS.

were always employed for unleavened bread. There was also another means of baking, by heating a large stone pitcher, rolling the dough out into thin cakes, and sticking these on the outside of the pitcher where they were quickly baked through. In the second chapter of Leviticus, in the instructions for bringing offerings to the Lord, reference is made to "a meat-offering baken in an oven," and a "meat-offering baken in a pan," and still another "baken in the frying-pan." We may here remind

PITCHERS.

the reader that a "meat-offering" was always a vegetable sacrifice, the Scriptural import of the word "meat" being simply food in general terms; as our Lord addressed the disciples on the seashore: "Children, have ye any meat?" (John xxi. 5) meaning food of any sort. Houses in the cities were usually provided with portable ovens of metal, earthenware, or stone, which were heated with grass, — "which to-day is, and to-morrow is cast into the oven" (Matt. vi. 30), — or brushwood, or the shrubby burnet, — a common thorn-bush with which the hills of Judæa, Galilee and Carmel still abound, — so that the "crackling of thorns under a pot" (Eccl. vii. 6) is a familiar sound even yet in Palestine. In Leviticus xi. 35 there is mention of "ranges for pots," which may have been similar to the Oriental kitchen-range of

HAND-MILL.

to-day, — a stone or brick stove within a chimney-place, with holes for the pots and to receive the charcoal.

The one utensil, universally found in an Eastern kitchen,

whether of the rich Dives or the destitute Lazarus, was the hand-mill,—the sort of which our Lord spoke when He said: "Two women shall be grinding at the mill: the one shall be taken and the other left" (Matt. xxiv. 41). It consisted of two circular stones, the "upper" and "nether" millstones: the upper revolved on a pivot fixed into the lower, while near the edge of the upper stone was a handle by which it was turned, crushing the grain and emitting that peculiar grating sound so often alluded to by preacher and prophet in the Bible as an essential feature in every scene of domestic activity in the cities of their time. The cessation of the "sound of the millstones" in an Eastern community was the type of a general ruin and desolation as by famine or the sword. The ancient Egyptians seem to have employed the mortar and pestle only, for preparing grain for household use. A small mill can be turned and filled by one person: but it was customary for two women to work together, sitting on the ground with the mill between them; each lent one hand to the wooden or iron handle, and with the other poured the wheat or barley into the hole in the upper stone, while the coarse meal produced fell upon the cloth spread under the mill.

WOMEN AT THE MILL.

This process was so tedious and laborious, that it was often imposed upon prisoners of war: when Samson was taken captive by the Philistines, we are told that "he did grind in the prison-house" (Judg. xvi. 21); and in a bold flight of Oriental imagery, Isaiah apostrophizes the doomed city: "Come down, and sit in the dust, O virgin daughter of Babylon, sit on the ground: there is no throne, O daughter of the Chaldeans: for thou shalt no more be called tender and delicate. Take the mill-stones, and grind meal" (Isa. xlvii. 2). It was one of the merciful enactments of the Levitical law that "No man shall take the nether or the upper millstone to pledge" (Deut. xxiv. 6).

The kneading-trough was an equally indispensable article for domestic use: in the houses of the poor it was simply an oblong shallow wooden basin, or the circular piece of leather that served them also as a table; but in those of the wealthy, of copper or iron. When the children of Israel went forth in haste out of the land of Egypt, "the people took their dough before it was

EGYPTIAN EARTHEN VESSELS.

leavened, their kneading-troughs being bound up in their clothes upon their shoulders" (Exod. xii. 34). Mortar and pestle were also commonly used for cracking grain, and when all Israel "did eat angels' food," we are told of the manna that "the people went about, and gathered it, and ground it in mills, or beat it in a mortar, and baked it in pans, and made cakes of it" (Num. xi. 8). These mortars were made of metal, earthenware, wood or stone, mostly of stone. There were caldrons, pans and frying-pans, "earthen vessels" and "brazen pots" (Lev. vi. 28);

FURNITURE AND UTENSILS.

bowls, cups and spoons, and "lordly dishes," that in the houses of kings were often of pure gold (Esth. i. 7; 1 Kings x. 21).

A characteristic feature of the Hebrew home was the stone water-pot; numbers of these stood even in the courts of the houses, usually of large size, such as those mentioned in the account of the marriage in Cana: "And there were set there six water-pots of stone, after the manner of the purifying of the Jews, containing two or three firkins apiece" (John ii. 6). These were probably used only when large quantities of water were needed, as on festive occasions when the feet of the guests were washed on entering the house. Besides these, there was a great variety of jars and bottles in metal, earthenware, or wood, to contain the domestic provisions of the store-room, — grain, dried fruit, vegetables, oil, wine, honey, and spices. The "pot of oil," miraculously multiplied by Elisha for the destitute widow (2 Kings iv. 2); the "barrel" and the "cruse" of the widow of Zarephath (1 Kings xvii. 12); the "four barrels" of water that figure in the miracle wrought by Elijah (1 Kings xviii. 33); and the water-pot left by the woman of Samaria at Jacob's well where the Messiah had talked to her of the Living Water (John iv. 28), are examples of these jars and "potter's vessels." Such, too, are the "pitchers" which the women took to the public wells and fountains morning and evening, to carry water to their homes, as "Rebekah came forth with her pitcher on

SKIN BOTTLES.

her shoulder; and she went down unto the well, and drew water" (Gen. xxiv. 45).

The most primitive bottles used for holding water, milk, and especially wine, were made of the skins of goats and kids, and sometimes of oxen. The shape of the animal was quite distinguishable, the neck frequently forming the neck of the bottle; while the legs constituted convenient handles in carrying them, for example, over the shoulder, — as Abraham gave the bottle of water to Hagar, ",putting it on her shoulder" when she set out on her sad journey with the lad Ishmael (Gen. xxi. 14).

It is of these skin bottles that our Lord speaks in the familiar text: "Neither do men put new wine into old bottles: else the bottles break, and the wine runneth out, and the bottles perish: but they put new wine into new bottles, and both are preserved" (Matt. ix. 17). New wine was put into new "green" skins that would stretch, without bursting, during the process of fermentation; the old skins, hard, shrivelled, and dry, would soon "break" under such an internal expansion. This is especially the case with skin bottles filled with wine, that have been long hung in the smoke to impart a desired flavor to their contents, according to David's apt simile: "I am become like a bottle in the smoke" (Ps. cxix. 83). In later times, large earthen jars, buried to the neck in the ground, were used by the Hebrews and by the Greeks, for the preservation of wine. One of these usually held as much as our modern barrel. Skin bottles are still used throughout the East, and in some parts of Spain.

EGYPTIAN BASKETS.

Baskets were in common use in all Oriental households: they were made of wicker or rushes, and various in shape and color. "White baskets" are mentioned in the history of Joseph (Gen. xl. 16). The expression "thy basket and thy store" (Deut. xxviii. 5) was derived from the general custom of gathering the fruits of the harvest and the vintage in deep, narrow, wicker baskets, as alluded to by Jeremiah: "Turn back thine hand as a grape-gatherer into the baskets" (vi. 9). In some texts it is evident that the word "basket" must signify some more substantial vessel, as that in which Gideon carried the seethed kid to the angel of the Lord, is supposed to have been of metal (Judg. vi. 19); while that by which St. Paul was let down from the city wall at Damascus must have been of rope. This article, simple as it is, assumes a dignified interest for us in its association with our Saviour's miraculous feeding of the five thousand in the "desert place apart," when the disciples "took up of the fragments that remained, twelve baskets-full" (Matt. xiv. 20); and again, on the mountain, "nigh unto the sea of Galilee," where, after the meal, "they took up of the broken meat that was left, seven baskets-full" (Matt. xv. 37).

Only those weights and measures which were used in the household, and familiarly associated with the lessons of the New Testament especially, need to be considered in this connection. The Jewish law took cognizance of this important provision for the public good in its two precepts,— the one referring to the certified standards preserved in the sanctuary: "Ye shall do no unrighteousness in judgment, in meteyard, in weight, or in measure. Just balances, just weights, a just ephah, and a just hin, shall ye have" (Lev. xix. 35, 36); the other, to those kept by every family for domestic purposes: "Thou shalt not have in thy bag divers weights, a great and a small: thou shalt not have in thine house divers measures, a great and a small: but thou shalt have a perfect and just weight, a perfect and just measure shalt thou have" (Deut. xxv. 13–15). In commercial transactions the Hebrews were required to be punctiliously just in the matter of weights and measures: inspectors went from shop to shop, from market to market; indeed, the law on this subject in later days was full of Pharisaical minutiae; "a wholesale dealer must cleanse the measures he used once every month, and a retail dealer twice a week; all weights were to be washed once a week, and the scales wiped every time they had been used," to remove even "the small dust of the balance" (Isa. xl. 15).

In the Mosaic period, the weight in common use was a "shekel," the word signifying weight: this was subdivided for con-

venience into a half, a third, and a fourth part of a shekel. The expression "shekel of the sanctuary," as found in Exod. xxx. 13, to denote the sum each Israelite must pay as "a ransom for his soul," is used only to prescribe the standard weight of precious metal, which in those days and for many centuries afterward, was their only form of money. The "mineh" and the "talent" were other weights of the same period. The shekel being equivalent to our half-ounce avoirdupois; the mineh (one hundred shekels) represented three pounds two ounces; while the talent, equal to three thousand shekels, or thirty mineh, was ninety-three pounds twelve ounces avoirdupois.

Of the dry measures, the one in daily use in the kitchen was the "measure" familiar to us in our Lord's Parable of the leaven: "The kingdom of heaven is like unto leaven, which a woman took, and hid in three measures of meal, till the whole was leavened;" and that of the unjust steward: "How much owest thou unto my lord? And he said, An hundred measures of oil. . . . Then said he to another, And how much owest thou? And he said, An hundred measures of wheat." (Luke xiii. 21. xvi. 5-7.) This was one-third of an "ephah," or twenty pints. The Greek word translated "bushel" in the Sermon on the Mount, "Neither do men light a candle, and put it under a bushel" (Matt. v. 15), is supposed to express this "measure." The Roman bushel corresponded to our peck. The "ephah," of Egyptian origin as the name denotes, occurs frequently in the

Old Testament, especially with reference to offerings in the sanctuary; the "omer," six pints, is interesting in its connection with the miraculous food supplied to the Israelites during the forty years' wandering: "This is the thing which the Lord commandeth, Fill an omer of it to be kept for your generations, that they may see the bread wherewith I have fed you in the wilderness" (Exod. xvi. 32). A "cab" was a small dry measure of two pints (2 Kings vi. 25).

The smallest measure for liquids was the "log," mentioned in the Old Testament only — a "log of oil" (Lev. xiv. 10); this was "six egg-shells full," or nearly one pint: the "hin" (Egyptian), commonly found in the Books of Exodus and Numbers, held ten pints. The "bath" was the largest of the liquid measures, and contained seven and a half gallons. When Solomon sent to the king of Tyre for skilled workmen to expedite the building of the Temple, he made this contract for their service: "Behold, I will give to thy servants, the hewers that cut timber, twenty thousand measures of beaten wheat, and twenty thousand measures of barley, and twenty thousand baths of wine, and twenty thousand baths of oil" (2 Chron. ii. 10).

The "firkin" was a Greek measure of the same capacity as the Hebrew "bath;" this is of interest in its connection with the marriage at Cana, the scene of our Lord's first miracle: "There were set there six water-pots of stone . . . containing two or three firkins apiece" (John ii. 6).

The balances, in their spiritual significance, are a favorite metaphor with the sacred writers; in his affliction, Job exclaims: "Oh that my grief were thoroughly weighed, and my calamity laid in the balances together!" and utters the prayer: "Let me be weighed in an even balance, that God may know mine integrity" (vi. 2. xxxi. 6). Hosea denounces the "balances of deceit" (xii. 7); and Amos hears the ungodly merchantmen impatiently longing for the "new moon" and the "sabbath" to be gone, that they "may set forth wheat, making the ephah small, and the shekel great, and falsifying the balances by deceit" (viii. 5). The prophet Daniel reads to the terror-stricken king of the Chaldeans his dreadful doom, written " over against the candlestick upon the plaster of the wall : " " Thou art weighed in the balances, and art found wanting" (Dan. v. 27). David stigmatizes those, whether of low or high degree, of whom it may be said: "To be laid in the balance, they are altogether lighter than vanity" (Ps. lxii. 9). Solomon declares that " A false balance is abomination to the Lord; but a just weight is His delight;" and that " A just weight and balance are the Lord's: all the weights of the bag are His work " (Prov. xi. 1, xvi. 11); and Micah interprets the mind of the Almighty when he pronounces the " scant measure " an " abomination," and asks, in His name, " Shall I count them pure with the wicked balances, and with the bag of deceitful weights ?" (vi. 11); while Isaiah magnifies the glory of the Creator, " who hath measured the waters in the hollow of His hand, and meted out heaven with the span, and comprehended the dust of the earth in a measure, and weighed the mountains in scales, and the hills in a balance " (xl. 12).

III.

MARRIAGE, WIDOWHOOD, AND DIVORCE.

THE forty-sixth chapter of Genesis, where we read how the venerable Jacob came into Egypt accompanied by "his sons, and his sons' sons, his daughters, and his sons' daughters, and all his seed," presents a faithful picture of the patriarchal system, as it prevailed among the ancient people of God. This intimate union of interests, domestic and material, was a feature in Eastern households strange to us, who are accustomed to see the closest family ties severed by the marriage of son or daughter, or even by less important exigencies.

When a son married, he brought his wife to his father's house, as Isaac met Rebekah, and "brought her into his mother Sarah's tent" (Gen. xxiv. 67); and as Tobias took Sara his wife to his father's house at Nineveh (Tob. xi.); he continued to live in filial subordination, and contributed his earnings to the common family purse. Where there were many sons, the household under a single roof might easily consist of fifty members, all rendering obedience to the acknowledged head; and when the father died, instead of scattering and forming new households, it was customary to invest the eldest son with the patriarchal authority, who henceforth became the representative of his entire family and kindred.

Up to the time of the Captivity, a plurality of wives prevailed among the patriarchs, notwithstanding the Mosaic dispensation, which, in both letter and spirit, declared its opposition to this practice, though not to the extent of prohibition. It must be acknowledged, however, that polygamy, as practised by the Hebrews, never became that revolting institution familiar to us in the history of pagan and Mohammedan nations: it was, rather, a carefully defined system, which permitted more than one wife, but recognizing always the chief or legitimate wife, whose superior rights were never disputed; and yet the others had, each, her own rights within certain limitations, equally well established.

Beside the chief wife and the secondary wife or wives, there was the concubine, who bore an inferior though legitimate conjugal relation to the master of the family. These were either young Jewesses bought of their fathers, or heathen captives taken in war. Concubines differed from wives in the absence in their case of any of the usual solemnities by which betrothal and marriage were consummated: they had no voice in the family government or interests; and though their children were not illegitimate, the children of the wives proper were preferred in questions of inheritance. It was customary for barren wives to give their handmaids to their husbands, to bear children in their stead: thus Sarah gave Hagar, her

HAGAR AND ISHMAEL.

Egyptian maid, to Abraham her husband (Gen. xvi. 3); and "when Rachel saw that she bare Jacob no children," "she gave him Bilhah her handmaid to wife" (Gen. xxx. 1, 4). There was no stigma attaching to the relation of concubine, but her social position was much inferior to that of the wife, and her influence upon her husband quite insignificant, unless, indeed, she chanced to be of exceptional charm and force of character. The rights of a concubine, even though a captive Gentile girl, were carefully protected by law: "When thou goest forth to war against thine enemies, and the Lord thy God hath delivered them into thine hands, and thou hast taken them captive, and seest among the captives a beautiful woman, and hast a desire unto her, that thou wouldest have her to thy wife; then thou shalt bring her home to thine house; and she shall shave her head, and pare her nails; and she shall put the raiment of her captivity from off her, and shall remain in thine house, and bewail her father and her mother a full month: and after that thou shalt go in unto her, and be her husband, and she shall be thy wife. And it shall be, if thou have no delight in her, then thou shalt let her go whither she will; but thou shalt not sell her at all for money, thou shalt not make merchandise of her, because thou hast humbled her" (Deut. xxi. 10–14). And in the more delicate question of one wife preferred to another,

the law again interferes for the protection of the "weaker vessel:" "If a man have two wives, one beloved, and another hated, and they have borne him children, both the beloved and the hated; and if the firstborn son be hers that was hated: then it shall be, when he maketh his sons to inherit that which he hath, that he may not make the son of the beloved firstborn before the son of the hated, which is indeed the firstborn: but he shall acknowledge the son of the hated for the firstborn, by giving him a double portion of all that he hath; for he is the beginning of his strength; the right of the firstborn is his" (Deut. xxi. 15-17). It is a significant consideration that the first instance of polygamy recorded in the Bible is found in the family of a near descendant of the accursed Cain: "Lamech took unto him two wives: the name of the one was Adah, and the name of the other Zillah" (Gen. iv. 19),—himself a murderer, as he confessed to his wives. It is recorded of that "mighty man of valor," Gideon, son of Joash, that he had "threescore and ten sons:" "for he had many wives." The law admonished kings, especially, not to "multiply wives," that their hearts "turn not away" (Deut. xvii. 17); nevertheless, the Sacred Books are full of illustrious offenders against this wholesome restriction, among whom David and his son Solomon are distinguished examples: "King Solomon loved many strange women, together with the daughter of Pharaoh, . . . and he had seven hundred wives, princesses, and three hundred concubines" (1 Kings xi. 1, 3). Polygamy was unknown in Egypt, nor can it be ascertained what was the Hebrew practice during their long sojourn in that land; doubtless the poverty and oppression under which they groaned had a salutary influence in correcting the evil. There is no doubt, however, that under their happier auspices in Canaan, they returned to the old sin; their prophets ceased not to inveigh against this practice, and the still more baleful mixed marriages with neighboring heathen women: nevertheless the wealthier classes continued to yield to the national temptation, even down to the New Testament era, where we find St. Paul limiting the qualifications for a bishopric or deaconship in the early Christian Church to "the husbands of one wife" (1 Tim. iii. 2, 12).

The most superficial Bible-reader can scarcely have failed to note the important part that Woman enacts in the Sacred Story, from Sarah, Rebekah, Leah, and Rachel, the "four mothers" of patriarchal Israel, to Dorcas, Lydia, Priscilla, Lois, and Eunice, of the New Testament, even to Her whom all nations call "Blessed," the exalted Mother of Our Lord!

The Hebrew women were not secluded after the manner of other Orientals; they mingled freely in society, and, so far as comported with modesty, took part even in public movements when those were of a beneficent or religious character. The title accorded to a wife, corresponding to that of her husband in every instance, testifies to the position she occupied in the family, — the possessor of equal dignity and rights; while "trusting in God" she was yet "in subjection" to her own husband, "even as Sarah obeyed Abraham, calling him lord" (1 Pet. iii. 5, 6). The law-givers, prophets, preachers, and poets of her own nation rise up to do honor to the faithful wife in Israel; and to her we owe the inspiration of one of the most exquisite pictures of home-life in the Bible: "the words of King Lemuel . . . that his mother taught him:" "Who can find a virtuous woman? for her price is far above rubies. The heart of her husband doth safely trust in her, so that he shall have no need of spoil. She will do him good and not evil all the days of her life. She seeketh wool, and flax, and worketh willingly with her hands. She is like the merchants' ships; she bringeth her food from afar. She riseth also while it is yet night, and giveth meat to her household, and a portion to her maidens. She considereth a field, and buyeth it; with the fruit of her hands she planteth a vineyard. She girdeth her loins with strength, and strengtheneth her arms. She perceiveth that her merchandise is good: her candle goeth not out by night. She layeth her hands to the spindle, and her hands hold the distaff. She stretcheth out her hand to the poor; yea, she reacheth forth her hands to the needy. She is not afraid of the snow for her household; for all her household are clothed with scarlet. She maketh herself coverings of tapestry; her clothing is silk and purple. Her husband is known in the gates, when he sitteth among the elders of the land. She maketh fine linen, and selleth it; and delivereth girdles unto the merchant. Strength and honor are her clothing; and she shall rejoice in time to come. She openeth

her mouth with wisdom; and in her tongue is the law of kindness. She looketh well to the ways of her household, and eateth not the bread of idleness. Her children arise up, and call her blessed; her husband also, and he praiseth her. Many daughters have done virtuously, but thou excellest them all. Favor is deceitful, and beauty is vain; but a woman that feareth the Lord, she shall be praised. Give her of the fruit of her hands; and let her own works praise her in the gates." (Prov. xxxi. 10–31.)

RUTH AND BOAZ.

The position of a widow or an unmarried woman in the East, especially in very ancient times, was peculiarly unhappy and insecure. A husband's house was her only sure refuge from servitude, insult, or neglect; hence it was called by the Hebrews the woman's "*mennehah*" (rest); so Naomi took leave of her two young widowed daughters-in-law with the affectionate invocation: "The Lord grant you that ye may find rest, each of you in the house of her husband" (Ruth i. 9). The old Mosaic law provided for the immediate succor and protection of a young widow, whose deceased husband had left brothers or near male relatives, whether married or unmarried. In Deuteronomy, twenty-fifth chapter, it is written: "If brethren dwell together, and one of them die, and have no child, the wife of the dead shall not marry without unto a stranger: her husband's brother . . . shall take her to him to wife." "And it shall be, that the firstborn which she beareth shall succeed in the name of his brother which is dead, that his name be not put out of Israel" (5, 6). The widow, on her part, was required to remain in the same house, and not to marry again, except the nearest kinsman of her deceased husband. If this person from any reason of expediency could not fulfil her claim upon him, he could transfer his obligation to the next nearest of kin. A widow no longer marriageable, who had no son, could relinquish her estate in favor of a childless and widowed daughter-in-law, — as Naomi did in the case of Ruth, for the Moabitess had no claim whatever upon the kinsman of her Jewish mother-in-law. The penalty that awaited the unworthy son of Israel who refused to fulfil his sacred obligation to the dead, is thus graphically described in the chapter of Deuteronomy last quoted: "Then shall his brother's wife come unto him in the presence of the elders, and loose his shoe from off his foot, and spit in his face, and shall answer and say, So shall it be done unto that man that will not build up his brother's house. And his name shall be called in Israel, The house of him that hath his shoe loosed" (9, 10).

This ancient privilege of the widow justified her in taking steps to secure her right which seem to us lacking in delicacy if not decorum, as in the cases of Tamar and Ruth.

It was concerning this law that "the Sadducees, which deny that there is any resurrection," came to inquire of Jesus, supposing, for argument's sake, an extreme case: "There were therefore seven brethren: and the first took a wife, and died without children. And the second took her to wife, and he died childless. And the third took her; and in like manner the seven also; and they left no children, and died. Last of all the woman died also. Therefore in the resurrection whose wife of them is she? for seven had her to wife" (Luke xx. 29–33). Our Lord's answer, while rebuking their grossly material representation of a future life, declares the truth of the doctrine they denied: "They which shall be accounted worthy to obtain that world, and the resurrection from the dead, neither marry, nor are given in marriage; neither can they die any more: for they are equal unto the angels; and are the children of God, being the children of the resurrection" (35, 36).

In apostolic times, widows were emancipated from their traditional reproach. St. Paul calls upon the Church to "honor widows that are widows indeed;" though even he makes a distinction (in respect of membership in a society, apparently) between her who is "desolate" and the "younger widows," for the reason that the latter "will marry" (1 Tim. v. 3, 11).

Of the few women whom the Saviour saw fit to select for His individual commendation, "a certain poor widow," who threw two mites into the treasury of the Temple, compelled his spontaneous tribute: "And he called unto him his disciples, and saith unto them, Verily I say unto you, that this poor widow hath cast more in, than all they which have cast into the treasury: for all they did cast in of their abundance; but she of her want did cast in all that she had, even all her living" (Mark xii. 43, 44); and the sorrow of another—who followed the bier of her only son out of the city of Nain—called forth the omnipotent deliverance by which "he that was dead sat up, and began to speak. And He delivered him to his mother" (Luke vii. 15). It was expected of a young Hebrew, even as a religious obligation in view of the promised Messiah, that he should marry at seventeen or eighteen years of age; but twenty was the extreme limit to which he might defer this vital event, unless he had so given himself up to study as to leave him neither time nor inclination to assume the responsibilities of the wedded state. It was not inconsistent with the freedom permitted in the intercourse of the sexes, for a young man to make personal choice of a bride; but he was not encouraged to expect a happy result from such self-assertion. The two wives that Esau took to himself at the mature age of forty were "a grief of mind to Isaac and Rebekah," his father and mother (Gen. xxvi. 35); and when it came to be a measure of safety for the younger son Jacob that he should be sent away from home, the doting mother comforted herself and said to Isaac: "I am weary of my life because of the daughters of Heth: if Jacob take a wife of the daughters of Heth, such as these which are of the daughters of the land, what good shall my life do me?" (Gen. xxvii. 46.) The sons, however, were sometimes suffered to express their personal preferences to their parents, of which we have two instances: it is related of the son of Hamor, "prince of the country" where Jacob had "bought a parcel of a field," and where he had "spread his tent," that "his soul clave unto Dinah the daughter of Jacob, and he loved the damsel, and spake kindly unto the damsel. And Shechem spake unto his father Hamor, saying, Get me this damsel to wife" (Gen. xxxiv. 3, 4); and of the mighty Samson, that he "went down to Timnath, and saw a woman in Timnath of the daughters of the Philistines. And he came up, and told his father and his mother, and said, I have seen a woman in Timnath of the daughters of the Philistines: now therefore get her for me to wife" (Judg. xiv. 1, 2).

But it was the common custom for the parents on both sides to negotiate this delicate transaction strictly without interference from the young people interested. Thus Hagar chose a wife for her son Ishmael "out of the land of Egypt" (Gen. xxi. 21); and "Judah took a wife for Er, his firstborn, whose name was Tamar" (Gen. xxxviii. 6); the patriarch Abraham sent his trusty servant hundreds of miles away from the land of his adoption to select a wife for his son, saying: "Thou shalt go unto my country, and to my kindred, and take a wife unto my son Isaac" (Gen. xxiv. 4). Indeed, this last chapter contains a comprehensive illustration of the marriage customs of that time. Abraham sought a daughter-in-law from among his own kindred; and Laban answered his nephew's proposal for his daughter Rachel in these words: "It is better that I give her to thee, than that I should give her to another man" (Gen. xxix. 19), although Jacob was so poor that he had to purchase his two wives by fourteen long years of labor; and Tobit warned his son Tobias, "Take not a strange woman to wife, which is not of thy father's tribe; . . . remember, my son, that our fathers from the beginning, even that they all married wives of their own kindred, and were blessed in their children" (Tob. iv. 12). Marriages between near relatives were preferred by the ancient Hebrews, from a strong feeling of exclusiveness, as well as with the object of keeping wealth in the family. The degrees of relationship between those intending marriage, which would render the alliance illegal, were sharply defined by the Mosaic Law (Lev. xviii. 6–18).

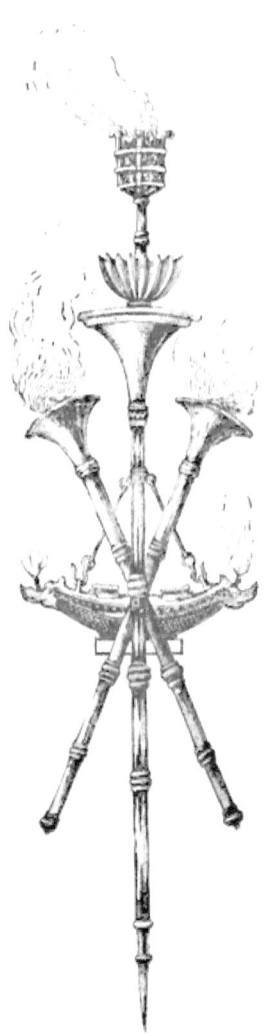

St. Paul's admonition to the Christians at Corinth to marry "only in the Lord" (1 Cor. vii. 39) is but a condensation of many Rabbinical exhortations to the young bachelors of his time: one affirms that "men marry for one of four reasons, — passion, wealth, honor, or the glory of God;" and after inveighing against the first three meretricious motives, and citing examples of the destructive tendency of each, as recorded in the holy Scriptures, he holds up for their emulation the marriage made "in the name of heaven," or "for the name of God," promising that the issue of such will be children who shall "preserve Israel."

We have said that the proposal of marriage came from the family of the bridegroom; and the few exceptions on record go far to prove the rule on this interesting subject: when "Moses fled from the face of Pharaoh, and dwelt in the land of Midian," Jethro, the priest, took compassion upon the desolate stranger, invited him to his house, and gave him Zipporah, one of his seven daughters, to wife (Exod. ii. 21). So Caleb gave Achsah, his daughter, to Othniel, her kinsman, to wife (Josh. xv. 16, 17); and Saul, the king, gave his daughter Michal to David, instead of the elder daughter Merab, who had been promised to him but treacherously married to another man (1 Sam. xviii. 27). It was of very old social custom that the elder daughter must be married first, no matter what might be her lack of personal attractions. It is probable, however, that this rule was subject to certain local limitations; for Jacob seems to have been ignorant of it until after his cruel disappointment, when his shrewd father-in-law explained to him that "it must not be so done in our country, to give the younger before the firstborn" (Gen. xxix. 26).

After the choice of the bride had been made, the formal contract followed, which was termed the betrothal or espousal: and it was always accompanied by presents according to the means of the bridegroom; for in Oriental marriages the primitive idea was evidently that the bride was to be purchased. The dowry came not with the bride, but was given for her: if not in money, jewels, flocks, or lands, it was paid in labor; as Jacob became herdman to Laban, and Moses, probably, to Jethro, while the love-stricken Shechem placed no limit upon the marriage portion that Jacob might demand for Dinah, his daughter. "And Shechem said unto her father and unto her brethren, Let me find grace in your eyes, and what ye shall say unto me I will give.

Ask me never so much dowry and gift, and I will give according as ye shall say unto me ; but give me the damsel to wife " (Gen. xxxiv. 11, 12).

No written contract of marriage was required among the Hebrews until after the Captivity: the acceptance of the bridegroom's presents, by the bride and her family, made the engagement as legally binding as wedlock itself. It will be remembered, that as soon as Rebekah had received the "jewels of silver, and jewels of gold, and raiment," that Abraham's steward had brought, and her mother and her brother had accepted the "precious things" (ten camels' load), the marriage was an accomplished fact, not to be set aside except by a bill of divorce : " And they called Rebekah, and said unto her, Wilt thou go with this man? And she said, I will go. And they sent away Rebekah their sister, and her nurse, and Abraham's servant, and his men. And they blessed Rebekah, and said unto her, Thou art our sister ; be thou the mother of thousands of millions, and let thy seed possess the gate of those which hate them. And Rebekah arose, and her damsels, and they rode upon the camels, and followed the man ; and the servant took Rebekah, and went his way. And Isaac came from the way of the well Lahai-roi ; for he dwelt in the south country. And Isaac went out to meditate in the field at the eventide : and he lifted up his eyes, and saw, and, behold, the camels were coming. And Rebekah lifted up her eyes, and when she saw Isaac she lighted off the camel. For she had said unto the servant, What man is this that walketh in the field to meet us? And the servant had said, It is my master. therefore she took a veil, and covered herself. And the servant told Isaac all things that he had done. And Isaac brought her into his mother Sarah's tent, and took Rebekah, and she became his wife : and he loved her : and Isaac was comforted after his mother's death" (Gen. xxiv. 58–67).

In the quaint apocryphal story of Tobit, we have an example of the marriage customs of a later period ; but this case may have been exceptional from the peculiar circumstances narrated.

The angel, travelling in the guise of a companion with Tobias,

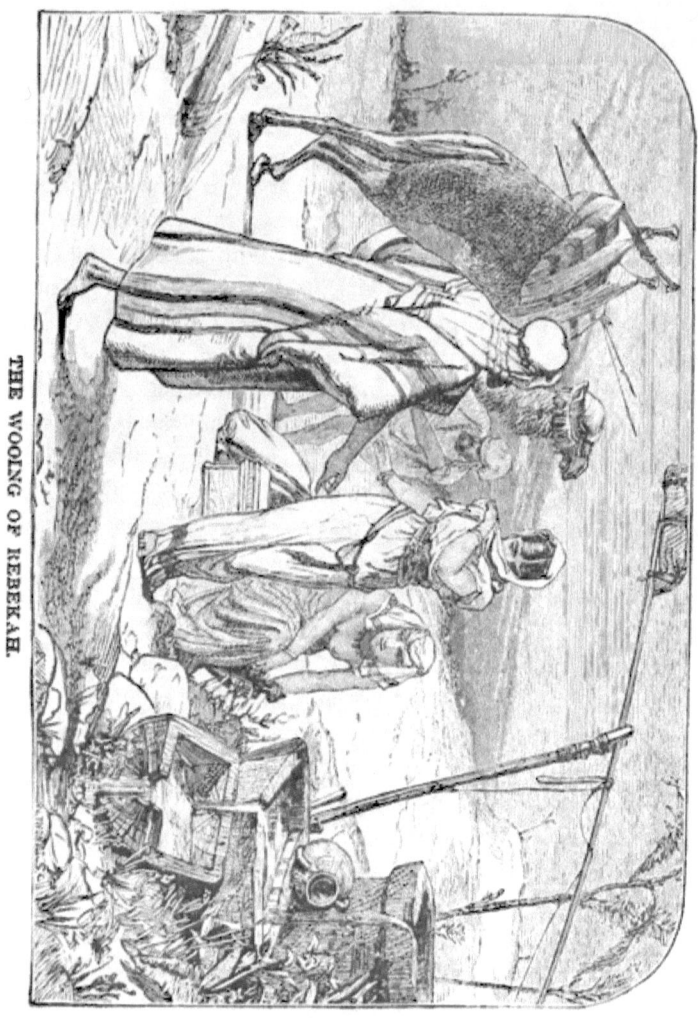

THE WOOING OF REBEKAH.

said to the young man, " Brother, to-day we shall lodge with Raguel, who is thy cousin; he also hath one only daughter, named Sara; I will speak for her, that she may be given thee for a wife. . . . The maid is fair and wise: now therefore hear me, and I will speak to her father; and when we return from Rages we will celebrate the marriage. For I know that Raguel cannot marry her to another according to the law of Moses, but he shall be guilty of death, because the right of inheritance doth rather appertain to thee than to any other."

After the preliminaries had been settled by the angel, who acted as the *paranymph* on this occasion, the father, Raguel, said to Tobias: " Then take her from henceforth according to the manner; for thou art her cousin, and she is thine; and the merciful God give you good success in all things."

" Then he called his daughter Sara, and she came to her father, and he took her by the hand, and gave her to be wife to Tobias: saying, Behold! take her after the law of Moses, and lead her away to thy father. And he blessed them; and called Edna his wife, and took paper, and did write an instrument of covenants, and sealed it. . . .

" And he kept the wedding feast fourteen days. . . . Then Raguel arose, and gave him Sara his wife, and half his goods, servants and cattle and money: and he blessed them, and sent them away, saying, The God of heaven give you a prosperous journey, my children. And he said to his daughter, Honor thy father and thy mother in law, which are now thy parents, that I may hear good report of thee. And he kissed her.

" Edna also said to Tobias, The Lord of heaven restore thee, my dear brother, and grant that I may see thy children of my daughter Sara before I die, that I may rejoice before the Lord: behold, I commit my daughter unto thee of special trust; wherefore do not entreat her evil." (Tob. vi., vii., x.)

Hence it will be seen that betrothal was the actual beginning of the married state: the maiden was regarded as a wife, and any breach of decorum or fidelity on her part was condemned as the gravest infringement of the marriage bond; even her property became her bridegroom's, unless he voluntarily relinquished his right. Thus in the Gospel story, Joseph is called the "husband" of the Blessed Virgin Mary, "before they came together," — she having been only as yet "espoused" to him (Matt. i. 18, 19).

TOBIAS AND SARA.

These espousals were often contracted in the very early childhood of the young couple, by their parents or brothers; but the marriage, in such a case, did not take place until the bride had attained her twelfth year. Even when both parties were of marriageable age, it was customary to allow at least a year to elapse between the betrothal and the actual marriage, — that interval of time being considered necessary to prepare the bridal outfit. On the other hand, a widow need postpone her nuptials only thirty days after the day of espousals.

The ceremony of betrothal was usually celebrated with a feast in the house of the bride, after which the prospective pair held communication with each other only through the "friend of the bridegroom." This important agent in Oriental marriage negotiations was the nearest friend of the young bridegroom; and upon him devolved the thousand and one delicate preliminaries to the actual union of the couple. Indeed, it is said that his good offices ceased not even here, but that after marriage he might reconcile differences, if any should arise, between the newly-wedded, and was constituted in all respects the confidant of the family. The "friend of the bridegroom" must not be confounded with the term "children of the bridechamber," used by Our Lord in answer to the Pharisees (Matt. ix. 15), and which simply signifies the guests invited to the wedding. This exalted office of *paranymph* was that which St. John the Baptist claimed for himself in his relation to Christ, as "preparing the way" for the heavenly Bridegroom to take possession of His bride, the Church — standing and hearing him, and rejoicing greatly because of his voice (John iii. 29). And in this character St. Paul wrote to the Corinthians: "I am jealous over you with godly jealousy; for I have espoused you to one husband, that I may present you as a chaste virgin to Christ" (2 Cor. xi. 2). And so, in the spiritual union of Jehovah with His people Israel, Moses fulfils the office of the "friend of the bridegroom," who leads out the mystical bride to the place of meeting at Sinai: "And Moses brought forth the people out of the camp to meet with God; and they stood at the nether part of the mount" (Exod. xix. 17). Indeed, in some hyper-spiritual commentary by an ancient Rabbi, it is represented that the "Almighty Himself took the cup of blessing, and spoke the benediction, while Michael and Gabriel acted the 'bridegroom's friends' to our first parents when they wedded in Paradise"!

When the time was finally appointed for the wedding, preparations to celebrate the happy consummation were made to the full extent of the means of the bridegroom, since his house was to be the special scene of rejoicing in view of the introduction of its new mistress. Invitations to the wedding feast were given some time in advance; and they were repeated at the time of celebration, by messengers sent to notify each guest. This custom of double invitations is of very ancient origin, and is still observed in some parts of the East: frequent allusion is made to it in Scripture narrative; Esther formally invited the king and Haman to a "banquet of wine," and when it was ready the chamberlains of the king "hasted to bring Haman unto the banquet that Esther had prepared;" so, too, the parable recorded by St. Luke affords a striking illustration: "A certain man made a great supper, and bade many: and sent his servant at supper-time to say to them that were bidden, Come; for all things are now ready" (Luke xiv. 16, 17); and again in that related by St. Matthew, where "A certain king, which made a marriage for his son," "sent forth his servants to call them that were bidden to the wedding," "saying, Tell them which are bidden, Behold, I have prepared my dinner; my oxen and my fatlings are killed, and all things are ready: come unto the marriage" (Matt. xxii. 2-4).

In many cases invitations to Oriental banquets were absolutely general in their character, addressed in the name of charity to rich and poor, friends and strangers. The last-quoted parable affords an example of this custom, in the ninth verse, where the king, justly indignant at the refusal of those that were bidden, bade his servants: "Go ye therefore into the highways, and as many as ye shall find, bid to the marriage. So those servants went out into the highways, and gathered together all as many as they found, both bad and good; and the wedding was furnished with guests." The allegorical banquet given by Wisdom is described as one of these peculiarly Oriental entertainments: "She hath killed her beasts; she hath mingled her wine; she hath also furnished her table. She hath sent forth her maidens; she crieth upon the highest places of the city" (Prov. ix. 2, 3).

It is to be observed that these invitations were made, evidently in the public streets, by women, through whose shrill voices, "upon the highest places of the city," she reached all classes of its inhabitants. A modern traveller relates his observation of a similar custom in Egypt: some ten or twelve women, veiled, and attended by eunuchs and other servants, went about the streets of

THE MARRIAGE FEAST AT CANA.

a town, uttering shrill and quavering notes, which he was informed were intended to express joy, and to constitute a public invitation to a festive gathering. In the days of Christ it would appear that only men-servants were charged with these hospitable announcements.

In the story of the marriage of Samson at Timnath to a daughter of the Philistines, reference is made to the custom of a farewell feast given by the bridegroom to his friends: "And Samson made there a feast; for so used the young men to do. And it came to pass, when they saw him, that they brought thirty companions to be with him" (Judg. xiv. 10, 11). This entertainment, being a part of the wedding festivities, began a week before the nuptial ceremony, and was supplemented by another week of feasting and rejoicing. It was on the seventh day of the young men's festivities that they proposed to the bride to "entice" her betrothed; and it was not until she had "wept before him the seven days while their (own) feast lasted," that he told her the answer of the riddle. On the occasion of Jacob's marriage, Laban, his father-in-law, "gathered together all the men of the place, and made a feast;" and when Jacob protested against the deceit practised upon him in giving him Leah, Laban told him to "fulfil her week" of festivities and rejoicing, and Rachel should also be given him to wife.

It was customary for Eastern monarchs and persons of distinction to present their guests with festal robes on all occasions of magnificent entertainment, but more especially at marriage-feasts; and the company were expected to put them on, and wear them throughout the festivities. This involved no trouble to the guest in changing the apparel; for the robe was simply an outer cloak or vest, with or without sleeves, to lay upon the shoulders. To reject, or neglect to make use of, this robe, was a flagrant insult to the host. Many cases are cited by historians of Eastern manners, where such presumption has cost a man his life at the hand of a despotic and irate monarch. In this connection the reader will recall the parable, in which, the king having come in "to see the guests, he saw there a man which had not on a wedding garment. And he saith unto him, Friend, how camest thou in hither, not having a wedding garment? And he was speechless. Then said the king to the servants, Bind him hand and foot, and take him away, and cast him into outer darkness; there shall be weeping and gnashing of teeth" (Matt. xxii. 11).

Mention has been made of the "governor of the feast," or, as we might say, "master of ceremonies," a very necessary officer on these occasions, when an immense concourse of people, inclined to be demonstrative, thronged an Oriental house in all the glory of its gala display. His duties were to escort distinguished guests to the places of honor,—a punctilious point of etiquette in the East,—and, with consummate tact, to dispose of all according to their relative positions in life: he prescribed the order of the amusement, preserved decorum, and tasted the wines before they were offered to the company. Among the Romans, the "master of the feast" was chosen by throwing dice: his rules for drinking, and for other details of the entertainment, were absolute. Thus at the marriage in Cana of Galilee,—hallowed above all other weddings by the presence of Jesus and His mother,—when, at her request, the Son of Mary changed the water into wine: "He saith unto them, Draw out now, and bear unto the governor of the feast" (John ii. 8). It would seem from our Lord's parable that the matter of seats, or "rooms," was sometimes left to the discretion of guests, but it was still subject to severe restrictions: "When thou art bidden of any man to a wedding, sit not down in the highest room; lest a more honorable man than thou be bidden of him; and he that bade thee and him come and say to thee, Give this man place; and thou begin with shame to take the lowest room. But when thou art bidden, go and sit down in the lowest room; that when he that bade thee cometh, he may say unto thee, Friend, go up higher: then shalt thou have worship in the presence of them that sit at meat with thee" (Luke xiv. 8–10). The Pharisees were repeatedly rebuked by Christ for their persistent appropriation of "the uppermost rooms at feasts, and the chief seats in the synagogues" (Matt. xxiii. 6).

THE BRIDEGROOM.

While these preparations have been going on in the home of the bridegroom, and while he himself, attended by his "friend" and his young companions, has put on the festive apparel, "perfumed with all powders of the merchant," and the nuptial turban representing the crown of King Solomon " wherewith his mother crowned him in the day of his espousals, and in the day of the gladness of his heart." the expectant lady has not been idle. Jeremiah exclaims, " Can a maid forget her ornaments, or a bride her attire?" and it is quite safe to deny any such imputation aimed at an Oriental bride, however passive. Surrounded by her

maidens and her young companions, she has for many hours submitted to the tedious processes of the toilet prescribed by tradition and custom; in which interesting connection we may mention that in later times so grave a code as the Talmud directed that one-tenth of a bride's dowry should be appropriated to perfumes and cosmetics. It is of vital moment that she should shine with tenfold charm, since so much depends upon this, presumably the first, glimpse her husband is to catch of her face, imaged to him heretofore only in dreams! The most costly garments attainable by her family have been prepared, together with a profusion of glittering, jingling jewelry, excessive to all but Oriental eyes; in fact, so incumbent was this display of gold and precious stones, upon both contracting parties, that if too poor to possess the necessary outfit they borrowed it from friends, — so that the simile of the prophet, "as a bridegroom decketh himself with ornaments, and as a bride adorneth herself with her jewels," was as familiar as household words.

The one complete description of a bridal toilet, procurable

MARRIAGE, WIDOWHOOD, AND DIVORCE.

from the Bible, is in the allegory wherein the Lord declares His love for Jerusalem under the figure of a marriage: "Yea, I sware unto thee, and entered into a covenant with thee, saith the Lord God, and thou becamest mine. Then washed I thee with water; . . . and I anointed thee with oil. I clothed thee also with broidered work, and shod thee with badgers' skin, and I girded thee about with fine linen, and I covered thee with silk. I decked thee also with ornaments, and I put bracelets upon thy hands, and a chain on thy neck. And I put a jewel on thy forehead, and earrings in thine ears, and a beautiful crown upon thine head. Thus wast thou decked with gold and silver; and thy raiment was of fine linen, and silk, and broidered work" (Ezek. xvi. 8-13). The "beautiful crown upon thine head" doubtless signified some one of the many curious headdresses assumed at marriage by Oriental women from very ancient times, and significant of the crown that wedlock was presumed to bestow upon the virgin, making her thenceforth a queen. Among these was the famous "Lebanon horn," still worn by Jewish married women resident at Tunis and Algiers; the large silver cup-shaped crown, fastened to the back of the head; the small silver trumpet, worn at the left side of the head above the ear; and silver disks, sometimes enclosing a talisman, worn on the top of the head.

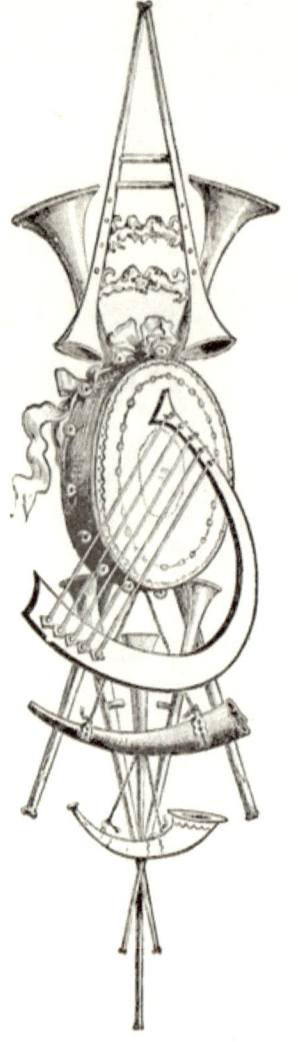

Another bridal crown was called the dodos, and is probably the most ancient of them all; a terra-cotta head has been found in Asia Minor, having a representation of the dodos encircled by a garland of flowers, which can scarcely be less than two thousand years old. This, however, was merely a tall foundation of pasteboard covered with flowers, and serving to confine the bridal veil; it was worn only during the wedding ceremonial, while the others, named above, were never laid aside.

The veil constituted an important and very ancient feature of the Jewish bridal costume: it might be worn by the bride alone, or spread over the young couple at a certain point of the formalities, as is the custom with modern Jews in the East. It is a curious illustration of the interference of the Rabbis in the minutiæ of social life, that they interdicted the wearing of the bridal veil, for a while, after the destruction of Jerusalem. The wearing of crowns, a still more ancient custom, was also prohibited after a certain epoch in the wars of Jewry. The instance of Rebekah, veiling herself at the approach of Isaac, might be cited as proof of the antiquity of the use of bridal veils; but the "veil," both in this text (Gen. xxiv. 65) and in that which describes Tamar as "she put her widow's garments off from her, and covered her with a veil" (Gen. xxxviii. 14) was a loose, flowing robe of some light diaphanous texture, which could readily be drawn up over the head. It is certain that the custom of veiling the face of women was not general in the patriarchal period, but has crept in under Mohammedan influence. It is asserted that no representation of this article of dress is found on Egyptian or Assyrian sculptures: yet it is well known that both Egyptians and Hebrews did make use of the veil on special occasions, when it became a significant addition to the costume. The veiling of the bride as she approached her bridegroom was a signal instance of this use of the veil, indicating her modesty as a virgin, and subjection as a wife.

The wedding procession is a peculiar feature of ancient Oriental social customs, graphically alluded to in the familiar Parable of the Ten Virgins (Matt. xxv.). On the night appointed for the nuptials, the bridegroom, attended by his friends, with bands of musicians, and bearers of lanterns and flaring torches, with songs and shoutings of joy, proceeds through the streets of the city to the home of the bride, — recalling to many a pious heart the words of Isaiah: " As the bridegroom rejoiceth over the bride, so shall thy God rejoice over thee."

All whom they meet are expected to join in the procession, and add to the boisterous demonstrations, — so characteristic of ancient Oriental cities that the prophet, in summing up the tremendous consequences of idolatry among the chosen people, adds to them all this significant " word of the Lord: " " Then

WEDDING PROCESSION.

will I cause to cease from the cities of Judah, and from the streets of Jerusalem, the voice of mirth, and the voice of gladness, the voice of the bridegroom, and the voice of the bride: for the land shall be desolate " (Jer. vii. 34).

But, long before the bridegroom reaches the house, the music and the shrill sounds of merry-making fill the night air, and announce his approach to the young maidens attendant upon the bride, who, in joyful excitement, cry out one to another: " Behold, the bridegroom cometh; go ye out to meet him!" and in great haste they light their lamps and their torches, and sally forth, singing and dancing, to meet the procession, which they escort into the house. After a short interval for rest and refreshment, the gay company again take up the line of march, to return to the home of the bridegroom, but this time escorting the bride and her family and friends.

A great abundance of light was an essential element in these midnight processions; hence the necessity, as exemplified in the parable, of carrying " vessels" of oil with which to replenish the lamps and torches. It was also customary to bear branches of palm and myrtle before the young pair, as symbols of joy and victory, while grain or small coins were scattered over them to bespeak their future prosperity. When the bridegroom reached his own house, " they that were ready went in with him to the marriage; and the door was shut." This was a necessary precaution, and obligatory in any case of private entertainment in the East, where the crowd offered a tempting opportunity for strangers to intrude themselves. A servant was stationed at the main entrance to receive guests who presented their tablets, or cards; and after the company was assembled no one was admitted, no matter how importunate. So it will be seen that the Five Foolish Virgins, who " took no oil with them," added to that folly their unavailing entreaty: " Lord, Lord, open to us!" The stringent character of this custom is equally insisted upon in one of the lessons of our Lord to the congregation in the synagogue: " When once the master of the house is risen up, and hath shut to the door, and ye begin to stand without, and to knock at the door, saying, Lord, Lord, open unto us; and he shall answer and say unto you, I know you not whence ye are" (Luke xiii. 25).

There is no mention, nor indirect evidence, of any religious ceremony in the marriages of the primitive Jewish people; the simple removal of the bride from her parents' protection, to the home of the bridegroom or of his father, constituted the public acknowledgment of the assumed relation. The " benediction" and " cup of blessing," common to both the ceremony of betrothal and that of marriage, in the days of the Rabbis, cannot be traced back to a very early date.

The week of wedding festivities being over, there yet remained the " bridal days" to the young couple, which comprehended an entire month, like our modern honeymoon. The Mosaic law was especially indulgent in view of these interesting conditions, and provided that " when a man hath taken a new wife, he shall not go out to war, neither shall he be charged with any business: but he shall be free at home one year, and shall cheer up his wife which he hath taken" (Deut. xxiv. 5). This enactment throws light upon the refusal of the one guest bidden to the Great Supper, who did not, like the others, "pray to be excused;" but said, as if the plea were unanswerable, "I have married a wife, and

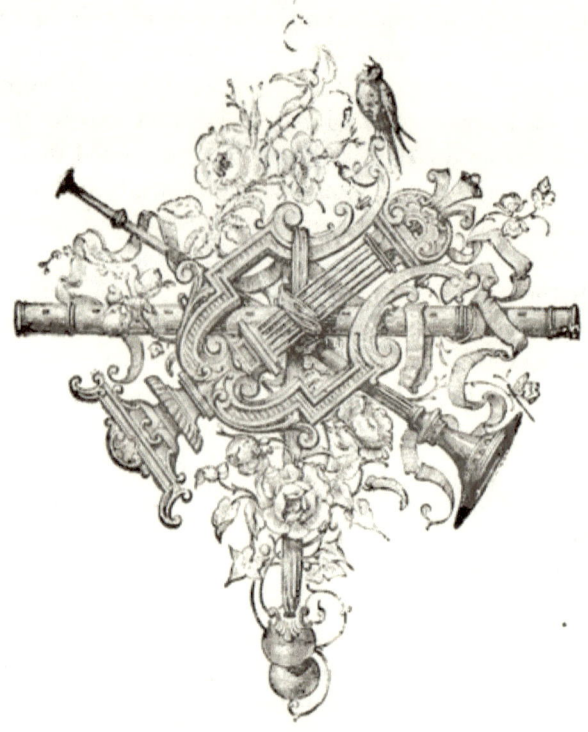

therefore I cannot come!" (Luke xiv. 20.) This generous dispensation for the bridegroom was extended even to the betrothed husband, who, in case of impending war, was thus addressed by the priest: "What man is there that hath betrothed a wife, and hath not taken her? Let him go and return unto his house, lest he die in the battle, and another man take her" (Deut. xx. 7).

The young Hebrew, who has with so many demonstrations of

joy brought his espoused bride to her new home, is thus exhorted by the wise men of Israel: "Rejoice with the wife of thy youth. Let her be as the loving hind and the pleasant roe; . . . and be thou ravished always with her love" (Prov. v. 18, 19); and, again: "Live joyfully with the wife whom thou lovest all the days of the life of thy vanity, which he hath given thee under the sun" (Eccles. ix. 9). He is assured that "whoso findeth a wife, findeth a good thing, and obtaineth favor of the Lord;" while the little "Song of degrees" (Ps. cxxviii.) is in itself a picture of a happy marriage crowned with the blessing of the Almighty: "Blessed is every one that feareth the Lord; that walketh in his ways. For thou shalt eat the labor of thine hands: happy shalt thou be, and it shall be well with thee. Thy wife shall be as a fruitful vine by the sides of thine house; thy children like olive-plants round about thy table. Behold, that thus shall the man be blessed that feareth the Lord. The Lord shall bless thee out of Zion: and thou shalt see the good of Jerusalem all the days of thy life. Yea, thou shalt see thy children's children, and peace upon Israel." For a later generation, the Apostle Paul sums up the whole duty of those who have entered the married state, in this comprehensive axiom: "Let every one of you in particular so love his wife even as himself; and the wife see that she reverence her husband" (Eph. v. 33). The same apostle precedes this admonition with the words: "So ought men to love their wives as their own bodies," — a sentiment apparently suggested by the following from the Talmud: "He that loveth his wife as his own body, honoreth her more than his own body, brings up his children in the right way, and leads them in it to full age, — of him the Scripture saith: 'Thou shalt know that thy tabernacle shall be in peace' (Job v. 24)." With a beginning so auspicious for a happy conjugal union, it is not pleasant to reflect for what trivial causes this hallowed compact might be dissolved, and the family ties irrevocably broken. This was especially true in the time of Christ, notwithstanding the fact that Rabbinical legislation had declared for the rights of the wife, even though the meanest of

MARRIAGE, WIDOWHOOD, AND DIVORCE. 85

Jewish slaves. The popular feeling on this vexed question of divorce is disclosed by the circumstance that it formed the subject of special inquiry to the Great Teacher, not only on the part of

"THY WIFE SHALL BE AS A FRUITFUL VINE."

the intolerant and jealous Pharisees, but of His own disciples. When Jesus had come "into the coasts of Judæa beyond Jordan," "the Pharisees also came unto him, tempting him, and saying unto him, Is it lawful for a man to put away his wife for every cause?" And he answered and said unto them, Have ye not read, that he which made them at the beginning made them male and female, and said, For this cause shall a man leave father and mother, and shall cleave to his wife: and they twain shall be one flesh. Wherefore they are no more twain, but one flesh. What therefore God hath joined together, let not man put asunder. They say unto him, Why did Moses then command to give a writing of divorcement, and to put her away? He saith unto them, Moses because of the hardness of your hearts suffered you to put away your wives: but from the beginning it was not so" (Matt. xix. 3–8); and He added to this comprehensive demonstration of the whole subject, the one cause, only, for which a man might righteously divorce his wife. "In the house his disciples asked him again of the same matter" (Mark x. 10), evidently amazed at their Lord's reply; from which they promptly drew the conclusion, that, "if the case of the man be so with his wife, it is not good to marry" (Matt. xix. 10).

The Mosaic law briefly enacted, that "when a man hath taken a wife, and married her, and it come to pass that she find no favor in his eyes. . . . then let him write her a bill of divorcement, and give it in her hand, and send her out of his house" (Deut. xxiv. 1); while the sole compensation granted to the wife was implied in her permission to marry another man. In later days, on the contrary, under Rabbinical supremacy, the wife could obtain a divorce on absurdly trivial grounds: as, for instance, that her husband was engaged in an offensive trade, such as that of a tanner or a fuller or a coppersmith; or that he had become afflicted with disease. Our Lord points to this possibility as a common practice, when He says, "If a wife shall put away her husband" (Mark x. 12); and the Apostle Paul, in discussing the subject to the Christian Church at Corinth, shows plainly that it was quite optional with the wife, at least of an "unbelieving" husband, to "depart" from him, with or without a formal divorce,—only it was stipulated, "let her remain unmarried" (1 Cor. vii. 10–16).

But without some knowledge of the gross, debasing immorality of pagan society in the days of the apostles, we shall fail to appreciate the wisdom of St. Paul's counsel on the vital topics of marriage and divorce — especially his exhortation: "Be ye not unequally yoked together with unbelievers" . . . for "what concord hath Christ with Belial?" (2 Cor. vi. 14.) Tertullian contrasts a Christian union with a mixed marriage; and in portraying the serious evils and hinderances to a pious life, which the converted wife encounters in the latter, he affords us indirectly a graphic picture of the manners of that time: "When the wife wishes to attend worship, her husband makes an appointment for the baths. Instead of hymns she hears songs; and his songs are from the theatre, the tavern, and the night-cellar. Her fasts are hindered by his feasts. He is sure to object against nocturnal services, prison visits, the kiss of peace, and other customs. She will have a difficulty in persuading him that such private observances as crossing and exsufflation are not magical rites."

It is true, that, under the Rabbinical dispensation, no "brother" or "sister" need be "under bondage" to live together after a change had taken place in the religious faith of either; but that was not according to the strict letter of the law: and when the apostle, "himself a Pharisee, and the son of a Pharisee," writes to the converts from Judaism at Rome, "to them that know the law," he elucidates the new doctrine by that law in regard to the marriage-bond: "The woman which hath a husband is bound by the law to her husband so long as he liveth; but if the husband be dead, she is loosed from the law of her husband" (Rom. vii. 2). The wife had no power of herself to be freed from that law: according to the Jewish axiom that "a woman is 'loosed from the law of her husband' by only one of two things,—death, or a letter of divorce."

In view of what appears to be the fatal facility with which wives could be put away with a bill of divorcement, it certainly speaks well for constancy of conjugal attachment among the early Hebrews, and for the popular sentiment with regard to the sanctity of the marriage bond, that there is no case of positive divorce recorded in the Old Testament. Indeed, the "mind of the Spirit," throughout both Old and New, declares for monogamy, as well as for the indivisibility of "that which God hath joined together." Those cruder and less worthy conditions in which the holy relation of marriage is found to have existed, in the various developments of national and spiritual life, both among the Jews and their Gentile neighbors, seem to have been temporary concessions made to the blindness and "hardness" of their hearts; but "from the beginning it was not so,"—not in that happy day in Eden when the Lord God "made a woman, and brought her unto the man" (Gen. ii. 22); nor will it be "so" in that glorious consummation of "things hoped for:" when "the marriage of the Lamb is come, and his wife hath made herself ready"! (Rev. xix. 7). What the inspired religious feeling on this subject was, even in the days of the prophets, it is easy to conjecture from an extract from one of them, the last: a pathetic representation of the altar of the Lord as covered "with tears, with weeping, and with crying out." And when the people ask of the prophet the reason of this, he answers: "Because the Lord hath been witness between thee and the wife of thy youth, against whom thou hast dealt treacherously: yet is she thy companion, and the wife of thy covenant. . . . And wherefore one? That he might seek a godly seed. Therefore take heed to your spirit, and let none deal treacherously against the

JEALOUSY.

wife of his youth. For the Lord, the God of Israel, saith that he hateth putting away" (Mal. ii. 14-16). A beautiful paraphrase by the Rabbis, of this passage of Scripture, has been translated by Dr. Sachs: —

> "If death hath snatched from thee the wife of youth,
> It is as if the sacred city were,
> And e'en the Temple, in thy pilgrim days,
> Defiled, laid low, and levelled with the dust.
> The man who harshly sends away from him
> His first-wooed wife, — the loving wife of youth,
> For him the very altar of the Lord
> Sheds forth its tears of bitter agony."

IV.

CHILDREN: THEIR TRAINING AND SCHOOLING.

THE eager expectation with which Israel waited for the promised Messiah, and the peculiar hope of each tribe or family that "from among their brethren" the divine "Prophet" should be "raised up" (Deut. xviii. 18), made a numerous offspring the coveted blessing of every home. No graver misfortune could befall a Hebrew than to die childless; to such a one, when dead, his neighbors applied the sad lament of Jeremiah: "Weep sore for him that goeth away, for he shall return no more" (xxii. 10): the childless man, alive and in health, was said in common parlance to be already dead; while the cry of every barren wife was voiced in that of Rachel: "Give me children, or else I die!" (Gen. xxx. 1.)

It is not without significance, as demonstrating the tenderness of parental affection among the Hebrews, that, beside the general terms *ben* and *bath* (son and daughter), they employed nine words for "child," expressive of its successive states of development. The *yeled* (as used in the second chapter of Exodus, in the touching story of the infant Moses) was the newly-born babe; *yonek* is literally suckling; *olel* signified the baby still at the breast, but beginning to eat and to "ask bread" (Lam. iv. 4). *Gamul* was the two-or-three-year-old child already weaned; while *Taph*, the "quickly stepping," indicated the merry restlessness of an older child, free from the nurse's arms; *elem*, "the strong," a sturdy boy, old enough to be of use in the household; such a lad it was to whom Jonathan said, "Run, find out now the arrows which I shoot" (1 Sam. xx. 36); *almah*, the term denoting the girl-child of this period, is the word used in the text so full of devout

CHILDREN: THEIR TRAINING AND SCHOOLING 93

interest for all Christians: "Therefore the Lord himself shall give you a sign; Behold, a virgin shall conceive, and bear a son, and shall call his name Immanuel" (Isa. vii. 14); next comes the *naar*, the manly youth entitled to a degree of freedom and

THE STAR IN THE EAST.

self-dependence; lastly, *bachur*, the fully-developed young man of marriageable age, and qualified for military service.

The firstborn son of every Jewish family was regarded with peculiar homage and affection, as the child set apart by command of God to be sanctified to Him. "Because all the firstborn are mine; for on the day that I smote all the firstborn in the land of Egypt I hallowed unto me all the firstborn in Israel, both man and beast" (Num. iii. 13). Thus the "firstborn" is one of the "thirteen things" enumerated by one of the most learned Rabbinical commentators, as being in the "sole ownership of the Holy One." He enjoyed special privileges over his brothers, exercising a certain authority among them; he received a double portion of the inheritance; and, in the absence or death of the father, he officiated as priest of the family. This sacerdotal dignity, however, no longer pertained to him after the priesthood

was delegated exclusively to the tribe of Levi: after that, the firstborn son was redeemed with a certain sum of money (five shekels, about two and a half dollars of our currency), which became a part of the sacred revenue throughout succeeding generations. The paternal blessing was an important feature of the birthright; which, however, could be withheld if the son proved unworthy, or transferred by the heir if he could be induced to part with a possession so sacred for a consideration. Perhaps no story of the Bible is better known than that which illustrates this sale of the father's blessing (Gen. xxv. 31).

The sons inherited their father's property at his death, to the exclusion of the daughters; but they were bound to support their sisters, however serious the inconvenience or loss to themselves, and in later times to provide a dowry for each, amounting to the tenth part of the entire inheritance. When Jacob represented to his wives the necessity of his leaving Laban their father, "Rachel and Leah answered and said unto him, Is there yet any portion or inheritance for us in our father's house? Are we not counted of him strangers? for he hath sold us, and hath quite devoured also our money" (Gen. xxxi. 14, 15); and it is recorded of Job as an extraordinary departure from common usage, that he gave his daughters "inheritance among their brethren" (Job xlii. 15).

Where there were only daughters, the father's goods were distributed equally among them, according to the law which reads: "If a man die, and have no son, then ye shall cause his inheritance to pass unto his daughter" (Num. xxvii. 8). But the daughters thus inheriting their father's estate were bound to marry within his own tribe. By Roman law also, the property was entailed on the sons at the father's death; and in certain Oriental lands the sons could demand a division of the estate during the father's lifetime, as described in the parable of the Prodigal Son; this was sometimes done among the Romans. These matters of family inheritance were fixed by law: there were no wills, and no need of any; for the inborn reverence for the law and for paternal authority would have made the modern device of "breaking" an obnoxious will a monstrous impossibility to a Hebrew son or daughter.

The birth of this much-desired son and heir was naturally an event of the utmost excitement and joy to every Oriental family. Its announcement was delegated to some favorite servant, who, waiting near the private apartments of his mistress, caught the first intimation of the happy event, and ran to inform his master. The afflicted prophet, in the bitterness of his soul, refers to this servant when he cries: "Cursed be the man who brought tidings to my father, saying, A man child is born unto thee; making him very glad" (Jer. xx. 15). In Persia this interesting office was endowed with certain perquisites: the confidential servant attached to the harem, being the first to receive the information, ran to his expectant master exclaiming, "*Mujdeh, Mujdeh!*" "Good news!" which entitled him to a considerable gift. Among the lower classes it was customary for the bearer of such happy tidings to seize upon the cap or shawl of the father, who was expected to redeem it with a present.

The birth of a son was an occasion of great joy to the Oriental mother as well, for other reasons than the gratification of her strong maternal love: it established her position in her husband's home and affections, and reconciled him to her if for any cause she had failed to secure his preference. Thus the despised Leah rejoiced at the birth of her son, the firstborn of Jacob, saying, "Now, therefore, my husband will love me!"

CHAPEL OF THE NATIVITY AT BETHLEHEM.

So Hannah prayed in the house of the Lord in Shiloh, after the birth of Samuel, offering her psalm of exultant thanksgiving: "My heart rejoiceth in the Lord, mine horn is exalted in the Lord; my mouth is enlarged over mine enemies; because I rejoice in thy salvation" (1 Sam. ii. 1). So Sarah rejoiced at the birth of the child of promise, when she was well stricken in years, saying: "God hath made me to laugh, so that all that

SIMEON AND ANNA.

hear will laugh with me. And she said, Who would have said unto Abraham, that Sarah should have given children suck? for I have borne him a son in his old age" (Gen. xxi. 6, 7). And so, when the venerable Elisabeth brought forth him who was to "prepare the way" of the Messiah, "her neighbors and her cousins heard how the Lord had showed great mercy upon her; and they rejoiced with her" (Luke i. 58;) while the *Magnificat* of the Blessed Mary, as she "entered into the house of Zacharias, and saluted Elisabeth" her kinswoman, is an outpouring of joy in the Holy Ghost, almost too sacred to be enumerated among merely human experiences: "And Mary said, My soul doth magnify the Lord, and my spirit hath rejoiced in God my Saviour. For he hath regarded the low estate of his handmaiden: for, behold, from henceforth all generations shall call me blessed" (Luke i. 46-55).

SHRINE OF THE ANNUNCIATION AT NAZARETH.

The new-born Hebrew baby was washed in salted water, or rubbed with salt, to harden the skin, and impart vigor to the body, not perhaps without reference to the purity and incorruption in which it was both an active agent and the symbol. When the prophet was commanded to depict the abominations of Jerusalem, he did so "under the similitude of a wretched infant," and, as such, addressed the backslidden city: "In the day thou wast born," thou wast not "washed in water to supple thee; thou wast not salted at all, nor swaddled at all" (Ezek. xvi. 4).

The "swaddling clothes," in which it is recorded that the Virgin Mother wrapped her divine Babe (Luke ii. 7), and which were specified by the angel to the shepherds: "This shall be a sign unto you: Ye shall find the babe wrapped in swaddling clothes, lying in a manger" (Luke ii. 12), were in common use at that time throughout the East, and are even to this day; they were bandages some three or four inches in width, and about three yards long, which were firmly wound around the newly-born from the neck to the feet, including the arms, which were confined to its sides. Thus swaddled, the baby could not move hand or foot; but it was considered necessary to support the frail bones in this manner until they had acquired substance and firmness. For a child of high rank these bandages were often very elegant and expensive; fine white shawls or silk scarfs confined

BETHLEHEM.

with a gold band sometimes answered this purpose; the poor used strips of common cotton or linen goods. In a superb metaphor, descriptive of the creation of the sea, Job refers to this well-known practice: "When I made the cloud the garment thereof, and thick darkness a swaddling band for it" (xxxviii. 9). The description by a modern lady traveller of a baby she saw in Bethlehem may not be inappropriate: "I took the little creature in my arms. His body was stiff and unyielding, so tightly was it swathed with white and purple linen. His hands and feet were quite confined; and his head was bound with a small, soft, red shawl, which passed under his chin and across his forehead in small folds."[1]

On the eighth day the infant son of a Hebrew received the rite of circumcision, according to God's covenant with Abraham, in which it was commanded, "he that is eight days old shall be circumcised among you, every man child in your generations, he that is born in the house, or bought with money of any stranger, which is not of thy seed" (Gen. xvii. 12). At a later period the ceremony took place in the father's house or in the synagogue, the godmother providing the officiator. Two chairs were placed, one for the godfather who held the child, the other for the Prophet Elijah, who was supposed to be invisibly present. It was customary to name the child at this important ceremony; and the Rabbis explain the custom by the fact that God changed the names of Abram and Sarai at the time He instituted the rite (Gen. xvii. 5, 15). Girls were named by the minister of the synagogue a month after birth. In the old, old story of the birth of our Lord we recall this custom: "When eight days were accomplished for the circumcising of the child, his name was called JESUS, which was so named of the angel before he was conceived in the womb" (Luke ii. 21); and a more detailed account in the case of St. John the Baptist: "It came to pass, that on the eighth day they came to circumcise the child; and they called him Zacharias, after the name of

[1] Miss Rogers's Domestic Life in Palestine.

his father. And his mother answered and said, Not so; but he shall be called John. And they said unto her, There is none of thy kindred that is called by this name. And they made signs to his father, how he would have him called. And he asked for a writing-table, and wrote, saying, His name is John. And they marvelled all" (Luke i. 59–63).

Other nations had certain name-days for their children, that Tertullian terms *Nominalia:* the Romans named their sons on the ninth day, their daughters on the eighth. The Greeks named the newly-born child on the tenth day; but on the fifth day the nurse with the child in her arms walked about a ceremonial fire, as a means of purification both for herself and the child. The Athenians gave names on the tenth day. The Persians appointed a certain night for naming a child. If the father could afford it he made a feast, and invited his friends, together with several priests. The infant was brought into the assembled company: five names were written upon separate slips of paper, which were placed within the leaves of the Koran. The first chapter of the Koran was read: then one of the slips of paper was drawn out at random by the father; and the priest, having read it, pronounced it in the ear of the child, placing the written name upon the swaddling clothes. The relatives gave money and other presents to the little one on this occasion.

All Oriental people, but especially the Jews, were fond of names with significations: indeed, it is doubtful if any pure Hebrew name is lacking in that distinctive feature. A few instances taken from Bible story will suffice to illustrate this interesting matter: When Leah, the hated wife of Jacob, bore a son, "she called his name Reuben" (*A son, I see!*); " for she said, Surely the Lord hath *looked* upon my affliction." The second son she named Simeon (*a hearing*), "because the Lord hath *heard* that I was hated;" the third son she called Levi (*joining*), and said, " Now this time will my husband be *joined* unto me, because I have borne him three sons;" at the birth of the fourth son "she said, Now will I *praise* the Lord: therefore she called his name Judah" (*praise*) (Gen. xxix. 32–35).

So the pious Hannah named her son, given in answer to prayer, Samuel (*asked of God*); Saul, the Hebrew form of the name of the great apostle to the Gentiles, has the same signification (*desired, asked for*); David (*beloved*); Absalom (*father of peace*); John (*beloved of God*), identical with Johanan (*to whom God is merciful*); Peter (*a rock*) — "On this rock will I build my Church;" and finally, that Name which is far above " every name

that is named, not only in this world, but also in that which is to come;" "for there is none other name under heaven given among men, whereby we must be saved," — JESUS (*Saviour*): " for He shall save His people from their sins."

The names bestowed upon daughters disclose a far different state of feeling, and usually express those personal charms and qualities most desired for this sex. Of Job's beautiful daughters, of whom it is recorded that, " In all the land were no women found so fair," it is also said. "He called the name of the first Jemima" (*bright as the day*); "and the name of the second Kezia" (*cassia*, one of the choicest spices); "and the name of the third Keren-happuch" (*horn of the eye-paint*, or *of beauty*). The exquisite grace and beauty of the palm-tree, *Tamar*, made it a favorite name with the ancients, as Solomon sings of the "fairest among women:" "Thy stature is like to a palm-tree." In the Old Testament there are three notable instances of women who bore this name, — the daughter-in-law of Judah, the sister and the daughter of Absalom: the beauty of the last two is specially mentioned, and is easily accredited to the near relation they bore to that son of David who was the handsomest man of his day. The name given to the only daughter of Jacob and Leah, Dinah (*avenged*), seems to have been strangely prophetic of her remarkable story (Gen. xxx. 21); Rebekah (*a cord with a noose, enchaining*) expresses the spell of beauty by which she won her husband's heart at first sight; Deborah (*a bee*) portrays the cheerfully busy housewife; Sarah (*princess*); Abigail (*source of joy*); Susanna (*a lily*); Hannah (*grace*); Esther (*star*); Ruth (*friend* or *beauty*); Naomi (*my delight*) — "Call me not Naomi," said the childless widow of this name, on her return to Bethlehem, the home of her youth: "Call me not Naomi, but call me Mara (*bitter*); for the Almighty hath dealt very bitterly with me" (Ruth i. 20). Adam called his wife's name Eve, because she was "the mother of all living" (Gen. iii. 20). But how shall we reconcile the signification of the name of the "second Eve," the Blessed Mary, with the nature of her who bore it, "full of grace," and richly adorned with that "meek and quiet spirit, which is in the sight of God of great price"? (1 Pet. iii. 4.) "Mary" is said to correspond with the name Miriam of the Old Testament, which signifies *rebellion!* But here we prefer to believe of the scientists of the nomenclature of the Bible, that somebody has blundered.

According to Mosaic law, the mother brought prescribed offerings to the priest (forty days after the birth of a son, and eighty days after the birth of a daughter), who offered them before the Lord. If her means sufficed, she brought a lamb of the first year, and a young pigeon or a turtle-dove; but " if she be not able to bring a lamb, then she shall bring two turtles or two young pigeons" (Lev. xii. 8). So we read of the Virgin Mother and her Child: "When the days of her purification according to the law of Moses were accomplished, they brought him to Jerusalem, to present him to the Lord;" "And to offer a sacrifice according to that which is said in the law of the Lord, A pair of turtle-doves, or two young pigeons" (Luke ii. 22, 24). She, who for her own purifying was "not able to bring a lamb," held in her bosom that Immaculate Lamb destined to

TURTLE DOVE.

be offered for " the sin of the world;" nor could she yet have sufficiently pondered " all these things " in her heart, — that tender heart to be pierced through as with a sword also, — else she might have whispered to her divine Babe, with Abraham of old, "My son, God will provide himself a lamb for a burnt-offering."

It was a pious custom of the Jews to bring their young children to men noted for sanctity, to invoke their blessing and their prayers. On the day that the little one was one year old, it was usually taken to the synagogue to receive the solemn benediction of the presiding Rabbi. In accordance with this usage, there were brought unto Jesus " little children, that he should put his hands on them, and pray: and the disciples rebuked them." " But when Jesus saw it, he was much displeased, and said unto them, Suffer the little children to come unto me, and forbid them not; for of such is the kingdom of God. And he took them up in his arms, put his hands upon them, and blessed them" (Matt. xix. 13; Mark x. 14, 16).

How sweetly and graciously does the Italian poet Filicaja find expression for the *maternal* quality, of wisdom blended with tenderness, displayed in the " love divine, all love excelling"!

> "Just as a mother, with sweet pious face,
>   Yearns toward her little children from her seat,
> Gives one a kiss, another an embrace,
>   Takes this upon her knees, that on her feet;
> And while from actions, looks, complaints, pretences,
>   She learns their feelings and their various will,
> To this a glance, to that a word dispenses,
>   And, whether stern or smiling, loves them still:—
> So Providence for us, high, infinite,
>   Makes our necessities its watchful task;
> Hearkens to all our prayers, helps all our wants;
>   And, e'en if it denies what seems our right,
> Either denies because 'twould have us ask,
>   Or seems but to deny, or in denying grants."

It is to the praise of Eastern mothers, that, whatever their rank, they delegated to no one the sacred office of nursing their infant children; and it was the practice to prolong this function until the child was two years and a half or three years old. It was a very ancient family custom to celebrate the weaning of a child by a festive gathering of friends, and an entertainment according to the means of the father: Abraham the mighty patriarch, for instance, " made a great feast the same day that Isaac was weaned" (Gen. xxi. 8). And when Hannah had weaned her son Samuel, " she took him up with her, with three bullocks, and one ephah of flour, and a bottle of wine, and brought him unto the house of the Lord in Shiloh" (1 Sam. i. 24). A " daily portion" was allotted to the Levites, set apart for the service of the Temple, " from three years old and upward;" hence it is inferred that the child Samuel was weaned at

THE OFFERING.

that age, and, being entered by his mother upon his life of consecration, "he ministered unto the Lord before Eli" (1 Sam. iii. 1).

The nurse was a very important personage in an Eastern family: there are repeated examples in the Bible of the esteem in which she was held, as well as of her own devotion that inspired it. Rebekah's nurse Deborah accompanied the young bride to Canaan; and when the faithful old servant died, having nursed her mistress's children's children, she was buried with heartfelt mourning under the Allon-bachuth, the "oak of weeping," near Bethel. When Ruth bore a son to Boaz, her mother-in-law, "Naomi, took the child, and laid it in her bosom, and became nurse unto it."

In times of rebellion and anarchy it was not unusual for the reigning family to put their entire trust for the safety of the young heir in the fidelity and affection of his nurse: thus was Mephibosheth, son of Jonathan, saved by the courage of his foster-mother; and Joash, the last of the royal seed of the house of Judah, was rescued from massacre, and hidden for six years with his nurse in the Temple, until he came to the throne of his father.

Several modes of carrying young children are described in the Bible; and we find two of them specially mentioned in the prophetic utterance of God to His ancient Church, in which He declares of the Gentiles that "they shall bring thy sons in their arms, and thy daughters shall be carried upon their shoulders. And kings shall be thy nursing fathers, and their queens thy nursing mothers" (Isa. xlix. 23). "In their arms" may be rendered, as in the margin, *bosom*, — that is to say, the baggy folds of the outer garment, overlaying the girdle, making a snug, soft bed for the little one. This disposition of children is indicated in the case of Naomi, who laid Ruth's baby "in her bosom;" and the custom is alluded to by Moses, when, weary of the complaints of the Israelites, he cries to the Lord, and asks, Are these my children, "that Thou shouldest say unto me, Carry them in thy bosom, as a nursing father beareth the sucking child,

unto the land which thou swarest unto their fathers?" (Num. xi. 12.) When old enough to sit upright with safety, the child was carried between the shoulders, with its little legs around the nurse's neck; or on one shoulder, usually the left, with one leg hanging down the back, and the other on the breast. In either of these cases the child held on to its bearer's head, and clung fast with its feet. Still another mode for young infants was to carry them astride the hips: reference to this particular custom is supposed to be found in the words, "Thy daughters shall be nursed at thy side" (Isa. lx. 4). Illustrations of Eastern manners represent nursing babies in a sort of basket-cradle, borne on the backs of poor mothers, probably on their way to daily labor in the field or vineyard.

The only mention in the Bible of the sports in vogue among the children is made by Christ to exemplify the peculiar perverseness of the Jews at the time of His visitation: "And the Lord said. Whereunto then shall I liken the men of this generation? and to what are they like? They are like unto children sitting in the market-place, and calling one to another, and saying, We have piped unto you, and ye have not danced; we have mourned to you, and ye have not wept" (Luke vii. 31, 32). From these few words we may be confirmed in the tradition that children are the same, not only all the world over, but in every age. These children, of whom our Lord speaks, were of the common people, familiar with the ordinary street scenes and sounds of an Oriental city; and for the child to reproduce these in his play was as natural in the days before the Flood as it is at this moment. The boisterous mirth, with dancing and music, — "the voice of harpers . . . and of pipers and trumpeters," — of the wedding processions, had often waked them out of sleep, to run to the housetop for a view of all the bravery of the show, — the glare of torches, the gorgeous dresses of the company; so, too, the melancholy, ghostlike march of mourners, following a bier, in garments of sackcloth, with weeping and wailing, was a scene that impressed itself with equal vividness upon the youthful imagination, busy with all its weird and awful suggestiveness. The text shows us these boys of the streets, "sitting in the market-place," and remonstrating with some perverse and perhaps dyspeptic playmates, for whom they had played at wedding and at funeral, but in vain — the fun for the day was spoiled. The prophet, foretelling the joyful restoration of Jerusalem, enumerates among its external signs of peace and gladness, that "the streets of the city shall be full of boys and girls playing in the streets thereof" (Zech. viii. 5). We are told that Sardis, the seat of one of the seven churches in Asia, was celebrated for the manufacture of children's toys: the neighborhood of this ancient city, as well as other parts of Western Asia, has yielded a great variety of the remains of its wares in this department, and in a tolerable state of preservation. They consist of mimic representations of animals, fowls, birds, asses with pack-saddles, dolls with arms and legs made movable on strings, whistles and marbles. The ruins and tombs of Egypt have also afforded many remains of these interesting objects. A conspicuous feature of antique toys — and one upon which we can congratulate ourselves of the nineteenth century, that it is quite impossible to this day of a better charity — were comic figures and caricatures of wretched hunchbacks, deformed negroes, and even idiots! together with mythological monstrosities, and grotesques born of nightmare horrors. There was doubtless a certain scruple among the Jews — as there was among the Mohammedans in later times — as to the representation of living things, prohibited by the law; and it is not probable that it was set aside for the amusement of their children. Happily, we need not waste sympathy on the ancient young folks for this apparently sad state of things in their nurseries; for the Eastern child was, no more than the Western, dependent upon mere externals for the "properties" of its every-day drama called play, — nor could be while with bewitched eyes it beheld a prancing steed in some withered branch, or a "love of a doll" in a cotton napkin tied about with a string.

Outside of the home circle, it is certain that the Jewish youth had no public games, such as the young Greeks and Romans delighted and excelled in. Indeed, these diversions were so opposed to the grave religious bias of the Hebrew character, that they were regarded with intense aversion, as calculated to undermine social morals. In New Testament times, when theatres and amphitheatres were erected in Jerusalem and other large cities by Herod the Great, the Jewish residents considered it

CORINTHIAN GAMES.
(From a Sculpture.)

disreputable to be present at these popular places of amusement, — much more so to take part in their spectacles. The Talmud records that a celebrated Rabbi was wont every day, on leaving the Academy, to pray in these terms: "I thank Thee, O Lord my

God, that Thou hast cast my lot among those who frequent the schools and synagogues, and not among those who attend the theatre and circus. For both I and they work and watch, — I to inherit eternal life, they for their destruction." Nevertheless, the development by training of the physical powers could not have been wholly neglected; for professional runners were employed as swift messengers from the battle-field or other points of excited interest. In connection with the great victory of the Philistines over Israel, one of these messengers is mentioned: "There ran a man of Benjamin out of the army, and came to Shiloh the same day with his clothes rent, and with earth upon his head" (1 Sam. iv. 12); and again where David is waiting for tidings of his beloved but rebellious son Absalom, the watchman,

WRESTLERS.
[From a Sculpture.]

noting the two racers, cried from the "roof over the gate:" "Methinketh the running of the foremost is like the running of Ahimaaz the son of Zadok. And the king said, He is a good man, and cometh with good tidings" (2 Sam. xviii. 27). In the "match" between the servants of David and those of the son of Saul at the pool of Gibeon: "Abner said to Joab, Let the young men now arise, and play before us. . . . And they caught every one his fellow by the head, and thrust his sword in his fellow's side; so they fell down together" (2 Sam. ii. 14, 16); and in the subsequent events of this encounter, begun apparently in good faith and ending in a mortal combat, it is recorded of one of the "three sons of Zeruiah," who were engaged in it, that "Asahel was as light of foot as a wild roe."

The Psalmist depicts the sun as a bridegroom coming out of his chamber, "and rejoiceth as a strong man to run a race" (Ps. xix. 5); while the Preacher "saw under the sun, that the race is not to the swift" (Eccl. ix. 11). There are many texts in Scripture setting forth so much dexterity in the use of the bow and the string as to imply a course of private, if not public, training and competition. Of the tribe of Benjamin it is written: "Among all this people there were seven hundred chosen men left-handed; every one could sling stones at a hair-breadth, and not miss" (Judg. xx. 16); and of the "mighty men, helpers of the war," who came to David at Ziklag, it is recorded, "They were armed with bows, and could use both the right hand and the left in hurling stones and shooting arrows out of a bow" (1 Chron. xii. 2).

The early Christians had good reason to shun and abhor those high seats of heathen amusement, wherein their brethren in the faith, in days of persecution, had been compelled to profess "a good profession before many witnesses," sealing it with their own blood, —

"Butchered to make a Roman holiday!"

What with the Jewish prejudice and the Christian horror of these public exhibitions, it is difficult to account for St. Paul's evident familiarity with the rules and customs pertaining to them, and his proneness to making metaphorical use of them in his epistles to the early Church. In his native city there was a *gymnasium* (a place for training) and a *stadium* (a ground for running), with both of which he must have been familiar in his early youth; while the famous Isthmian games were celebrated near Corinth, where he lived for some time. In the well-known text beginning, "None of these things move me" (Acts xx. 24), the concluding words, "finish my course," are equivalent to "end my race." In another, equally familiar, all the figures are of this character: "I have fought the good fight," refers to an *athletic*, not a warlike, contest. "I have finished my course" (I have ended my race), "I have kept the

CHILDREN: THEIR TRAINING AND SCHOOLING.

faith: henceforth there is laid up for me a crown of righteousness, which the Lord, the righteous judge, shall give me at that day" (2 Tim. iv. 7, 8), the last allusion being to the wreaths of palm or laurel with which the judges crowned the victor. To the Galatians he writes: "Ye did run well, who did hinder

you?" to the Philippians: "I press toward the mark for the prize;" to the Corinthians: "I so run, not as uncertainly; . . . so fight I, not as one that beateth the air,"—a few of many references to the training, regimen, and active participation in the Greek games, or in the brutal encounters of men and beasts in gladiatorial arenas.

HOME DISCIPLINE.

Whatever may have been the practice of domestic discipline in Jewish households, it is evident that their theories on this subject, as demonstrated in the Bible and the Apocrypha, did not err on the side of weak indulgence. Profound reverence for parental authority was strictly inculcated and enforced, both by the law and by family rule: the relation between parents and children was invested with peculiar sanctity, as typical of that existing between the Almighty Father and His chosen people. It is not an exaggeration to assert that in a Jewish community no crime was regarded with more unqualified horror than any breach, whether in the letter or the spirit, of the "commandment with promise." For a child to be lacking in respect or loving attention to a parent, would have met with the severest condemnation; while crimes against parents, so common in our day, were happily almost unknown.

It is only necessary to review a few of the enactments under the Mosaic dispensation, to read the Jewish mind on this vital subject: "Cursed be he that setteth light by his father or his mother" (Deut. xxvii. 16); "He that smiteth his father or his mother shall be surely put to death" (Exod. xxi. 15); "Every one that curseth his father or his mother shall be surely put to death: he hath cursed his father or his mother; his blood shall be upon him" (Lev. xx. 9); and lastly, the terrible duty exacted from the parents of an incorrigible son, against whom there is not even an accusation of crime: "If a man have a stubborn and rebellious son, which will not obey the voice of his father, or the voice of his mother, and that, when they have chastened him, will not hearken unto them: then shall his father and his mother lay hold on him, and bring him out unto the elders of his city, and unto the gate of his place; and they shall say unto the elders of his city, This our son is stubborn and rebellious, he will not obey our voice; he is a glutton, and a drunkard. And all the men of his city shall stone him with stones, that he die: so shalt thou put evil away from among you; and all Israel shall hear, and fear" (Deut. xxi. 18-21). It was concerning one of these laws that Jesus spoke, when He accused the Jews of His time of having "made the commandment of God of none effect" by their tradition (Matt. xv. 6); in evident allusion to the interpretation of the law by the Mishnah, which reads: "He that curseth his father or his mother is not guilty, unless he curses them with express mention of the name of Jehovah" — otherwise he was declared innocent!

The Rabbinical ordinances carefully specified the duties of parents, and in a measure restricted their authority. A son was his own master from the time he could support himself; a

THE PATRIARCH.

daughter continued under her father's control until her marriage, but after she was of age he could not bestow her hand without her own consent; if a daughter had been given away before her legal "majority," twelve years and one day, she had afterwards the right of insisting upon a divorce.

A father might chastise a young child, even then not to excess of severity; but it was forbidden to beat a grown-up son, on pain of excommunication. These examples show a decided amelioration of the uncompromising rigor recommended to the head of the family in an earlier and more orthodox period, by that Wise King, who was not himself, perhaps, the best illustration of his own axiom: "Train up a child in the way he should go, and when he is old he will not depart from it." But here are some others, concerning this training: "Chasten thy son while there is hope, and let not thy soul spare for his crying" (Prov. xix. 18); "Foolishness is bound in the heart of a child; but the rod of correction shall drive it far from him" (Prov. xxii. 15); "Withhold not correction from the child: for if thou beatest him with the rod, he shall not die. Thou shalt beat him with the rod, and shalt deliver his soul from hell" (Prov. xxiii. 13, 14). In like spirit writes the son of Sirach in the Apocrypha: "He that loveth his son causeth him oft to feel the rod. . . . He that chastiseth his son shall have joy in him." "Cocker (indulge) thy child, and he shall make thee afraid; play with him, and he will bring thee to heaviness. Laugh not with him." . . . "Give him no liberty in his youth." . . . "Bow down his neck while he is young, and beat him on the sides while he is a child, lest he wax stubborn, and be disobedient unto thee, and so bring sorrow to thine heart" (Ecclus. xxx. 1, 2, 9–12). This of the sons; but he continues: "Hast thou daughters? have a care of their body, and show not thyself cheerful toward them" (Ecclus. vii. 24); yet this severe teacher suffers the tenderness of his heart to overflow unwittingly toward the girls, in one little verse of true paternal feeling: "The father waketh for the daughter when no man knoweth; and the care for her taketh away sleep: when she is young, lest she pass away the flower of her age; and being married, lest she should be hated" (Ecclus. xlii. 9).

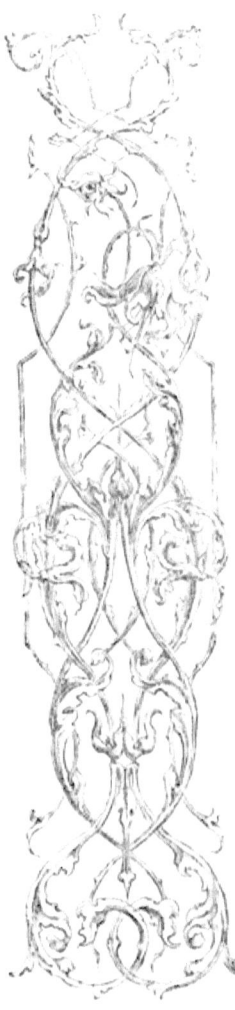

The great Pharisee of the New Testament insists no less upon the parental discipline under which he himself was reared. Writing to Timothy concerning the officers of the infant Church, St. Paul says of the bishop, he must be "one that ruleth well his own house, having his children in subjection with all gravity. (For if a man know not how to rule his own house, how shall he take care of the church of God?") (1 Tim. iii. 4, 5.) And again: "Let the deacons be the husbands of one wife, ruling their children and their own houses well" (1 Tim. iii. 12); and finally he sums up the Christian doctrine of family relationship and its mutual duties in these comprehensive words: "Children, obey your parents in the Lord: for this is right. Honor thy father and mother; which is the first commandment with promise; that it may be well with thee, and thou mayest live long on the earth. And, ye fathers, provoke not your children to wrath: but bring them up in the nurture and admonition of the Lord" (Eph. vi. 1-4).

As illustrations of the fulfilment of this beautiful law of corresponding authority and submission, ordained and blessed of God, we shall do well to remember Isaac and Joseph of the Old Testament, especially as prototypes of that Holy Child of the New Dispensation, who, born of Mary and reared by the carpenter, "went down with them, and came to Nazareth, and was subject unto them. . . . And Jesus increased in wisdom and stature, and in favor with God and man" (Luke ii. 51, 52).

In treating of the education of Jewish children, it must be borne in mind, that, in the scholastic system of the chosen people, religious discipline held the first place,—all merely intellectual development being subordinated to the love of God, and the knowledge of His holy Law. Philo wrote of the Jews of his day, that they "were from their swaddling-clothes, even before being taught either the sacred laws or the unwritten customs, trained by their parents, teachers, and instructors to recognize God as Father and as the Maker of the world;" and that, "having been taught the knowledge (of the laws) from earliest youth, they bore in their souls the image of the commandments."

Josephus adds his testimony to the same effect, that "from their earliest consciousness" they had "learned the laws so as to have them, as it were, engraven upon the soul." And these authorities, though of comparatively modern date, are but the repetition of what may be gathered throughout the pages of Scripture,—the Book of Proverbs being exceptionally rich in details affording an insight into family life, with special reference to "training up a child in the way he should go" (Prov. xxii. 6).

On no subject is the law more emphatic than in its commands to parents to teach the "statutes, judgments, and commandments of the Lord," to their children, thus: "These words, which I command thee this day, shall be in thine heart: and thou shalt teach them diligently unto thy children, and shalt talk of them when thou sittest in thine house, and when thou walkest by the way, and when thou liest down, and when thou risest up" (Deut. vi. 6, 7); and again in the thirty-first chapter: "Gather the people together, men and women and children, and thy stranger that is within thy gates, that they may hear, and that they may learn, and fear the Lord your God, and observe to do all the words of this law: and that their children, which have not known any thing, may hear, and learn to fear the Lord your God."

Six or seven was the age at which a Jewish parent was required to enter his son upon a course of study; but even before the child could speak, his religious education had begun in his nurse's arms when, carried into or out of any "clean" apartment in the house, he would be taught to touch the revered "Mesusah," and kiss the tiny finger that had approached the sacred Name exposed for adoration. Then with its first lispings the baby was fed with the "sincere milk of the Word,"— simple verses of

"SUFFER LITTLE CHILDREN TO COME UNTO ME."

Scripture, little morsels of prayer, and especially that "birthday text" which began or ended with the same letters as its own name, and which it was a later custom to teach a child always to repeat with its daily prayer. Thus in the apostolic days had Lois the grandmother, and Eunice the mother, of the pious

"THE ANGEL WHICH REDEEMED ME FROM ALL EVIL, BLESS THE LADS!"

Timothy, taught him so faithfully that St. Paul could say with confidence to his "own son in the faith:" "Continue thou in the things which thou hast learned and hast been assured of, knowing of whom thou hast learned them. And that from a child" (baby) "thou hast known the holy scriptures, which are able to make thee wise unto salvation through faith which is in Christ Jesus" (2 Tim. iii. 14, 15).

The Talmud records the interesting fact, that before the coming of Christ, and probably during His time, there were small parchment rolls prepared specially for the use of children, containing certain portions of the Law, "the history of the Creation to the Flood, and the first eight chapters of the book of Leviticus." An ancient Rabbi lays down the following formula for the education of sons: "At five years of age, reading of the Bible (of course in the original Hebrew); at ten years, learning the Mishnah; at thirteen years, bound to the commandments; at fifteen years, the study of the Talmud; at eighteen, marriage,"—which was necessarily an abrupt and final interruption to the scholastic course. Wiser sayings on this important topic warn the parent against setting a child to "regular study before it is six years old." At this age the Jewish boy of the better class passed from the exclusive care of his mother and his nurse to that of some faithful servant of the household, usually the steward or ruler of the house, who enjoyed to the fullest extent his master's respect and confidence. His duty was not to impart instruction, but to guard the young heir from whatever might corrupt him in mind or body, to exercise over him an unceasing moral restraint, to attend him to and from school, the bath, sightseeing, or whatever else should take him out of doors. Such a personal guardian is referred to by St. Paul, when he wrote to the Galatians: "The law was our schoolmaster to bring us unto Christ" (iii. 24).

The Jewish lad became "of age" morally, so to speak, when he was thirteen years old and one day: he was then made a "son of the covenant," responsible before God for his own actions. He put on the *Talith*, or "fringed garment," and the phylacteries; and thrice a day, if possible, he was obliged to attend the religious exercises of the synagogue, undertaking the strict fulfilment of the law.

Daughters remained in charge of the mother and the nurse until marriage: there was very slight provision made for the education of girls, since, certainly as late as the days of Rabbinical control, those wise doctors declared their opposition to any more than a rudimentary course of study for the frailer sex. For this opposition they gave several reasons, so indisputably excellent that it seems somewhat supererogatory that they should dismiss the whole subject with the dogmatical assertion: " Women are of a light mind!" Yet, for all that, there were learned women in that day, learned even from the Rabbinical standpoint; but how the reverend teachers disposed of such perverse and strong-minded facts, has not been disclosed for our edification.

Before the Captivity, children were taught by their parents and the Levites, and later by the Rabbis, to read and write, and to commit the law to memory; after the Captivity, when synagogues were built in every considerable town, there were elementary schools attached to each, where young children were exercised by their appointed teachers in learning the Hebrew characters, preparatory to the first lessons in reading the Bible, beginning always with Leviticus, the book of the law. The alphabet was taught by drawing the letters on a board until the child became familiar with them, and able to name each at sight. He was then required to decipher them one by one in perfect manuscript, to combine them, and to read them aloud — special care being taken to instruct the pupil in his choice of language and pronunciation. The training of the memory was considered of the highest importance in early education, and mnemonic rules were devised to that end.

The rules and regulations for these infant-schools were of the most careful and salutary character: as the teacher was to promote the moral welfare of his pupils, still more than the intellectual, he must keep them strictly from every vicious association; he must suppress in them all desire for revenge, all

CHILDREN: THEIR TRAINING AND SCHOOLING. 127

ill-feeling one toward another. He must by no means promise a child any thing that he did not intend to perform, lest the child should become accustomed to the idea of falsehood; he must not lose patience with a pupil, however slow and stupid; if, after all

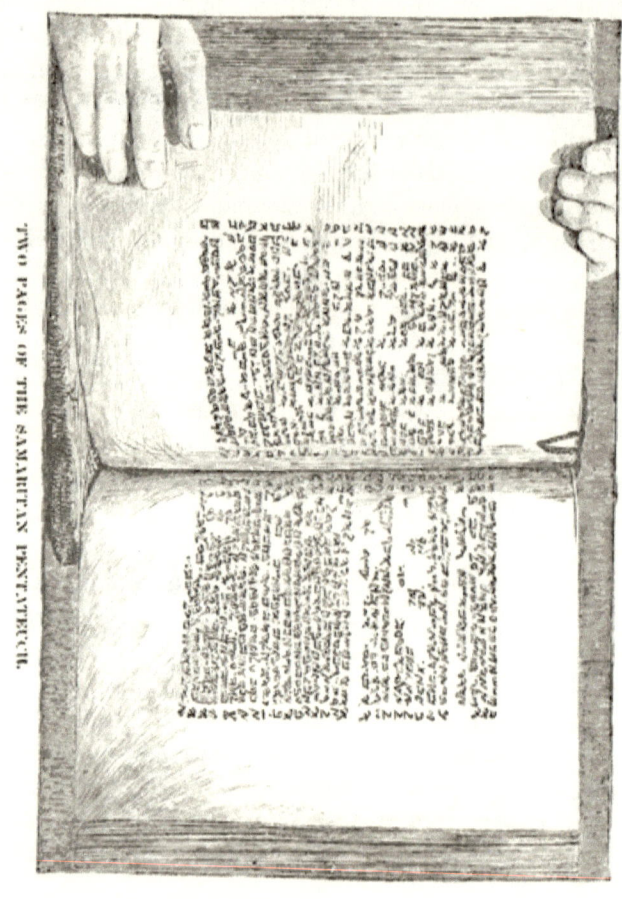

TWO PAGES OF THE SAMARITAN PENTATEUCH.

kindness had failed, the teacher must resort to punishment, he might administer correction only with a strap, and that with moderation. Lest he should show favor to the children of rich parents, the teacher was salaried by the congregation, and all expenses of the school were defrayed by charitable contributions.

The hours of study were regulated according to the age of the pupil, and the season of the year; only four hours were permitted for instruction during July and August; nor was a teacher allowed to chastise his pupils during these months! Lastly, he must be a married man, and bring to his delicate duties the sympathies of a paternal heart.

It was the custom in Oriental schools for the master to sit on a high chair: his elder pupils sat on a low bench, while the youngest sat on the floor,--the scholars were literally "at the feet" of their teacher. So St. Paul said of himself that he "was brought up in this city" (Jerusalem), "at the feet of Gamaliel" (Acts xxii. 3); so the pious Mary, who had "chosen that good part," "sat at Jesus' feet, and heard his word" (Luke x. 39); and so, when the Great Teacher was about to teach the assembled people in the synagogue at Nazareth, "he closed the book, and he gave it again to the minister, and sat down" (Luke iv. 20). In like manner it was "when he was set," that "his disciples came unto him, and he opened his mouth, and taught them" in the wonderful Sermon on the Mount (Matt. v. 1, 2). In the Temple "all the people came unto him, and he sat down and taught them" (John viii. 2); and in that hour of the "power of darkness," He testified to them that had "come out as against a thief, with swords and staves;" "I sat daily with you teaching in the temple" (Matt. xxvi. 55).

This system of public school instruction prevailed at the time of our Lord's dwelling among us, and theoretically, at least, it would seem difficult to improve upon its liberal provisions and its great good sense. A most beautiful feature of this system was the kindness extended to the children of poor members of the congregation, as well as to orphans. In the Temple there was a separate receptacle provided to receive contributions, which, with much delicacy, were privately appropriated to these children, whose helplessness constituted an eloquent appeal to the hearts of the faithful. Indeed, we are told that orphans were a special charge to the whole congregation,—"not thrust into poorhouses; and the parochial authorities were even bound to provide a fixed dowry for the girls."

V.

THE HIGHER EDUCATION.

OF a very different character were the important "Schools of the Prophets," mentioned very early in the history of the Jewish people. These theological seminaries, as we may term them, are said to have been established in the service of religion by the holy Samuel, in a heroic effort to restore the purity of the priesthood. Through his influence, schools were opened in Ramah, Bethel, Jericho, Gilgal, and other cities: students, termed the "Sons of the Prophets," were selected among those young men of intellectual promise, as well as of unblemished character, who were desirous of further instruction in the law, and in the arts of music and poetry as connected with the liturgy of public devotion. When they had completed the prescribed course of study, they were installed in the sacred office of expounders of holy things to the people, — an office they were expected to magnify by an austere and strictly spiritual mode of life. Numerous allusions are made to these theological schools and to their students, the "Sons of the Prophets." We will indicate a few for the curious reader, as found in the Second Book of the Kings. ii. 3, 5, 7; iv. 1, 2, 38, 43; vi. 1, 2 (1 Sam. x. 5, 10, xix. 19, 20).

But, beside these special seats of learning, there were, at a later period, academies for lads of sixteen or eighteen, as well as class-rooms presided over by distinguished Rabbis, and even debates of the mighty Sanhedrim, to which maturer scholars were admitted; but entrance to the two last supposed a very advanced degree of acquirement. In these schools, though the profound study of the law, as expounded by the Rabbis, constituted a feature of the first importance; yet certain concessions were made to the growing demand of the age for instruction in science and in the languages of their polite neighbors, the Greeks and Romans, with whom the people were brought into continual commercial contact. Up to this period all teaching of heathen science or literature had been absolutely prohibited. One learned Rabbi declared that "he who reads foreign books" forfeits his inheritance of eternal life; while another explained that the "foreign books" meant "those of Aristotle and his followers, the chronicles of Gentile kings, and the amatory verses of the poets." A third and still greater Rabbi disposed of the subject to the total discomfiture of any contemporaneous aspirant to profane attainments: he refers the young Israelite of "advanced thought" to the first Psalm: "Blessed is the man" whose "delight is in the law of the Lord; and in His law doth he meditate day and night." "Find the hour," says the great Rabbi, "which is neither day nor night, and in that you may, without offence, study heathen writings."

The earliest books, so frequently mentioned in the Sacred Volume, were written on linen or cotton cloth, on skins, or on leaves made of the stalk of the Egyptian water-reed called *papyrus*, from which paper was first made and derives its name. When written on cloth or parchment, the ancient book was made in the form of a sheet, attached at both extremities to cylindrical rods, as our modern maps are mounted: the rods were then rolled up and met midway. To use the book, the reader unrolled the manuscript to the desired point, keeping only a small portion exposed for perusal, as required. Thin strips of parchment were fastened to each roll, indicating its contents, to save the student the trouble of unrolling the wrong book. The subject matter of each roll was written in columns about four inches wide and some fifty lines long, corresponding to the pages of our books. Ancient rolls were often furnished with a case or cover, more or less ornamental according to the esteem in which the manuscript was held.

Modern books in the East, whether of parchment or paper, are made of separate sheets bound together at the back, and, if valuable, are kept in cases elaborately decorated in gold, pearls, and precious stones. A recent traveller took the pains to count over four hundred gems in the embroidered wrapper of a copy of the Koran. A convent in Jerusalem boasts of possessing "one hundred manuscript volumes on vellum;" and in the monastic libraries on Mount Athos, there are "six rolls of parchment, each ten inches wide and ten feet long." But these are insignificant when compared with the ancient manuscript roll of the Pentateuch, preserved in the public library at Cambridge, Eng.: it is made of thirty-seven goat-skins dyed red, and measures forty-eight feet in length by about twenty-two in breadth. As a part of it is lacking, it is computed that originally it must have been some ninety feet long. In his Second Epistle to Timothy, St. Paul directs him, when he comes, to bring "the books, but especially the parchments" (iv. 13). Such was the book that Jehudi read "in the ears of the king" (Jehoiakim).

THE BOOK, OR ROLL IN ITS CASE.

"And it came to pass that when Jehudi had read three or four leaves, he cut it with the penknife, and cast it into the fire that was on the hearth, until all the roll was consumed" (Jer. xxxvi. 23). The "flying roll" that was shown to Zechariah in a vision was thirty feet long and twenty wide. Such was the book, a parchment roll, made use of by our Lord when He " went into the synagogue (at Nazareth) on the sabbath day, and stood up for to read. And there was delivered unto him the book of the prophet Esaias. And when he had opened the book, he found the place where it was written : The Spirit of the Lord is upon me, because he hath anointed me to preach the gospel to the poor ; he hath sent me to heal the broken-hearted, to preach deliverance to the captives, and recovering of sight to the blind, to set at liberty them that are bruised ; to preach the acceptable year of the Lord" (Luke iv. 16-19). To these rolls the prophet refers in the words : " The heavens shall be rolled together as a scroll " (Isa. xxxiv. 4).

In Job we find allusion to three ancient methods of preserving records: " Oh that my words were now written ! Oh that they were printed in a book ! That they were graven with an iron pen and lead in the rock forever!" (xix. 23, 24.) Books were often engraved on tablets of stone, brick, lead, copper, or wood, or bark of trees. Lead tablets, especially, are of great antiquity ; some of these thin sheets of lead in the British Museum date back to the fourth century before Christ ; they were excavated from the ruins of a heathen temple in Cnidus, an ancient Greek city of Asia Minor. It would be pleasant to say of the inscriptions on these tablets that have lived so long, that they record something noble, something that can never die ; but alas for poor human nature in the days of her extreme poverty ! they contain only the names of the men and women of Cnidus, whom other men and women of Cnidus hated, and which were thus reported to the gods of the temple for their special malediction and vengeance.

A book of these tablets was purchased in Rome some two centuries ago, made entirely, even to the hinges and nails of the cover, of lead. It was about four inches long by three in width, and contained six " leaves." Its matter consisted of Egyptian gnostic figures, and inscriptions in Greek and Etruscan characters.

It is probable that Job refers, not to leaden tablets or leaves,

THE HIGHER EDUCATION. 133

but to the ancient custom of cutting letters in stone, and then filling them with molten lead. Important truths or events were recorded in this manner: thus "Joshua built an altar unto the Lord God of Israel in Mount Ebal. . . . And he wrote there upon

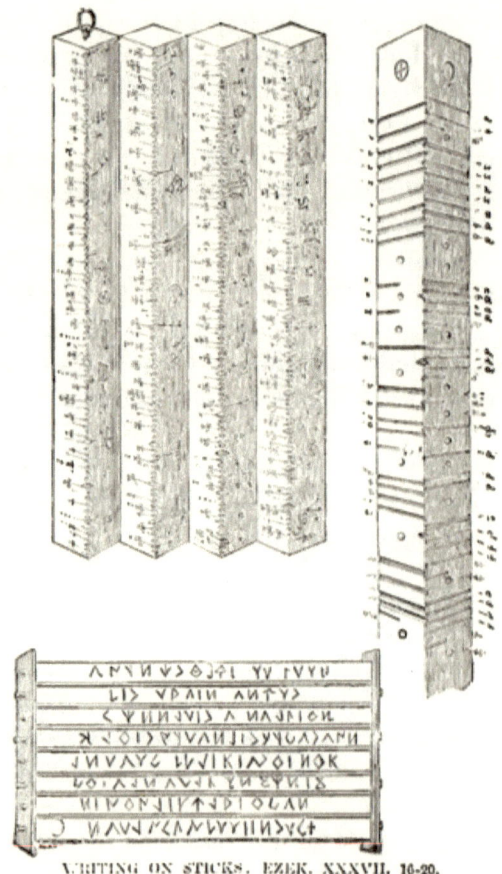

WRITING ON STICKS. EZEK. XXXVII. 16-20.

the stones a copy of the law of Moses, which he wrote in the presence of the children of Israel" (Josh. viii. 30, 32); and scholars devoted to Oriental research find indications of incised letters, filled with lead or copper, in the Assyrian and other ancient monuments. Many of these stone records are invaluable, as confirming and even supplementing Biblical facts and history: the famous Moabite Stone, for instance, discovered in 1868, contains the Moabitish account of the battle between the three kings, — of Israel, Judah, and Edom, — and the king of Moab, who had rebelled against the king of Israel, refusing his customary tribute of "a hundred thousand lambs, and a hundred thousand rams, with the wool" (2 Kings iii.)

The Rosetta Stone in the British Museum is a famous example of writing on stone: it contains a proclamation of the coronation of an Egyptian monarch, 196 B.C. Nineveh and Babylon have furnished many of these valuable "books" of stone, as well as bricks and tiles with inscriptions.

The Greeks and Romans used the papyrus and parchment for manuscripts. The papyrus was put to a great variety of uses: for many ages it was the staple product of Egypt, and its manufacture became a royal monopoly. An instructive writer on the "Trades of the Bible" says: "In the whole compass of inspired prophecy, there is nothing more surprising than the declaration made by Isaiah of the utter failure of the papyrus crop: 'The reeds and flags shall wither. The paper-reeds by the brooks, by the mouth of the brooks, and every thing sown by the brooks, shall wither, be driven away, and be no more'" (xix. 7), — a prophecy that has been literally fulfilled." It was among these tall water-plants, in the lair of the crocodile, that the infant Moses was hidden on the banks of the Nile.

In reviewing these tedious processes of book-making, we may infer that the calling of a scribe was one of acknowledged importance: indeed, the enrolment of the "families of the scribes which dwelt at Jabez," in the genealogical tables contained in the opening chapters of the First Book of the Chronicles, would indicate that they occupied no mean position among their brethren. There were the secular, the military, and the sacred scribes, — distinctions scarcely necessary to be explained in detail here: the sacred scribe had the custody of the holy oracles, and the responsibility of their reproduction; and the mere copyist

THE PHARAOH OF THE NILE.

under his orders had a task requiring the utmost patience, skill, and reverence for his work. The Rabbinical books prescribed stringent rules for the writing of the sacred rolls of the Law. The material must not be papyrus, nor ordinary parchment, but the finest *vellum* made of the inner side of the sheepskin. The letters must be of that form — the "square Hebrew" — which, by Jewish tradition, was identical with that used on Mount Sinai in the tables of the law. They must be written with black ink, not with gold or colors; minute directions were given for breaking off the lines, and especially for writing the Divine Name: the pen which had recorded the name JEHOVAH was consecrated solely to that sacred purpose. If an error was detected in the manuscript, the whole skin had to be destroyed, as no erasure or correction was permitted.

SAMARITAN COPY OF THE LAW.

In those dark days for Israel, during the Syrian persecutions which finally roused the Maccabees to desperate defence of their race, it was common for private families to possess at least portions of the Word of God in the form we have described. It is on record that a feature of those persecutions was the monthly search for the Scriptures in the homes of the Jewish people; and, in the words of the historian: "When they had rent in pieces the books of the Law which they found, they burnt them with fire; and whosoever was found with any book of the Testament, or if any consented to the Law, the king's commandment was that they should put him to death" (1 Macc. i. 56, 57).

After the triumph of the Maccabees, there was a period of great religious revival, and it may be supposed that scribes were multiplied to repair the losses sustained in the destruction of the precious manuscripts; and that in the time of Christ few pious Hebrew homes — such as that of Elisabeth, or Anna, or Dorcas Lydia, Phœbe, Priscilla, or the mother of Zebedee's children, or St. John's "elect lady," or Lois or Eunice, or Mary the mother of Mark, or, lastly, that greater Mary whom all generations call Blessed — were without some portion of the written Word from which to teach their children the way of eternal life.

In these days the scribe added to his laborious art of transcrib-

MEDIÆVAL BIBLES.

ing, the perilous responsibility of commenting upon and expounding the Law; and, finally, his devotion to the *letter* seems to have led to the perversions that characterized that time, when our Lord was constrained to say to His disciples, "in the audience of all the people:" "Beware of the scribes, which desire to walk in long robes, and love greetings in the markets, and the highest seats in the synagogues, and the chief rooms at feasts; which devour widows' houses, and for a show make long prayers: the same shall receive greater damnation" (Luke xx. 46, 47). Quite distinct from these pretentious scribes, who were also identified with certain legal functions, was the writer who earned his modest living by conducting correspondence, or keeping accounts, for the large class of the community who had no knowledge of writing. This art was, especially in early times, a rare accomplishment among the Hebrews and other Orientals; letter-writing was, for the most part, a polite interchange of formal expressions of courtesy according to the prevailing etiquette, which could be delegated to a public scribe without sensitive reluctance.

Ancient letters were probably written on fine parchment, specially prepared for the purpose, on palm-leaves, or on papyrus. There were also writing-tablets in common use among the Greeks and Romans, as well as the Hebrews; small "leaves" sometimes made of ivory, but generally of wood,—citron, beech, or fir. One side was covered with a thin coating of wax, in which the letters were formed by the *stylus*,—a sort of pen made of gold, silver, or cheaper metals, or even of bone. One end of the stylus was pointed for writing; the other was broad and flat for erasions, and for smoothing the wax, so that it could be used again. Five or six of these tablet leaves might be fastened together at the back by wires; and, when used for letter-writing, all could be tied together with a strong cord, the ends of which were sealed with the writer's signet. Such was the "writing-table," or tablet, that Zacharias called for at the circumcision and naming of his son, St. John the Baptist: the company "made signs to his father, how he would have him called. And he asked for a writing-table, and wrote, saying, His name is John" (Luke i. 62, 63). There were several varieties of pens, to correspond with the materials upon which the writing was to be inscribed. In very early times it was common to paint the letters or hieroglyphic characters with a hair pencil finely pointed; afterward, the *calamus*, or reed pen, was introduced, and still later the improvement of splitting the point of the reed, as we prepare goose-quills, with a knife made for that purpose; this penknife is mentioned in Jer. xxxvi. 23. Job speaks of "an iron pen;" Jeremiah declares that "the sin of Judah is written with a pen of iron, and with the point of a diamond" (xvii. 1). Inks of various sorts were manufactured, and for brilliancy and durability have certainly never been equalled by modern compositions. The commonest preparation was made of pulverized charcoal, or ivory or lamp black, mixed with gum and water: the Greeks used an ink similar to our Indian ink, rubbing it from a solid block and mixing it with water. The Romans made ink of soot with pitch, and by boiling and straining the dregs of wine: they also used a black secretion of the cuttle-fish, hence its name *sepia*. The Romans were also skilled in the manufacture of colored inks, and of invisible or sympathetic inks for secret correspondence: a very costly red ink was made for the imperial signature; but, if the emperor was a minor, his regent signed for him in green ink. The Egyptians were also fond of red ink, and that found on their papyrus writings of ancient date is as fresh as if written recently. Josephus speaks of writing in gold letters, probably in the style of later illuminated manuscripts. The ink so frequently mentioned in the New Testament was almost certainly black, as indicated by its name in that connection.

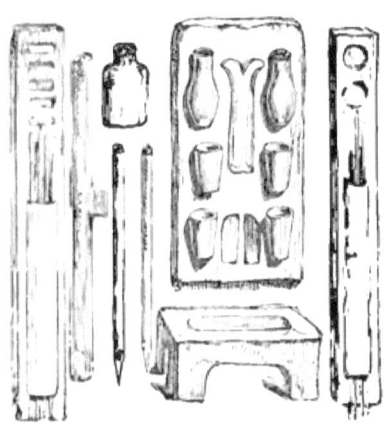

EGYPTIAN WRITING IMPLEMENTS.

The writer's inkhorn is spoken of but once in the Bible, though it is one of the most familiar articles in use in the East, even to this day: in vision the prophet Ezekiel saw "six men;" and "one man among them was clothed with linen, with a writer's inkhorn by his side" (ix. 2). This was a convenient case for writing-materials, consisting of a receptacle for pens and paper, with a small box, having a hinged lid, for the ink at one end. The whole case is about ten inches in length, usually made of brass, copper, or silver, and often exhibiting exquisite workmanship: one in the writer's possession is of brass, elaborately engraved in delicate arabesque designs. It is still customary in the East for public letter-writers to carry these inkhorns in their girdles, and at the street-corners to write impassioned confessions for lovers, or bitter denunciations for mortal enemies, with equal placidity and skill. "It came to pass in the morning, that David wrote a letter to Joab, and sent it by the hand of Uriah. And he wrote in the letter, saying, Set ye Uriah in the forefront of the hottest battle, and retire ye from him, that he may be smitten, and die" (2 Sam. xi. 14, 15). This is the first letter recorded in the Bible. We may safely conclude that it was penned by the king's own hand, not by one of the four scribes of his royal household. Short as it is, few readers need to be reminded of the terrible part it bore in bringing to a tragic crisis the shameful story that, through the Divine mercy, found a blessed sequel in the Fifty-first Psalm.

Another royal personage, the infamous Jezebel, accomplished a murderous purpose, in the interest of her husband King Ahab, by means of letters: "She wrote letters in Ahab's name, and sealed them with his seal, and sent the letters unto the elders and to the nobles" (1 Kings xxi. 8). The seventh chapter of the Book of Ezra contains "the copy of the letter that the king Artaxerxes gave unto Ezra the priest, . . . a scribe of the law of the God of heaven." In the beautiful story of the cleansing of Naaman the leper, we read that the king of Syria sent a letter to the king of Israel (2 Kings v. 5).

These primitive letters were in the form of rolls, closed at the ends with clay or wax, and then sealed. In writing to persons of distinction, it was the custom in Persia, as well as other Oriental lands, to enclose the scroll in a very elegant bag or purse: the opening of the bag was tied, and covered with clay or wax, which then received the impression of the writer's seal. This elaborate form of letter was a polite recognition of the respect due to the rank or worth of the person addressed: an open letter, on the contrary, was an intentional expression of contempt, or simply the usual manner of indicating that it was sent to an inferior. Such was evidently the etiquette as to correspondence prevailing in Persia in the days of the devout Nehemiah; for he lays stress upon the fact that Sanballat (who wished to intimidate and insult him) sent " his servant unto me in like manner the fifth time with an open letter in his hand" (Neh. vi. 5). It was so unusual in the East for persons to write their own letters, that the seal became of more importance than the signature, and was often used in its stead. Seals were often fastened upon rings, and worn on the finger. The gift of such a ring was a transfer of authority: thus " Pharaoh took off his ring from his hand, and put it upon Joseph's hand" (Gen. xli. 42); and Ahasuerus invested Haman with royal power in the same way, and again gave it to Mordecai (Esth. iii. 10–12). Many specimens of these seals and signet-rings are preserved in public and private collections: they present a great variety of forms, and are made of gold, silver, brass, precious stones, or even pottery; some were perforated, to be hung on a chain about the neck; others were cylindrical and in a metal frame, so as to revolve as the impression was taken: Chaldæa and Assyria have furnished beautiful specimens of this sort of seal. The art of engraving stone seals is very ancient: it is first mentioned in connection with the precious stones of the high-priest's ceremonial vestments: " With the work of an engraver in stone, like the engravings of a signet, shalt thou engrave the two stones with the names of the children of Israel" (Exod. xxviii. 11). The devices preferred for seals were figures and characters of symbolical significance: a favorite design for the convex surface of an Egyptian seal was the sacred scarabæus, or beetle. Clay was used in preference to wax; because the heat of the Oriental climate hardened the clay, while it would melt the wax. Job says of the earth: "It is turned as clay to the seal" (xxxviii. 14). It must be remembered that seals were used for countless other purposes than the closing or signing of letters: in Egypt, Babylonia, and Assyria, bricks were stamped with a seal; wine-jars and mummy-pits in Egypt were covered

SEALS AND SIGNETS.

and sealed with clay; the doors of granaries or treasure-rooms throughout the East are to this day thus sealed, so that they cannot be opened without first breaking the seal. Even tombs are secured in this manner, as is written of the grave of Jesus: "They went and made the sepulchre sure, sealing the stone" (Matt. xxvii. 66). So was the pit of lions fastened, into which Daniel was cast: "A stone was brought, and laid upon the mouth of the den; and the king sealed it with his own signet, and with the signet of his lords" (vi. 17). Many precautions were necessary to maintain the inviolability of signatures and seals; since, in later times especially, their imitation and fraudulent use was a crying public evil. Josephus dwells upon this fact; and almost every epistle of St. Paul, written by amanuenses, contains at its close a special assurance from the apostle of its genuineness: "The salutation of Paul with mine own hand, which is the token in every epistle: so I write" (2 Thess. iii. 17); "The salutation by the hand of me Paul" (Col. iv. 18); "Ye see how large a letter I have written unto you with mine own hand" (Gal. vi. 11).

VI.

EMPLOYMENTS AND SERVANTS.

BETHANY.

A STRIKING feature in the education of Jewish children — in strong contrast to the system prevailing among the Gentiles — was the enactment that compelled the Hebrew parent, however wealthy or distinguished, to teach his son a trade. While the luxurious and corrupt Greeks and Romans contemned all manual or mechanical labor as mean and vulgar, the wiser Jewish people delighted to honor it with their lips, and even to engage in it with somewhat ostentatious humility. It was a Rabbinical principle, that "whoever does not teach his son a trade is as if he brought him up to be a robber;" and a multiplicity of laudatory proverbs from high sources demonstrate the popular esteem in which honest labor was held. Yet certain trades, it must be confessed, were regarded with virulent prejudice, by reason of the uncleanliness of their surroundings, — such as those of tanners, dyers, and miners; while the Mishnah (one of the Rabbinical books) warned a man not to instruct his son in a trade which must necessarily bring him into contact with women. It is evident that this caution was not too strictly observed, or there would have been a notable deficiency of jewellers, perfumers, weavers, manufacturers of various household appointments, and other tradesmen delegated more especially to the ministration of the fair sex. After a period in Jewish social history in which the mechanical arts had been held in contempt, as incompatible with the pursuit of learning, the Rabbis carried their appreciation of the dignity of labor to an opposite extreme. It became the fashion for these exalted scholars, profound in the mysteries of the law, to engage personally in severe manual toil, so that the celebrated names of that epoch handed down to us are coupled with the trades of smiths, potters, shoemakers, tailors, sandal-makers, — in short, throughout the entire list of common crafts: an extreme case is recorded of a stone-cutter, who was summoned from his shop to be invested with the office of high-priest.

In this connection, it is edifying to consider how the great Apostle Paul pursued his occupation as a tentmaker while he was burdened with " the care of all the churches ;" and while in Corinth, at the house of Aquila and Priscilla, because he " was of the same craft, he abode with them and wrought : for by their occupation they were tentmakers" (Acts xviii. 3). That he was not alone in thus combining spiritual with secular pursuits, St. Paul declares in writing to the Corinthians of the other apostles as well : " We have no certain dwelling-place; and labor, working with our own hands" (1 Cor. iv. 11, 12).

Nor must we fail to dwell upon the fact, so difficult to realize, that the " Only Begotten of the Father, full of grace and truth," passed years of patient waiting in daily toil at the carpenter's bench in the little shop at Nazareth, where, with his reputed father, he labored for the modest support of his family. And yet when only twelve years of age he had said to his mother: "Wist ye not that I must be about my Father's business?" (Luke ii. 49.)

The daughters of the family were instructed in the household duties incumbent upon the women of their times. Of the ideal wife and mother of Israel, as depicted in the Book of Proverbs, it is said, "She seeketh wool and flax, and worketh willingly with her hands. . . . She layeth her hands to the spindle, and her hands hold the distaff" (Prov. xxxi. 13, 19); and at the building of the tabernacle it is recorded that "all the women that were wise-hearted did spin with their hands, and brought that which they had spun, both of blue, and of purple, and of scarlet, and of fine linen. And all the women whose heart stirred them up in wisdom spun goats' hair" (Exod. xxxv. 25, 26). It is therefore reasonable to conclude that spinning wool for winter garments, and flax for the fine linen so highly prized, constituted perhaps the most important domestic industry. The task of preparing the yarn for weaving belonged to the young girls of the family, hence our word *spinster* for an unmarried woman; while the more delicate operation of weaving the cloth was the mother's work, and is expressed in her title *wife*. The ancient sculptures represent Egyptian women busy with the distaff and at the loom. From the choice flax of Egypt the finest linen was produced, especially a transparent fabric of exquisite texture, represented on mural pictures as draping but not concealing the outlines of the figure. The prophet, in his "burden of Egypt," alludes to them "that work in fine flax, and them that weave net-works" (Isa. xix. 9). Spinning and weaving may have been

A CARPENTER'S SHOP IN MODERN NAZARETH.

the employments of which the righteous Tobit speaks in his quaint autobiography: "My wife Anna did take women's works to do; and when she had sent them home to the owners, they paid her wages, and gave her also besides a kid" (Tob. ii. 11, 12).

We observe, from the examples presented in the first books of the Bible, that it was customary for women of the highest rank to engage personally in what are now, by a perverted social sense, considered the menial offices of the household, — cooking, serving, drawing water; and in the rural districts taking part in the farm-labor and the tending of flocks. Sarah, the wife of Abraham, — receiving her title, "the Princess," from the Almighty, — "makes cakes upon the hearth," and prepares the savory meat for her husband's guests (Gen. xviii. 6); and so the wife of the Bedouin chief of to-day dispenses with her own hands the sacred rites of family ministration and hospitality. To the younger women pertained the task of bringing water from the well or public fountain for the use of the family, — a duty they were not averse to, since it brought them in contact with their young companions to interchange the social gossip of the hour. In his prayer to God for the success of his mission, the servant of Abraham said: "Behold, I stand here by the well of water; and the daughters of the men of the city come out to draw water: . . . and it came to pass, before he had done speaking, that, behold, Rebekah came out . . . with her pitcher upon her shoulder" (Gen. xxiv. 13. 15); and so when Saul and his servant went to seek the prophet Samuel, "as they went up the hill to the city, they found young maidens going out to draw water" (1 Sam. ix. 11). This custom still prevails in many parts of the East: the girls carry the pitchers with broad bottoms on their heads, protected by a small cushion; those that are pointed (*amphoræ*) are carried on the shoulder, also with a cushion. It is permissible now for a passing stranger to ask a drink of these fair water-carriers, even as it was in the far-away time when Eliezer begged that favor of the beautiful Rebekah (Gen. xxiv. 45); and later, when at Jacob's well "there cometh a woman of Samaria to draw water: Jesus saith unto her, Give me to drink" (John iv. 7).

The washing of the family linen in small towns and villages was, and is still, done at the public fountain, — a rude structure being erected for the accommodation of the officiating matrons.

The gathering of fuel in the rural districts has been from a remote period the peculiar duty of Eastern women and children, and is another household custom still preserved in Palestine. Maidens are seen at the barley-harvest of Boaz, who said to Ruth: "Go not to glean in another field, neither go from hence, but abide here fast by my maidens; let thine eyes be on the field that they do reap, and go thou after them" (Ruth ii. 8, 9). They tended their fathers' flocks, as in the example of Rachel, who came to the well of Haran "with her father's sheep, for she kept them" (Gen. xxix. 9); and of Jethro's seven daughters in the land of Midian, who "came and drew water, and filled the troughs to water their father's flock" (Exod. ii. 16). They also took part in the gathering of the vintage, and of the harvests of grains and fruits.

Fine embroidery and needlework form so prominent an industry among modern Oriental women, that it is not unreasonable to conclude that it was a feminine accomplishment at a very early period. It would be pleasant to know that the "embroidery" and "cunning work," mentioned so frequently in the Book of Exodus in connection with the adornment of the tabernacle and the priests' garments, was wrought by the nimble fingers of those "women that were wise-hearted" to spin fine linen and goats' hair for the house of the Lord; and may it not be surmised from the proclamation of Moses throughout the camp of zealous contributors?—" Let neither man nor woman make any more work for the offering of the sanctuary" (Exod. xxxvi. 6).

Under the new dispensation, the apostles left no room for "doubtful disputations" as to the "sphere" of woman and her work, whether in the church or in the family. St. Paul, instructing Timothy as to the essential qualifications for membership in a certain pious sodality of women, describes the elderly Christian widow, "she that is a widow indeed:" "Well reported of for good works; if she have brought up children, if she have lodged strangers, if she have washed the saints' feet, if she have relieved the afflicted, if she have diligently followed every good work." "But," he continues, "the younger widows refuse. . . . I will therefore that the younger women marry, bear children, guide the house, give none occasion to the adversary to speak reproachfully" (1 Tim. v. 5, 10, 11, 14). Again in his Epistle to Titus the apostle urges him to exhort "the aged women likewise, that they be in behavior as becometh holiness, not false accusers, not given to much wine, teachers of good things; that they may teach the young women to be sober, to love their husbands, to love their children, to be discreet, chaste, keepers at home, good, obedient to their own husbands, that the word of God be not blasphemed" (ii. 3–5). Both St. Paul and St. Peter covet for all "women professing godliness," the adornment of "good works" (1 Tim. ii. 10); not that "of wearing of gold or of putting on of apparel," but "the ornament of a meek and quiet spirit, which is in the sight of God of great price" (1 Pet. iii. 4).

"Whosoever shall do the will of my Father which is in

heaven, the same is my brother, and sister, and mother," is the Saviour's inspiring assurance to the weakest of that sex whose lives, for the most part, are spent in a weary round of daily tasks. To the fretting housewife, " cumbered about much serving," He administers the gentle rebuke: " Martha, Martha, thou art careful and troubled about many things; but one thing is needful; and Mary hath chosen that good part, which shall not be taken away from her" (Luke x. 41, 42); while His commendation of her who came to Him "in Bethany, in the house of Simon the leper,"—"She hath done what she could" (Mark xiv. 8),—is the supreme tribute attainable by the most exalted among women, and yet equally within the reach of the lowliest drudge.

SLAVERY is found in Israel in the earliest records of the nation; but, like polygamy, it was, in their practice, a system eminently humane and protective. The "bondmen" and "bondmaids," so often indicated in the law and narrative of the Old Testament, were, for the most part, captives taken in war from the heathen nations whom the Hebrews were commanded to drive out before them, as they took possession of the promised land. But in certain circumstances a Jew might purchase one of his own people: as where a man too poor to pay a debt sold himself to his creditor, in which case the law mercifully provided: "If thy brother that dwelleth by thee be waxen poor, and be sold unto thee; thou shalt not compel him to serve as a bondservant: but as a hired servant, and as a sojourner, he shall be with thee, and shall serve thee unto the year of jubilee: and then shall he depart from thee, both he and his children with him, and shall return unto his own family, and unto the possession of his fathers shall he return" (Lev. xxv. 39–41); or as when a man, having stolen something he could not restore or replace, was "sold for his theft." Parents might sell their daughter as a maidservant, but it was understood that she was to be her master's concubine; if, however, she became his son's wife, the law compelled her master to "deal with her after the manner of daughters" (Exod. xxi. 9).

THE SISTERS OF BETHANY.

This state of servitude could last by law only six years; but, where it was entered into for debt, it might be still shorter, that is, cancelled when payment was made. Otherwise the Hebrew bondman served six years; and, it was written, " in the seventh he shall go out free for nothing." Frequently, however, the master had given one of his own bondmaids to his servant to wife, in which case he must "go out by himself," since wife and children belonged to the master; for this emergency the law also provided: " If the servant shall plainly say, I love my master, my wife, and my children; I will not go out free: then his master

EASTERN LANDSCAPE.

shall bring him unto the judges; he shall also bring him to the door, or unto the door-post; and his master shall bore his ear through with an awl; and he shall serve him forever" (Exod. xxi. 5, 6). Even when discharged free in the seventh year, the master was commanded not to "let him go away empty." "Thou shalt furnish him liberally out of thy flock, and out of thy floor, and out of thy winepress: of that wherewith the Lord thy God hath blessed thee thou shalt give unto him" (Deut. xv. 14). A Hebrew bondmaid might not go free in the seventh year; but, if not married to her master or his son, she must be returned to her father, or given to another Hebrew master.

A peculiar feature of Oriental slavery was the possibility of promotion it offered to a faithful, intelligent servant, devoted to the interests of his owner. This is exemplified in the remarkable history of Joseph, where, from a slave in a dungeon, he rose to be " even as Pharaoh " the king ; and in the elevation of Abraham's steward, Eliezer of Damascus, to be the " eldest servant of his house, that ruled over all that he had," and to whom was intrusted the delicate mission of procuring a bride for the patriarch's son Isaac. It was by no means impossible for the ambitious slave to become the son-in-law of his master, even though a heathen and a " stranger." An instance of this promotion is recorded in 1 Chron. ii. 34, 35 : " Sheshan had no sons, but daughters. And Sheshan had a servant, an Egyptian, whose name was Jarha. And Sheshan gave his daughter to Jarha, his servant, to wife."

The honorable office of steward is very ancient, and pertained necessarily to a wealthy establishment. Its duties comprised the entire management of the business of the house, the keeping of accounts ; ordering of supplies ; overseeing of servants, giving them " their portion of meat in due season," and " paying their hire," as shown in the parables of the Gospel. This head-servant, or steward, was generally an old slave, identified with the interests of the family, whose fidelity and capacities had been abundantly tested. To him also was delegated special guardianship over the son and heir of his master, from early childhood until the lad reached marriageable age; not with reference to instruction, but as to his morals and health. Accordingly St. Paul writes: "The heir, as long as he is a child, differeth nothing from a servant, though he be lord of all; but is under tutors and governors until the time appointed of the father" (Gal. iv. 1, 2); and in the third chapter of the same Epistle he refers to the same trustworthy servant (not a teacher, as the text would imply), where he makes use of this comprehensive figure: "The law was our schoolmaster to bring us unto Christ."

The position of nurse in an Israelitish family was one of great dignity and importance: her authority was inferior only to that of a parent, while her devotion to her young charges merited all the reciprocity they could render her in affection and gratitude. She was esteemed for her sagacity, for skill and experience in the delicate arts of her profession, for patience and gentleness, and, above all, for well-tried fidelity and friendship. She was preeminently identified with the fortunes of the family, and held, perhaps, a nearer place in its affections than any other dependent. When the eldest daughter was given in marriage, it was expected that the nurse should accompany the young bride, whom she had carried in her bosom, to her new home, and in a strange family circle to be her constant friend and adviser in every possible domestic emergencies; especially was she to re-assume the duties of nurse when the bride became a mother.

Thus, when Rebekah consented to go with the steward Eliezer, to become the wife of his master's son, her mother and brother sent her away on her long journey to Canaan, attended by her damsels, and her nurse Deborah (Gen. xxv. 59), — a woman of such distinguished superiority, that her burial-place was recorded by the sacred historian (Gen. xxxv. 8). The aged Naomi fulfilled this office for Obed, the first-born son of her kinsman Boaz and Ruth, and the immediate ancestor of the inspired Psalmist: she "took the child and laid it in her bosom, and became nurse unto it" (Ruth iv. 16).

The crippled Mephibosheth owed his life to the devotion of his nurse, who in a time of great public peril "took him up and fled;" but in such haste, poor woman! that the five-year-old boy fell from her trembling arms and "became lame." Another notable example of devotion was the nurse of Joash, infant son of King Ahaziah, who at his father's death was saved by his aunt from the general massacre of the seed royal, ordered by Athaliah his grandmother. The child was hidden with his nurse, first in a

THE HEBREW NURSE.

"bed-chamber," and afterward "he was with her, hid in the house of the Lord six years,"— until he began to reign, at seven years of age (2 Chron. xxii. 12). Beside these confidential upper servants of a large and wealthy household, there was a numerous retinue of slaves and hirelings, men and women, for the menial offices of the house: such as cooking, washing, sweeping, scrubbing, the hewing of wood and drawing of water (the latter no sinecure in Eastern lands), grinding the corn, cleaning the lamps, running on messages, and lastly — lowest service of all — taking off and putting on the master's sandals, and those of his guests, or carrying them when the master preferred to walk unshod. Reference to this service is contained in the familiar words of John the Baptist, concerning his coming Lord: "He that cometh after me is mightier than I, whose shoes I am not worthy to bear" (Matt. iii. 11); and again, "the latchet of whose shoes I am not worthy to stoop down and unloose" (Mark i. 7). There were also social functionaries brought in for special occasions of entertainment, such as the "governor of the feast," as at the marriage in Cana of Galilee (John ii. 8), whose duty it was to taste the wine before it was offered to the guests, and to oversee the servants in attendance.

In the presence of master or mistress, the servant stood apart, attentively watching for orders, which were commonly indicated by gestures of the head or hands; this familiar custom serves as an illustration to the sacred poet: "Behold, as the eyes of servants look unto the hand of their masters, and as the eyes of a maiden unto the hand of her mistress; so our eyes wait upon the Lord our God, until that he have mercy upon us" (Ps. cxxiii. 2).

The condition of the Hebrew bondsman was in edifying contrast to that of the slave in heathen communities. In Greece no household was complete without its quota of slaves, who were, in the words of Aristotle, so many "living working tools and possessions" only. The smaller islands of the Archipelago and the mountainous regions of Asia Minor were scoured by the pirates who furnished the slave-marts of Athens and other large cities with their human commodities. The Roman master, especially, held his slaves in absolute subjection: their very lives were in his hand, — the same system of bondage that we find in the New Testament. Both master and slave, however, met as brethren in the "household of faith," as exemplified in the early Church; and to each in his place St. Paul addressed the "wholesome words:" "Servants, be obedient to them that are your masters according to the flesh, with fear and trembling, in singleness of your heart, as unto Christ;" "And, ye masters, do the same things unto them, forbearing threatening: knowing that your Master also is in heaven; neither is there respect of persons with him" (Eph. vi. 5, 9); while another Epistle contains the admirable summary: "He that is called in the Lord, being a servant, is the Lord's freeman: likewise also he that is called, being free, is Christ's servant" (1 Cor. vii. 22), — having in tender remembrance, doubtless, the parting words of the great Master to his disciples: "Henceforth I call you not servants, . . . but I have called you friends" (John xv. 15).

VII.

LARDER, KITCHEN, AND TABLE.

TO recline at meals was not an original practice of the Jews, but one which they adopted, probably from the Persians, who are supposed to have introduced the extraordinary fashion of "dinner-beds." The Greeks and Romans also found it quite in accordance with their taste for foreign luxuries, and vied with each other in the elegance of these appointments. The first chapter of the Book of Esther affords a striking picture of Persian luxury, in its description of the feast given by King Ahasuerus, "when he showed the riches of his glorious kingdom and the honor of his excellent majesty many days, unto all his princes and servants."

At the seven days' feast given by the king in Shushan, the palace, "in the court of the garden of the king's palace," there were even greater displays of royal magnificence, in which figure hangings, "white, green, and blue;" and "beds of gold and silver, on a pavement of red and blue and white and black marble." These "beds," it will be remembered, were the dinner-couches already described in the "Furniture of the House;" and tables stood in front of them within easy reach of the guests.

In the New Testament, wherever allusion is made to "sitting at meat," this custom of reclining is to be understood. This is especially noticeable in the accounts of the Last Supper, where the "beloved disciple" is described as leaning on the bosom of the Lord (John xiii. 23); and in the touching scene at the feast given by Simon, where "a woman in the city," "when she knew that Jesus sat at meat in the Pharisee's house, brought an alabaster box of ointment, and stood at his feet behind him weeping, and began to wash his feet with tears, and did wipe them with the hairs of her head, and kissed his feet, and anointed them with the ointment" (Luke vii. 38). Here the attitudes described leave no room for doubt as to the prevailing mode of "sitting" at table at that time.

ASSYRIANS FEASTING.

The ancient table (still in use among the peasants of remote rural districts of the Holy Land) was simply a circular leathern bag, furnished with holes around the edge, through which a cord was run. At meal-time this bag was spread upon the ground or the floor, with sometimes a small wooden stool placed in the centre to receive the principal dish. At the conclusion of the repast, the crumbs and bits of refuse were thrown out to the dogs

ROMANS AT TABLE.

or fowls, and the "table," drawn up by the cord, was hung on a peg or nail. It is easy to perceive how such a table could fulfil, in a figure, the malediction of the Psalmist upon his enemies: "Let their table become a snare before them; and that which should have been for their welfare, let it become a trap" (Ps. lxix. 22): "snares" and "traps" being laid upon the ground to catch the prey of the huntsman.

The ancient Egyptians used at meals a small, low table of wood or stone; they sat on chairs and stools or on the floor, with the right knee raised to form a support for the hand. When Joseph received his brethren in his own house, and had given orders to "set on bread" (having before told the "ruler of his house" that guests should dine with him at noon), "they set on for him by himself, and for

EGYPTIAN TABLES.

them by themselves, and for the Egyptians, which did eat with him, by themselves: because the Egyptians might not eat bread with the Hebrews; for that is an abomination unto the Egyptians. And they sat before him, the first-born according to his birthright, and the youngest according to his youth: and he took and sent messes unto them from before him" (Gen. xliii. 32–34). This narrative affords a very particular account of the Egyptian manner of entertaining at dinner, at that remote period; it will be observed that it differs essentially from the primitive practice among the Hebrews of sitting around a common dish, and eating from it with the fingers or with bits of bread. In the beautiful Book of Ruth we find an example of this homely custom, where Boaz, "a mighty man of wealth," said to the young stranger who had gleaned in his fields all the day: "At meal-time come thou hither, and eat of the bread, and dip thy morsel in the vinegar. And she sat beside the reapers: and he reached her parched corn, and she did eat, and was sufficed, and left" (ii. 14). In this connection also we are reminded of the solemn words of our Saviour, as he ate at the passover with his disciples: "And he answered and said, He that dippeth his hand with me in the dish, the same shall betray me" (Matthew); "It is one of the twelve, that dippeth with me in the dish" (Mark); "Behold, the hand of him that betrayeth me is with me on the table" (Luke); "He then lying on Jesus' breast saith unto him, Lord, who is it? Jesus answered, He it is, to whom I shall give a sop, when I have dipped it. And when he had dipped the sop, he gave it to Judas Iscariot, the son of Simon" (John).

The religious as well as the social life of the Jews afforded many occasions of feasting; since their holy convocations, as well as their domestic recurrences of birthdays, marriages, weaning of children, treaties of any sort, sheep-shearings, and even burials, were all celebrated after this manner. But in general the Jew led the life of the Oriental of to-day, — one of extreme simplicity and abstemiousness, breaking his fast with the "kindly fruits of the earth," and eating meat, if at all, only once a day.

It was the pious custom to give thanks at the commencement of each meal: the usual forms being, "Blessed be Thou, O Lord our God, the King of the world, who produced bread out of the earth!" and, "Blessed be Thou, O Lord, the King of the world, who created the fruit of the vine!" In allusion to this usage, St. Paul calls the consecrated wine of the Lord's Supper, "the cup of blessing" (1 Cor. x. 16). When our Saviour fed the five thousand with the "five barley-loaves and two small fishes." he "took the loaves, and when he had given thanks, he distributed" them (John vi. 11); and after his resurrection, when he walked with the two disciples to Emmaus, it was not until, "as he sat at meat with them, he took bread and blessed it," that "their eyes were opened, and they knew him" (Luke xxiv. 30, 31).

The food of the "chosen people," in common with all other intimately personal considerations, was regulated as to its quality by the Mosaic Law; beasts, birds, fishes, and insects were clean or unclean, according to certain distinctions carefully specified in the eleventh chapter of Leviticus. They were extremely scrupulous about eating or drinking with the Gentile nations, who in their turn had the same prejudices against the Jews; as exemplified of the Egyptians at the dinner in Joseph's house. So, at Jacob's well, the woman of Samaria answered our Lord's request, "Give me to drink," with the retort: "How is it that thou, being a Jew, askest drink of me, which am a woman of Samaria? for the Jews have no dealings with the Samaritans" (John iv. 9): the Jews themselves carrying the prohibition still further, to include particular classes of their own nationality. One of their chief accusations against the Lord Jesus was that he ignored such self-righteous distinctions; when the scribes and Pharisees saw him sitting at meat with these despised Jews, "they said unto his disciples, How is it that he eateth and drinketh with publicans and sinners?" (Mark ii. 16;) "Behold a gluttonous man, and a winebibber, a friend of publicans and sinners!" (Luke vii. 34.) The story of the Hebrew Judith in the Assyrian camp furnishes an example in point: Holofernes bade his servants to "prepare for her of his own meats, and that she should drink of his own wine. And Judith said, I will not eat thereof, lest there be an offence; but provision shall be made for me of the things that I have brought" (Jud. xii. 1, 2). So too, when the four young men of the tribe of Judah were taken captive by Nebuchadnezzar, to become members of the royal household, "the king appointed them a daily provision of the king's meat, and of the wine which he drank;" but, rather than violate the law of his nation, "Daniel purposed in his heart that he would not defile himself with the portion of the king's meat, nor with the wine which he drank" (Dan. i. 5, 8).

One of the first gracious effects of the gospel dispensation was to emancipate the Christian from this bondage of meats and drinks, and to assure him that "God is no respecter of persons."

From the day when, on the tanner's housetop in Joppa, St. Peter saw in a vision the vessel let down from heaven, "wherein were all manner of four-footed beasts of the earth, and wild beasts, and creeping things, and fowls of the air" (Acts x. 12), and heard the voice saying, "Rise, Peter, kill and eat," until he witnessed before Cornelius the centurion, and his friends, the "good confession:" "Ye know how that it is an unlawful thing for a man that is a Jew to keep company, or come unto one of another nation; but God hath showed me that I should not call any man common or unclean" (Acts x. 28), — this glorious truth, that "on the Gentiles also was poured out the Holy Ghost," was preached and contended for by the apostles until the last barrier of national prejudice in the Jewish convert was broken down. On this important subject St. Paul's *dictum* to the church at Corinth is final: "Whatsoever is sold in the shambles, that eat, asking no question for conscience' sake;" "Whether therefore ye eat, or drink, or whatsoever ye do, do all to the glory of God. Give none offence, neither to the

Jews, nor to the Gentiles, nor to the church of God" (1 Cor. x. 25, 31, 32).

Orientals have always been large consumers of bread, so that the word anciently stood for any sort of food; the expressions, "set on bread," "sat down to eat bread," were equivalent to serving and partaking of a various meal. Wheat and barley were generally used in bread-making, with or without leaven. The first description of the primitive baking of bread appears in Gen. xviii. 6: to entertain the three angels in the plains of Mamre, "Abraham hastened into the tent unto Sarah, and said, Make ready quickly three measures of fine meal; knead it, and make cakes upon the hearth." Other methods of baking are already described in connection with "ovens." In later times, when the Israelites dwelt in cities, there was, in addition to the household appliances, a public oven in every town, while in large cities there were many; in Jerusalem, for example, there was a locality known as "the bakers' street" (Jer. xxxvii. 21). In Hosea, the allusions are evidently to one of these public bakers, and they expressly indicate the processes then in vogue among them: "As an oven heated by the baker, who ceaseth from raising after he hath kneaded the dough, until it be leavened. . . . For they have made ready their heart like an oven. while they lie in wait: their baker sleepeth all the night; in the morning it burneth as a flaming fire" (Hos. vii. 4, 6).

There were various preparations of cereals, coarse and unsifted, of which bread, or rather thin cakes, were made by simply mixing with milk or water, and baking on the hearth. Thus the prophet was commanded to make bread of "wheat, and barley, and beans, and lentiles, and millet, and fitches," and to eat of it, to typify the coming siege of Jerusalem.

The husks, with which the Prodigal Son would fain have appeased his pangs of hunger, were the long-podded fruit of the carob-tree, sweetish to the taste. This fruit is often called "St. John's bread," because it has been suggested that this was what the great prophet ate in the wilderness; the carob-tree being of the same family as our locust, and sometimes called by that name.

Corn, in the Bible, is simply a general name for all kinds of cereals: there was no grain in Palestine to correspond to our maize, or Indian corn. The "parched corn," so often mentioned in the Old Testament, was prepared from the unripe grains of wheat: they were sometimes roasted in a pan; or the heads, tied together, were held over a blaze until parched. This was the primitive refreshment offered by Boaz to Ruth, after her first day's gleaning (Ruth ii. 14); Abigail took "five measures of parched corn" to David, as part of her conciliatory gift (1 Sam. xxv. 18); in the second chapter of Leviticus it is called "green ears of corn dried by the fire." The wheat was also palatable in its green state, and the law permitted the "standing corn" to be gathered by any one passing through it (Deut. xxiii. 25); so when our Lord, on a sabbath day, "went through the cornfields, his disciples plucked the ears of corn, and did eat, rubbing them in their hands" (Luke vi. 1). But there is still another bread of the Bible, — that great miracle of the wilderness, whereby some three or four million souls were sustained for forty years, with " bread from heaven:" typical of the "Hidden Manna"—that " Living Bread," which after a lapse of so many centuries " came down from heaven, that a man may eat thereof and not die:" " Then said the Lord unto Moses, Behold, I will rain bread from heaven for you; and the people shall go out and gather a certain rate every day: . . . and in the morning the dew lay round about the host. And when the dew that lay was gone up, behold, upon the face of the wilderness there lay a small round thing, as small as the hoar frost on the ground. And when the children of Israel saw it, they said one to another, It is manna: for they wist not what it was. And Moses said unto them, This is the bread which the Lord hath given you to eat. And the house of Israel called the name thereof Manna: and it was like coriander seed, white; and the taste of it was like wafers made with honey" (Exod. xvi. 4, 13–15, 31). This supply of "corn of heaven," "angels' food," manna (*what is this?*), failed not until the Lord brought his people into the good land of promise; " a land of wheat and barley and vines and fig-trees and pomegranates;

a land of oil olive, and honey;" a land wherein they ate "bread without scarceness," and lacked nothing (Deut. viii. 8, 9) The manner of preparing meat for the table is illustrated by many examples in Scripture: in primitive times, the master of the house, whether rich or poor, was his own butcher; and it was customary to cook the entire animal as soon as killed and dressed, probably on account of the difficulty of preserving fresh meat in a hot climate. On the two occasions referred to, while his supernatural guests waited, "Abraham ran unto the herd, and fetched a calf tender and good, and gave it unto a young man, and he hasted to dress it" (Gen. xviii. 7). And when Joseph gave orders to his steward for the entertainment of his brethren, he charged him to bring them to the house, and then to "slay and make ready;" yet the dinner was to take place at noon. With the same rude haste, the Witch of Endor killed the "fat calf" she had in the house, and set it before Saul and his servants, during a visit that could have lasted only a few hours (1 Sam. xxviii. 24).

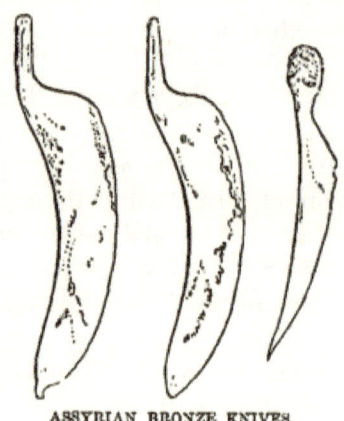

ASSYRIAN BRONZE KNIVES.

EGYPTIAN COOKS.

Egyptian monuments abound in representations of the household custom as to the killing of animals for the table: it was done by the menservants in the courtyards of private dwellings; and, while poulterers' shops are largely represented, there are no meat-markets or butchers' shops,— from which omission it is inferred that flesh-meat was used only on occasions of special feasting. The cow was held sacred by the Egyptians, and never used for food; swine were regarded with abhorrence.

The fatted calf was esteemed the choicest dish to offer a guest, but the flesh of the ox was also used as in our own day. Solomon assured his readers that, "Better is a dinner of herbs where love is, than a stalled ox and hatred therewith" (Prov. xv. 17); while the historian records of that magnificent prince that the daily provision for his royal table included "ten fat oxen, and twenty oxen out of the pastures, and a hundred sheep, besides harts, and roebucks, and fallow deer, and fatted fowl" (1 Kings iv. 23). Nehemiah says of his own hospitable table, where he entertained "one hundred and fifty of the Jews and rulers," during the rebuilding of the wall of Jerusalem: "Now that which was prepared for me daily was one ox and six choice sheep; also fowls were prepared for me, and once in ten days stores of all sorts of wine" (Neh. v. 18).

In the parable of the marriage of the king's son, the royal proclamation went forth: "Behold, I have prepared my dinner; my oxen and my fatlings are killed" (Matt. xxii. 4); and the feast with which the rejoicing father makes merry over the return of the repentant prodigal is furnished with "the fatted calf" (Luke xv. 23).

The sheep does not appear ever to have been used as food by the Egyptians, to whom even its keepers, the shepherds, were an abomination. It is often mentioned in Scripture as an article of food in great request among the Jews: "five sheep ready dressed" constituted a part of the handsome present with which Abigail hastened to appease the anger of David against Nabal her husband (1 Sam. xxv. 18); Adonijah, the son of David, "slew sheep and oxen and fat cattle by the stone of Zoheleth," for a treasonable feast (1 Kings i. 9); and the Psalmist complained to God: "Thou hast given us like sheep appointed for meat; and hast scattered us among the heathen" (Ps. xliv. 11).

Of our familiar barnyard fowls there is no mention in the Old

Testament; and the only place in the New Testament in which the hen with her brood appears is in our Lord's compassionate lament over the Holy City, as he foretold her destruction: "O Jerusalem, Jerusalem! thou that killest the prophets, and stonest them which are sent unto thee, how often would I have gathered thy children together, even as a hen gathereth her chickens under

"HOW OFTEN WOULD I HAVE GATHERED THY CHILDREN TOGETHER."

her wings, and ye would not!" (Matt. xxiii. 37.) The Rabbis prohibited the keeping of fowls within the walls of Jerusalem; but that the ordinance was probably not enforced, we may infer from the cock-crowing in connection with St. Peter's cowardly denial of his Master. It is supposed that the Romans introduced these domestic fowls into Judæa. The use of hens' eggs for food is probably indicated by the words of our Lord: "If he shall ask an egg, will he offer him a scorpion?" (Luke xi. 12.) Jeremiah employs the figure: "As the partridge sitteth on eggs, and hatcheth them not" (xvii. 11), perhaps because she was ruthlessly hunted then as she is now, in the East; and Job asks: "Is there any taste in the white of an egg?" (vi. 6.)

The arts of the hunter and the fowler were ardently studied and pursued by the ancient peoples of the Bible, at first for food, the legitimate objects of such pursuits, but afterwards for the recreation and excitement they afforded. Solomon thinks of the amateur sportsman when he says: "The slothful man roasteth not that which he took in hunting" (Prov. xii. 27). In Esau we meet with the ideal Oriental hunter, — the purveyor of meat for the family, wild and fierce in his pleasures, with great strength and endurance, courting the hardships and the danger for the love of them: his weapons, "thy quiver and thy bow," are invoked by his aged father, who longed for the venison and the "savory meat;" while allusions to traps, pitfalls, and snares, gins and nets, are frequent, in both the Old and New Testaments, especially in their metaphorical application to the souls of men. The Psalmist sings of the godly: "Surely he shall deliver thee from the snare of the fowler" (Ps. xci. 3); and assures his own soul of the same divine protection: "He shall pluck my feet out of the net." St. Paul, in a forcible figure, represents the great Enemy as a mighty hunter, and indicates the only means by which "they may recover themselves out of the snare of the devil, who are taken captive [taken alive, *marginal reading*] by him at his will" (2 Tim. ii. 26). The earliest reference to the chase in the Bible is to "Nimrod, the mighty hunter before the Lord" (Gen. x. 9).

The ancient Egyptians were enthusiasts in the chase: their monuments are rich in representations of the weapons, traps, hounds, game-beaters, game-bags, and every other requisite for the successful prosecution of the sport. The Assyrian tablets also abound in scenes of the chase. The lion was their noblest game; and on the monuments of Nineveh royal triumphs over this king of beasts are recorded side by side with martial victo-

ASSYRIANS HUNTING: SCULPTURE.

LARDER, KITCHEN, AND TABLE.   173

ries. The palaces of Babylon were in like manner adorned with mural paintings of noted encounters in the chase.

The spoils of the commercial hunter and fowler were in great request for the tables of the Egyptians and the luxurious Assyrians and Babylonians. They consisted of wild goats,— the flesh closely resembling venison,— gazelles, hares, wild geese and ducks, teal, quails, partridge, and an endless variety of birds. The Hebrews partook of these delicacies within the wholesome restrictions of the law, which pronounced even upon the uncleanness of birds and "creeping things." Only three of the latter class were permitted to be eaten,— the grasshopper, beetle, and locust. The locust is especially interesting in its connection with the great Baptist, of whom the early Gospel narrative relates that "his meat was locusts and wild honey" (Matt. iii. 4). There were

HUNTING WILD BULLS: ASSYRIAN SCULPTURE.

various methods of preparing this peculiarly Oriental article of food: sometimes they were stewed, and dressed in oil; or they might be roasted, minus the legs, by setting them on long wooden spits before the fire. When breadstuffs were scarce, it was not unusual to dry them, and to make cakes of their pulverized flesh, which were baked on the hearth. The Arabs and other wandering tribes of the desert use the locust as food to this day: they roast or dry them in the sun, pack them in salt, and cut slices from the compact mass as required.

The Orientals have always been large consumers of fish: the Hebrews were restricted by law to those having scales and fins. The Nile, the Sea of Galilee, and all the lakes and rivers of Palestine, abounded in fish: so that fishing was a most important industry, especially in the time of our Saviour, and occupied a large proportion of the peasant population. This calling was pursued in small skiffs usually at night, and chiefly with nets and drag-nets. Jerusalem received its supply of fish mainly from Joppa, forty miles off, the seaport associated in the Old Testament with Jonah, the recalcitrant prophet, and in the New with the raising of the benevolent Dorcas from the dead by St. Peter, as well as with that apostle's visit to Simon the tanner, and all its incalculable results (Acts ix. 36, 43). Fish was also brought to Jerusalem from the Sea of Galilee, a distance of eighty miles. We read again and again of the "fish-gate" of Jerusalem, which was probably the principal market-place in the city for that important article of food. When the pious Nehemiah undertook the repairs of the holy city, he records of this locality, "But the fish-gate did the sons of Hassenaah build, who also laid the beams thereof, and set up the doors thereof, the locks thereof, and the bars thereof" (Neh. iii. 3); and he complains of certain "men of Tyre" (that "renowned city," "strong in the sea"), "which brought fish and all manner of ware, and sold on the sabbath unto the children of Judah, and in Jerusalem" (Neh. xiii. 16). A great variety of shell-fish, prohibited to the Jews, were consumed by their Gentile neighbors: among these were the oyster, clam, shrimps, crabs, lobsters, and many others quite unfa-

SEA OF GALILEE.

miliar to modern palates. When Moses blessed the tribes of Israel before his death, he said of the tribe of Zebulun, on the Mediterranean shore: "They shall suck of the abundance of the seas, and of treasures hid in the sand" (Deut. xxxiii. 19): this prophetic utterance is interpreted to refer to the fish, and especially to the shell-fish which burrow in the sand of the sea-shore.

It will be remembered, that, in the first plague sent upon Egypt, the destruction of the fish was a calamity of incalculable gravity to a people who depended upon this diet; and in the "burden of Egypt," the most alarming utterances of the prophet touched upon this subject: "The fishers also shall mourn, and all they that cast angle into the brooks shall lament, and they that spread nets upon the waters shall languish. And they shall be broken in the purposes thereof, all that make sluices and ponds for fish" (Isa. xix. 8, 10). One of the homesick longings of the Israelites in the wilderness was for this familiar food: "We remember the fish which we did eat in Egypt freely" (Num. xi. 5).

This whole subject of fish, fisheries, and fishermen is replete with interest for Bible-lovers in its intimate association with our Lord's ministry, as we follow it step by step through the Gospel records. In both instances of the miraculous feeding of the multitude (John vi.; Matt. xv. 34), "two small fishes" and "a few little fishes" bear their important part; to pay the tribute-money demanded by the collectors at Capernaum, our Lord elects a fish from the Sea of Galilee to bring the coin in its mouth to Peter, the apostle; on two occasions he commands a miraculous draught of fishes to fill the nets of his humble disciples, who have toiled all night and caught nothing (Luke v. 6; John xxi. 6). The second of these miracles took place after the Saviour's glorious resurrection; as soon as the fishermen " were come to land, they saw a fire of coals there, and fish laid thereon, and bread. . . . Jesus then cometh, and taketh bread, and giveth them, and fish likewise" (John xxi. 9, 13). On another solemn and mysterious occasion, the risen, but not yet ascended, Lord met his timid disciples on a Sunday evening, when they were assembled with closed doors " for fear of the Jews," and, to re-assure them, asked for food: "they gave him a piece of a broiled fish, and of an honeycomb; and he took it, and did eat before them" (Luke xxiv. 42).

During the persecutions of the early Christian Church, the word "fish" became a watchword with the faithful; because its Greek name, *ichthus*, is formed of the initials of the Greek words. "Jesus Christ, Son of God, Saviour." Several kinds of fish were held sacred in Egypt, and the priests were prohibited from any sort of fish food. Dagon, the great god of the Philistines, was half man, half fish: he was worshipped also in Assyria and in India.

NOTWITHSTANDING the abstemious and simple diet affected by the Orientals, they have from the earliest times been excessively addicted to highly seasoned food, prepared with spices, condiments, and various aromatic herbs. The "mint, and anise, and cummin," on which the Pharisees so scrupulously paid tithes, to the omission of "weightier matters of the law" (Matt. xxiii. 23), were among these condiments, to which may be added saffron, garlic, and onions. Dishes dressed in this manner constitute the "savory meat," such as Isaac loved (Gen. xxvii. 14). Salt was of course a necessary ingredient in these dishes: "Can that which is unsavory be eaten without salt?" (Job vi. 6.) The salt which has "lost his savor," mentioned in the Sermon on the Mount, was that which is produced by the evaporation of sea-water, and which is liable, from the extreme heat, to lose its saline properties, when it is indeed "good for nothing but to be cast out, and to be trodden under foot of men" (Matt. v. 13). Salt was invested with peculiar significance by the Orientals: it was the symbol of perpetuity, purity, and fidelity. In the charge to Aaron, concerning his "part and inheritance among the children of Israel," it is declared to be "a covenant of salt forever before the Lord," — something absolutely indissoluble. To "eat salt" with a person, even among

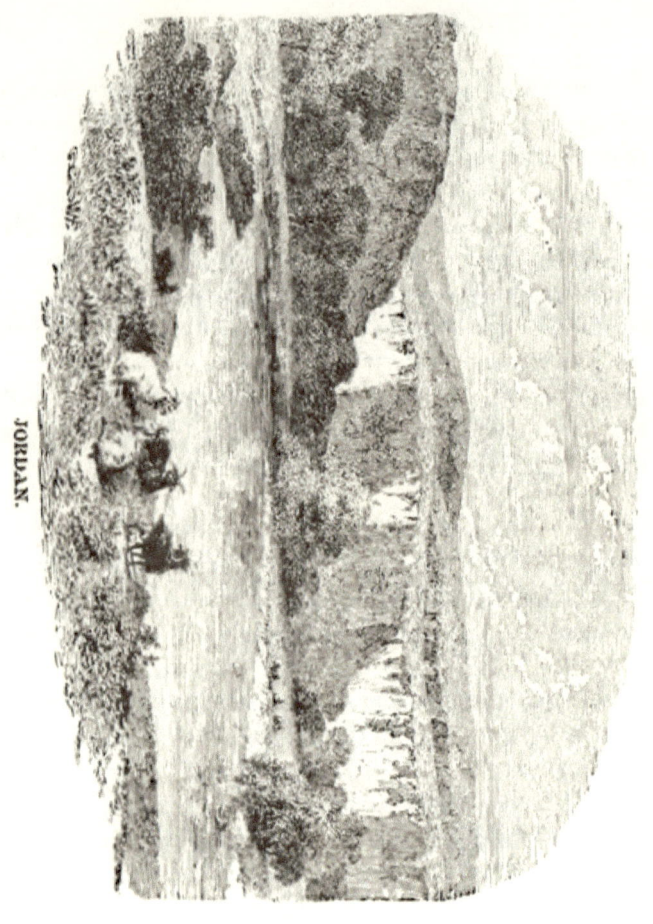
JORDAN.

the modern Arabs, is a pledge of mutual and perpetual friendship.

The oil of olives was another indispensable element in Eastern cookery, and used, as we use butter and lard, in the composition of almost every dish: the olives themselves were eaten, and, when pickled, formed an agreeable relish. The culture of the olive was only second to that of the vine in Palestine, where the failure of the crop was deplored as a national calamity. The sacred writers employ the olive as the emblem of beauty, luxuriance, strength, and the divine blessing. Its leaf has been the symbol of peace, reconciliation, ever since the dove returned with it to the ark. Olive-trees and cellars of oil are enumerated among the royal treasures of David and Rehoboam (1 Chron. xxvii. 28; 2 Chron. xi. 11); and the Psalmist in exulting confidence exclaims, "I am like a green olive-tree in the house of God" (Ps. lii. 8). One of the methods for gathering the fruit of the olive-trees was by beating; hence the humane law, in the interest of the poor: "When thou beatest thine olive tree, thou shalt not go over the boughs again: it shall be for the stranger, the fatherless, and for the widow" (Deut. xxiv. 20). The tree lives to a great age, — for several centuries, we are told, — producing fruit when it is little more than a hollow shell.

When the Israelites "fell a-lusting" in the wilderness, it was not only for the flesh-pots, and the fish of Egypt, but for its tempting variety of vegetable food, — "the cucumbers, and the melons, and the leeks, and the onions, and the garlic" (Num. xi. 5). In her days of fruitfulness Palestine abounded in these summer vegetables, many of them growing wild: such as asparagus, and artichokes, egg-plant, and cauliflower. The lentiles, of which Esau's pottage was made, are of the same family as our garden-pea, but smaller; red lentiles, still sold in Eastern markets, are considered the best, and are made into a pottage pronounced very savory by modern travellers. Mandrakes, or *love-plants*, are stemless, with long narrow leaves, bearing rich purple blossoms, and, "in the days of wheat-harvest," a yellow and pulpy fruit, the size of a large plum. It is said that the same superstitious notions attach now to the effects of eating these plants that prevailed in the days of Rachel, who begged them of her fruitful sister (Gen. xxx. 14–16). This plant was particularly esteemed for its strong odor, so offensive to Europeans: it still grows in Syria and in the neighborhood of Jerusalem, where the women are fond of dressing their bosoms with its flowers. This explains the allusion in Solomon's Song: "The mandrakes give a smell; and at our gates are all manner of pleasant fruits" (vii. 13).

The "beans" mentioned in 2 Sam. xvii. 28, and in Ezek. iv. 9,

OLIVE-JARS.

is quite a different article of diet from that known to us by the same name. It is of the same family, but bears in its pods large coarse seeds, that are eaten only by the poorer classes, and fed to animals.

"Butter of kine, and milk of sheep," asses, goats, and cows, and even camels, were highly prized as articles of daily consumption in the East. The first butter and milk mentioned in the Bible is that which was set before his angel-guests by Abraham (Gen. xviii. 8). The word rendered "butter" in this passage commonly signifies curdled milk, — the same that Jael gave to Sisera, and of which Deborah and Barak sang: "He asked water, and she gave him milk; she brought forth butter in a lordly dish" (Judg. v. 25). Here, again, the butter is evidently a preparation of curdled milk, much esteemed as a beverage from remote antiquity. The Arabs have a tradition that its composition was divinely revealed to Abraham; while another legend asserts that an angel brought Hagar a draught of sour milk (*leben*), when she and the youth Ishmael were perishing with thirst in the wilderness. But we have Solomon's proverb, or rather a part of it, which goes to prove that there was some preparation called butter, made according to our own processes: "Surely the churning of milk bringeth forth butter" (Prov. xxx. 33). This churning was done by shaking or treading upon a goat-skin, until the separation of the butter took place.

Isaiah prophesied of the Virgin-born Immanuel: "Butter and honey shall he eat" (Isa. vii. 15). This seems to have been a favorite combination in ancient times, and is supposed to indicate a beverage of the curdled milk, sweetened with honey, or preparations of those two ingredients, to be spread upon bread: they are used in these forms by the modern Arabs, and esteemed a great delicacy. "Honey and butter" were among the supplies sent to David in his sore straits at Mahanaim (2 Sam. xvii. 29). Job speaks of "brooks of honey and butter" (xx. 17); and the mystic Bridegroom: "Thy lips, O my spouse, drop as the honeycomb: honey and milk are under thy tongue" (S. of Sol., iv. 11). Palestine was described as "a land flowing with milk and honey," while yet "Moses kept the flock of Jethro, his father-in-law" (Exod. iii. 8): such it proved to the weary wanderers of the wilderness, and even now it scarcely belies that attractive title. David writes of the "honey out of the rock" (Ps. lxxxi. 16), referring to the swarms of wild bees that deposited their honey in hollow trees or the clefts of rocks, — the "wild honey" that St. John the Baptist ate in the wilderness; in Solomon's Song, the bridegroom sings: "I have eaten my honeycomb with my honey" (v. 1); and in his Proverbs he warns the lovers of this dainty: "Hast thou found honey? eat so much as is sufficient for thee. . . . It is not good to eat much honey" (xxv. 16, 27).

Cheese was a very common article of food to these peoples of flocks and herds. The entire Tyropœon Valley of the Holy City was occupied by dairies and their products: hence its name, "valley of cheesemongers." Cheese was also in later times imported for epicures from the Roman province of Bithynia. This article is mentioned but three times in the Bible, and in each instance the different word employed indicates a different variety. The ten cheeses sent by Jesse, father of David, to the captain in Saul's camp, seem to have been soft cheeses, "ten sections of curds" (1 Sam. xvii. 18); the "cheese of kine," sent to David at Mahanaim, implies that it was grated (2 Sam. xvii. 29); while the reference in Job x. 10, evidently is to curdled milk: "Hast thou not poured me out as milk, and curdled me like cheese?" The cheese now used in the East is made into small cakes, strongly salted, and of quality very inferior to the products of our dairies.

The Holy Land abounded in "summer fruits," of almost every kind: grapes, figs, dates, apples, mulberries, quinces, pomegranates, oranges, bananas, apricots, olives, almonds, a variety of delicious melons, and a few pears, do not complete the list. The fruit of the vine has been from earliest ages the principal product of the lands of the Bible: the soil and climate of Palestine, and especially of particular districts of Judaea, were so perfectly adapted to grape-culture, that they became famous for the production of

THE GRAPES OF ESHCOL.

certain varieties. The finest grapes came from the western slopes of Mount Lebanon, from Helbon, En-gedi, and the vales of Eshcol (*cluster*) and Sorek (*a choice vine*), in Judea. With the exception of the delicious white grape of Sorek, the vines of the Holy Land produced only red and black fruit: hence, in Scripture, the juice is called "the blood of the grape," translated "red wine" (Isa. xxvii. 2). Various sorts of wine were produced from the vineyards of Palestine, all highly esteemed for their strength and aroma: the wine of Helbon and the wine of Lebanon were particularly choice, and are distinguished by name, by Ezekiel (xxvii. 18) and by Hosea (xiv. 7).

Wine, throughout the Bible, is accounted one of the great blessings of the Almighty to his dependent creatures: the Psalmist, calling upon his own soul to bless the Lord, gratefully enumerates the "wine that maketh glad the heart of man, and oil to make his face to shine, and bread which strengtheneth man's heart" (civ. 15). It formed part of the domestic stores of every well-to-do household, and was freely dispensed at all social entertainments. The first cultivator of the vine, mentioned in Scripture, was Noah; and of his indulgence in the fruit of his labor it is recorded that "he drank of the wine, and was drunken" (Gen. ix. 21). There is no doubt that succeeding generations were not lacking in those who followed this example of the illustrious patriarch, and that strong drinks were used to great excess, not only by the Gentile nations, but by the Jews. The sacred writings abound in denunciations of this abuse and perversion of a recognized blessing; and, in vivid portraiture of the effects of gross indulgence, Isaiah pronounces his maledictions: "Woe unto them that rise up early in the morning, that they may follow strong drink; that continue until night, till wine inflame them! woe unto them that are mighty to drink wine, and men of strength to mingle strong drink! Woe to the drunkards of Ephraim; . . . but they also have erred through wine, and through strong drink are out of the way; the priest and the prophet have erred through strong drink, they are swallowed up of wine, they are out of the way through strong drink" (Isa. v. 11, 22, xxviii. 1, 7);

and Solomon sums up his "winged words" of warning against the prevailing vice, in this masterly presentation of the subject: "Who hath woe? who hath sorrow? who hath contentions? who hath babbling? who hath wounds without cause? who hath redness of eyes? They that tarry long at the wine; they that go to seek mixed wine. Look not thou upon the wine when it is red, when it giveth his color in the cup, when it moveth itself aright. At the last it biteth like a serpent, and stingeth like an adder" (Prov. xxiii. 29–32). In "the words of king Lemuel, the prophecy that his mother taught him," however, is embalmed this epitome of feminine wisdom (not less profound, perhaps, because, by the verdict of all the ages, it can only be intuitive) on a question more "vexed" to-day, if possible, than in the reign of the magnificent Solomon: "It is not for kings, O Lemuel, it is not for kings to drink wine; nor for princes strong drink: lest they drink, and forget the law, and pervert the judgment of any of the afflicted. Give strong drink unto him that is ready to perish, and wine unto those that be of heavy hearts. Let him drink, and forget his poverty, and remember his misery no more" (Prov. xxxi. 4–7). From the Wisdom of the Son of Sirach of a later period, some two centuries before Christ, is evolved a like conclusion: "Wine is as good as life to a man, if it be drunk moderately; what life is then to a man that is without wine? For it was made to make men glad. Wine, measurably drunk and in season, bringeth gladness of the heart, and cheerfulness of the mind. But wine drunken with excess maketh bitterness of the mind, with brawling and quarrelling" (Ecclus. xxxi. 27–29).

By "mixed wine" the Greeks and Romans always meant wine diluted with water; the Hebrews, on the contrary, meant wine made more intoxicating by the addition of opiates, strong spices, honey, and other ingredients. It was customary with the Romans to administer to a criminal, about to be executed, a stupefying potion to alleviate his sufferings: it is said that a society of charitable women in Jerusalem pledged themselves to this office of mercy. So, in our Saviour's passion: "They gave him to drink wine mingled with myrrh: but he received it not" (Mark xv. 23).

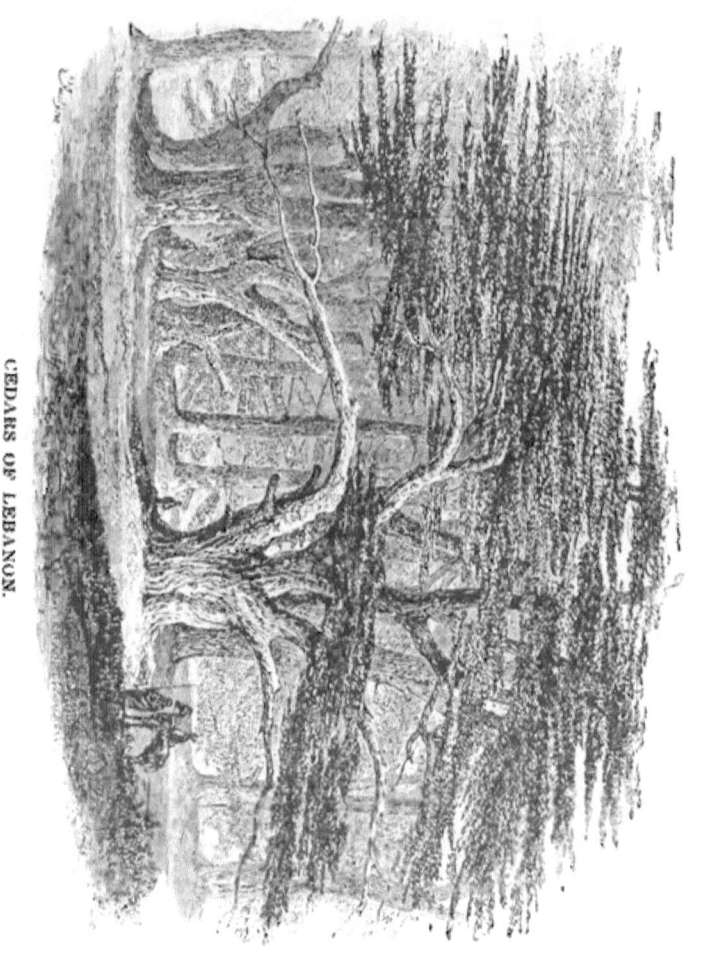

CEDARS OF LEBANON.

The grape was highly prized in Egypt, and the various stages of its cultivation are exhibited in the ancient sculptures. The Babylonians were famous for their high living, which included

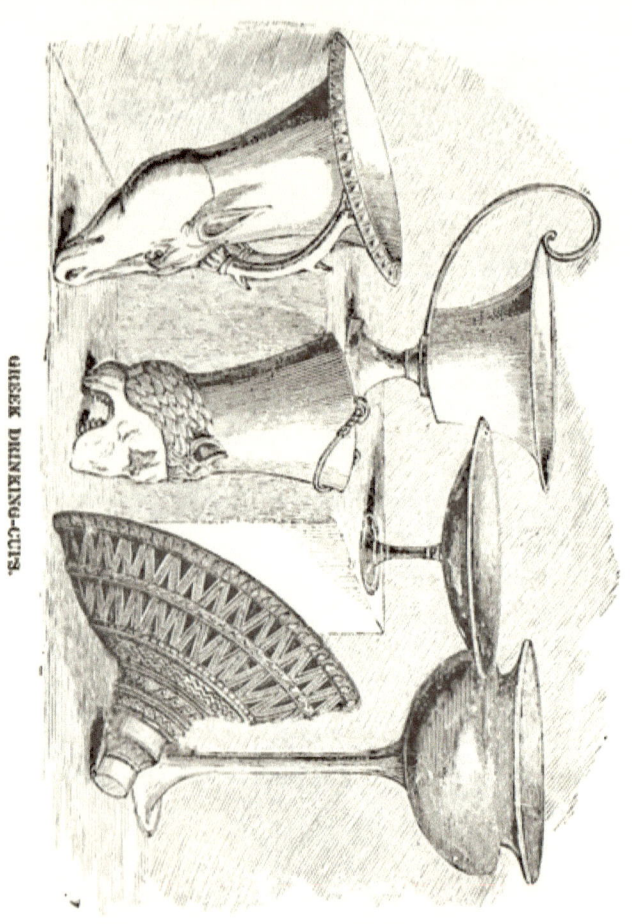

GREEK DRINKING-CUPS.

excessive indulgence in the finest wines. Of the Ninevite monuments, Rawlinson says: " In the banquet-scenes of the sculptures it is drinking, and not eating, that is represented. Attendants dip the wine-cups into a huge bowl, or vase, which stands on the ground and reaches as high as a man's chest, and carry them full of liquor to the guests, who straightway fall into a carouse. . . . Every guest holds in his right hand a wine-cup of a most elegant shape."

The Jews, in common with other Oriental people, were careful to strain their wine before drinking, to rid it of the lees and of the insects that in a hot climate would naturally swarm around the sweet mixture; and for fear of violating the law, which forbade the eating of "creeping things" (Lev. xi. 23, 43). The Buddhists have the same practice in deference to a similar scruple. In denouncing the scribes and Pharisees, our Lord points to this familiar custom: "Ye blind guides, which strain at (*out*) a gnat, and swallow a camel!" (Matt. xxiii. 24.) A very elegant wine-strainer, found in the ruins of Herculaneum, is described by Winckelmann.

It is common in the East at the present day to cool wines and summer drinks with snow or ice; and it is supposed from this Proverb, "As the cold of snow in the time of harvest, so is a faithful messenger to them that send him: for he refresheth the soul of his masters" (xxv. 13), that it was the practice in Solomon's luxurious time; Mount Lebanon probably then, as now, supplied snow to the neighboring country from its inexhaustible stores, for this refreshing purpose. The raisins produced by drying the ripe fruit in bunches were considered a very important provision for domestic use: "a hundred bunches of raisins" constituted part of the present brought on "a couple of asses" by Ziba to King David (2 Sam. xvi. 1); and his offering from Abigail, his future wife, contained "a hundred clusters" of the same dried fruit (1 Sam. xxv. 18). The Hebrew word translated "flagon" in various Old Testament texts means a "cake" of compressed raisins; the "vessels of flagons," in Isa. xxii. 24, is an exception, and is correctly expressed by our English word.

A sort of treacle, obtained by boiling down the juice of the grapes until it becomes a thick sirup, was much esteemed by the ancients, and is still used in the East. It is called by the

ASSYRIAN ENTERTAINMENT: SCULPTURE.

Mohammedans *dibs*; and its Hebrew name is honey. It is this sweet compound, and not bees' honey, that must be understood in many passages where it occurs in the Bible. This sirup was eaten on bread, and drunk mixed with water or sour milk; children were especially fond of it.

Several kinds of vinegar, or sour wine, were used as a beverage by the ancient Romans and by the Hebrews; or as a stimulating sauce, into which to sop their bread or parched corn at a harvest meal or on a fatiguing march. Such was the vinegar into which Boaz invited Ruth to dip her morsel, after the day's gleaning. The "wine mingled with myrrh," to which we have already referred in connection with the solemn details of the crucifixion, is in the other Gospel records termed vinegar: "They gave him vinegar to drink mingled with gall; and when he had tasted thereof, he would not drink" (Matt. xxvii. 34); an incident prophetically presented by David: "They gave me also gall for my meat; and in my thirst they gave me vinegar to drink" (Ps. lxix. 21).

There was also a stronger and more sharply aciduous kind of vinegar, not intended for a beverage: this is referred to in Prov. x. 26: "as vinegar to the teeth;" and in xxv. 20: as "vinegar upon nitre."

We may not close a necessarily brief demonstration of this most fruitful subject of the vine, — alike in its literal and spiritual significance an almost inexhaustible theme, — without reminding the reader of Him of whom the Church sings: "For thy love is better than wine" (Solomon's Song i. 2); who said to his apostles on the night of the last paschal supper: "I will not drink henceforth of this fruit of the vine, until that day when I drink it new with you in my Father's kingdom;" and after supper when "he took the cup, and gave thanks, and gave it to them, saying, Drink ye all of it; for this is my blood of the new testament which is shed for many for the remission of sins" (Matt. xxvi. 29, 27, 28).

Among the most important of the strictly Oriental fruits were figs, dates, and pomegranates. Figs were, and still are, a staple product in all Eastern countries. There are several varieties of this fruit, of which two kinds only are named in the Bible: the "early fig," which ripens in June, is described by Isaiah as "the hasty fruit before the summer" (xxviii. 4), and by Hosea (vii. 1). as "the first ripe" fruit. The "green figs," of Solomon's Song ii. 13, constitute the main crop, which does not ripen until August. Bethphage of the New Testament, near the village of Bethany, signifies "*house of green figs*." Some varieties of the fig were eaten fresh as they came from the tree; while others were allowed to remain to dry on the branch, and were then pressed for home consumption. In early times they seem to have been a common article of food, and to have been esteemed for certain medicinal properties. "Two hundred cakes of figs" are enumerated in the present of Abigail to David, already referred to (1 Sam. xxv. 18). The fig-tree was regarded by the Egyptians as one of the choicest products of the earth, especially the sycamore-fig, which is still common in their country. The small, sweet fruit of this tree closely resembles the fig; but it requires to be punctured, several days before it is fully ripe, with a sharp instrument or with the finger-nail. This was at one time the humble occupation of the prophet Amos: " I was no prophet," he said to Amaziah, " neither was I a prophet's son; but I was an herdsman, and a gatherer of sycamore fruit" (Amos vii. 14). The fig-tree does not grow to a great height; but it affords a very grateful shade, and on this account is often planted in private courtyards: to " sit every man under his vine and under his fig-tree" (Mic. iv. 4), became the synonyme of domestic peace and repose.

The palm-tree, and its fruit of dates, was another rich source of profit and pleasure to the ancient dwellers in the Holy Land. Jericho was called " the city of palm-trees" (Deut. xxxiv. 3); and Bethany—the home of Lazarus and his sisters, those dear friends of Jesus—means " *the house of dates*," as it might well have been from its situation on the Mount of Olives, where the multitude " took branches of the palm-trees, and went forth to meet him," at the time of our Lord's victorious entry into Jerusa-

TREE OF THE "APPLES OF SODOM."

lem. Properly speaking, the palm-tree has no "branches," but immense leaves, often twelve feet in length, drooping in graceful curves toward the ground. The fruit grows in clusters, weigh-

DATE-PALMS.

ing from fifteen to twenty pounds each: when ripe, they are plucked by hand, or shaken into a net held to receive them. Some are eaten fresh, and some laid aside for household stores.

The date yields a rich sirup, which, duly prepared, became the date-wine so highly esteemed by the ancients.

The pomegranate was equally admired for its beauty as a flowering bush, and for its agreeable fruit. The flowers are of a brilliant scarlet or orange; the fruit is the size of an orange, and of a ruddy flesh-color: "As a piece of a pomegranate are thy temples within thy locks" (S. of Sol., vi. 7): it has a hard rind, and is filled with a pulp of delightful flavor. Its juice was anciently made into wine, and used for a summer drink: thus, in Solomon's Song: "I would cause thee to drink of spiced wine of the juice of my pomegranate" (viii. 2). The pomegranate was chosen, for its graceful shape, as a decoration for the skirt of the high priest's robe: "Beneath upon the hem of it thou shalt make pomegranates of blue, and of purple, and of scarlet, round about the hem thereof; and bells of gold between them round about: a golden bell and a pomegranate, a golden bell and a pomegranate, upon the hem of the robe round about" (Exod. xxviii. 33. 34). That this fruit was well known to the Egyptians, is attested by their monuments, and by the complainings of the Israelites in the wilderness of Zin: "It is no place of seed, or of figs, or of vines, or of pomegranates" (Num. xx. 5).

The apple proper is very rare in the Holy Land, and its fruit inferior: learned writers disagree as to the particular fruit meant by the "apple" of Scripture; they have urged the claims, successively, of the citron, orange, quince, and apricot, without positively deciding in favor of either. The name, in the Hebrew, signifies *breathing forth*, which would seem to indicate a peculiar fragrance.

"Nuts and almonds" were among the gifts sent by Jacob to Joseph in Egypt: "Take of the best fruits in the land in your vessels, and carry down the man a present, a little balm, and a little honey, spices and myrrh, nuts and almonds" (Gen. xliii. 11). The bridegroom in the Canticles "went down into the garden of nuts, to see the fruits of the valley" (S. of Sol., vi. 11). In the first text, the reference is to the fruit of the pistachio-tree, not known to the Egyptians, — a thin-shelled nut, having a green meat similar to the walnut; and to the oval fruit, familiar to us, of the light and graceful almond-tree, whose delicate white blossoms are used by "the Preacher" in a figure, to depict the hoary head of old age (Eccles. xii. 5). There are two kinds of almond-trees: the one, less common, producing soft-shelled nuts; the other, the hard-shelled and bitter. The nuts referred to in Canticles were probably a variety, including almonds and filberts, the pistachio, and the walnut: this last is known to us as the "English walnut," the fruit of a noble tree, common to all parts of the East.

In conclusion, it may not be unprofitable to consider the lessons of spiritual significance and application, drawn from this general subject of meats and drinks by Christ and his apostles. One of the most pointed of these is found in the Sermon on the Mount: "I say unto you, Take no thought for your life, what ye shall eat, or what ye shall drink; nor yet for your body, what ye shall put on. Is not the life more than meat, and the body than raiment? . . . But seek ye first the kingdom of God, and his righteousness; and all these things shall be added unto you" (Matt. vi. 25, 33). When our Lord's disciples, fearing the effect of his long fasts, "prayed him, saying, Master, eat," he answered them: "I have meat to eat that ye know not of. . . . My meat is to do the will of Him that sent me, and to finish his work" (John iv. 31, 32, 34); and, in the same spirit, he exhorts the multitude whom he had miraculously fed: "Labor not for the meat which perisheth, but for that meat which endureth unto everlasting life" (John vi. 27). It remained for him to announce himself to the people as the "Living Bread which came down from heaven," explaining to his startled hearers: "The bread that I will give is my flesh, which I will give for the life of the world. . . . For my flesh is meat indeed, and my blood is drink indeed" (John vi. 51, 55). St. Paul, seeking to emancipate the early converts to the Christian faith from the "carnal ordinances" familiar to both Jew and Gentile, taught them that "the kingdom of God is not meat and drink; but righteousness, and peace, and joy in the Holy Ghost" (Rom. xiv. 17); while for himself, in deference to the lingering prejudices of some feeble saint, he nobly declared: "If meat make my brother to offend, I will eat no flesh while the world standeth" (1 Cor. viii. 13). Finally, the apostle sums up the Christian's duty, in that which must of necessity be a concession to the lower appetites, by a comprehensive exhortation, inspired, as it were, by a holy impatience: "Whether therefore ye eat or drink, or whatsoever ye do, do all to the glory of God" (1 Cor. x. 31).

VIII.

DRESS AND ORNAMENTS.

THE dress of men and women of the Bible differed but little, and chiefly in the outer garments,—the veil being the distinguishing feature; for the young girl, this represented the modesty of her virginal state, and for the matron, her dutiful subjection to her husband. The every-day attire of both sexes consisted of the "inner garment" or tunic, an "outer garment," a girdle and sandals.

The "coat" mentioned in the Bible generally means a kind of shirt, with or without sleeves, reaching usually to the knees, but sometimes to the ankles, and confined at the waist, together with the outer garment, by a wide girdle. This "inner garment," "coat," or shirt, was of wool, cotton, or linen, in several degrees of fineness and decoration, according to the means of the wearer; it was sometimes woven in one piece, and such an one is described as worn by our Lord: "The coat was without seam, woven from the top throughout" (John xix. 23). It is worthy of note that a person was said to be "naked," who had on this garment only: as in the example of Saul, who "lay down naked," after prophesying before Samuel (1 Sam. xix. 24); of St. Peter, who "girt his fisher's coat unto him (for he was naked), and did cast himself into the sea" (John xxi. 7); and of the youth in the Garden of

Gethsemane, who "when the young men laid hold on him," as on one who had followed Jesus to the scene of his betrayal, fled from them, naked" (Mark xiv. 52); and clad only in this long tunic, having "laid aside his garments," our Lord washed the disciples' feet (John xiii. 4).

The upper garment, or cloak, was nothing so elaborate as its name implies, but simply a square or long strip of cloth to wrap about the body. When very full, and girded at the waist, the long ends formed a sort of skirt or apron, and were so used: the "veil" that Ruth held for the "six measures of barley" was doubtless this skirt of her outer garment (Ruth iii. 15). The loose, baggy folds at the waist, above the girdle, formed an ample pocket, in which were carried weapons, money, or other articles portable on the person. Of this "pocket," our Lord said, "Good measure, pressed down and shaken together, and running over, shall men give into your bosoms;" and these same warm, woolly folds are to be remembered in connection with the tender promise that the Good Shepherd "shall gather the lambs with his arm, and carry them in his bosom."

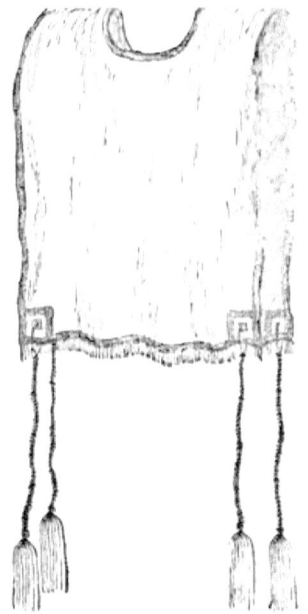
THE FRINGED GARMENT.

This upper robe was peculiarly susceptible of decoration: those worn by the wealthy were often brilliant in color, as well as of great value and beauty.

Allusion is made to this upper robe in the Mosaic law, which compelled the Hebrews to "make them fringes in the borders of their garments throughout their generations, and that they put upon the fringe of the borders a ribbon of blue" (Num. xv. 38, 39). The ostentatious "enlargement" of these borders by the self-righteous Pharisee was the

DRESS AND ORNAMENTS.

subject of severe rebuke from our Lord, as a "work" done "to be seen of men." The superstition of later times invested this border or fringe with peculiar virtue: it was used to cover the head in prayer, and it was in this spirit that the poor, diseased woman "came behind" Jesus, in the crowd, and "touched the hem of his garment;" while the people of Gennesaret "laid the sick in the streets," that "they might touch if it were but the border of his garment."

In connection with the fringed garment of the pious Israelite, may be mentioned the use of the "phylacteries." This singular observance arose from the literal interpretation of certain passages of Scripture, in Exodus and Deuteronomy, which are equally susceptible of a purely spiritual significance. One of these, in the sixth chapter of Deuteronomy, reads thus: " These words which I command thee this day, shall be in thine heart . . .

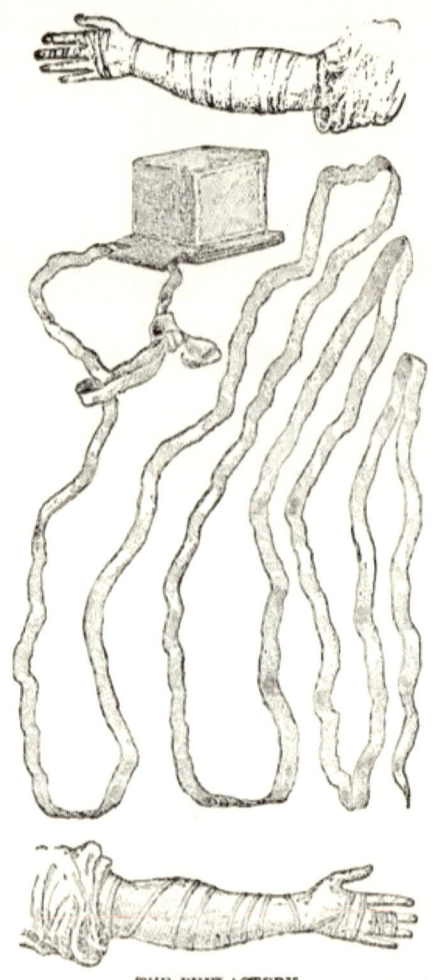

THE PHYLACTERY.

and thou shalt bind them for a sign upon thine hand, and they shall be as frontlets between thine eyes." Whatever the original intention may have been, it is certain that for ages the Jews fulfilled the command literally; and in the time of our Saviour it was still observed after this manner, except by the Karaite Jews and the Samaritans. The phylacteries were of two sorts, as the text quoted above implies, — one for the head, the other for the arm. That for the head consisted of four strips of parchment, on which were written in Hebrew these four passages of Scripture: Exod. xiii. 1–10, Exod. xiii. 11–16, Deut. vi. 4–9, and Deut. xi. 13–21. These were enclosed in a small square case of parchment or black calfskin having four cells: it was fastened on the forehead, between the eyes, by leather straps. The phylactery for the arm was a similar case, containing the same texts written on one strip of parchment; this was fastened to the inside of the left arm, so that the law might be near the heart: the straps were wound in a peculiar manner, seven times around the arm and three times about the fingers, the ends hanging loose from the middle finger: "Bind them upon thy fingers, write them upon the table of thine heart" (Prov. vii. 3). Phylacteries were not worn by women; and the men displayed them only during prayers, except the Pharisees, who never laid them aside. It will be remembered that our Lord did not condemn the wearing of phylacteries, but only the practice of making them "broad," in a spirit of ostentatious hypocrisy (Matt. xxiii. 5). It is not unlikely that they came to be worn as amulets, and that certain occult influences were attributed to their use.

That the art of dyeing, as well as of weaving, was known to the early Hebrews, even before they occupied the cities of their conquered foes, there is abundant proof. Beside Joseph's "coat of many colors," — which, in the light of the latest exposition, may be rejected as an example in point, — there was the "blue, and purple, and scarlet," and "rams' skins dyed red," employed in the construction of the tabernacle (Exod. xxv. 4, 5); there was the scarlet thread, bound on the hand of one of the twin-sons of Tamar, as well as that which was hung from the window of Rahab's house in Jericho; and the "white, green, and blue hangings" that decorated "Shushan the palace," at the superb feast given by Ahasuerus to his nobles (Esth. i. 6).

The ancient Egyptians were well acquainted with the art of dyeing; but the Phœnicians excelled all other peoples of their time in the brilliancy and permanency of their dyes; the famous Tyrian purple, for instance, obtained from certain shell-fish, was for ages the imperial color, and is mentioned by all writers of ancient history or classics.

The "soft raiment" worn "in king's houses" was the costly result of these ancient arts of the weaver and the dyer, and is often minutely described in the Bible, as at the court of Ahasuerus: "Mordecai went out from the presence of the king in royal apparel of blue and white, and with a great crown of gold, and with a garment of fine linen and purple" (Esth. viii. 15); and in the Apocrypha, where that monarch himself is described: "Who sat upon his royal throne, and was clothed with all his robes of majesty, all glittering with gold and precious stones" (Esth. xv. 6).

Ezekiel's impassioned allegory represents images of the nobles of Assyria sculptured "upon the wall," and "portrayed with vermilion;" as "clothed in blue," "clothed most gorgeously," and "exceeding in dyed attire upon their heads" (Ezek. xxiii. 12, 15); and the Assyrian marbles preserved to us attest the truth of his description. They reproduce the famous fringed garments of the Assyrians, ample and flowing, but differing in form from those of the Egyptians or the Hebrews. They consisted of tunics varying in length, of mantles, long-fringed scarfs, and embroidered girdles; the wide borders of these costly robes were ornamented with figures of men, animals, flowers, and foliage. Ezekiel, in his bitter lamentation for Tyre, thus apostrophizes that luxurious but guilty city: "Blue and purple from the isles of Elishah was that which covered thee." Merchants "occupied in thy fairs with emeralds, purple, and fine linen, ... in blue clothes and broidered work, and in chests of rich apparel" (Ezek. xxvii. 7, 16, 24). So, the rich man in the parable is described as "clothed in purple and fine linen;" of the "virtuous woman," it is recorded that "her clothing is silk and purple," while "all her household are clothed with scarlet;" David, lamenting over the dead king, calls upon the "daughters of Israel" to "weep over Saul, who clothed you in scarlet, with other delights; who put on ornaments of gold upon your apparel" (2 Sam. i. 24). And it will be remembered that Lydia, the first-fruits of St. Paul's ministry in Europe, was a "seller of purple," of the city of Thyatira.

Outer garments of fur or skin were worn in winter, some of them sufficiently rich and costly to be included in the royal apparel. The common skins of domestic animals, or a coarse cloth woven of goats' hair, were used by the poorer classes: the "mantle of Elijah, with which he "smote the waters," the "rough garment to deceive," the "sheep's clothing" of the false prophets, and John the Baptist's "raiment of camel's hair," are examples of these rude but warm and ample cloaks. St. Paul, in his Epistle to the Hebrews, writes of those "of whom the world was not worthy," that "they wandered about in sheep-skins and goat-skins: being destitute, afflicted, tormented" (Heb. xi. 37); and so, too, in "coats of skins," our father Adam, and the "mother of all living," went forth, out of the home which had witnessed their innocent happiness and their fall (Gen. iii. 21).

This coarse cloak was the poor man's bed-covering; hence the humane provision of the law for his necessity to the usurer: "If thou at all take thy neighbor's raiment to pledge, thou shalt deliver it unto him by that the sun goeth down: for that is his covering only, it is his raiment for his skin: wherein shall he sleep?" (Exod. xxii. 26, 27.) And, again: "Thou shalt deliver him the pledge again when the sun goeth down, that he may sleep in his own raiment, and bless thee" (Deut. xxiv. 13).

The girdle was a most important article of Eastern costume, and indispensable to comfort and convenience; since without it the long flowing outer garments would have effectually impeded the wearer when walking or at work. It was a wide belt or band, with a clasp, to be tightened or loosened at pleasure, and was made of cloth, leather, or linen, and often richly adorned with metals, jewels, and embroidery. This article, in a woman's costume, was known as a "stomacher;" and, where the means of the wearer permitted, it was very ornamental and expensive, being often made of cloth of gold, studded with precious stones. Girdles of this sort are still worn in the East. The "virtuous woman," praised by Solomon, is described as delivering "girdles unto the merchant" (Prov. xxxi. 24). Such a belt braced the whole body, seeming to impart strength and firmness; hence to "gird up the loins," denoted a condition of readiness for active, vigilant service; while to "loose the girdle," became the significant expression for repose and self-indulgence. The sacred writings abound in figurative allusions to this article of dress: in St. Paul's stirring exhortation to the Christians at Ephesus, to "stand, therefore, having your loins girt about with truth" (Eph. vi. 14), the allusion is to the military girdle, the indispensable adjunct to every warrior's outfit. Our Saviour warned his disciples to let their

"loins be girded about" (Luke xii. 35); and when he washed their feet (on the night of his last supper), he "laid aside his garments, and took a towel, and girded himself," as a servant. But to St. John, the beloved disciple, our Lord revealed himself in the glorious vision on Patmos, as "girt about the paps with a golden girdle," significant of his everlasting priesthood (Rev. i. 13).

HORNED HEAD-DRESSES.

In the third chapter of Isaiah, that eloquent prophet administers a scathing rebuke to the "haughty daughters of Zion;" and in an enumeration of the articles with which they adorned their persons, as he beheld them walking with "stretched-forth necks and wanton eyes," presents a very comprehensive inventory of the wardrobe of a fashionable lady of that day.

Among these, the "changeable suits of apparel" were rich garments designed specially for occasions of ceremony and social entertainment: the same word in the Hebrew is used to describe the "change of raiment" with which Joshua was clothed in the vision disclosed to the prophet Zechariah.

Beautiful cloths, woven or wrought with the needle in different colors and with gold or silver threads, were highly prized for these costly garments; and the Israelites probably learned the art of their manufacture from the Egyptians. Such were the rich spoils imagined by the "wise ladies," when comforting the anxious mother of Sisera: "a prey of divers colors, a prey of divers colors of needlework, of divers colors of needlework on both sides;" and such the raiment of "silk and broidered work" mentioned by Ezekiel (xvi. 13), and the "garment of divers colors" that Tamar wore (2 Sam. xiii. 18).

Babylon was so renowned for these stuffs, that she gave her name to the elaborate costumes composed of them: in the Book of Joshua (vii. 21) the miserable Achan confesses, that, tempted by "a goodly Babylonish garment," among other meretricious considerations, he had "sinned against the Lord God of Israel." So, in ecstatic inspiration, the "King's daughter" is depicted by David, not only as "all glorious within," but in "clothing of wrought gold," "in raiment of needlework" (Ps. xlv. 13, 14).

"Wimples" were full and flowing upper tunics of rich materials, with decorations of jewels and embroideries; the "mantle" was still another form of outer garment, a wide cloak of silk or woollen goods.

The "fine linen" described a woman's undergarments of exquisite texture and fashion; "bonnets" and "hoods" were adornments for the head, with distinctions too subtle to be discovered at this late day; only it appears that the "hood" was a simple handkerchief or scarf wound about the head, while the

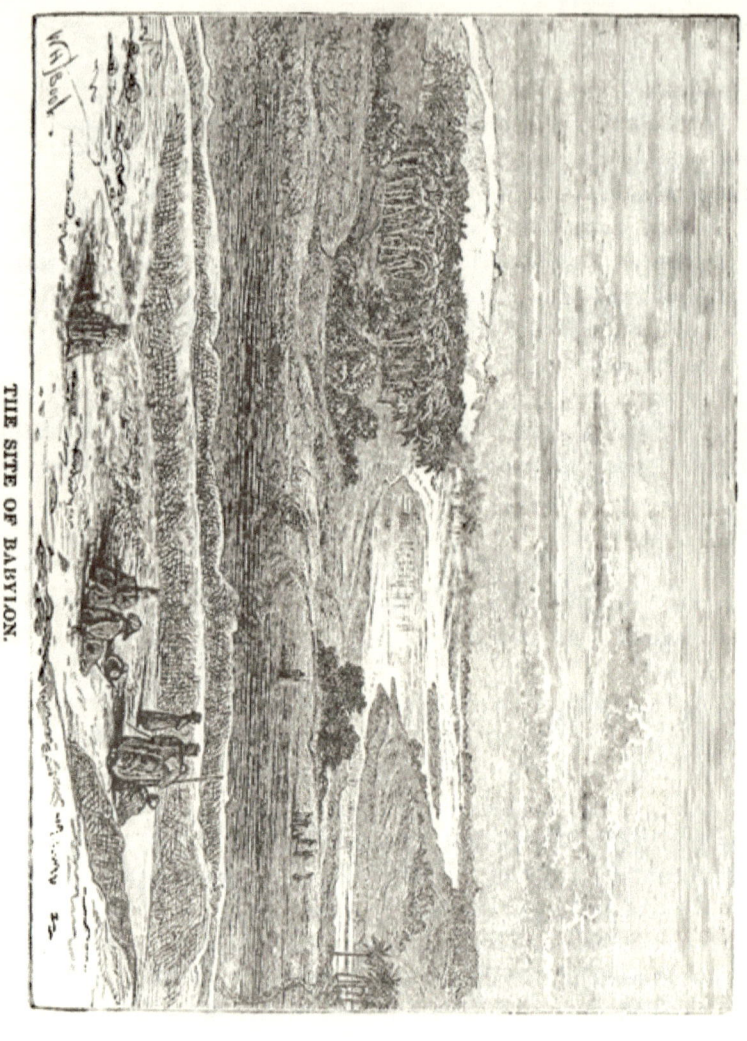

THE SITE OF BABYLON.

DRESS AND ORNAMENTS.

"bonnet" was a cap trimmed with silk or gauze draperies, and decorated with gold, silver, and jewelled ornaments, so as to resemble a diadem.

So, too, there were veils, and veils; though the one termed "muffler" in the text seems to suggest an out-of-door headdress with a face veil, as its Hebrew name points to the coquettish flutter of a thin gauze in a breeze about the fair head which it covers but is loath to conceal.

There is no description in the Bible of a headdress for men among the ancient Hebrews, except the "mitre of fine linen and goodly bonnets of fine linen," constituting a part of the official dress of the high priest, worn only during the sacred service of the tabernacle. In the time of Christ, a sort of turban or pointed cap was worn by the wealthy, in large cities where

VEILS.

the resident Jews adopted many of the prevailing modes of dress; as we read in the Apocrypha, that the wicked high priest Jason, desiring to introduce "Greek fashions and increase of heathenish manners" among his own people in Jerusalem, "brought the chief young men under his subjection, and made them wear a hat" (2 Macc. iv. 12). In remote rural districts it is probable, that, as in primitive times, the folds of the wide outer garment constituted a sort of hood that could be drawn over the head in bad weather. The word "hat" found in Dan. iii. 21 is literally rendered "upper tunic," a fold of which may have been thus used. It certainly was not customary to cover the head, since this (like uncovering the feet) was a recognized token of great affliction. When Haman was disgraced at the court of Ahasuerus, he "hasted to his house mourning, and having his head covered" (Esth. vi. 12). Thus David and his friends covered their heads when they fled from Jerusalem (2 Sam. xv. 30). The primitive covering for the foot was of the rudest sort: it consisted merely of a piece of wood or skin shaped to the sole, and bound upon the foot with straps or strings. The Hebrew word translated "shoe" in most of the texts where it occurs in the Old Testament, signifies this simple sandal, which has descended in its original form to the desert Arab of to-day.

EGYPTIAN SHOES.

The illustration affords us a correct representation of the sandals worn by the upper classes in ancient Egypt: turned up at the toes like skates, or rounded at both heels and toes. Boots and shoes have been found depicted upon the monumental remains of Thebes, but only as worn by foreigners, hence they are supposed to have belonged to the later era of Grecian supremacy. The ordinary sandal was made of several thicknesses of leather stitched together: it was fastened to the foot by two straps, one of which passed between the great and second toes, while the other enclosed the heel and instep. This shoe was never worn in doors, but was slipped off with ease at the entrance of the house or apartment, the latchets being loosed by a servant specially assigned to that menial office, as well as to the kindred duty of washing the feet of the guest, to whom the shoe we have described afforded but slight protection against the dust of road or street. This act of hospitality was so obligatory upon the host, that its omission emphasizes our blessed Lord's mild reproach to Simon the Pharisee: "I entered into thine house, thou gavest me no water for my feet" (Luke vii. 44).

In the time of Christ it is certain that there were more elabo-

THE PRODIGAL'S RETURN.

rate coverings for the feet, bearing some resemblance to our modern shoe; various models of the ancient shoe, as distinguished from the sandal, represent them as sometimes covering the entire foot, sometimes leaving the toes bare. Ladies of fashion wore, besides sandals of delicate workmanship, embroidered slippers of costly fabric, often decorated with precious stones and highly perfumed. A suggestive allusion in Judith's "song of praise" is made to these dainty adjuncts of coquetry: "her sandals ravished his eyes" (Jud. xvi. 9).

That shoes were regarded, even at this comparatively late date, as articles of luxury, may be inferred from our Lord's command to his disciples whom he was sending out on their ministry, to "be shod with sandals." It was on a festal occasion of great rejoicing, when the prodigal son was clad in the "best robe," that his father ordered shoes to be put on his feet. In one of the mystic allegories in the Book of Ezekiel, which includes the description of a most sumptuous feminine toilette, it is written: I "shod thee with badgers' skin;" and in the Song of Songs, we find the significant apostrophe: "How beautiful are thy feet with shoes, O prince's daughter!"

To go barefoot was a token of mourning or humiliation: a touching example of this is the account of King David's ascent of Mount Olivet when he left Jerusalem, pending the conspiracy and rebellion of his son Absalom: "David went up by the ascent of Mount Olivet, and wept as he went up, and had his head covered, and he went barefoot: and all the people that was with him covered every man his head, and they went up, weeping as they went up" (2 Sam. xv. 30). When Ezekiel was forbidden to mourn for the death of his wife, the "desire of his eyes," he was commanded to put on his shoes (Ezek. xxiv. 17). And so, at the command of the Lord, Isaiah "walked naked and barefoot three years, for a sign and wonder upon Egypt, and upon Ethiopia," to predict the captivity of the Egyptians and Ethiopians at the hand of the king of Assyria (Isa. xx. 3).

The shoe played an important part in two very ancient customs in Israel: the man who refused to marry his brother's widow was required by law to submit to the indignity of having his shoe loosed "from off his foot" by the humiliated woman, and his name was "called in Israel, the house of him that hath his shoe loosed" (Deut. xxv. 9); and, in making a bargain, we read: "Now this was the manner in former time in Israel concerning redeeming and concerning changing, for to confirm all things; a man plucked off his shoe, and gave it to his neighbor: and this was a testimony in Israel" (Ruth iv. 7). In this way did the "kinsman" transfer his right to Boaz to purchase the field of Naomi, and with it Ruth, the fair Moabitess, to wife. The transfer of a sandal seems a very appropriate representation of the transfer of landed property, as the sign of the owner's exclusive right to tread that particular soil. This custom is said still to exist in the East.

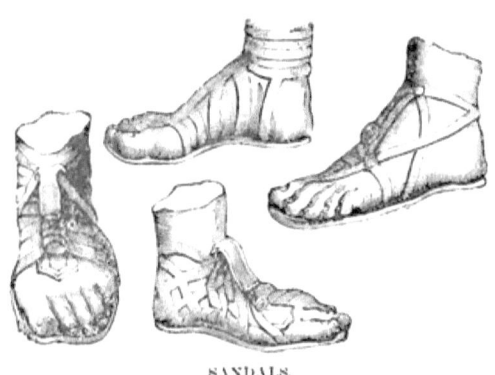

SANDALS.

Having described what may be termed the necessary articles of clothing in use among the peoples of the Bible, it now remains to consider some of the merely ornamental accessories, as they increased in number, value, and artistic excellence, with the multiplied luxuries of successive periods. Of the Hebrews, it is scarcely necessary to say, that, in respect of love of splendor and display in gold and jewels, they have always been conspicuous examples of a characteristic common to all Orientals. In the time of Isaiah, as we have seen, that prophet stooped from the highest soarings possible to the human intellect, to inveigh in detail against the excesses in dress indulged in by the wealthy women of his time; and in the early Christian era this condition of things still prevailed, so that the apostles again and again warned the women converts to the faith against the "braided hair," the "gold, pearls, and costly array," so prized by the heathen women about them. It cannot be denied, however, that the fashionable gentleman of the same epochs, whether Jew or Gentile, with his curled and perfumed locks, his bracelets, rings, and chains of gold, his embroidered tunics of purple or even white, and his girdle of gorgeous beauty, constituted an equally "shining mark" for the rebukes of prophet and apostle.

Necklaces of gold or silver, close-fitting about the throat, or hanging far below the girdle, sometimes made of pearls or other precious stones strung together, were worn by both sexes: the gold chain, like the signet-ring, was among the ancients a mark of distinction, affected by persons of high rank only. Thus, at the elevation of Joseph: "Pharaoh took off his ring from his hand, and put it upon Joseph's hand, and arrayed him in vestures of fine linen, and put a gold chain about his neck" (Gen. xli. 42). the gift of the ring being an actual conferring of royal dignity and power. In like manner, Ahasuerus gave his ring to Haman, and afterward to Mordecai. Chains were also made of crescent-shaped gold coins, and suspended from gala headdresses, described as "round tires like the moon."

The "nose-jewels," enumerated by Isaiah (iii. 21), were ornaments peculiar to Oriental women, and are still to be seen in the East among the lower classes. They were rings, from one to three inches in diameter, made of gold, silver, coral, moth-

EARRINGS AND NOSE-JEWELS.

er-of-pearl, or even horn, and were left open, so that one end might be inserted into the pierced nostril, or into the middle cartilage of the nose. The other end was strung with jewels or beads or other pendent devices. The "golden earring of half a shekel weight" that Eliezer put upon the "face" of Rebekah, the bride elect of his master's son Isaac, was a nose-jewel. This singular ornament is alluded to in one of Solomon's caustic sayings: "As a jewel of gold in a swine's snout, so is a fair woman which is without discretion" (Prov. xi. 22); and in Ezekiel's powerful allegory: "I put a jewel on thy forehead," which the marginal reading translates "nose."

But there were also earrings, in our modern interpretation of the word, worn in ancient Israel by both men and women. They were not simply articles of jewelry, but amulets, engraved with mystic figures and symbols, and distinctly associated with the idolatrous superstitions and practices of the heathen among whom the chosen people dwelt. Earrings are still worn in the East as charms against evil spirits, and to procure good fortune. In the second chapter of Hosea, the wearing of earrings is directly connected with the burning of incense to Baal; and when Jacob, in obedience to the divine command, went to Bethel to renew his covenant with God, he first required his household to give up "all the strange gods which were in their hand, and all their earrings which were in their ears; and Jacob hid them under the oak which was by Shechem" (Gen. xxxv. 4), by that act putting away those open expressions of idolatry.

Bracelets, armlets, and anklets were essential to the outfit of an Oriental woman, of whatever rank or means. For the wealthy these articles were made of the precious metals, massive and richly decorated; while the women of the poorer classes set off their shapely arms, often from wrist to elbow, with bracelets of the cheapest materials, — brass, wire, horn, or even beads. Specimens of ancient Assyrian and Egyptian bracelets are to be found in public museums, and to their curious, if not always graceful, designs the artistic jeweller of to-day is indebted for an endless variety of suggestion and reproduction.

EGYPTIAN JEWELRY.

Among the "jewels of silver and jewels of gold" presented

by Abraham's servant to Rebekah were "two bracelets for her hands, of ten shekels weight of gold" (Gen. xxiv. 22). Bracelets were also worn by men. Monarchs wore them above the elbow, and they constituted a part of their royal insignia. Thus the young Amalekite who slew King Saul brought to David "the crown that was upon his head, and the bracelet that was on his arm" (2 Sam. i. 10); and Tamar, Judah's daughter-in-law, required as a pledge his "signet" and his "bracelets" (Gen. xxxviii. 18).

EGYPTIAN BRACELET.

There seems to be no question that the "tinkling ornaments" about the feet, and the "ornaments of the legs," specified in the third chapter of Isaiah, refer to the gold and silver anklets worn by the fashionable women of his time, and to the "step-chains," which, joining one ankle to the other, compelled the "mincing" movement in walking alluded to in this connection. The "tinkling" was produced by tiny bells or small ornaments attached to the anklet, that jingled with every movement of the coquettish wearer. When the wife of Jeroboam went to consult the blind prophet Ahijah concerning her sick son, it is said that "Ahijah heard the sound of her feet as she came in at the door" (1 Kings xiv. 6); and it has been suggested that the sound was the jingling of her anklets.

The "tablets," literally "houses of the soul," mentioned in this list (which we have followed somewhat irregularly), are supposed to have been gold or silver ornaments of a certain mystic significance, in the form of a temple, and corresponding to those of similar import commonly worn by the Greek and Roman ladies of a later date. These tablets were suspended from the necklace or girdle.

Another favorite and very ancient adjunct to the toilet was a small metal mirror ("glasses") with highly-polished surface, worn also at the girdle. In Exod. xxxviii. 8 it is recorded of the furnishing of the sanctuary, that Moses made the laver of brass, and the foot of it of brass, of the looking-glasses of the women assembling, which assembled at the door of the tabernacle of the congregation."

These "looking-glasses" were what we call hand-mirrors, small and exquisitely made, the handles especially artistic in shape and

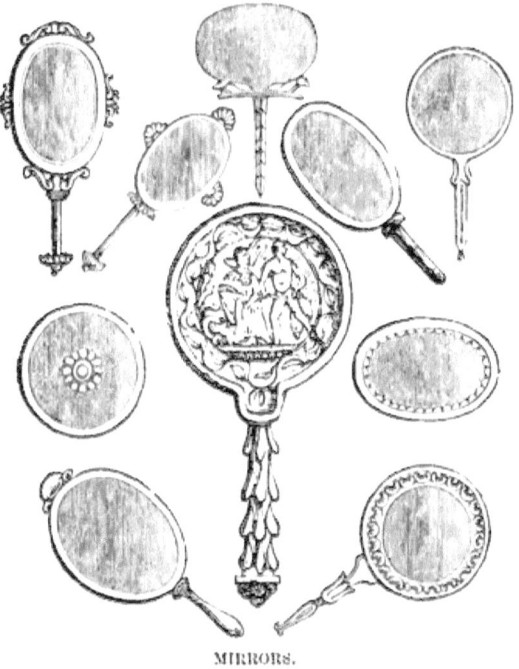

MIRRORS.

highly ornamented. Job eloquently likens the sky to a "molten looking-glass" (xxxvii. 18); and the apostles Paul and James, in their Epistles to the early Christian Church, make use of this familiar article to illustrate their pious exhortations (2 Cor. iii. 18; Jas. i. 23). Among other expensive trifles were the "crisping-pins" mentioned by Isaiah, which by our modern light we are disposed to connect with the art of ancient hair-dressing, but which appear to have been long bags or purses of highly ornamental needlework, or even of gold links, worn by women, suspended from the girdle or neck-chain. The same word, translated "bags," will be found in 2 Kings v. 23. "Cauls" and "head-bands" were nets or fillets to cover the hair: they were strung with gold ornaments or small coins, in patterns more or less intricate. Gold cords were also worn around the head, from which a fringe of precious stones delicately set depended upon the brow and face. This latter ornament is indicated in Solomon's Song: "Thy cheeks are comely with rows of jewels, thy neck with chains of gold" (i. 10).

FROM the second chapter of Genesis, where we learn of "the land of Havilah," rich in gold and the "onyx-stone," to the closing scenes of Revelation, made luminous with the vision of the heavenly Jerusalem, the sacred volume is full of allusions to the precious metals and the precious stones; but, though described by their names, it is by no means easy to identify the latter with those of our own time. Besides those mentioned separately, there are three noticeable enumerations of precious stones in the Bible. The first comprises the twelve jewels (four rows of three stones each) that composed the "breastplate of judgment" worn by the high priest as he ministered before the Lord. Their names are given as "sardius, topaz, carbuncle, emerald, sapphire, diamond, ligure, agate, amethyst, beryl, onyx, and jasper." On each of these was the name of one of the twelve tribes of Israel, "like the engravings of a signet" (Exod. xxviii. 11).

The second of these enumerations describes the crown jewels of the king of Tyre, consisting of nine precious stones, — the "sardius, topaz, diamond, beryl, onyx, jasper, sapphire, emerald, and carbuncle (Ezek. xxviii. 13). In the Apocalypse of "the new Jerusalem, coming down from God out of heaven, prepared as a bride adorned for her husband," there are twelve stones ("all manner of precious stones") enumerated, besides the twelve pearls of the twelve gates, — "jasper, sapphire, chalcedony, emerald, sardonyx, sardius, chrysolite, beryl, topaz, chrysoprasus, jacinth, and amethyst" (Rev. xxi. 19, 20).

Though these twelve stones bear different names from those on the high priest's breastplate (being translated from the Greek instead of the Hebrew), they represent, with mystical significance, the same jewels, the order in which they are named being the only change. It is interesting to examine the results of scientific research in the difficult matter of identifying some of these precious stones with those with which we are familiar. The sardius or sard, we are told, is an agate: its original Hebrew name is "red," and the Talmud says that "the color of this stone represented the blushes of Reuben, because of shame for his iniquity." The topaz is the same yellow or greenish-yellow gem that we know as a favorite with our grandmothers, but no longer in fashion: the ancients ascribed certain pacifying and salutary attributes to this stone. The carbuncle of the Bible is identical with our garnet, while the emerald is supposed to be the modern carbuncle. The sapphire is identified, almost beyond a doubt, with our precious stone of the same name. It is a Jewish tradition that the tables of the Ten Commandments were of sapphire: hence we are not surprised to learn that it was supposed "to invigorate both body and soul, to prevent evil thoughts, and to be so potent an enemy to poison, that, placed in a glass with a spider or venomous reptile, it would kill it." It was deemed a specific against fevers, and was worn by the priests as an emblem of chastity.

Job says of the earth: "The stones of it are the place of sapphires;" and of wisdom, that "it cannot be valued with the gold of Ophir, with the precious onyx, or the sapphire" (Job xxxviii. 6, 16). In the vision of the glory of God, the prophet describes "the likeness of a throne, as the appearance of a sapphire stone" (Ezek. i. 26); and when Moses was called up into the mountain with "Aaron, Nadab, and Abihu, and seventy of the elders of Israel, they saw the God of Israel: and *there was* under his feet as it were a paved work of a sapphire stone" (Exod. xxiv. 10).

The sixth stone in the high priest's breastplate is translated "diamond," but it is by no means probable that the ancient Hebrews were possessed of this most precious stone. Jeremiah writes: "The sin of Judah is written with a pen of iron, and with the point of a diamond" (xvii. 1); but he makes use of another Hebrew word, indicating a stone of great hardness.

The mystic Spouse sings of her Beloved: "His hands are as gold rings set with the beryl: his belly is as bright ivory overlaid with sapphires" (S. of Sol., v. 2). Job and Ezekiel both tell of coral, but it cannot be identified with the dainty article so admired now. The pearl is seldom mentioned in the Old Testament, but frequently named in the New, especially in connection with solemn lessons of Christian faith, from the lips of Him who "spake as never man spake;" "The kingdom of heaven is like unto a merchantman seeking goodly pearls: who, when he had found one pearl of great price, went and sold all that he had, and bought it" (Matt. xiii. 45). "Pearls" are specially mentioned by the Apostle Paul in his admonition to the women of the early Church, against the extravagant modes of the time; and the woman shown to St. John in vision was "decked with gold and precious stones and pearls" (Rev. xvii. 4). This chaste and exquisite jewel was held in great esteem by the ancient Egyptians, Babylonians, and Romans: it was considered next in value to the diamond, and fabulous prices were paid for single specimens of exceptional size and beauty.

The arts of polishing, cutting, and mounting precious stones were well understood at a very early period in the history of Oriental nations, as well as the less reputable art of imitating the true gems: it is almost amusing to read of ancient Thebes, that in the manufacture of emeralds and amethysts she excelled the cunning workmen of modern Paris. This branch of industry was probably stimulated by the demand for fictitious gems in the adornment of heathen temples and tombs, though these decorations were not confined to imitated jewels.

"THE PEARL OF THE EAST,"—DAMASCUS.

IX.

THE TOILET AND THE BATH.

THE care of the hair and beard was of sufficient importance among the Hebrews to be considered in Levitical enactments. While the Egyptians, and other Oriental people among whom they dwelt, shaved their heads and beards, Israelites were required to cut their hair, much after the fashion of the present day: only the law admonished them: "Ye shall not round the corners of your heads, neither shalt thou mar the corners of thy beard" (Lev. xix. 27). The first clause of this law is generally supposed to signify a prohibition against shaving the hair off the temples, and was probably suggested by certain idolatrous practices.

In the ordinances for the priests, recorded by Ezekiel, it is even more carefully insisted upon: "Neither shall they shave their heads, nor suffer their locks to grow long; they shall only poll their heads" (Ezek. xliv. 20): lest they should resemble the priests of heathen tem-

ORIENTAL BARBER.

ples, or, on the other hand, the Nazarites, a sect of which Samson and probably Samuel and John the Baptist, were notable examples.

The beard was an object of special veneration to the Jew, who regarded it as a symbol of his dignity and free manhood, since slaves were required to shave to denote their servile condition.

The beard was most scrupulously cared for, trimmed and perfumed, and its luxuriant growth promoted by every known art of the toilet: to neglect or shave it was a sign of profound affliction, and an insult offered to it an unpardonable offence. The implements used by the ancient barber were identical with those of our day, — the razor, scissors, basin, and mirror. A razor found in an ancient tomb is similar in shape to the modern instrument. Among the several instructions to Ezekiel from "the voice of One that spake," was one containing an allusion to this familiar implement, then, as now, in daily use: "Son of man, take thee a sharp knife, take thee a barber's razor, and cause it to pass upon thine head and upon thy beard" (Ezek. v. 1). The barbers' shops of Rome and Athens were famous resorts for the wits and gossips of fashionable society, as recorded in the annals of those luxurious cities.

In notable contrast to the Jewish custom, the Egyptians shaved the whole head and beard, except in times of mourning; but the men wore, in doors and out, wigs of elaborate workmanship, — a fine specimen of the art being preserved in the British Museum. They also wore false beards, made of braided hair, and graduated in size and length according to the rank of the wearer. That Egyptian ladies wore large and expensive wigs as late as the Christian era, is proved by their presence in mummies; and examples of the head-dresses of that time, as exhibited in terra-cotta models found in the ruins of Smyrna, show that the Grecian ladies had adopted the same fashion.

Elaborate hair-dressing has been the common practice among Eastern women "from the beginning;" and long hair, especially if black or very dark brown, was considered the perfection of this natural ornament, so that even the ascetic St. Paul could pause in his polemics to the early Church to declare: "If a woman have long hair it is a glory to her" (1 Cor. xi. 15). Solomon twice sings in praise of "the fairest among women:" "Thy hair is as a flock of goats that appear from Mount Gilead" (S. of Sol., iv. 1), — the black goats whose hair furnished the covering for the "tents of Kedar;" and she, in her turn, sings of her beloved: "His locks are bushy, and black as a raven" (v. 11). Baldness in men or women was such a calamity, and even reproach, that the prophecy fulminated at the "daughters of Zion," that "instead of well-set hair" they should have "baldness" (Isa. iii. 24), was fraught with peculiar horror.

Laborious weaving of the hair in multitudinous braids is an Oriental custom of great antiquity, as we find by the plaited hair found on the heads of mummies. Even in modern times, Lady Wortley Montagu relates that she had counted one hundred and

EGYPTIAN HEAD-DRESSES.

ten braids on the head of a Turkish lady, all of her own hair; and it is evident that in the days of the apostles the practice must have been carried to great excess to have elicited the particular prohibition of both St. Paul and St. Peter, in their epistles, against the "braided hair" and "that outward adorning of plaiting the hair," common to the fashion of the period. The luxurious Greeks and Romans of both sexes were excessively fond of scented pomades and oils for the hair. Curious research has brought to light at least ten varieties known to have been commonly used by Roman barbers. In Capua, a city noted for the effeminate manners of its people, there was a famous street called the "Seplasia," occupied entirely by shops for the sale of rare perfumes, scented powders, and unguents.

In "artistic" hair-dressing the ancient *coiffeur* far excelled his fellow-craftsman of to-day; it was required of him, not only to dispose the tresses of his fair patron to the enhancement of her personal charms, but to crown her devoted head with reproductions in hair of many curious devices, well calculated to inspire the beholder with awe, if not admiration. "Figures of coronets, harps, wreaths, diadems, emblems of public temples and conquered cities, were formed by the mimic skill of the ancient *friseur*," who used in these marvellous structures a mucilaginous preparation similar to our bandoline, together with choice ointments, combs, and hair-pins.

Another and more natural fashion of dressing the hair, sufficiently elaborate withal, consisted of many braids hanging down the back, into which ribbons were introduced to increase their apparent length; and coins or jewels were added to enhance their glossy darkness. Some writers contend that the Hebrews abstained from the use of hair-dyes and false hair; others affirm, that, at least as late as the days of our Saviour, Jewish belles preferred a reddish auburn to the natural color of their abundant tresses, and that to obtain it they employed dyes, or had their heads sprinkled with gold-dust.

The sacred writings abound in beautiful and touching expressions of reverence for gray hairs. Solomon says, "The hoary head is a crown of glory" (Prov. xvi. 31); and, "The beauty of old men is the gray head" (Prov. xx. 29). The law admonishes the faithful Israelite: "Thou shalt rise up before the hoary head, and honor the face of the old man, and fear thy God: I am the Lord" (Lev. xix. 32). The paternal heart of every age has responded to the pathetic remonstrance of the aged patriarch Jacob, trembling for Benjamin, the son of his beloved Rachel: "If mischief befall him by the way in the which ye go, then shall ye bring down my gray hairs with sorrow to the grave"

(Gen. xlii. 38). And who, in the shadow of declining years, makes not David's prayer his own? "Now also, when I am old and grayheaded, O God, forsake me not!" (Ps. lxxi. 18.) The blossoming of the almond-tree constitutes a prominent feature in that inimitable allegory of old age contained in the final chapter of Ecclesiastes; and Hosea nicely describes the stealthy approach of our common enemy in one little line: "Gray hairs are here and there upon him, yet he knoweth it not" (Hos. vii. 9). Our Saviour forbade the ancient Oriental custom of swearing by the hair and by the beard: "Neither shalt thou swear by thy head, because thou canst not make one hair white or black" (Matt. v. 36); while he left us the gracious assurance: "The very hairs of your head are all numbered" (Matt. x. 30). The Bible student will reverentially recall the two instances in which white hair is described as pertaining to the person of the Divine Majesty as revealed to his servants: in the Book of Daniel (vii. 9) we read: "I beheld till the thrones were cast down, and the Ancient of days did sit, whose garment was white as snow, and the hair of his head like the pure wool;" and in the Apocalypse of St. John "in the isle that is called Patmos," that beloved disciple beholds one "like unto the Son of man," whose "head and hairs were white like wool, as white as snow." With more of human interest we dwell upon the three notable heads of hair in Scripture: the seven wonderful locks in which lay the strength of the mighty Samson, "a Nazarite to God from the womb

to the day of his death" (Judg. xiii. 7); the hair of the Prince Beautiful of all Israel, Absalom, of which it is recorded, that, "when he polled his head (for it was at every year's end that he polled it; because the hair was heavy on him, therefore he polled it), he weighed the hair of his head at two hundred shekels after the king's weight" (2 Sam. xiv. 26), and which finally procured his ignominious death; and those softly flowing, long, luxuriant locks of Mary Magdalene, honored above all that have been a "glory" to women since the world began, in that they served her Master's use, and elicited his tender acknowledgment: "She hath washed my feet with her tears, and wiped them with the hairs of her head" (Luke vii. 44).

OINTMENTS and perfumes are first mentioned in the Bible in connection with the service of the Tabernacle, where Moses receives the Divine command to "compound after the art of the apothecary" the "sweet incense" to be burned morning and evening on the altar, and the "holy anointing oil" for the consecration of the priests, and the furniture of the sacred place (Exod. xxx. 23, 34). Into these compositions entered the precious spices well known to the ancients: "pure myrrh, sweet cinnamon, cassia, sweet calamus, stacte, onycha, and galbanum, with pure frankincense."

There is a Rabbinical tradition that a Levite, one of the fifteen prefects of the Temple, was specially assigned to the duty of making this precious compound, and that a laboratory was fitted up for him within the sacred building. Various theories have been advanced as to the significance of the use of incense in public worship: it seems most reasonable to regard it as the symbol of prayer, as it was offered while the assembled congregation were in the posture and act of devotion. Even to the angel in the Apocalypse, there was given "much incense, that he should offer it with the prayers of all saints" (Rev. viii. 3). Dr. Wilson aptly remarks of incense as an agent in public worship, that "this symbolical mode of supplication had this one advantage over spoken or written prayer, that it appealed to those who were both blind and deaf,— a class usually excluded from social worship by their affliction: the hallowed impressions shut out by one avenue were admitted to the mind and heart by another."

So holy were the purposes to which the incense and the anointing oil were devoted, that the children of Israel were forbidden to make either of these confections for personal use, under the dire penalty of being "cut off" from their people (Exod. xxx. 32, 37).

This very prohibition goes far to prove that the use of perfumes in the toilet was already common, and the art of their compounding a commercial fact. The ancient trade of perfumer, however (like that of the barber), was held in decided disrepute; so that when the prophet Samuel wished to emphasize his warning to the Jews, when they demanded a king to rule over them, he said, "He will take your daughters to be confectionaries, and to be cooks, and to be bakers" (1 Sam. viii. 13).

ALTAR OF INCENSE.

It is necessary to note that the original signification of the term "confectioner" is simply one who compounds various ingredients; and in the text it is applied to those who prepared the sweet spices so liberally used by Oriental peoples. The word "ointment," also, as found in the Bible, means highly-scented oil, extract of spices, or perfume, and is in no case susceptible of its modern application to healing salves or emollients. Solomon's proverb, that "ointment and perfume rejoice the heart," was not more true of the Orientals of his time than of those before and since; the excessive use of sweet and pungent odors has always been common to every action of their daily life. Not only were they worn on the person, in dainty boxes or vials of gold, silver, and alabaster; but the rooms of their houses, their beds and furniture, were filled with the aromatic fumes of burning resins, or perfumed with spices and gums. Even in natural flowers, those of the strongest odor have always been preferred in the East. This universal fondness has been accounted for, with some show of reason, by the necessity of neutralizing the offensive smells which are engendered, especially in their cities, by the excessive heat, and the absence of all "modern improvements" of a sanitary character.

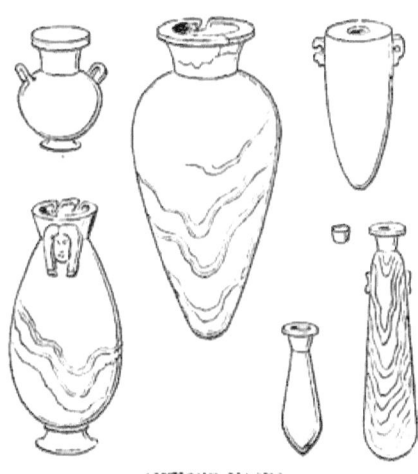

ANTIQUE VASES.

The personal use of fragrant oils and powders is frequently referred to in the Scriptures. Thus in David's "Song of loves," of Him who is "fairer than the children of men," he says, "Thy God hath anointed thee with the oil of gladness above thy fellows. All thy garments smell of myrrh and aloes and cassia" (Ps. xlv. 7, 8). Again, in the "Song of songs," the Church triumphant takes up the inspired strain:

"Who is this that cometh out of the wilderness like pillars of smoke, perfumed with myrrh and frankincense, with all powders of the merchant?" "The smell of thy garments is like the smell of Lebanon." (S. of Sol. iii. 6, iv. 2.)

The custom of perfuming the clothing was universal among Orientals; and for this purpose they employed camphor, civet, sandalwood, and other strong scents. The extreme antiquity of the practice is proved by its early mention in the Bible, in the pathetic scene where the aged patriarch, deceived by Jacob, bestows upon him the blessing: "And his father Isaac said unto him, Come near now, and kiss me, my son. And he came near, and kissed him: and he smelled the smell of his raiment, and blessed him, and said, See, the smell of my son is as the smell of a field which the Lord hath blessed" (Gen. xxvii. 26, 27).

Anointing was very anciently practised by the Egyptians and the Hebrews, and later by the Greeks and Romans. It is probable, that originally it was a feature of occasions of religious or civil solemnity only, such as the consecration of priests and the coronation of kings; but in course of time it became a daily habit of the people, in connection with the bath and other refined luxuries of private life. The Bible abounds in examples of this custom, both in its ceremonial and its domestic aspects. Olive-oil was used, pure, or mixed with rare and costly spices of exquisite fragrance; and when employed as a cosmetic it was applied not only to the head, but to the entire person.

At the coronation of the son of David, it is written: "Zadok the priest took a horn of oil out of the tabernacle, and anointed Solomon. And they blew the trumpet; and all the people said, God save king Solomon" (1 Kings i. 39); and, in the case of the sons of Aaron, Moses was thus instructed: "Thou shalt anoint them, as thou didst anoint their father, that they may minister unto me in the priest's office: for their anointing shall surely be an everlasting priesthood throughout their generations" (Exod. xl. 15). When Naomi "sought rest" for her daughter-in-law Ruth, in the heart and home of her rich kinsman Boaz, she bade her: "Wash thyself therefore, and anoint thee, and put thy raiment upon thee, and get thee down to the floor" (Ruth iii. 3). Again, when "David perceived that the child was dead," for whose recovery he had fasted and wept before the Lord, he "arose from the earth, and washed, and anointed himself, and changed his apparel, and came into the house of the Lord, and worshipped" (2 Sam. xii. 20).

It was especially the custom to anoint the head on all happy and festal occasions; so that the act became symbolical of the luxury of joy. On the other hand, its omission was a token of mourning. The prophet depicts the sinful pleasures of them that were "at ease in Zion," "that drink wine in bowls, and anoint themselves with the chief ointments" (Amos vi. 6); and the Lord, recounting his mercies to backslidden Israel, says, "Then washed I thee with water, . . . and I anointed thee with oil" (Ezek. xvi. 9).

The Psalmist likens brotherly love to the "precious ointment upon the head, that ran down upon the beard, even Aaron's beard; that went down to the skirts of his garments" (Ps. cxxxiii. 2); and in that most lovely outpouring of the devout heart in childlike faith and trust, the twenty-third Psalm, he exclaims, "Thou anointest my head with oil: my cup runneth over."

"Words softer than oil;" "oil to make his face to shine;" "the oil of joy for mourning;" "a kindness, an excellent oil;" "the Lord will bless thy wine and thy oil;" "the oil of gladness."—are a few of the numerous expressions in Scripture that denote the esteem, both literal and symbolical, in which this "labor of the olive" was held. The expression, "fresh oil," employed by the Psalmist in Ps. xcii. 10, is interpreted literally *green* oil; that is, oil newly made, or made from unripe olives, or that which is pressed from the nut without the usual process of boiling. This "cold-drawn" oil was used for medicinal purposes, as being the purest, and was preferred especially for anointing the person; but it was also much more expensive than the ordinary kinds.

To omit washing and anointing the body was so conspicuous a sign of distress, that our Lord condemned the practice in connection with ostentatious fasting, and enjoined precisely the opposite course upon his disciples: "But thou, when thou fastest, anoint thine head, and wash thy face; that thou appear not unto men to fast, but unto thy Father which is in secret" (Matt. vi. 17, 18).

The Jews adopted from the Egyptians the custom of anointing guests on festal occasions. Servants were appointed to the office of sprinkling the garments of their master's friends with rose-water or other scented essences; while their heads, and even the garlands with which they were crowned, were anointed with choice unguents. So universal was this custom, that its omission could be construed only as premeditated insult. And in this light, new, perhaps, to some readers, let us look again at that most beautiful incident in the social life of our Lord, where, though the chief guest, at the house of a wealthy Pharisee, he was yet indebted to "a woman in the city" for his anointing, as well as for the necessary refreshment of washing his feet. "He said unto Simon, Seest thou this woman? I entered into thine house, thou gavest me no water for my feet: but she hath washed my feet with tears, and wiped them with the hairs of her head. Thou gavest me no kiss: but this woman, since the time I came in, hath not ceased to kiss my feet. My head with oil thou didst not anoint: but this woman hath anointed my feet with ointment." (Luke vii. 44–46.)

The "alabaster box of ointment" in this record; and the "alabaster box of ointment of spikenard, very precious," mentioned in the Gospel of St. Mark, and of which the apostle adds, "She brake the box, and poured it on his head" (xiv. 3), — were the familiar receptacles at that time for medicines and perfumes, and as such are to this day. Alabaster is a kind of soft white marble, easily carved, and susceptible of a high polish. Specimens of antique vases and vials made of this stone, to contain ointments and cosmetics, were among the Layard discoveries at Nineveh, and a fine collection is preserved in the British Museum. Alabaster was so called from Alabastron, an Egyptian town, near which it was procured. The vessels were called *alabastra* by the

Greeks from this circumstance, and finally all perfume boxes, or vases, or vials, whether of ivory or glass, bone, shell, or even gold, were known as alabastra. The Gospel phrase, "she brake the box," is interpreted to mean that (making her offering still more lavish) she broke the slender neck of the sealed bottle or pitcher that contained the ointment; because the word signifying "oil-vessel" is in several Old-Testament texts translated indifferently "box" or "vial." The two following will serve as an illustration: when Elisha wished to anoint Jehu king over Israel, he sent one of the "children of the prophets," with a "box" of oil in his hand for the purpose; and Samuel, in a like case, took a "vial" of oil, and poured it upon the head of Saul. In these two texts the Hebrew word is the same, having the same derivation from the verb "to drop," thereby indicating a flask with a narrow, tube-like mouth, such as have been found in Egyptian and Assyrian excavations.

Oil was highly esteemed in the East as an article of the *materia medica*: certain kinds were prized as specifics in pains and diseases of the head, while others were carefully avoided as productive of delirium and insanity. The Psalmist praises, under the figure of the "excellent oil which shall not break" his head, the smiting and reproof of the righteous, alluding to the ancient custom of administering domestic correction upon the crown of the head. It is curious, in this connection, to learn that the Hindoos have traditional expressions almost identical with the text referred to: "Let a holy man smite my head! And what of that? it is an excellent oil." "My master has been beating my head, but it has been good oil for me."

In the parable of the Good Samaritan, it is said, to the honor of his humanity, that he went to his suffering neighbor, "and bound up his wounds, pouring in oil and wine" (Luke x. 34), — a practice doubtless familiar to the "beloved physician" who records the story. This was a favorite treatment in ancient surgery, especially for wounds resulting from violent assaults: wool, lint, or pounded olive was first laid upon the wound, and the mixture poured into the gash, — the wine to cleanse, and the

GREEK AND ROMAN ALABASTRA.

oil to soothe and heal. Indeed, the healing properties of oil and ointments were so firmly believed in, that it was a common practice to anoint the sick with them. In St. Mark's Gospel we read that the disciples (sent forth on their mission of mercy by our Lord, "two and two"), beside their preaching, and casting-out of devils, "anointed with oil many that were sick, and healed them;" showing that though their cures were miraculous, they preferred to make use of natural means. And St. James the Apostle, among his injunctions to the early Christians, lays stress upon this custom, which in the Roman Catholic Church has ever since held the place of a sacrament, under the name of "extreme unction:" "Is any sick among you? let him call for the elders of the church; and let them pray over him, anointing him with oil in the name of the Lord" (Jas. v. 14).

THE excessive heat of the climate, as well as certain peculiarities of costume and custom among the Orientals, made the refreshment of frequent bathing a necessity: running water was preferred by the Hebrews for their personal ablutions, but in the large cities families made use of the pools and fountains in the courts of their own houses. As wealth and the love of sensuous pleasures increased, the bathing custom, especially among the Greeks and Romans, became in the highest degree luxurious: public baths were erected at great cost, and were extensively patronized by the elegant society of that day, to whom they were favorite lounging-places, similar to the modern clubs.

Bathing constitutes a distinctive feature of the Mosaic code, by which, in connection with the ceremonial of the sanctuary, it was elevated from a sanitarial necessity into a rite symbolical of inward purity, and of that "holiness without which no man can see the Lord." In this spirit David, overwhelmed with a sense of his spiritual uncleanness, cries out to God: "Wash me thoroughly from mine iniquity, and cleanse me from my sin;" "Wash me, and I shall be whiter than snow;" "Create within me a clean heart" (Ps. li. 2, 7, 10). The priests who ministered before the Lord were required to observe very strictly these ordinances for personal cleanliness; when Solomon built the Temple he constructed a superb copper lavatory, or "molten sea," for the priests, which contained from sixteen to twenty-four thousand gallons of water (1 Kings vii. 26; 2 Chron. iv. 2).

We learn from the charming story of the infant Moses, that it was possible for a royal princess to bathe in a river, probably enclosed at a specified point to secure her privacy; in the Second Book of Moses the historian tells us that "the daughter of Pharaoh came down to wash herself at the river; and her maidens walked along by the river's side" (Exod. ii. 5). It does not follow, however, that this was on an ordinary occasion; for the Nile was regarded as a sacred river, and it has been customary in later times, for young maidens to bathe in its waters in the spring of the year, singing songs in honor of the rise and overflow at that season.

A favorite mode of Eastern bathing was by having water poured on the body, after submitting to the usual processes of lathering with soap, and manipulations by the attendant. Egyptian monuments afford many examples of this sort of bathing as applied to men and women. Snow-water was supposed to possess superior qualities for brightening and cleansing the skin, and for preventing perspiration by contracting the fibres. Job, in his despair of establishing his innocency before God, exclaims: "If I wash myself with snow-water, and make my hands never so clean," he would still be foul in His sight. Frequent washing of the hands was made expressly essential to comfort and decency by certain Oriental customs. At meals, for example, it was required that the hands should be scrupulously clean; because the meats and fowls were "carved" only by pulling apart with the fingers, and, being passed from guest to guest, were eaten in the same primitive fashion. Thus it may be seen, that, under the pressure of these etiquettes, the services of the attendant with basin, ewer, and towel, would be required repeatedly before the close of the meal.

THE FOUNTAIN IN THE COURT.

THE TOILET AND THE BATH.

It was characteristic of the Pharisees that they should magnify this every-day custom into a religious observance, and define it with many fantastic regulations: " For the Pharisees, and all the Jews, except they wash their hands oft, eat not, holding the tradition of the elders. And when they come from the market, except they wash, they eat not. And many other things there be, which they have received to hold, as the washing of cups,

BY THE NILE.

and pots, brazen vessels, and of tables" (Mark vii. 3, 4). Extracts from the ancient Rabbinical writings discover some of these "traditions of the elders," against which Christ so vehemently protested, as " making the word of God of none effect:" " of the quantity of water sufficient for this washing; of the washing of the hands, and the plunging of them; of the first and second waters; of the manner of washing; of the time; of the order, when the number of those that exceeded five, or did not exceed; and other such like niceties." It is added, that, not content with the ordinary usage of washing after a meal, they did so before eating, for fear of being injured by Shibta, "an evil spirit which sits upon men's hands in the night, and, if any touch his food with unwashen hands, that spirit sits upon that food, and there is danger from it." The common mode of washing the hands is exemplified in the Biblical notice of the servant of Elijah: "Elisha the son of Shaphat, which poured water on the hands of Elijah." The hands are held over a basin or laver, which has a double bottom, the upper compartment being full of holes, through which the water poured on

EWER AND BASIN.

the hands runs into the lower. In the centre of the basin is a projection contrived as a receptacle for the soap. These utensils, in the houses of the wealthy, were sometimes made of solid silver, or even gold. Various vegetable preparations were used by the ancients to cleanse the body. So the beautiful but maligned Susanna, going into her garden at noonday to bathe, said to her two maids: "Bring me oil and washing balls, and shut the garden doors, that I may wash me" (Sus. i. 17). The Lord declared to Jerusalem, in the days of her backsliding, "Though thou wash thee with nitre, and take thee much soap, yet thine iniquity is marked before me" (Jer. ii. 22); and the last of the prophets says of the expected Redeemer: "But who may abide the day of his coming? and who shall stand when he appeareth? for he is like a refiner's fire, and like fuller's soap" (Mal. iii. 2). The soap referred to in these passages of Scripture was made by burning a variety of alkaline plants that grow in the vicinity of the Dead and Mediterranean seas, and mixing their ashes with the inferior qualities of olive-oil, or other fatty substances.

This soft soap was used by the Jews from very early times, both for bathing purposes and for cleansing their clothes. "Nitre," or more properly *natron*, was an earthy alkaline salt that rose to the surface of the Egyptian lake Natron, where it was condensed into a hard substance similar to soap, and used as such. This natron is an impure carbonate of soda, and is found in parts of Egypt and Syria on the surface of the ground: it was extensively employed, especially by fullers, whose trade was a favorite one in Jewish communities. But because the fuller

SUPPOSED SCENE OF THE TRANSFIGURATION.

must of necessity make use of unclean materials in his calling,— such as animal secretions, as well as vegetable and mineral alkalies,— he was compelled to set up his shop outside the walls of the Holy City. Even Roman fullers were required to live in the suburbs, or in back streets. Fuller's-earth and other strong detergents were placed in the water in which the soiled articles were to be washed; and these, after being dried, were subjected to the fumes of sulphur, or a finer sort of fuller's-earth was rubbed into them, to intensify their whiteness.

A singular allusion is made to this familiar workman in St. Mark's graphic account of the transfiguration of our Saviour, in which he says: "His raiment became shining, exceeding white as snow, so as no fuller on earth can white them" (Mark ix. 3).

On the great Day of Atonement of the Jewish ceremonial, the high priest laid aside his splendid robes and his jewelled breastplate, and put on the white garments emblematic of purity and holiness; and so St. John, rapt in apocalyptic vision, beheld the "great multitude, which no man could number," "clothed with white robes;" for they "have washed their robes, and made them white in the blood of the Lamb" (Rev. vii. 9, 14).

The use of cosmetics in connection with the bath prevailed among the wealthy women of a very remote period. At the magnificent court of Ahasuerus, in the seventh year of his reign, the following elaborate processes of "purification" were prescribed for the maidens destined for the king's harem: being "gathered together unto Shushan the palace, . . . to the custody of Hegai, keeper of the women," they abode in the "women's house," and "so were the days of their purifications accomplished, to wit: six months with oil of myrrh, and six months with sweet odors, and with other things for the purifying of women" (Esth. ii. 8, 12). The Song of songs is rich in figurative allusions to these "sweet odors," its last rapturous note echoing from "the mountains of spices;" "myrrh and frankincense, with all powders of the merchant;" "camphire, with spikenard and saffron; calamus and cinnamon, with all trees of frankincense; myrrh and aloes, with all the chief spices;" "my hands dropped myrrh, and my fingers sweet-smelling myrrh;" "his cheeks are as a bed of spices, as

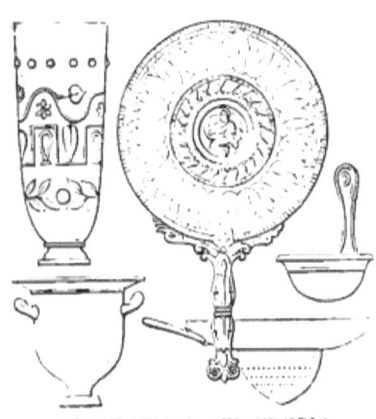
ROMAN MIRROR AND VESSELS.

sweet flowers; his lips like lilies, dropping sweet-smelling myrrh;" the "mandrakes" and the "pleasant fruits."

It is most interesting to learn, in connection with another couplet of this exquisite song, "My beloved is unto me as a cluster of camphire in the vineyards of En-gedi," that En-gedi is the one only place in all Palestine where camphor still grows. This plant is better known by its Arabian name *henna:* it is a tall shrub, whose white-and-yellow flowers grow in clusters, like our familiar lilac. The Eastern women are still fond of wearing these fragrant blossoms in their hair or their bosoms; but it is as an ancient dye that the plant has come into special notice. The dried leaves of the henna were crushed and made into a paste with water, and applied to the palms of the hands, to the nails of fingers and toes, and to the hair, if the discovery of gray threads should be unwelcome. It was used by the men to dye the hair and beard, and even applied sometimes to color the mane and tail of a favorite horse. The antiquity of this custom is demonstrated by its frequent mention by writers of a very early period, and even more conclusively by the fact that the nails of some Egyptian mummies (especially those of women) still retain the stain of the dye.

Painting the eyelids and eyebrows with *kohl* was another Eastern fashion (not yet extinct) of equal popularity. The large, languishing black eye, shaded with long dark lashes, has doubtless always been the distinguishing feature of beauty in the dusky daughters of the East; and it is not surprising that they have tenaciously retained a practice supposed to enhance its size and brightness. The black powder called *kohl* was made of several substances: stibium or antimony, with zinc and oil; or burnt almond-shells, mixed with *liban*, a sort of frankincense, also burnt; another sort was made of powder of lead ore, and was considered not only ornamental, but beneficial by reason of certain medicinal properties. This kohl was kept in boxes or vials of wood, stone, or pottery, having several compartments, and often highly ornamented. It was applied with a small stick of wood, ivory, or silver, which was first wet in rose-water, dipped into the black powder, and drawn carefully along the edges of the eyelids, both upper and under. In the same way the arch of the eyebrow was darkened and elongated. This practice of eye-painting must have been in great popularity as early as

the time of Job; for Keren-happuch, the name of the youngest of his three beautiful daughters, signifies "a horn for paint;" that is, "a bottle for kohl." It was esteemed a great mark of beauty, that the eyebrows should meet over the nose in the form of a bow; and it was common to imitate nature in this respect by the use of the kohl; but this had to be removed in seasons of mourning, and, if the hair actually grew there, it must be plucked out. It will be remembered, however, that this was not permitted to the Hebrews, who were forbidden in their law to "make any baldness between their eyes for the dead" (Deut. xiv. 1). It is written, "When Jehu was come to Jezreel, Jezebel heard of it; and she painted her face, and tired her head, and looked out at a window" (2 Kings ix. 30). The phrase "painted her face" is literally "put her eyes in paint," an evident allusion to the use of the kohl. In Jer. iv. 30, "Though thou rentest thy face with painting," again the marginal reading substitutes "eyes" for "face." In Ezek. xxiii. 40 is still another allusion: "So they came, for whom thou didst wash thyself, paintedst thine eyes, and deckedst thyself with ornaments." And the wise man pays an unconscious tribute to this alluring decoration, when he warns his son against a meretricious beauty with the words: "Neither let her take thee with her eyelids" (Prov. vi. 25).

In the toilet of that rare Jewish beauty of the apocryphal story, Judith, the widow of Manasses, — which was made in the highest interests of religion and patriotism, as expounded in the day of that historical fiction, — there is so full a recapitulation of the several customs in connection with women's dress, that it seems appropriate to introduce the description in closing the subject. The narrative reads thus: "She put off the garments of her widowhood, and washed her body all over with water, and anointed herself with precious ointment, and braided the hair of her head and put a tire upon it, and put on her garments of gladness. . . . She took sandals upon her feet, and put about her her bracelets and her chains and her rings and her earrings and all her ornaments, and decked herself bravely" (Jud. x. 3, 4).

X.

DOMESTIC AND PUBLIC WORSHIP.

OF a people like the Hebrews, who imbibed the spirit of religion with their mothers' milk, whose every act of domestic or social life was hedged about with holy law, we are prepared to learn that they laid great stress on the ceremonial observances connected with devotion, both private and public. And this is not less to be noted of the Gentile Orientals than of the Jews, with whom was deposited the inestimable treasure of a true faith.

It was a saying of a Rabbi in the time of our Lord, that "he who prays in his house surrounds and fortifies it with a wall of iron;" and long before his day of advanced "traditionalism," the saints and sinners of successive ages had afforded him precedents upon which to erect his theory. It was an ancient custom of the Jews to pray three times a day,—at nine, twelve, and three o'clock in the afternoon; or, as the pious David writes, "Evening, and morning, and at noon, will I pray, and cry aloud: and he shall hear my voice" (Ps. lv. 17). To these were added less formal acts of devotion at the beginning and end of the night, and the thanksgiving at meals. For those who were called to a more strictly devout order of life, there were "night watches" unto prayer, to which David alludes in Ps. cxix.: "At midnight I will rise to give thanks unto thee, because of thy righteous judgments" (62); and again: "Mine eyes prevent the night watches" (148). The reader will remember that it was the custom in every Jewish house to have a light brightly burning all through the night; but for one of these pious watchers "who sleeps in a dark house, and does not know the time for

DOMESTIC AND PUBLIC WORSHIP. 253

saying the '*shema*' (the Hebrew creeds), when it is," a Rabbi provides for the situation by deciding that "when the wife speaks to her husband, and the babe sucks its mother" (indicating the "third watch," from midnight to three hours before sunrise). "he may rise up and say the prayer."

The superior efficacy of morning prayer, and its special obligation, were insisted upon by all Oriental teaching. The Talmud, as an exposition of the popular sentiment on this subject, declares: "Every one that eateth and drinketh, and after that says his prayers, of him the Scripture saith, 'But Me hast thou cast behind thy back;'" and again, "It is forbidden to a man to go about his business before praying."

The spirit of the Koran is the same: "The prayer of daybreak is borne witness to;" and Hafiz, the Persian lyric poet, addressing the mystic Beloved, says: "In the morning hours be on thy guard (lest thou be compelled to hear and answer), if this poor stranger make his complaint." So the sweet singer of Israel takes up the strain: "My voice shalt thou hear in the morning, O Lord; in the morning will I direct my prayer unto thee, and will look up" (Ps. v. 3); and "Unto thee have I cried, O Lord; and in the morning shall my prayer prevent thee" (lxxxviii. 13).

The custom of going even to public morning prayer, fasting, is established by the answer of St. Peter to those who accused the newly inspired disciples, assembled for worship, of being "full of new wine:" "These are not drunken, as ye suppose, seeing it is but the third hour of the day" (Acts ii. 15), — the third hour corresponding with our nine o'clock of the morning.

The posture in devotional exercises was not arbitrarily pre-

MOONLIGHT ON THE NILE.

scribed: standing, kneeling, the head bowed or raised, and the hands uplifted, were all accepted attitudes of reverence. Thus, at the dedication of the temple, Solomon "kneeled down upon his knees before all the congregation of Israel, and spread forth his hands toward heaven" (2 Chron. vi. 13); and again, "Solomon stood before the altar of the Lord in the presence of all the congregation of Israel, and spread forth his hands toward heaven"

(1 Kings viii. 22). So, in defiance of the blasphemous proclamation of Darius, it is written of Daniel: " His windows being open in his chamber toward Jerusalem, he kneeled upon his knees three times a day, and prayed, and gave thanks before his God" (Dan. vi. 10); and Ezra records of his ministry: " I fell upon my knees, and spread out my hands unto the Lord my God;" and at the conclusion of his prayer, he is described as " weeping, and casting himself down before the house of God."

In the New Testament all these attitudes of devotion are mentioned: our Lord, teaching his disciples how to pray, said. " When ye stand praying " (Mark xi. 25); of the two men in the parable, who " went up to the temple to pray," he said. "The Pharisee stood, and prayed;" and " the publican, standing afar off," prayed also. St. Paul writes to Timothy: " I will therefore that men pray everywhere, lifting up holy hands, without wrath and doubting" (1 Tim. ii. 8); and to the saints at Ephesus: " For this cause I bow my knees unto the Father of our Lord Jesus Christ" (Eph. iii. 14); while of Him who " ever liveth to make intercession for us," the Evangelists record that, on one solemn occasion of mediatorial supplication, he condescended to the most abject expressions of human guilt and suffering: it was in the garden. "a place called Gethsemane," that " he went a little farther, and fell on his face, and prayed" (Matt. xxvi. 39); or, after St. Luke: " He was withdrawn from them about a stone's cast, and kneeled down, and prayed" (xxii. 41); while in connection with the sublime " sacerdotal prayer," uttered just before he entered upon the awful scenes of his passion, there is no allusion to any change of posture, only: " These words spake Jesus, and lifted up his eyes to heaven" (John xvii. 1).

When our Lord gave us the matchless prayer which is called by his name, his preliminary instruction was as to the place in which it was to be offered: " Enter into thy closet, and, when thou hast shut thy door, pray to thy Father" (Matt. vi. 6). The instinctive requirement for all true prayer is privacy, except, of course, as to the solemn assembly for the public worship of the Most High. Hence we find the saints of the Bible praying in the "secret places" of their homes, — the little "chamber over the gate," or the "inner chamber," or the housetop: as St. Peter, lodging "with one Simon, a tanner," at Joppa, "went up upon the housetop to pray about the sixth hour" (Acts x. 9). Christ's prohibition against the "vain repetitions" of the heathen, and the "long prayers" of the scribes and Pharisees, was intended to rebuke the false teachings and practices of that time. "Long prayers make a long life," was one of the Rabbinical sayings;

PRAYER IN THE GARDEN.

"Much prayer is sure to be heard," was another; while the posture prescribed for a Pharisee's devotion was to "bend so low that every vertebra in his back would stand out separate;" or, at least, until "the skin over his heart would fall into folds."

The Hebrew seventh day "of rest," a marked feature of Judaism, was instituted in the first home of the Bible, as it is written: "God blessed the seventh day, and sanctified it; because that in it he had rested from all his work which God created and made " (Gen. ii. 3). It is first called sabbath in connection with the gathering of manna in the wilderness; on the sixth day of the miracle, Moses said to the people, "To-morrow is the rest of the holy sabbath unto the Lord: . . . Six days ye shall gather it: but on the seventh day, which is the sabbath, in it there shall be none" (Exod. xvi. 23, 26); and, in the twentieth chapter of the same book, the commandment for the strict observance of the day is recorded in the Mosaic Decalogue: "Remember the sabbath day, to keep it holy" (8–12). "When Moses came down from Mount Sinai, with the two tables of testimony" in his hand, he again declared this word of the Lord to the people, concerning the seventh day of rest, adding the penalty of its violation: "Whosoever doeth work therein shall be put to death. Ye shall kindle no fire throughout your habitations upon the sabbath day" (Exod. xxxv. 2, 3). This latter prohibition related to the cooking of the family meals, which would have debarred the servants from their privilege of rest. For this reason it was necessary to make provision the day before, especially as even the straitest sects of the Jews were agreed in the custom of honoring the sabbath with fare much choicer than the ordinary daily diet. Hence Friday was termed the day of preparation, or simply the preparation: St. Mark and St. Luke speak of Good Friday, the day of the crucifixion, as "the preparation, that is, the day before the sabbath" (Mark xv. 42): "that day was the preparation, and the sabbath drew on" (Luke xxiii. 54). St. John calls it "the preparation of the passover," because it was also the paschal Friday. In Jerusalem the sabbath was ushered in by six blasts by the silver trumpets so freely employed in the temple ritual: three to interdict the people from work, and three to set apart the day as one of holy rest; in other towns, from the roof of the synagogue. There were two additional offerings in honor of this day, and more if it should chance to be a new moon or any festival. The making and baking of the shewbread, though involving in its composition three offences against the law, was done on the sabbath day, — a fact of which the Pharisees were reminded by "One greater than the temple:"

"Have ye not read in the law, how that on the sabbath days the priests in the temple profane the sabbath, and are blameless?" (Matt. xii. 5.) At home it was in early times a family festival of innocent joy, and rest from the daily toil of the week. While the father was in the temple or synagogue on sabbath eve, the mother and her maidens were busy decorating the best rooms, spreading the table with the choicest fare they could afford, and

lighting the sabbath lamp, to greet him on his return, as at the threshold he bestowed upon each child the blessing of Israel. Friendly intercourse among neighbors and kinfolk was the order of the day, while the poor and afflicted were comforted with some act of delicate sympathy.

All this sweet spirit of keeping holy the seventh day was turned at a later epoch into the cruel burden of the law, of which St. Paul said well, "the letter killeth," and against which, both by precept and practice, the "Lord of the sabbath day" so uncompromisingly protested. The scribes and Pharisees had so completely lost sight of the fundamental truth that "the sabbath was made for man," that a man of their day might well have bewailed the *fact* that he was "made for the sabbath." Except that we are taught by all record and experience that there are no limitations to the excesses of a perverted conscientiousness, we could not credit the absurdities which finally came to be considered essential to the pious observance of this holy seventh day. Let us look at a few of the Rabbinical rules on this subject: "To preserve life on the sabbath is to violate it, and to kill a flea is as bad as to kill a camel. A woman must not go out with her ribbons about her, unless they are part of her dress; a false tooth must not be worn; no one was to write two letters of the alphabet; the sick must not send for a physician; a tailor must not carry a needle out on Friday night, lest he should forget it, and so break the sabbath by carrying it about on that day." A sect of extremists on this question carried their scruples so far as to refuse to save a drowning woman on the sabbath, because they must not touch a female; while, even where a child was in similar peril, they must put off the phylacteries before lending a hand to its rescue. A Rabbi of this sect of "pietists" refused to rebuild his demolished house, because he had thought about it on the sabbath: another saved himself from a violent death as an accused murderer, by disclosing the name of the criminal; but he wrote that name on a sabbath day, and he passed the remainder of his life in severe penance.

Bearing in mind this state of things, it is easier to comprehend the bitter animosity with which the merciful ministrations of our Saviour were received, on that day wherein it was not lawful for a Pharisee even to "do well." After the miraculous healing of "the man which had the withered hand," in the synagogue on the sabbath-day, we are told that the people "were filled with madness, and communed one with another what they might do to Jesus" (Luke vi. 11). St. Mark writes that "the Pharisees went forth, and straightway took counsel with the Herodians against him, how they might destroy him" (iii. 6). On a similar occasion, when the Lord made straight the woman "which had a spirit of infirmity eighteen years, and was bowed together, and could in no wise lift up herself," "the ruler of the synagogue answered with indignation, because that Jesus had healed on the sabbath-day" (Luke xiii. 14).

A very remarkable element in the household worship of the early Hebrews was the *teraphim*, or images, that seem to have been identical with the *lares* and *penates* of the Romans. It is supposed that they were introduced to the Jews by the family of Laban; and we know that when Jacob fled secretly from his father-in-law, his wife Rachel stole the "images" (*teraphim*) that belonged to her father, and " put them in the camel's furniture, and sat upon them" (Gen. xxxi. 34). These family gods were probably rude representations of the human form, more or less decorated: they must have been of various sizes, since Laban's images were small enough to be concealed under the camel's saddle, while that in David's house was large enough to serve his wife Michal in her clever deception (1 Sam. xix. 13, 16). Although familiarly mentioned in the historical books of the Bible, there is no conclusive evidence that they were worshipped as idols, but rather consulted as oracles: the image wore on its breast a casket containing lots that determined the consultation, and a sort of mask (whence its name, signifying " a nodding countenance or living mask ") from which the priest deduced his mystic conclusions. The most graphic account of these objects of superstitious reverence (especially curious in their undoubted connection with the worship of the Almighty) is to be found in chapters xvii. and xviii. of the Book of Judges, where it is related of Micah, " a man of Mount Ephraim," that he had these images in " an house of gods," and a Levite for his priest. The teraphim are classed with " the familiar spirits, and the wizards, . . . and all the abominations" (2 Kings xxiii. 24), that the zealous Josiah sought to abolish in his reign; but among a people so tenacious of old domestic traditions this was well-nigh impossible, and allusion to their continued use of the oracles is found so late as the days of Hosea. " For the children of Israel shall abide many days without a king, and without a prince, and without a sacrifice, and without an image, and without an ephod, and without teraphim " (iii. 4).

Among the Romans the *lares* and *penates*, familiar to the classic scholar, occupied the same position in the household: they were kept in the inner part of the house, and " their altar was the domestic hearth." These divinities were small figures in terra-cotta, wax, bronze, or silver. Such, too, were the miniature copies of the great Temple of Diana at Ephesus, and the " silver shrines " for that goddess, manufactured by Demetrius the silversmith, and " the image that fell down from Jupiter" (Acts xix. 24, 35); such the little brass, bronze, or clay figures, preserved in museums, of Ashtaroth, the great Venus of the Zidonians, the Syrians and Phœnicians, the Astarte of the Greeks and Romans; as well as of the innumerable divinities of the classic mythology: they were worn on the person, and worshipped in the home. An act of idolatrous devotion to the goddess Astarte, it is supposed, in which an entire family are engaged, is thus described in Jeremiah: "Seest thou not what they do in the cities of Judah and in the streets of Jerusalem? The children gather wood, and the fathers kindle the fire, and the women knead their dough, to make cakes to the queen of heaven." (vii. 17, 18.)

Among the many methods of divination, universally practised by ancient Oriental nations, were those by rods and by examination of the viscera of animals, especially the liver, and by the divining-cup. Divination by rods is said to have had its origin in Chaldæa, but it was widely used by the Scythians, Persians, Assyrians, and Arabians. It is curious to trace the final remains, perhaps, of this superstition, in England and our own country, where wells of water or petroleum are discovered by the use of willow rods in the hands of the "seventh son of the seventh son," or some one of equally occult pretension. That the Hebrews were involved in this foolish practice of their Gentile neighbors, is seen by the divine reproof at the mouth of the prophet: "My people ask counsel at their stocks, and their staff declareth unto them" (Hos. iv. 12). Divination by inspection of the liver — the organ supposed by the ancients to be the seat of the passions — was a favorite method among the Babylonians, Greeks, and Romans; but there is nothing in Scripture to prove that it was practised by the Jews. Two other modes are mentioned in connection with this one, in a prophecy of Ezekiel against Jerusalem: "The king of Babylon stood at the parting of the way, at the head of the two ways, to use divination: he made his arrows bright, he consulted with images, he looked in the liver" (Ezek. xxi. 21). Divining-cups were commonly consulted by the Egyptians, and other Orientals: they were inscribed on the inside with mystic signs and characters, or with emblematic figures, and when used were filled with water. Various devices were employed to procure an answer from this oracle: rays of sunlight falling into the water produced figures, each endowed with its peculiar significance; melted wax dropped into the water revealed the will of the gods by the shapes it assumed on the surface; plates of gold and silver, or precious stones, appropriately engraved with mystic characters, were also used. That Joseph, in his character of an Egyptian functionary of high rank, consulted this cup, or pretended to do so, is proved by his order to the steward of his house on the occasion of his brethren's visit: "And put my cup, the silver cup, in the sack's mouth of the youngest;" and by the message he puts in the steward's mouth: "Is not this it in which my lord drinketh, and whereby indeed he divineth" (Gen. xliv. 2, 5).

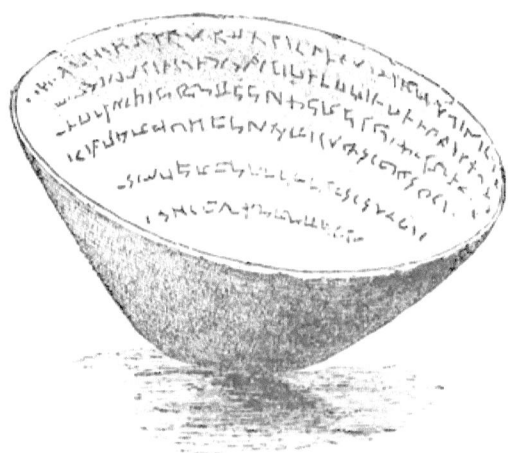

EARTHEN DIVINING BOWL: BABYLON.

All these practices of divination were expressly prohibited to the Hebrews in the words of the law, which apply with wonderful wisdom to our own day of so-called "spiritualism" and "new lights:" "When thou art come into the land which the Lord thy God giveth thee, thou shalt not learn to do after the abominations of those nations. There shall not be found among you any one that maketh his son or his daughter to pass through the fire, or that useth divination, or an observer of times, or an enchanter, or a witch, or a charmer, or a consulter with familiar spirits, or a wizard, or a necromancer. For all that do these things are an abomination unto the Lord" (Deut. xviii. 9, 14).

The obligation solemnly to celebrate public worship was established throughout the generations of the Jews by the divine institution of the tabernacle in an early period of their history as a theocracy, when the Lord said to the meek leader of the children of Israel, "Let them make me a sanctuary, that I may dwell among them" (Exod. xxv. 8). As the name implies, this elaborate tabernacle, erected to the glory of the Most High, was in the form of a tent, and constructed with special reference to convenient removal and reconstruction, as the encamped nation journeyed, or tarried by the way in the wilderness. In the court of the tabernacle stood the altar of burnt-offering, and the brazen laver, containing water for the priests' ablutions when about to enter the sanctuary. The holy place of the tabernacle proper was furnished with the golden candlestick with its seven lamps, the sacred table on which were placed every sabbath the twelve mystic loaves, the altar of incense, the golden pot of manna, and the miraculous rod of Aaron. In the awful holy of holies stood "that one object of absolute sanctity," the Ark of the Covenant, whose lid of solid gold, the mercy-seat, enclosed the tables of the divine law, even as the Lord had commanded Moses: "Thou shalt put into the ark the Testimony which I shall give thee" (Exod. xxv. 16). In this sacred tent the prescribed offerings and the daily sacrifices were made for Israel by the consecrated Levites. Here the holy feasts were kept unto the Lord; and in its courts the people assembled to receive the declarations of the Divine Will, and the manifestations of the Divine Presence.

This tabernacle of the congregation fulfilled its sacred purpose to the families of Israel, until their happy entrance into the promised land of Canaan. It was then more permanently established, — first at Gilgal, and afterward at Shiloh, where it stood between three and four centuries. Two other cities, Nob and Gibeon, enjoyed the distinction of possessing the tabernacle before the erection by Solomon of the great Temple at Jerusalem, which henceforth superseded its prototype, and was possessed of its priceless treasures.

Of the sacred city thus augustly crowned with the chosen habitation of Jehovah, it is no wonder that the Psalmist of Israel breaks forth in prophetic song, though he might never behold the glorious sight: "Great is the Lord, and greatly to be praised in the city of our God, in the mountain of his holiness. Beautiful for situation, the joy of the whole earth, is Mount Zion, on the sides of the north, the city of the great King" (xlviii. 1, 2); while in the later days of Rabbinical sententious-

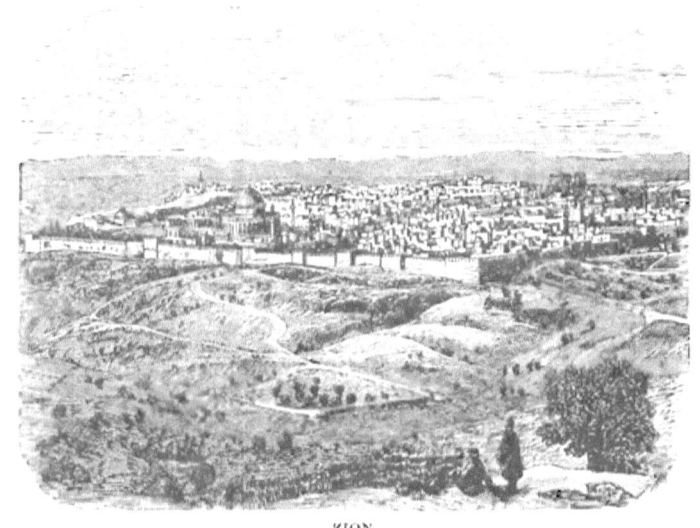

ZION.

ness the Jewish heart as truly responded to the axiom, "God hath bestowed ten measures of beauty upon the world, and nine of these fall to the lot of Jerusalem." It was to this beloved city, after the building of the Temple, that every pious Israelite made his pilgrimages according to the Mosaic laws: "Three times thou shalt keep a feast unto me in the year," and "Three times in the year all thy males shall appear before the Lord" (Exod. xxiii. 14, 17). Previous to that happy event the people had assembled in whatever city was sanctified by the presence

THE FLIGHT INTO EGYPT.

of the tabernacle; and, though only the able-bodied men were under obligation to make the journey, it became customary for the women and children to accompany their husbands and fathers, and to take part in the religious solemnities. Thus Hannah accompanied Elkanah, her husband, when he "went up out of his city yearly to worship, and to sacrifice unto the Lord of hosts in Shiloh" (1 Sam. i. 3). And after Hannah had "lent" her baby-boy Samuel to the Lord, and left him in Shiloh in performance of her vow, it is sweetly written of the pious mother, that "she made him a little coat, and brought it to him from year to year, when she came up with her husband to offer the yearly sacrifice" (1 Sam. ii. 19). So, too, so long after, the Blessed Mary and her Son went with Joseph "to Jerusalem every year at the feast of the Passover" (Luke ii. 41). The three great feasts commanded to be celebrated with peculiar ceremonies before the Lord were the Passover, the feast of harvest, or Pentecost, and the feast of Tabernacles. Each of these festivals was preceded by a season of preparation, lasting fifteen days, during which the devout worshipper must needs meditate on the events and the mercies about to be commemorated, and submit himself to the prescribed legal purifications. St. John refers to this preparation when he says, "Many went out of the country up to Jerusalem before the Passover, to purify themselves" (John xi. 55). There was also much preparation of a material sort to be made for so vast an influx of travellers upon the highways leading to Jerusalem, and in the city itself, and the many adjacent villages. Roads, bridges, and public water-tanks were carefully inspected and repaired for the convenience of the multitude. The primitive modes of travel, as depicted in the Bible, were exceedingly slow, and devoid of comfort: journeys were made on foot, or on camels or asses, and rarely in rude carriages or chariots. Rebekah, with her damsels, "rode upon the camels, and followed the man." Abraham's servant, on her long journey to "the south country," where her expectant bridegroom dwelt (Gen. xxiv. 61). And when the aged patriarch set out on his gloomy errand to the land of

Moriah, where by faith "he that had received the promises offered up his only-begotten son," he "rose up early in the morning, and saddled his ass" for his own use, while Isaac and the two young men-servants travelled afoot (Gen. xxii. 3). The luxury of a chariot was enjoyed only by the distinguished and opulent traveller. Pharaoh, on the occasion of the exaltation of the Hebrew Joseph, "made him to ride in the second chariot which he had" (Gen. xli. 43); and Naaman, the "mighty man in valor" of Syria, "came with his horses and with his chariot, and stood at the door of the house of Elisha" (2 Kings v. 9); and so the royal treasurer of Ethiopia was returning in his chariot from his devotions in Jerusalem, when St. Philip was sent by God to teach and baptize him (Acts viii. 27). In marked contrast to the many ostentatious visitors that thronged her streets, the "daughter of Zion" beheld her King, on the occasion of his entry into Jerusalem, coming unto her "lowly, and riding upon an ass, and upon a colt the foal of an ass" (Zech. ix. 9); and even this humble convenience was accepted by him only "that it might be fulfilled which was spoken by the prophet" (Matt. xxi. 4).

In the annual pilgrimages to Jerusalem it was customary for families, friends, and neighbors of each village or city to travel in company for mutual safety and comfort, and to beguile the tedium of the way. It would appear from a suggestion in Isaiah, as well as from modern usage in the East, that it was common with travellers to relieve the monotony of their slow march with vocal and instrumental music: "Ye shall have a song, as in the night when a holy solemnity is kept; and gladness of heart, as when one goeth with a pipe to come into the mountain of the Lord, to the Mighty One of Israel" (xxx. 29). The mode of travelling to and from the sacred city in parties is exemplified in the Gospel account of the visit of the Holy Family when Jesus was twelve years old: "And when they had fulfilled the days, as they returned, the child Jesus tarried behind in Jerusalem; and Joseph and his mother knew not of it. But they, supposing him to have been in the company, went a day's journey; and

IN THE STABLE AT BETHLEHEM.

they sought him among their kinsfolk and acquaintance" (Luke ii. 43, 44). "A day's journey" is a very ancient term in estimating distances, and is repeatedly employed in the Scriptures. It may stand for from eighteen to thirty miles, though ordinarily computed at twenty. A "sabbath day's journey" was about three-quarters of a mile, — never over two miles: so it is written of the apostles, that, having witnessed the ascension of our Lord, "Then returned they unto Jerusalem from the mount called Olivet, which is from Jerusalem a sabbath day's journey" (Acts i. 12). The public accommodations for wayfarers were the rudest imaginable. A simple shelter for man and beast might be obtained in the "inns" or temporary lodging-places provided by private charity or municipal enterprise; but each family was compelled to provide its own provisions, cooking utensils, and bedding, besides fodder for the horses, camels, and asses. The Eastern inn, or caravansary, of the present time is made familiar to us by illustrated books of Oriental travel: it is probably identically the same as those of old, and presents nothing more inviting than a series of stone-floored and stone-walled apartments opening upon a common quadrangular court, in which the animals and baggage of travellers are usually stored, and where a well or fountain supplies the general need. Sometimes, however, there are stables for the domestic animals, or at least caves, connected with these rude resting-places; and these have for us a profound interest, from the fact that approved students of the Gospels find in these out-houses a probable counterpart to the place in which Mary " brought forth her first-born son, . . . and laid him in a manger, because there was no room for them in the inn" (Luke ii. 7). Two such "inns" are mentioned in the story of Joseph (Gen. xlii. 17; xliii. 21), wherein his brethren stopped to give their asses provender. No payment was demanded of the passing traveller, except in emergencies of sickness or other accident, when the man in charge, like the "host" of the parable of the Good Samaritan, would render service for a certain price (Luke x. 35).

Once in or near Jerusalem, whatever may have been the discouragements "because of the way," the strangers were received with warm-hearted hospitality into houses that were not for hire, but thrown open freely as to brethren. If the city proper proved too small for the accommodation of her vast concourse of guests, there was still room outside her walls for tents to be pitched, beside villages to supply additional lodgings. It is pleasant to learn that Bethany and Bethphage were especially noted for their prompt response to the necessities of the pilgrim visitors, who counted among them "devout men out of every nation under heaven" (Acts ii. 5). To the Hebrews hospitality was in all time and at all times an observance of religious obligation. The Rabbis declared that "the entertainment of strangers was as great a matter as the reception of the *Shechinah*; in which connection we are reminded of St. Paul's admonition, "Be not forgetful to entertain strangers; for thereby some have entertained angels unawares." It was a custom in Jerusalem at the annual feasts to hang a curtain at the doors of such houses as were not already full of guests, and to set a table in front of it to indicate that still there was room. It would be unjust to Oriental peoples of far lower privileges to seem to omit them from the general praise in this particular. Job calls his own righteous soul to witness, if I "have eaten my morsel myself alone, and the fatherless hath not eaten thereof" (xxxi. 17); and the wretched Arab of to-day refuses to sit down to his meal of mean pottage, before he "calls out thrice with a loud voice to all his brethren (*the sons of the faithful*) to come and partake, though perhaps none may be within a hundred miles."

The sacred obligation of friendship between those Orientals who have eaten bread or salt together is, perhaps, their most universally recognized characteristic. David denounces as an act of peculiar baseness the violation of hospitality: "Yea, mine own familiar friend, in whom I trusted, which did eat of my bread, hath lifted up his heel against me" (Ps. xli. 9); and our betrayed Lord, disclosing the treachery of Judas to his disciples, quotes this very passage as thus fulfilled by him (John xiii. 18). Even more pathetic are the words of Zechariah, as he saw in the spirit the kindred indignities to be heaped upon the Messiah: "And one shall say unto him, What are these wounds in thine hands? Then he shall answer, Those with which I was wounded in the house of my friends" (xiii. 6),—those hands that had broken unto them the bread of life.

To return to the occasion of the pilgrimages we have considered: the three great feasts of the Jewish ecclesiastical year were the Passover, the feast of Harvest, or Pentecost, and the feast of Tabernacles. The exact time of their celebration was calculated by the division of the year into lunar months. In the absence of almanacs and astronomical processes, and of any means of rapid communication with all parts of the country, it is not difficult to appreciate the obstacles that must have been overcome to procure a simultaneous convocation of the people at Jerusalem. We read in Brown's "Antiquities of the Jews" a citation from Maimonides which explains the ingenious system of signals employed to this end: "The first appearance of the new moon was the starting-point. To ascertain this, the Sanhedrim took the deposition of two impartial witnesses as to the time they had seen it. They next spread the intelligence through the country by means of beacons: a person with a bundle of brushwood or straw went to the top of Mount Olivet, where he kindled his torch, and waved it back and forth till he was answered by similar fires from the surrounding hills. From these, in like manner, the intelligence was spread to others until the whole land was notified."

The Passover commemorated the "passing over" of the houses of the Israelites, during their cruel bondage in Egypt, on that awful night when "the Lord smote all the firstborn in the land of Egypt, from the firstborn of Pharaoh that sat on his throne unto the firstborn of the captive that was in the dungeon; and all the firstborn of cattle" (Exod. xii. 29), and their final deliverance from their oppressors. The Paschal Supper took place, according to the law, "in the fourteenth day of the first month at even" (Lev. xxiii. 5), which was Abib or Nisan, and corresponded to our month of April. The next day was the beginning of the feast of unleavened bread, which lasted seven days, for which time all leaven was banished from every Jewish household (Exod. xii. 19); but the term "Passover" was applied to the entire period. The observance of this feast was specially incumbent upon every Hebrew family, quite apart from its celebration in the Temple. The most exact instructions for keeping it were given by Moses in the twelfth chapter of Exodus, even before the miraculous events commemorated had taken place. In after-time there were some trifling deviations from the ancient customs; for example, our Lord and his disciples reclined at the Paschal table, instead of standing with their loins girded, shoes on their feet, and staff in hand, as originally prescribed in Egypt (Exod. xii. 11).

UNLEAVENED BREAD.

The ordinary usage was for the head of the family to select and slay a male lamb of the first year, and without blemish. It was roasted whole, care being taken that the body should be kept intact; for, concerning the Paschal Lamb of God (of whom this innocent creature was a feeble prototype), the divine decree had gone forth: "A bone of him shall not be broken" (John xix. 36; Ps. xxxiv. 20).

The lamb was eaten by the family with a salad of bitter herbs, with unleavened bread, and a cup of wine and water, over which the father, or his representative, pronounced the benediction: "Blessed be He who created the fruit of the vine." Not less than four cups of wine were to be drunk during the feast. At a certain point in the supper the youngest child present was instructed to rise, and formally ask the meaning of so peculiar a meal; to which the father responded with a brief and simple story of the whole national history of Israel, in accordance with the Mosaic injunction (Exod. xii. 26, 27). The child was taught that the lamb had been slain in commemoration of the death of the firstborn of the Egyptians, and of the escape of the firstborn of Israel; that the bitter herbs he had eaten with his morsel of unleavened bread were typical of the hard bondage of his own people in the land of Egypt; while the peculiar bread of flour and water, hastily mixed and baked, told him of their hurried flight from the oppressor. At successive stages in the supper, parts of the "Hallel," or hymn of praise, were chanted: it began with Ps. cxiii. inclusive to the end of Ps. cxviii. The "hymn" referred to in the Gospel accounts of the Passover celebrated by our Lord just before he suffered — "and when they had sung a hymn, they went out into the Mount of Olives" (Mark xiv. 26) — consisted of the three last Psalms cited above.

The public services of the Temple, proper to this season, were solemnly imposing. Congregations of devout worshippers thronged the superb courts at different hours of the day of preparation; some having assembled soon after midnight, in order to be present at the daily morning sacrifice. The daily evening sacrifice was slain half an hour after noon, to gain time for the offering at intervals of the additional Paschal sacrifices; the people dispersing at nightfall to take part in the household ceremonial made ready in their homes or their temporary lodgings.

Thus the disciples of Jesus came to him on the day of unleavened bread, saying,

"Where wilt thou that we prepare for thee to eat the Passover?" (Matt. xxvi. 17); the King of the Jews and his lowly followers being among the few of all the assembled thousands in that royal city for whom nothing had been provided. The reader need scarcely be reminded of that one great Paschal feast at Jerusalem, in which its ancient types and promises

THE WAY OF THE CROSS· JERUSALEM.

were fulfilled "once for all;" when "Christ, our Passover, was sacrificed for us" (1 Cor. v. 7); and it was not without solemn significance, we may believe, that the "Pure Offering" of "the Lamb slain from the foundation of the world" (Rev. xiii. 8) was made on the Lord's Passover at the very hour of the Paschal sacrifices offered in the Temple on the previous day;

"About the ninth hour Jesus cried with a loud voice, saying, Eli, Eli, lama sabachthani? that is to say, My God, my God, why hast thou forsaken me? . . . Jesus, when he had cried again with a loud voice, yielded up the ghost" (Matt. xxvii. 46, 50). The feast of Harvest, sometimes called the feast of Weeks, because of its occurrence seven weeks after the Passover, and again known as Pentecost, from the Greek word meaning *fiftieth*, — the fiftieth day from the Passover, — took place after the harvest of breadstuffs, and before the vintage. Originally it was designed to give public expression of gratitude for blessings bestowed upon the agricultural labors of the Jewish people. The distinctive offering at this feast consisted of two loaves of leavened bread made of the finest flour of the last crop of wheat, beside the prescribed sin and peace offerings; and each person was thus admonished in the law: "Thou shalt take of the first of all the fruit of the earth, which thou shalt bring of thy land that the Lord thy God giveth thee, and shalt put it in a basket, and shalt go unto the place which the Lord thy God shall choose to place his name there" (Deut. xxvi. 2).

In later times, after the destruction of Jerusalem, and the dispersion of the Jews among nations where the harvest-seasons were widely different, the feast assumed another character, and was commemorated in honor of the proclamation of the law on Mount Sinai, which (according to tradition) took place on the fiftieth day after the escape from Egypt. As a Christian festival Pentecost is kept, seven weeks after Easter, as the hallowed anniversary of the outpouring of the Holy Spirit upon the early Church — as recorded in the Acts of the Apostles, second chapter, — in fulfilment of the risen Saviour's promise: "Ye shall be baptized with the Holy Ghost not many days hence" (Acts i. 5); and of the prophecy of Joel, as quoted by St. Peter in his address to the mixed assembly in Jerusalem on that day (Acts ii. 17).

A much more important and joyful feast was that of the Tabernacles, or the ingathering: it took place in the seventh month, corresponding to our October, and lasted eight days. During this time the multitude left their houses, and dwelt in arbors or booths, according to the Mosaic law: "Ye shall take you on the first day the boughs of goodly trees, branches of palm trees, and the boughs of thick trees, and willows of the brook; and ye shall rejoice before the Lord your God seven days. . . . Ye shall dwell in booths seven days; all that are Israelites born shall dwell in booths" (Lev. xxiii. 40, 42).

Every adult male whose health would permit was required to sleep and take his meals in such an arbor, in commemoration of the many years his people had dwelt in tents after the captivity in Egypt. The feast was also one of general thanksgiving for the ingathering of the products of the earth for the whole year, — the corn, summer fruits, wine, and oil. We can imagine very imperfectly, perhaps, the picturesque beauty of Jerusalem during this season of her people's rejoicing, when, as in Nehemiah's day, they went "forth unto the mount," and brought "olive branches, and pine branches, and myrtle branches, and palm branches, and branches of thick trees, . . . and made themselves booths, every one upon the roof of his house, and in their courts, and in the courts of the house of God, and in the street of the water gate, and in the street of the gate of Ephraim" (Neh. viii. 15, 16). An impressive ceremony, introduced at a later date into the celebration of this festival, was the drawing of water from the Pool of Siloam by the priest, in commemoration of the water miraculously provided for their fathers in the desert (Exod. xvii. 6), as a symbol of "latter rain," so necessary to the expectant husbandman; and to represent the promised outpouring of the Holy Spirit at the coming of the "Consolation of Israel." Every morning of the seven days at daybreak the priest carried a golden pitcher, holding two or three pints, from the Temple to the pool, in the midst of a procession of the people and a band of musicians. Having filled the pitcher, he was escorted back to the Temple, where, at the west side of the altar, he poured the water into a silver basin, having perforations from which the water was carried off through an aperture in the marble pavement. This memorial service was hailed by the shouts and songs of the congregation, as well as with blasts from the silver trumpets so constantly used in the Jewish ritual.

Another interesting ceremonial was performed in the woman's court of the Temple at the close of the first day of the feast, which was a day of "holy convocation." A great golden candelabrum, having four branches, was erected in this court. Ladders were placed at each branch, which were mounted by four young priests, who poured oil into the large receptacles supported by the candelabrum. Then wicks, made of the old girdles and sacred vestments of the priests, were thrust into the oil-vessels; and an illumination was created that was visible from all parts of the city. Men with torches in their hands danced and rejoiced before the people, singing hymns; while the priests chanted to an accompaniment of the chief musicians, and other priests blew the silver trumpets at the gate of the Court of Israel.

The children, when very young, were taught to join in the sacred songs of the Temple, and especially to take part in this joyful feast by waving the branches of palm and willow and myrtle which it was customary to carry at this season. It was this early training in the active worship of God that prompted the children in the Temple to join in the "Hosanna to the Son of David" on the triumphal entry of our Lord into Jerusalem. The priests and scribes were "sore displeased," and said unto him, Hearest thou what these say? And Jesus saith unto them, Yea; have ye never read, Out of the mouth of babes and sucklings thou hast perfected praise?" (Matt. xxi. 15, 16.)

On the first and last days certain portions of the law were read to the people. It was on the last day — the apostle John calls it "that great day of the feast" — that Jesus stood and cried, saying, "If any man thirst, let him come unto me and drink" (John vii. 37), — an allusion, it is supposed, to the ceremonial use of water at that feast, with which all were familiar. The intermediate days were passed in much innocent merry-making and social feasting.

The celebration of the joyous season of harvest by a certain period of rest and relaxation was not peculiar to the Hebrews,

but was common to many of the primitive Gentile nations. The
ancient Arabs observed two stated festivals in the spring and
autumn; the Babylonians, their great Sakeau feast at harvesting;
the Romans, their bacchanalian revels.

After the Babylonish captivity two other annual feasts were
instituted by the Sanhedrim, — those of Purim and the Dedication.
The first was a festival of great triumph and rejoicing in honor
of the preservation of the Jewish people from a general massacre through the devotion of the Jewess Esther, wife of Ahasuerus, King of Persia, and Mordecai, her uncle. This feast occurs
about the middle of our March. The fourteenth and fifteenth
days of Adar were, by the decree of Mordecai, to be honored " as
the days wherein the Jews rested from their enemies, and the
month which was turned unto them from sorrow to joy, and from
mourning into a good day: that they should make them days of
feasting and joy, and of sending portions one to another, and
gifts to the poor. . . . And that these days should be remembered
and kept throughout every generation, every family, every province, and every city; and that these days of Purim should not
fail from among the Jews, nor the memorial of them perish from
their seed" (Esth. ix. 22, 28). We are witnesses at this late
day of the hearty enthusiasm with which this popular holy day
is still enjoyed by the Hebrew citizens of our own land.

Like the Purim, the feast of Dedication, also called the feast
of Lights, is one of much household rejoicing. It was instituted
to commemorate the restoration of the divine worship in the
Temple B.C. 164, after its defilement at the hands of the heathen conqueror, Antiochus Epiphanes. A detailed account of the
purification of the sanctuary, and its re-dedication " with songs,
and citherns, and harps, and cymbals," and " the sacrifice of deliverance and praise," is given in the Apocryphal book of 1 Macc. iv.
This feast is mentioned only once in the New Testament: St John,
in his Gospel, prefaces a sermon of our Lord to the Jews by the
incidental remark, " It was at Jerusalem, the feast of the Dedication, and it was winter. And Jesus walked in the Temple in
Solomon's Porch" (x. 22, 23). It began on our Christmas Day,

the twenty-fifth of Chisleu (December), the anniversary of the profanation of the Holy Place. The peculiar feature of this feast was the general illumination of Jewish houses: the family assembled in the evening, and one lamp or candle was lighted for each member on the first night, two for each one on the second, and so on to the eighth; while the children joined in the Hallel, or some simpler Hebrew hymn. This pleasing custom sprang from a tradition of the Rabbis, that, when the Jews under Judas Maccabæus drove out the heathen from the Temple, they found one bottle of the sacred oil that had escaped the profane ransacking. With this they lighted the lamps of the altar, and by a miracle it was made sufficient for the eight days of "mirth and gladness" before the Lord.

It will be necessary to omit description of the many recurring seasons of religious significance to the Jewish people, as prescribed in their law; such as the feast of New Moons, and that of Trumpets; the sabbatical year, the year of Jubilee, and others appointed under the Rabbinical dispensation to commemorate contemporaneous events of national deliverance or humiliation; as well as fasts, annual and accidental, that formed no part of the original Hebrew ritual.

The only fast of Mosaic obligation was the great Day of Atonement, commanded as a "statute for ever:" "In the seventh

month, on the tenth day of the month, ye shall afflict your souls,
and do no work at all, whether it be one of your own country,
or a stranger that sojourneth among you: for on that day shall
the priest make an atonement for you, to cleanse you, that ye
may be clean from all your sins before the Lord" (Lev. xvi.
29, 30). The seventh month (Tisri) corresponds to our early
October. This day was marked by a most rigid fast from sunset
to sunset, and otherwise kept with profoundest solemnity. The
Rabbis not only forbade eating and drinking, but one must neither wash, nor anoint, nor put on shoes, nor delight himself with
wife or children. Two notable exceptions were permitted: to
this general prohibition as to personal preparation the king
and a bride might wash and anoint even on that holy day, —
the king, because he must always preserve his majesty and beauty
in the eyes of his subjects; the bride, lest unhappily she should
forfeit the admiring preference of her new husband. The children, though not required to fast, were gradually inured to abstinence, and instructed in the solemn significance of the day. The
sick were likewise exempt, and such as providentially came
under the following curious conditions: "any one faint with
hunger, or injured by accident, or by the fall of a wall, or by the
bite of a mad dog, or a violent sore throat." For these the traditional maxim, "Danger of life supersedes the sabbath," was
applied to the Day of Atonement. On this day, alone of all the
year, the high priest, laying aside his gorgeous robes of office,
put on his white linen vestments, and entered the Holy of Holies, — first with incense, and a second time with the atoning blood
of the appointed victim, which he sprinkled upon the mercy-seat.
This rite was so awful that it was always feared the high priest
would not survive its solemnization: he was therefore warned
not to tarry in the Most Holy Place, even to pray, lest a panic
should seize the attending priests and congregation. The distinctive feature of the ceremonial for this day was the sacrifice
of one goat, and the sending away of another, called the scape-goat, according to the command given to Moses: "Aaron shall
lay both his hands upon the head of the live goat, and confess

over him all the iniquities of the children of Israel, and all their transgressions in all their sins, putting them upon the head of the goat, and shall send him away by the hand of a fit man into the wilderness: and the goat shall bear upon him all their in-

THE MOUNTAIN OF THE SCAPEGOAT.

iquities unto a land not inhabited: and he shall let go the goat in the wilderness" (Lev. xvi. 21, 22). During the prayer over the scapegoat the high priest uttered the Divine Name, at which, though it was "rather a sound than a name," so great was the awe it inspired, priests and people fell on their faces in profound adoration. The animal was then led forth, and passed from one person to another, previously appointed to the office, along the road from Jerusalem to the mountain called Tzuk. Huts had been erected at ten stations on the road, so that each conductor of the goat should travel only the distance termed a sabbath day's journey. The news of the ceremonial liberation of the scapegoat was "telegraphed" to Jerusalem by the waving of signals from station to station along the road it had been led. On one occasion, as tradition relates, the sin-laden victim found its way back to the city, to the superstitious consternation of the citizens; and afterward it was the custom to push the goat over a precipice of the mountain to break its neck or its legs in the fall, — a summary proceeding, which can scarcely be regarded as a literal fulfilment of the law above quoted, that the "fit man" should "let go the goat in the wilderness."

The sins of all the people were thus transferred to the devoted creature; and to see it thus driven forth with its imputed guilt, to suffer for sin though incapable of sin, alone in the desolate wilderness, is a spectacle of profoundest significance to the Christian, who beholds in it a remote type fulfilled in him of whom it was written, "He was wounded for our transgressions, he was bruised for our iniquities: . . . and the Lord hath laid on him the iniquity of us all" (Isa. liii. 5, 6); of whom the apostle, supplementing the prophecy, writes to the church at Corinth: "He hath made him (Christ) to be sin for us, who knew no sin; that we might be made the righteousness of God in him" (2 Cor. v. 21).

Dancing is mentioned very early in the Sacred Record as an act of triumphant worship; and it seems originally to have had no part in social festivities, except in their connection with religious feasts. Among the Hebrews it was accompanied with sacred song, and usually practised by the women: thus, after the glorious deliverance of Israel by way of the Red Sea, Moses led the people in a song of exalted joy; and the women responded with dancing and singing, as it is written, "Miriam the prophetess, the sister of Aaron, took a timbrel in her hand; and all the women went out after her with timbrels and with dances" (Exod. xv. 20).

At the yearly feast of the Lord in Shiloh, during the days when the tabernacle was in that city, the "daughters of Shiloh" came out "to dance in dances;" and it was at one of these

ECCE HOMO!

festivities that the young Benjaminites, lying in wait in the vineyards, sprang out and caught "every man his wife of the daughters of Shiloh" (Judg. xxi. 21),— an example which was followed after a modified fashion in the days of the Rabbis, when the young Hebrews were exhorted to make choice of wives from among "the damsels of Jerusalem who went out in white garments, and danced amid the vines," at the feast of Harvest and at the close of the Day of Atonement.

Sometimes men only participated in these religious dances, as in the feast of Tabernacles, where men with torches danced by the light of the great lamps in the woman's court of the Temple. An illustrious example is found in King David on the occasion of his bringing up the ark of the Lord from the house of Obededom to Jerusalem, when "David danced before the Lord with all his might, . . . leaping and dancing before the Lord" (2 Sam. vi. 14, 16). In the Psalms he calls upon the people thus to be "joyful in their king:" "Let them praise his name in the dance," "praise him with the timbrel and dance" (Ps. cxlix. 3; cl. 4).

Dancing also formed a prominent feature in the religious ceremonies of the Egyptians and other idolatrous nations.

The origin of the synagogue, so familiarly alluded to in the New Testament, is wrapt in obscurity, though tradition boldly traces it back to patriarchal times. There is no trace of synagogue worship, either in the law or the prophets, — certainly nothing in common with that of the ancient ritual, wherein the sacrificial services were wholly typical. But during the Babylonish captivity, while the Jews were deprived of their Temple services, it was necessary to substitute some forms of religious meeting, lest the people, especially the young, should become tainted with the pagan practices about them. Attentive students discover the beginnings, the early germs, of the synagogue institution in the days of Ezra and Nehemiah, when the dispersed Israelites, returning to the strongholds of their faith, sought to be spiritually revived by renewed instruction, both for themselves and their children, many of whom, as Nehemiah records, "spake half in the speech of Ashdod, and could not speak in the Jews' language" (xiii. 24). At all events, we know certainly that in the time of our Lord there was no town of any importance that had not its synagogue, while large cities had several, — wherever, indeed, there was a foreign settlement of Jews in which ten men could be found to devote themselves exclusively to holy things, being supported meanwhile by the revenues of the synagogue. The inhabitants of small villages could attend the services of the nearest township on market-days, — a happy combination of commercial and spiritual interests.

The highest ground in the town or city was always selected for the erection of the synagogue, which was usually very simple in its construction; that of Alexandria, described in both the Talmuds, being exceptionally gorgeous in displays of decorated architecture. It was even a matter of superstition with the citizens that no building should be above the one consecrated to religious teaching and to prayer. It was considered a very meritorious act of devotion to build a synagogue; thus in Capernaum, "the elders of the Jews," coming to Jesus to implore him to heal the sick servant of the Roman centurion, "besought him instantly, saying he was worthy for whom he should do this; for he loveth our nation, and he hath built us a synagogue" (Luke vii. 4, 5). Of that wonderful sermon contained in the sixth chapter of St. John's Gospel, it is written, "These things said he in the synagogue, as he taught in Capernaum" (59).

But synagogues were usually built at the expense of the congregation, with such assistance as might be offered by wealthy citizens. In small communities of Jews, one large room in a private house was sometimes secured for the purpose. This practice, we know, was adopted by the early Church, where the

brethren broke bread "from house to house" (Acts ii. 46). The
apostle Paul specifies some of these consecrated apartments:
"The church in thy house" (Epistle to Philemon); "Nymphas,
and the church in his house" (Col. iv. 15); "Aquila and Priscilla
salute you much in the Lord, with the church that is in their
house" (2 Cor. xvi. 19). The earliest Christian church edifices
seem to have been constructed on the model of the synagogue,
which in its turn retained some suggestive resemblance to the
Temple. The separate apartments for men and women was a
feature of Temple worship reproduced in the synagogue by
means of a partition and different entrances: this appears to
have been simply a concession to Eastern manners and opinions.
At first it is probable that the congregation stood in praying or
hearing the reading of the law; but, after the services became
more protracted, seats were provided. It will be remembered
that our Lord warned the people against those scribes who "love
the chief seats in the synagogues" (Matt. xxiii. 6), which, we
are told, were placed facing the worshippers.

The substitution of outward performances, in the mere "letter" of devotion, for the symbolical and typical worship of the
Temple, showed a great spiritual decline in that day and generation. Still there was nothing in the services themselves to pro-
hibit the presence of the Lord or his disciples: on the contrary,
the studied informality of proceedings afforded the best of all
opportunities to preach the gospel tidings to the "common people," who "heard him gladly." The main object of the synagogue
service was teaching, as attested by Josephus and other writers, as
well as by the indirect reports of the Gospels, where "teaching"
is almost always mentioned as connected immediately with our
Lord's appearance in the synagogue of any town whatever.
There was no service of "praise;" but the liturgy in general use
consisted of prayer and the Aaronic benediction by the priest,
according to command: "On this wise ye shall bless the children
of Israel, saying unto them, The Lord bless thee, and keep thee:
the Lord make his face shine upon thee, and be gracious unto
thee; the Lord lift up his countenance upon thee, and give thee

peace" (Num. vi. 23–26). The ordinary "teaching" included the reading of a portion of the law, and of the prophets, which was followed by an address or sermon. This was preceded, however, by the repetition of the "Shema," a sort of creed, composed of certain texts of Scripture. We learn from the Mishnah that "all males were bound to repeat this creed twice every day; but women, children, and slaves were exempt from the obligation." If the sermon was a profound theological discussion by some learned Rabbi, he whispered his subtile deductions into the ear of a speaker who translated it, so to say, into popular language for the mixed congregation; on the other hand, lighter addresses and monitions were made quite extemporaneously, and were called "talks."

In view of this meagre spiritual diet, we are not surprised to learn that when Christ the Lord became their preacher, opening his "mouth in parables," and "uttering things" which had been "kept secret from the foundation of the world" (Matt. xiii. 35), "the people were astonished at his doctrine, for he taught them as one having authority, and not as the scribes" (Matt. vi. 28, 29). Even in his own country, where he testified to the unbelief of his kindred and neighbors, they could not withhold the general tribute: "He taught them in their synagogue, insomuch that they were astonished, and said, Whence hath this man this wisdom, and these mighty works?" (Matt. xiii. 54.) In Nazareth "all bare him witness, and wondered at the gracious words which proceeded out of his mouth" (Luke iv. 22); in Capernaum "they were astonished at his doctrine: for his word was with power" (Luke iv. 32); and in Jerusalem, at the feast of Tabernacles, when he was boldly preaching in the Temple to the thronging multitude, "the Pharisees and the chief priests sent officers to take him" (John vii. 32); but these men, disarmed of their purpose, had no explanation to make before the council of their failure in official duty, — nothing but to echo the popular voice, "Never man spake like this Man!" (Matt. vii. 46).

The Jews had other places of prayer, whether in connection

with the synagogue, or in towns where they were not permitted to build a sacred edifice, or were too poor to do so, is not known. It is certain that there were such resorts, — a plain building, or often only a grove, — and that they were generally situated near the water for convenience in the ablution required before engaging in religious offices. To such a meeting-place St. Paul and Timothy conduct us in their missionary visit to Philippi: "On the sabbath we went out of the city by a river side, where prayer was wont to be made; and we sat down, and spake unto the women which resorted thither" (Acts xvi. 13). Dr. Pusey quotes from a decree of the Halicarnassians, which permitted "that those of the Jews who willed, men and women, should keep the Sabbaths, and perform their rites according to the Jewish laws, and make *oratories by the sea*, according to their country's wont." And here that lovely lament of the Psalmist finds its appropriate place: —

PSALM CXXX.

"By the rivers of Babylon, there we sat down, yea, we wept, when we remembered Zion.

"We hanged our harps upon the willows in the midst thereof.

"For there they that carried us away captive required of us a song; and they that wasted us required of us mirth, saying, Sing us one of the songs of Zion.

"How shall we sing the Lord's song in a strange land?

"If I forget thee, O Jerusalem, let my right hand forget her cunning.

"If I do not remember thee, let my tongue cleave to the roof of my mouth; if I prefer not Jerusalem above my chief joy."

XI.

MUSIC: SACRED AND SECULAR.

MUSIC — both instrumental and vocal — filled so exalted an office in the sacred liturgy of the Hebrews, that to omit all allusion to the art in this connection would be a serious inadvertence. Its antiquity is truly primeval; for the first mention of music in the Bible is, that Jubal, sixth in descent from Cain, was "the father of all such as handle the harp and organ" (Gen. iv. 21). The social use of the "divine art," even in the age of the patriarchs, is demonstrated in the remonstrance of Laban to his absconding son-in-law: "Wherefore didst thou flee away secretly, and steal away from me; and didst not tell me, that I might have sent thee away with mirth, and with songs, with tabret, and with harp!" (Gen. xxxi. 27.) While, as late as the second century before Christ, the son of Sirach declares, with the somewhat extravagant simile of an Oriental, that a "concert of music in a banquet of wine is as a signet of carbuncle set in gold. As a signet of an emerald set in a work of gold, so is the melody of music with pleasant wine" (Ecclus. xxxii. 5, 6). But it is chiefly as an element of worship that music appears in the Bible, and in this relation to the homes of the people it is desirable to consider it. From the banks of the Red Sea, after "Israel saw that great work which the Lord did upon the Egyptians" in delivering his people out of their hands, ascended the first grand sacred song of joy and thanksgiving recorded in the Scriptures. — a song accompanied by Miriam the prophetess, and all the women, "with timbrels and with dances" (Exod. xv. 1, 20). So, again, in a later day of Israel's triumph, — this time delivered by "the hand of a woman," — Deborah, prophetess and judge of the nation, sang an inspired pæan to the praise of God that is scarcely excelled in the Biblical anthology (Judg. v.).

When the king brought the ark of God from the house of Abinadab, we are told that "David and all Israel played before God with all their might, and with singing, and with harps, and with psalteries, and with timbrels, and with cymbals, and with

GLORIA IN EXCELSIS!

trumpets;" and its final moving "out of the house of Obed-edom" was accompanied with every demonstration of religious rejoicing, — "with shouting, and with sound of the cornet, and with trumpets, and with cymbals, making a noise with psalteries and harps" (1 Chron. xiii. 8; xv. 28). David was endowed with remarkable musical gifts, and personally proficient in the handling of at least one instrument. While keeping "those few sheep in the wilderness" near Bethlehem, he had become so "cunning a player on an harp," that he was sent for from court to soothe with his melodious numbers the melancholy of the king (1 Sam. xvi. 16). During his own reign, therefore, we are prepared for those indications of progress in music which are chronicled pre-eminently in connection with the service of the sanctuary. In assigning certain families to the various offices

ANCIENT STRINGED INSTRUMENTS.

of the house of God, a decided prominence is given to those who figure in the musical department. Of the thirty-eight thousand Levites, "four thousand praised the Lord with the instruments" (1 Chron. xxiii. 5); of the twenty-four courses, or classes, of musicians, each numbered one hundred and fifty members and three leaders, — all being under the general management of Asaph and his brethren. On festival occasions, when all were required to be present, the grand choir consisted of four thousand musicians and singers, the priests accompanying on silver trumpets. Josephus, whose statements may be received with some grains of doubt, says that there were two hundred thousand vocalists, and the same number of instrumental performers, employed in the service of Solomon's Temple; and their exact training is to be inferred from the words of the sacred historian: "The trumpeters and singers were as one, to make one sound to be heard in praising and thanking the Lord" (2 Chron. v. 13).

The musical instruments specified in the Bible may be classed under three heads,—wind and stringed instruments, with those of percussion, or such as emit sound on being struck. The organ, pipe, and flute were the earliest as well as the simplest of musical instruments. Originally they were merely reeds, such as Eastern shepherds still use, perforated at intervals, and played by the mouth. The primitive organ is supposed to be that which the Greeks termed the "pipe of Pan," and which consisted of seven or more reeds of unequal length. These rude pipes, especially the double pipe, are represented on Egyptian monuments, and were played as our flute is. When Solomon was anointed King of Israel "the people piped with pipes, and rejoiced with great joy" (1 Kings i. 40). This instrument was especially appropriate for occasions of merrymaking: the children in the parable say one to another, "We have piped unto you, and ye have not danced" (Luke vii. 32). In later times these wind instruments were constructed more elaborately of various materials,——brass, copper, box-wood, horn, bone, or ivory, and ingeniously decorated.

The horn and cornet, as their names denote, were doubtless at first only the horns of animals. When they came to be manufactured of metal, they retained both the shape and name of the original article. There are several Hebrew words variously translated "trumpet," "horn," and "cornet;" but these seem to have differed only in trifling particulars, if at all. The priests' silver trumpets were straight and about eighteen inches long. The Greeks had six varieties of trumpets; the Romans, four: these were used on the battle-field, and constituted their sole equipment for martial music. The Psalmist invokes the congregation of the faithful: " With trumpets and sound of cornet make a joyful noise before the Lord, the King " (Ps. xcviii. 6).

Of stringed instruments the harp was regarded as of the first

CHOIR OF ANGELS.

importance by the lovers and patrons of early Oriental music. Much research and fancy have been expended upon discussions as to the shape and other particulars of this charming instrument. Judging from Assyrian and Egyptian monuments, where it often appears, it seems probable that the most ancient form of the harp was a triangular frame within which the strings of camel-gut were stretched. The Babylonian and Assyrian harps were " carried under one arm, and played with both hands, one

on either side of the strings," as our own is to-day. It has been
conjectured by some inquirers that the ancient harp was played
by means of a *plectrum*, — a small bit of quill, ivory, or bone.
There are also contending opinions as to the number of strings:
"from seven to forty-seven" have been "ascertained." This
instrument, so popular with the Hebrews, Egyptians, and Assyrians, has, — unlike most of the others of Biblical fame, — in a
measure, disappeared from Oriental countries. The Psalmist,
exhorting the people to "make a joyful noise unto the God of
Jacob," enumerates "the pleasant harp with the psaltery" (Ps.
lxxxi. 2); and again, he says, "Sing unto him with the psaltery,
and an instrument of ten strings" (Ps. xxxiii. 2); and again,
"Awake, psaltery and harp!" (Ps. cviii. 2). The "psaltery"
was a species of harp, about which there is much difference of
opinion; it being severally termed a lyre, a lute, a guitar, and
a viol. Josephus says it had twelve strings. The psalteries of
David, we are told, were made of fir-wood (2 Sam. vi. 5); those
of Solomon, of the algum-tree. — a novel experiment, doubtless,
as the historian adds. "There were none such seen before in the
land of Judah" (2 Chron. ix. 11).

The "sackbut" was still another variety of harp, supposed to
resemble that of the Egyptians, which rested on the ground, and
was almost identical with our modern instrument. The *sambuca*
of the Romans was a triangular harp with four or more strings,
which emitted a sharp, twanging sound.

The ancient guitar, having from three to twenty-four strings,
is known to us as the cithern. or cittern: it was of Greek origin,
but was extensively adopted by the Chaldeans, Egyptians, and
Assyrians, and is still popular in the East. The proverb that
"there is no new thing under the sun" (Eccles. i. 9) is not more
aptly illustrated perhaps than by the fact that the original of
the modern banjo has been found at Thebes. and described by
Wilkinson, with "the wooden body covered with leather, the
handle extending down to the lower side. and part of the string
remaining to which the plectrum was attached."

The "dulcimer" is regarded by the best Biblical authorities as a sort of bagpipe, still in use among the peasantry of Northwestern Asia and Southern Europe. It consisted of two pipes attached to a leather bag, which, inflated with wind from the mouth, was held in the arms, and pressed to the body.

All these instruments are enumerated in connection with the famous decree of Nebuchadnezzar after he had set up the golden image in the plain of Dura: "Then a herald cried aloud, To you it is commanded, O people, nations, and languages, that at what time ye hear the sound of the cornet, flute, harp, sackbut, psaltery, dulcimer, and all kinds of music, ye fall down and worship the golden image that Nebuchadnezzar the king hath set up" (Dan. iii. 4). The Babylonians were extremely fond of music, as their monuments testify: they had an ample variety of instruments, and organized large bands of skilled performers in concert. "Annarus, a Babylonian noble, entertained his guests at a banquet with music, vocal and instrumental, performed by a band of one hundred and fifty women."

Lastly, among musical instruments of percussion, we find the "cymbals," the "sistrum," and the "timbrel." The cymbals of remote antiquity resembled those in use at the present day, and consisted of two circular concave plates of brass, which, when struck forcibly together, produced a loud, clanging sound. They were of two sorts, as exemplified in the words of David: "Praise him upon the loud cymbals; praise him upon the high-sounding cymbals!" The first are supposed to have been used like castanets,—two small metal plates in each hand, clapped by the thumb and second finger; while the

EGYPTIAN CYMBALS.

"high-sounding cymbals" were the larger plates, such as we see in military bands. St. Paul refers to this clanging accompaniment in the opening sentence to his sublime eulogium of charity: "Though I speak with the tongues of men and of angels, and have not charity, I am become as sounding brass, or a tinkling cymbal" (1 Cor. xiii. 1).

The "sistrum" was pre-eminently the sacred instrument of the Egyptians, essential to their public religious service. It was made of brass, from eight to eighteen inches long, having three or four movable bars, on which hung several loose rings. The instrument was often highly ornamented with silver and gold; and it was "played" by simply holding it upright, and producing a clattering noise by shaking the rings. Only a queen, or some noble Egyptian lady who enjoyed the distinction of being one of the "women of Amun" (an exalted sodality of the temple), was permitted to hold the sacred sistrum during worship. It is asserted that the drum was used by the Egyptians in war; and their sculptures represent an instrument of wood or copper covered at the extremities with skin or parchment, and suspended from the neck of the drummer.

The "timbrel," or "tabret," is almost identical with the familiar tambourine of our street-singers. It was equally popular

THE TIMBREL.

with the Assyrians, Egyptians, and Hebrews, and is frequently mentioned in Scripture. Job speaks of those careless, worldly men who "take the timbrel and harp, and rejoice at the sound of the organ" (Job xxi. 12). The prophet promises the "virgin of Israel," "Thou shalt again be adorned with thy tabrets, and shalt go forth in the dances of them that make merry" (Jer. xxi. 4); even as the sweetly submissive daughter of Jephthah, all unconscious of her father's vow, "came out to meet him with timbrels and with dances" (Judg. xi. 34); and David, describing an act of worship in the sanctuary, writes, "The singers went before, the players on instruments followed after; among them were the damsels playing with timbrels" (Ps. lxviii. 25).

In the New Testament we find very meagre notice of music, either in its social or spiritual connection. St. Paul, in his Epistle to the Ephesians, alludes to the simple hymns that constituted a characteristic of the public worship of the early Christian Church: "Be filled with the Spirit; speaking to yourselves in psalms and hymns and spiritual songs, singing and making melody in your heart to the Lord" (v. 19); and again to the Colossians: "Let the word of Christ dwell in you richly in all wisdom; teaching and admonishing one another in psalms and hymns and spiritual songs, singing with grace in your hearts to the Lord" (iii. 16). But in the Apocalyptic Vision, Music once more assumes her exalted place in the solemn worship of the Almighty. St. John, beholding the heavenly Mount Zion, "heard the voice of harpers harping with their harps: and they sung as it were a new song before the throne" (Rev. xiv. 2, 3). Of the victorious multitude standing "on the sea of glass, having the harps of God," he writes, "And they sing the song of Moses the servant of God, and the song of the Lamb, saying, Great and marvellous are thy works, Lord God Almighty; just and true are thy ways, thou King of saints (Rev. xv. 3).

XII.

ALMS AND HOSPITALITIES.

THE pious practice of "almsdeeds," as enjoined by the law and inculcated by parental exhortation, was a prominent feature in the religion of the Jews; and it was not subject to the spasmodic sympathies of the individual, but was made the habit of his life by a well-ordered system of benevolence, whereby one-tenth of his substance was consecrated to God; and he was further stimulated to voluntary offerings of expiation or thanksgiving. It was with this tithe that the tribe of the Levites, who had no inheritance with their brethren, were supported, according to the divine ordinance: "Behold, I have given the children of Levi all the tenth in Israel for an inheritance, for their service which they serve, even the service of the tabernacle of the congregation" (Num. xviii. 21). That this system was in force, however, long before the time of Moses, is shown by the " tithes of all" given to Abram by Melchizedek, king of Salem (Gen. xiv. 20); and by the vow made to God by Jacob after waking out of the sleep of his wonderful vision: "For all that thou shalt give me, I will surely give the tenth unto thee" (Gen. xxviii. 22). The Book of Leviticus abounds in requirements addressed to landowners for the benefit of their less fortunate neighbors: the corners of the fields must not be wholly reaped, nor the gleanings of the harvest or the vineyard closely gathered. "Thou shalt leave them for the poor and stranger," was the holy law of God (xix. 9, 10); thus Boaz, in behalf of Ruth, who came to gather after the reapers in his barley-field, "commanded his young men, saying, Let her glean even among the sheaves, and re-

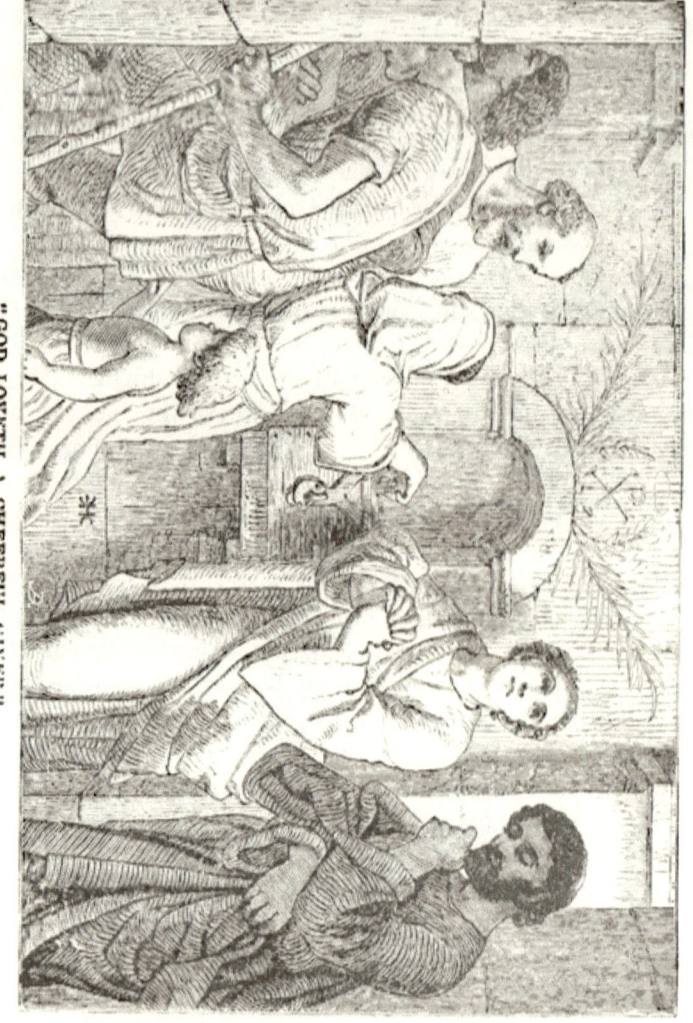

"GOD LOVETH A CHEERFUL GIVER."

proach her not; and let fall also some of the handfuls on purpose for her, and leave them that she may glean them, and rebuke her not" (Ruth ii. 15, 16). Every third year there was a feast of the farmer's tithe, made in his own house, for the Levite and for the destitute: "At the end of three years thou shalt bring forth all the tithe of thine increase the same year, and shalt lay it up within thy gates: and the Levite, (because he hath no part nor inheritance with thee,) and the stranger, and the fatherless, and the widow, which are within thy gates, shall come, and shall eat and be satisfied; that the Lord thy God may bless thee in all the work of thine hand which thou doest" (Deut. xiv. 28, 29).

From Genesis to Revelation one and the same Spirit speaks on this vital subject, whether from the code of Mosaic law, or through the voice of the Word made flesh. If we read in Deuteronomy, "For the poor shall never cease out of the land: therefore I command thee, saying, Thou shalt open thine hand wide unto thy brother, to thy poor, and to thy needy, in thy land" (xv. 11), we have but to turn to the Gospel of St. Mark to hear Jesus saying, "For ye have the poor with you always, and whensoever ye will ye may do them good" (xiv. 7); and to St. Luke: "He that hath two coats, let him impart to him that hath none; and he that hath meat, let him do likewise" (iii. 11). Of all subjects in the Bible inviting "doubtful disputation," "hard to be understood," and capable of being wrested unto the destruction of the "unlearned and unstable" (as St. Peter writes of the Epistles of St. Paul), we think the passages prescribing the duty of large and liberal contributions to the poor may be discharged of any such misconstruction. The references in proof are so numerous, that it is embarrassing to choose from the accumulated stores of sacred lawgiver, historian, prophet, priest, king, of Him who is all in One, and of his apostles. Even the Rabbis, of whose didactic formalism we are disposed to be suspicious, afford a grateful surprise by their truly devout admonitions on this subject of charity. One of their oldest commentaries thus enlarges upon the word of the Psalmist. "He shall stand at the right hand of the poor" (cix. 19): "Whenever," says the commentator, "a poor man stands at thy door, the Holy One, blessed be his name, stands at his right hand. If thou givest him alms, know that thou shalt receive a reward from him who standeth at his right hand." The Talmud exhorts to imitation of God in these four acts of mercy: "He clothed the naked (Gen. iii. 21); He visited the sick (Gen. xviii. 1); He comforted the mourners (Gen. xxv. 11); and He buried the dead" (Deut. xxxiv. 6). As to the tender care of the destitute and the sick, they took the highest ground of even Christian devotion and self-sacrifice: " Let thy house be wide open, and let the poor be the children of thy house," was a saying of Jose, a Rabbi of Jerusalem.

We are bound to remind the reader that liberal charities have ever been a characteristic feature of all Oriental religions. When our Lord, for instance, gave this instruction to the people, — which sounds strangely to our ears, except in connection with annual festival occasions, in prisons, hospitals, and asylums, perhaps, — " But when thou makest a feast, call the poor, the maimed, the lame, the blind; and thou shalt be blessed, for they cannot recompense thee" (Luke xiv. 14), — he spoke to those who not only were accustomed to this act of charity, but who, when entertaining their own " friends, and brethren, and kinsmen, and rich neighbors," always made additional provision for the poor, who gathered about the house in expectation of being called in to an outer room, where they might consume all that remained of the repast. There was doubtless much room, in these large public ministrations to the needy, for that self-glorification which our Saviour took occasion to rebuke in his Sermon on the Mount: "Take heed that ye do not your alms before men, to be seen of them; otherwise ye have no reward of your Father which is in heaven. Therefore when thou doest thine alms, do not sound a trumpet before thee, as the hypocrites do in the synagogues and in the streets, that they may have glory of men. Verily I say unto you, They have their reward. But when thou doest alms, let not thy left hand know what thy right hand doeth; that thine alms may be in secret; and thy Father which seeth in secret himself shall reward thee openly" (Matt.

"IF THINE ENEMY HUNGER, FEED HIM."

vi. 1–4). It may be that all unconsciously it was in this spirit the afflicted patriarch recalled his acts of mercy in happier days: "When the ear heard me, then it blessed me; and when the eye saw me, it gave witness to me: because I delivered the poor that cried, and the fatherless, and him that had none to help him. The blessing of him that was ready to perish came upon me: and I caused the widow's heart to sing for joy. I put on righteousness, and it clothed me: my judgment was as a robe and a diadem. I was eyes to the blind, and feet was I to the lame. I was a father to the poor: and the cause which I knew not I searched out" (Job xxix. 11–16),—a noble record that may well command our admiration and inspire our zeal.

In the pious story of Tobit, in the Apocrypha, we read the advice of the godly father to his son in this matter: "Give of thy bread to the hungry, and of thy garments to them that are naked; and according to thy abundance give alms;" "For alms is a good gift, unto all that give it in the sight of the Most High;" "If thou have but a little, be not afraid to give according to that little: for thou layest up a good treasure for thyself against the day of necessity" (Tob. iv. 16, 11, 8). The Psalms of David and the Proverbs of Solomon, his son, abound in assurances of the Almighty's peculiar solicitude for the poor, and in denunciations of the "wicked, who, in their pride, do persecute" them: as well as in declarations of the blessings awaiting him "that considereth the poor;" him "that hath mercy on the poor;" him that "stoppeth not his ears" at their cry; him that "defends the poor and the fatherless; that does justice to the afflicted and needy; that delivers the poor and needy, and rids them out of the hand of the wicked."

Zaccheus, the rich publican, confessed before Jesus, as he passed through Jericho, "Behold, Lord, the half of my goods I give to the poor; and if I have taken any thing from any man by false accusation, I restore him fourfold" (Luke xix. 8). Cornelius, the centurion of the Italian band, "gave much alms to the people," and was rewarded, while fasting and praying unto God, with a visit from "a man . . . in bright clothing," who said, "Cornelius, thy prayer is heard, and thine alms are had in remembrance in the sight of God" (Acts x. 31). Dorcas of Joppa, raised from the dead by St. Peter, was a "woman full of good works and almsdeeds which she did" (Acts ix. 36). The family of Stephanas, converts under St. Paul's preaching in Achaia, "addicted themselves to the ministry of the saints" (2 Cor. xvi. 15). Phœbe, Priscilla, and Aquila, Epenetus, Mary, Urbane, are a few of the faithful mentioned by the apostle Paul, in his Epistle to the Romans, as his "helpers in Christ," "servants of the Church," doubtless foremost among them who were pleased "to make a certain contribution for the poor saints which are at Jerusalem" (Rom. xv. 26); but, of all "whose names are in the book of life," none have won more precious words of praise than she of whom Jesus spoke, as he sat over against the treasury in the Temple: "And he looked up, and saw the rich men casting their gifts into the treasury. And he saw also a certain poor widow casting in thither two mites. And he said, Of a truth I say unto you, that this poor widow hath cast in more than they all. For all these have of their abundance cast in unto the offerings of God: but she of her penury hath cast in all the living that she had" (Luke xxi. 1–4). Who shall tell, if perchance this woman had been in the "innumerable multitude of people" on that day when Jesus taught them those rich lessons of the things concerning the kingdom of God, and, hearing his word, — "Sell that ye have, and give alms; provide yourselves bags which wax not old, a treasure in the heavens that faileth not, where no thief approacheth, neither moth corrupteth" (Luke xii. 33), — had thus responded in the simple obedience of her heart by an act of faith that called forth the spontaneous commendation of the Saviour!

In the Temple in Christ's day were two safety chambers for the reception of these voluntary gifts of the people, as distinct from the payment of their tithes and other legal offerings. One was for the money put into the collecting chests, as referred to above; the other for storage of valuable articles and vessels of plate, given for the service or decoration of the Temple. We

ALMS AND HOSPITALITIES.

read in St. Luke that some spake to Christ " of the Temple, how it was adorned with goodly stones and gifts" (xxi. 5). Josephus writes, that among these costly offerings were golden vines, from which depended golden clusters of grapes as tall as a man. The custom of adorning the temples of their gods with rich spoils of battle, and gifts from wealthy devotees, was common to all the heathen nations mentioned in the Bible. The treasurers opened one of these chambers in the Temple once a month, and disposed of such gifts as could not be used in the sanctuary; the other was inspected three times a year, immediately before the celebration of the three great feasts. The priests who counted the contents of the thirteen collecting boxes were not allowed to wear " shoes, sandals, phylacteries, or a folded dress," lest they should be tempted to secrete any of the dedicated coins. The Mishnah explains that the residue of the offerings, after all legitimate expenses had been paid, was devoted to providing the gold plates with which the most holy place was covered.

SAMARITAN COINS.

One of the most striking scenes of the Gospel story is that wherein our blessed Saviour, "meek and lowly of heart," cleansed by summary process the polluted courts of the Temple, in fulfilment of David's prophecy: "The zeal of thine house hath eaten me up" (Ps. xlix. 9).

From Capernaum, whither he had gone with " his mother and his brethren and his disciples," he went up to Jerusalem to the Passover, "and found in the Temple those that sold oxen and sheep and doves, and the changers of money sitting: and when he had made a scourge of small cords, he drove them all out of the Temple, and the sheep, and the oxen; and poured out the changers' money, and overthrew the tables; and said unto them that sold doves, Take these things hence; make not my Father's house a house of merchandise" (John ii. 14–16). These traders were naturally of great convenience to those who came to make their prescribed offerings according to the law, since, on paying a certain sum, they were at once provided with all the essential articles,—the victims, the meal, oil, frankincense, and wine. The money-changers supplied the exact coin for the payment of the Temple tax incumbent upon every Israelite.

THE SHEKEL OF THE SANCTUARY.

It is easy to see how such apparently innocent, and even essential, accommodations for a large crowd of strangers might become mere traps for the unwary, making the "house of prayer" a "den of thieves," even as our Lord said to those whom he dislodged (Matt. xxi. 13).

Another class, constant in their attendance upon the gates of the Temple and of the synagogues, and even of rich men's houses, were the beggars, that have always formed so large a community in Oriental lands. Thus the blind man, restored to sight by Jesus, was seen of him as he "went out of the Temple," where he daily "sat and begged" (John ix. 8); and the lame man, healed by Peter and John, was "laid daily at the gate of the Temple which is called Beautiful, to ask alms of them that entered into the Temple" (Acts iii. 2); and Lazarus, a beggar, "was laid at the rich man's gate, full of sores" (Luke xvi. 20).

But, while so many rules were prescribed to the giver of alms, there were not wanting — at least during the supremacy of the Rabbi — certain restrictions upon the eligibility of the recipient. No one who had a yearly income of so trifling a sum as two hundred denarii (about thirty American dollars), or who had so much as one-fourth that amount in ready cash, with which he might invest in a small trade, had any claim to the "corner of the field," or the "gleaning," or to a share in the "tithes of the poor," already described. Indeed, the Mishnah solemnly warned man or woman, who should take alms beyond their actual necessities or right, that beggary sooner or later would be the inevitable penalty; but, on the other hand, whoever refused alms, although in pressing need, might confidently expect to be able to succor the destitute before leaving this life.

Finally, for us, as Christians, the whole law and gospel on this matter of personal almsgiving, whether of money or time, or both, is summed up in these immortal words: " I was an hungred, and ye gave me meat: I was thirsty, and ye gave me drink: I was a stranger, and ye took me in: naked, and ye clothed me: I was sick, and ye visited me: I was in prison, and ye came unto me. Then shall the righteous answer him, saying, Lord, when saw we thee an hungred, and fed thee? or thirsty, and gave thee drink? When saw we thee a stranger, and took thee in? or naked, and clothed thee? Or when saw we thee sick, or in prison, and came unto thee? And the King shall answer and say unto them, Verily I say unto you, Inasmuch as ye have done it unto one of the least of these my brethren, ye have done it unto me" (Matt. xxv. 35–40).

Yet must we not forget that higher heavenly love with which these material sacrifices must be offered to be acceptable; and of which St. Paul writes to the Corinthians, and through them to all the world: "Though I bestow all my goods to feed the poor, and though I give my body to be burned, and have not charity, it profiteth me nothing" (1 Cor. xiii. 3).

XIII.

SEEDTIME AND HARVEST.

IN the earliest history of the Jewish people the tilling of the soil and the care of flocks and herds were, without doubt, the chief national occupation; and the wise and beneficent laws of the Pentateuch, by which it was regulated for the best interests of the commonwealth, have commanded the profound respect of all succeeding generations. When God created Adam he also "planted a garden eastward in Eden. . . . And the Lord God took the man, and put him into the garden of Eden to dress it and to keep it" (Gen. ii. 8, 15). After the fall, "the Lord God sent him forth from the garden of Eden, to till the ground from whence he was taken." Hence Adam was the first farmer of all this teeming earth; and his son Cain followed his father's calling, with the generations of them that came after, even unto Noah (*rest*), who was so named by Lamech his father, saying, "This same shall comfort us concerning our work and toil of our hands, because of the ground which the Lord hath cursed" (Gen. v. 29). After the Deluge, it is written of Noah that he "began to be an husbandman, and he planted a vineyard" (Gen. ix. 20); but it was not until the Hebrews had passed through their Egyptian trial, their subsequent wanderings, and their entrance into the possession of the Promised Land, — into the enjoyment of "vineyards and olive-trees" which they had planted not" (Deut. vi. 11), — that they applied themselves strictly to the cultivation of the soil, and adopted the agricultural methods employed by its former owners. The inexhaustible fertility of the hillsides and plains of Palestine, its wonderful variety of climate, capable of producing the vegetation of both temperate and torrid zones, the abundant water-supply, and the natural enrichment of the soil by the disintegration of its limestone rocks, — all more than fulfilled to the Israelite the promise vouchsafed to his fathers during their oppression in the country of their adoption: "And the Lord said, I have surely seen the affliction of my people which are in Egypt, and have heard their cry by reason of their taskmasters; for I know their sorrows; and I am come down to deliver them out of the land of the Egyptians, and to bring them up out of that land unto a good land and a large, unto a land flowing with milk and honey" (Exod. iii. 7, 8).

A remarkable requirement of the Mosaic law was the *rest* prescribed for the land one year in every seven: "The seventh year shall be a sabbath of rest unto the land, a sabbath for the Lord: thou shalt neither sow thy field, nor prune thy vineyard" (Lev. xxv. 4). Each husbandman held his share of the ground for himself and his heirs by an everlasting tenure, — a system of tenantry, so to speak, under God, by which he might not even rent it beyond the fiftieth year, the Year of Jubilee: "The land shall not be sold forever: for the land is mine; for ye are strangers and sojourners with me" (Lev. xxv. 23). The Hebrews learned much from the Egyptians, who were adepts in that pursuit which endowed their country with the distinction of being the granary of the world. The monuments of that most interesting land abound in representations of agricultural processes, and the implements proper to them. The methods of artificial irrigation practised by the Egyptians were as ingenious and various as they were effective in carrying the waters of the Nile at its annual inundation, far and wide, through fields and gardens divided by narrow channels to receive them. "Watering with the foot"—a practice referred to in the Bible, and by Virgil in the *Georgics*, as in vogue in his time—is supposed to indicate the manner of directing these artificial water-courses by opening or shutting their sluices with a touch of the foot, or by treading the soft soil to admit or cut off the water. Of these laborious

EGYPTIAN CARTS.

processes, however, the Israelites needed not to bring away any knowledge from the land of their sojourning: the Almighty had anticipated their possible apprehensions in this particular: "The land, whither thou goest in to possess it, is not as the land of Egypt, from whence ye came out, where thou sowedst thy seed, and wateredst it with thy foot, as a garden of herbs: but the land, whither ye go to possess it, is a land of hills and valleys, and drinketh water of the rain of heaven" (Deut. xi. 10, 11). In a later day of greatly advanced civilization Solomon applied artificial irrigation to his fruit-gardens: "I made me pools of water, to water therewith the wood that bringeth forth trees" (Eccles. ii. 6). But his royal father had already given the praise and glory to God for the fulfilment of his word in a bucolic

PEACOCK OF THE OLD TESTAMENT.

poem full of the inspiration of Nature: "Thou visitest the earth, and waterest it: thou greatly enrichest it with the river of God, which is full of water: thou preparest them corn, when thou hast so provided for it. Thou waterest the ridges thereof abundantly: thou settlest the furrows thereof: thou makest it soft with showers: thou blessest the springing thereof. Thou crownest the year with thy goodness; and thy paths drop fatness. They drop upon the pastures of the wilderness: and the little hills rejoice on every side. The pastures are clothed with flocks; the valleys also are covered over with corn; they shout for joy, they also sing" (Ps. lxv. 9–13).

The implements employed in the various processes of primitive agriculture were necessarily simple, even to rudeness. At first the plough was probably only a stout and forked branch of a tree, having one end sharpened, while the other served as a handle. A wooden "share," shod with a triangular bit of iron, requiring frequent sharpening, constituted the improved machine, such as is still used in Asia Minor. Fortunately the fruitful earth of the Holy Land needed only a slight scratching to prepare it for sowing. Steep places, inaccessible to the animals yoked to the plough, were tilled with the mattock or hoe. Oxen and asses were trained to the plough, being coupled to it by yokes attached to the end of a stout "tongue." The driver used a long "goad," one end having a broad blade of iron to free the ploughshare from clods of earth; the other armed with a sharp spike with which to control the cattle. It is recorded of Shamgar, son of Anath, that he "slew of the Philistines six hundred men with an ox goad" (Judg. iii. 31). It is this primitive instrument that is meant in the account of the conversion of St. Paul in his defence before Agrippa: "And when we were all fallen to the earth, I heard a voice speaking unto me, and saying in the Hebrew tongue, Saul, Saul, why persecutest thou me? it is hard for thee to kick against the pricks" (Acts xxvi. 14). The yoke and goad are familiar Biblical symbols for chastisement and restraint, as they were of slavery among the heathen. The Romans required their prisoners of war to pass under a yoke in acknowledgment of their submission: hence "subjugation." "Take my yoke upon you," says our gracious Redeemer, "for my yoke is easy, and my burden is light" (Matt. xi. 29, 30). And in the same spirit of freedom from "the law of sin

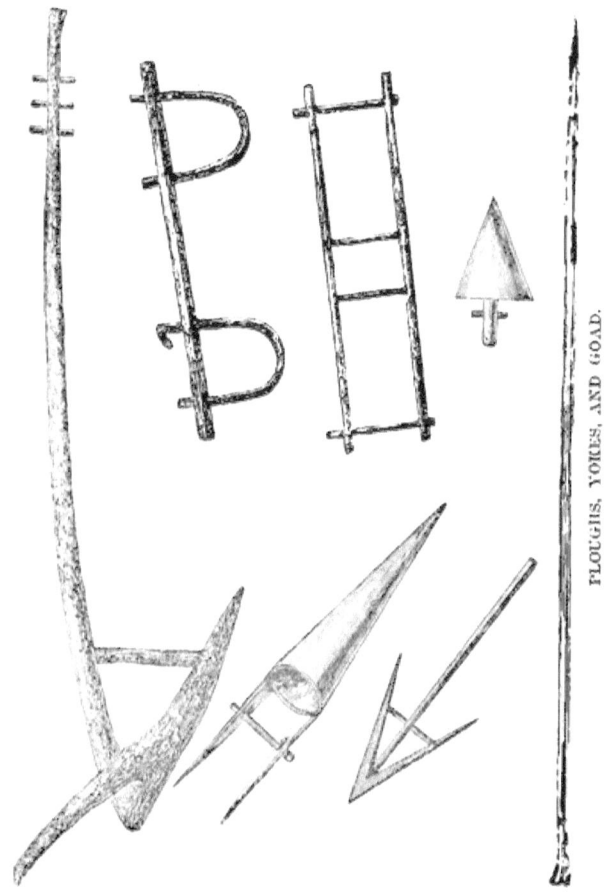

PLOUGHS, YOKES, AND GOAD.

and death," St. Paul exhorts the "foolish Galatians:" "Stand fast therefore in the liberty wherewith Christ hath made us free, and be not entangled again with the yoke of bondage" (Gal. v. 1). Justin Martyr informs us that the manufacture of these implements belonged to the trade of carpenters, and that our blessed Lord had, up to his thirtieth year, followed the craft of his reputed father, " making ploughs and yokes for oxen."

The Egyptian monuments represent the ancient sickle as closely resembling the one in modern use. The scythe was unknown among these early farmers, nor is the harrow mentioned in the Scriptures. Job asks, " Will he (the unicorn) harrow the valleys after thee?" (xxxix. 10); but the verb rendered *harrow* signifies to " break the clods."

In Palestine the agricultural year was practically divided into the dry and rainy seasons, variously designated " seedtime and harvest," " summer and winter," " cold and heat." Seedtime continued from October until December, following the " former rain," which prepared the earth for the sower. The method of sowing grain seems to have been nearly the same in all times and with all peoples. Scattered broadcast over the prepared soil, the seed was ploughed in, according to the present practice, and as described by Isaiah: " Doth the ploughman plough all day to sow? doth he open and break the clods of his ground? When he hath made plain the face thereof, doth he not cast abroad the fitches, and scatter the cummin, and cast in the principal wheat and the appointed barley and the rye in their place? (xxviii. 24, 25.) In Egypt, asses, pigs, sheep, and goats were employed to tread the grain into the muddy soil, saturated by the overflow of the Nile: " Blessed are ye that sow beside all waters, that send forth thither the feet of the ox and the ass" (Isa. xxxii. 20).

The simple processes of sowing and reaping the " bread which strengthened man's heart" (Ps. civ. 15) have, apparently more than any other, furnished imagery and methods of instruction to the sacred writers. The reader will recall as prominent examples the Parable of the Sower; that of " the man who sowed good seed in his field" (Matt. xiii. 3; xxiv.); and that of a " certain rich man" whose ground " brought forth plentifully;" and St. Paul's profound demonstration of the resurrection of the body in his First Epistle to the Corinthians; and the solemn words of our Lord of similar import relative to his own approaching death: "Verily, verily, I say unto you, Except a corn of wheat fall into the ground and die, it abideth alone: but if it die, it bringeth forth much fruit" (John xii. 24).

Grain-harvest began about the middle of April, and continued until mid-June; the season of fruits comprised August, September, and November. Snow in the mountains, hail and thunder storms, and frequent rains, characterized the winter months, but without intense cold: the fields becoming green in the latter part of January. The "latter rain," so longed for by the husbandman to mature his crops of grain, fell early in April; and on the sixteenth day after the first new moon in this month the first sheaf of ripe barley was solemnly presented to the Lord at the Passover, thus consecrating the entire returns. When the harvest had been plentiful, Pentecost was a season of great mirth and festivity, with appropriate songs and games for the children, hired laborers, and slaves of the landowner, who all had shared the toil of reaping the fields. "They joy before thee according to the joy in harvest," sang the Prophet of the coming kingdom of the Messiah (Isa. ix. 3); and the Psalmist encourages the spiritual laborer in his Master's field by reminding him of these well-known customs: "He that goeth forth and weepeth, bearing precious seed, shall doubtless come again with rejoicing, bringing his sheaves with him" (Ps. cxxvi. 6). The grain was cut with a sickle, or at first even plucked up by the root; and the practice of binding the ripe grain into sheaves, or rather large bundles, is one of remote antiquity. The youthful Joseph unconsciously laid the foundation of his future greatness when he said to his brethren, "Hear, I pray you, this dream which I have dreamed: for, behold, we were binding sheaves in the field, and, lo, my sheaf arose, and also stood upright; and, behold, your sheaves stood round about, and made obeisance to my sheaf" (Gen. xxxvii. 5, 6). Ruth's request of the servant set over the reapers in the barley-field of Boaz was, "I pray you, let me glean and gather after the reapers among the sheaves" (Ruth ii. 7). And we read in Amos, "Behold, I am pressed under you, as a cart is pressed that is full of sheaves" (ii. 13). So in the parable the reapers were commanded, "Gather ye together first the tares, and bind them in bundles to burn them: but gather the wheat into my barn" (Matt. xiii. 30).

As the time for ingathering approached, the Oriental husbandman must protect his crop from the invasion of wild beasts or thieves: to do so effectually it was usual to build a small hut or lodge on an eminence, in which a watchman was installed, for security against enemies far or near. The prophet compares the condition of the Church to the desolation of such a watch-tower: "The daughter of Zion is left as a cottage in a vineyard, as a lodge in a garden of cucumbers" (Isa. i. 8).

The threshing-floors of Egypt, as well as Palestine, have been, from their earliest history, out of doors. They were simply flats of high ground from fifty to one hundred feet in diameter, levelled and rolled from year to year, so that they became in course of time literally "floors" of clay. Of the threshing-floors of the Bible the most famous is that of Ornan the Jebusite, which was purchased by David for a place of sacrifice to God, and which afterward was chosen as the site for the magnificent Temple of Solomon (1 Chron. xxi. 18–25).

THRESHING-FLOOR.

One of these tablelands usually served the agricultural purposes of an entire encampment or village, the farmers taking turns in threshing their harvests. The bundles of breadstuffs were scattered loosely on the surface of the floor, and the primitive threshing-machine, the "sharp threshing instrument having teeth," spoken of by Isaiah (xli. 15), was dragged over them, round and round the floor, until the grain was accumulated in a great heap in the centre. The machine was a heavy square frame with rollers, each furnished with several iron rings, or "wheels," serrated like the teeth of a saw; sometimes the frame was in the form of a rude cart. Isaiah enumerates four methods of threshing: "For the fitches are not threshed with a threshing instrument, neither is a cart wheel turned about upon the cummin; but the fitches are beaten out with a staff, and the cummin with a rod. Bread corn is bruised; because he will not ever be threshing it, nor break it with the wheel of his cart, nor bruise it with his horsemen" (xxviii. 27, 28).

The fitches and cummin—plants raised for their small seeds, which were highly pungent and aromatic condiments—were threshed with a rod or flail, which was used also for very small quantities of grain, as when Ruth "beat out" the result of her day's gleaning in the field of her future husband (Ruth ii. 17); or when it was necessary to do the work by stealth, as Gideon "threshed wheat by the wine-press to hide it from the Midianites," his enemies (Judg. vi. 11). As the threshing-floor was not protected by enclosure, it was incumbent upon the owner of the grain, and his trusted servants, to keep watch night and day until the whole harvest was threshed, winnowed, and stored for safe keeping. So, in the lovely pastoral story of Ruth, we read, "When Boaz had eaten and drunk, and his heart was merry, he went to lie down at the end of the heap of corn" (iii. 7). The threshed heap was winnowed by tossing it against the wind (usually in the evening sea-breeze) with broad shovels, and thus separating the chaff from the grain,—the "shovel" and the "fan" are both mentioned in this connection by Isaiah (xxx. 24), —when the chaff was collected and burned. These processes are employed in a forcible figure by St. John the Baptist, to describe the coming Messiah: "Whose fan is in his hand, and he will thoroughly purge his floor, and gather his wheat into the garner; but he will burn up the chaff with unquenchable fire" (Matt. iii. 12); and the Psalmist compares the wicked to "the chaff which the wind driveth away" (Ps. i. 4). The Egyptians and Romans used primitive threshing-sledges,—the Roman *tribulum*, heavy and sharply grinding, having given us the expressive word "tribulation." One description of "fan" is supposed to have been an instrument with which an artificial breeze was created, in the absence of a natural supply. A still finer separation of the grain from the chaff was effected by sifting; and sieves of different degrees of fineness, made of rushes or papyrus, were used by the ancients. A prophecy concerning the Jews, fulfilled long before our day, alludes to this ordinary utensil: " I will sift the house of Israel among all nations, like as corn is sifted in a sieve" (Amos ix. 9). And in our Lord's

CEDARS OF LEBANON.

solemn address to St. Peter, concerning his spiritual danger, and that of his brother apostles: "Simon, Simon, behold, Satan hath desired to have you" (*all*), " that he may sift you as wheat: but I have prayed for thee, that thy faith fail not: and when thou art converted, strengthen thy brethren" (Luke xxii. 31).

When the grain had been thoroughly prepared for household consumption, it was stored in ample pits or cisterns dug in the earth, some six or eight feet deep, either under a retired portion of the house, — such as the apartments of the women, — or in the open country, where their location was carefully concealed by sodding. These receptacles were cool and dry, and effectually protected from vermin by a packed layer of earth at the opening. Such subterranean granaries are alluded to in several passages of Scripture: in the enumeration of King David's officials of the royal household, "Jehonathan, the son of Uzziah," was "over the storehouses in the fields, in the cities, and in the villages, and in the castles" (1 Chron. xxvii. 25); and " ten men" saved themselves from the massacre of Ishmael, the son of Nethaniah, by confessing that they had "treasures in the field, of wheat, and of barley, and of oil, and of honey" (Jer. xli. 8). The "barns" mentioned in the parable (Luke xii. 18) were evidently built above ground; since it was in their self-complacent owner's mind to pull them down, and "build greater."

It is recorded of Joseph, that, in view of the impending famine in Egypt, "he gathered up all the food of the seven years, . . . and laid up the food in the cities" (Gen. xli. 48). The ancient monuments of that land, famous for its agricultural achievements, in spite of great natural obstacles, represent a variety of these granaries that afforded every facility for the holding, and subsequent delivery, of their stores. Some were low, flat roofed structures, divided into convenient rooms or vaults to receive the grain "in bulk" from the sacks. The Romans had such storehouses raised above the ground on stone pillars. In the subterranean grain-pits, we are told, that "corn" (the Bible term for all sorts of cereals) will keep perfectly sound for several years. Chenier, a French traveller, asserts that among the Moors it was customary for wealthy men to fill a granary of this sort at the birth of a child, not to be opened until its wedding-day; and that, even after twenty-five years, the grain had been found in good condition, except in the loss of its whiteness.

The cultivation of the vine claimed the care and skill of the Oriental husbandman equally with the tilling of the ground. The earliest mention of its culture, as already quoted, is after the Deluge, when Noah, beginning "to be a husbandman," "planted a vineyard" also. To Armenia and the adjacent territory belongs the distinction of being the original birthplace of the Eastern grape-vine; but Palestine, of all countries in the world, seems best adapted by soil, climate, and natural features, to its successful cultivation. The table-lands and mountain-slopes were selected as the choice sites for vineyards; but the plains and valleys, as well, have produced the preferred varieties, such as the famous clusters from the vales of Eshcol and Sorek, and the vale of Rephaim between Bethlehem and Jerusalem.

It appears that there were various modes of making a vine-

A VINEYARD.

yard in the East. A very ancient method was to plant beside natural ridges of stone, or by heaps of stones (called by the Arabs "grape-mounds"), gathered and piled for the purpose, over which the vines crept, and which afforded an admirable exposure for ripening the fruit, beside keeping the clusters off the ground. Miles of these stone-heaps are to be seen now in districts of Palestine east of the Jordan, once teeming with luxuriant vineyards, but now utterly sterile and desolate. Another plan was to plant on the sunny side of a terraced hill, the branches of the vine trailing along the dry ground, while the fruit-bearing shoots were propped up on forked sticks; or the young vines were simply set in rows eight or ten feet apart, and so trained as to form a mutual support.

The fruit of the vine was highly esteemed in Egypt: the royal butler pressed grapes into Pharaoh's cup as early as Joseph's days of humiliation (Gen. xl. 11), and the ancient sculptors show us the Egyptian modes of grape-culture. In these the vines are trained on lattices, or rafters, or on circular frames; and the various methods of making wine are depicted, which will be described farther on. The pruning and training of the vine, the annual use of the primitive spade — the *bepalium* of the Romans — to loosen the earth and eradicate weeds, and the gathering of stones, comprised the processes of cultivating a vineyard; the vinedressers constituting a humble class of laborers, distinct from farmers or growers of other fruits. In the dreadful siege and destruction of Jerusalem by Nebuchadnezzar, king of Babylon, it is recorded by the historian, that " the captain of the guard left of the poor of the land to be vinedressers and husbandmen" (2 Kings xxv. 12).

To defend them from the ravages of wild beasts, vineyards were enclosed with stone walls, or with hedges of thorny plants, or with both stones and hedge combined. Balaam, riding on his ass, found himself " in a path of the vineyards, a wall being on this side, and a wall on that side" (Num. xxii. 24); and we find another example in Solomon's graphic " moral maxim:" " I went by the field of the slothful, and by the vineyard of the man void of understanding: and, lo, it was all grown over with thorns, and nettles had covered the face thereof, and the stone wall thereof was broken down" (Prov. xxiv. 31). David, mourning over the mystical vineyard whose vine had been " brought out of Egypt," complains to his God, " Why hast thou then broken down her hedges, so that all they which pass by the way do pluck her? The boar out of the wood doth waste it, and the wild beast of the field doth devour it" (Ps. lxxx. 12, 13); while Isaiah's beautiful " song of my Beloved, touching his vineyard," affords a picture of the two enclosures: "I will tell you what I will do to my vineyard; I will take away the hedge thereof, and it shall be eaten up; and break down the wall thereof, and it shall be trodden down" (v. 5). The towers, always mentioned in connection with vineyards, seem to have been durable edifices of stone, round or square, and varying in height from fifteen to fifty feet, according to the location of the field. This building was sometimes occupied as a summer residence by the proprietor until after the vintage ; and for defence against wild beasts attracted by the ripening fruit, as well as the assaults of thieves, it was necessary to make it in a manner impregnable. Our Lord is supposed to allude to one of these agricultural strongholds in his lesson " in the house of one of the chief Pharisees : " " For which of you, intending to build a tower, sitteth not down first, and counteth the cost, whether he have sufficient to finish it!" (Luke xiv. 28;) and Maundrell describes an unfinished tower he saw in a garden near Beirut, which, with walls twelve feet thick, had been built to the height of about sixty feet, and then abandoned. Van Lennep describes one he had seen in Western Asia as " a square building of solid masonry, rising to the height of forty feet, on the top of which is a story containing several apartments with windows, whose elevated position makes it the recipient of every breeze, and an excellent post of observation. The lower portion of this building has a small, solid door, and a few narrow windows at a considerable height from the ground." They are called by the Greeks *pyrgos*, the very word used by our Saviour in the parable: " A certain man planted a vineyard, and set a hedge about it, and digged a place for the wine-fat, and built a tower, and let it out to husbandmen, and went into a far country" (Mark xii. 1).

To express the juice of the ripe grapes for the manufacture of wine, wine-presses were hewn out of the ledges of rock abounding on the hillsides of Canaan, or were constructed of rude masonry. They consisted of two parts, — the shallow tank for the reception of the fruit, and a " wine-fat," or vat, into which the juice ran through a hole in the upper tank. The fruit in the wine-press was crushed by the bare feet of the laborers. Usually from two to seven men worked in company, lightening their labor with the songs and shouts peculiar to both the Egyptian and Hebrew grape-treaders. It is written of the men of Shechem, that they "went out into the fields, and gathered their vineyards, and trode the grapes, and made merry" (Judg. ix. 27); and Isaiah laments, in the downfall of Moab, the absence of these familiar sounds of rustic glee: "Gladness is taken away, and joy out of the plentiful field; and in the vineyards there shall be no singing, neither shall there be shouting: the treaders shall tread out no wine in their presses; I have made their vintage shouting to cease" (xvi. 10). The prophet repeats the figure of the labor of the vintage in one of his most impressive presentations of the coming Messiah in the form of exalted and poetic colloquy: "Wherefore art thou red in thine apparel, and thy garments like him that treadeth in the wine-fat? I have trodden the wine-press alone; and of the people there was none with me: for I will tread them in mine anger, and trample them in my fury; and their blood shall be sprinkled upon my garments, and I will stain all my raiment" (Isa. lxiii. 2, 3).

Some very ancient wine-presses, hewn from the solid rock, still remain in Palestine in as perfect condition as when last used at the merry vintage harvest of a dimly distant past.

The law humanely stipulated, "Thou shalt not glean thy vineyard, neither shalt thou gather every grape of thy vineyard; thou shalt leave them for the poor and stranger" (Levit. xix. 10). It was the privilege of the poor, moreover, to eat on the ground as much fruit as they wished, only they might not take it away in vessels to their houses (Deut. xxiii. 25). It was common to plant fruit-trees of various sorts in vineyards, after the manner of the ancient Egyptians: hence, in the parable, "a certain man had a fig tree planted in his vineyard" (Luke xiii. 6). And to "sit under one's vine and fig tree" was a proverbial saying, expressive of domestic peace and satisfaction (1 Kings iv. 25; Mic. iv. 4). This content was quite attainable by an Oriental within the modest limits of his courtyard; since it was customary

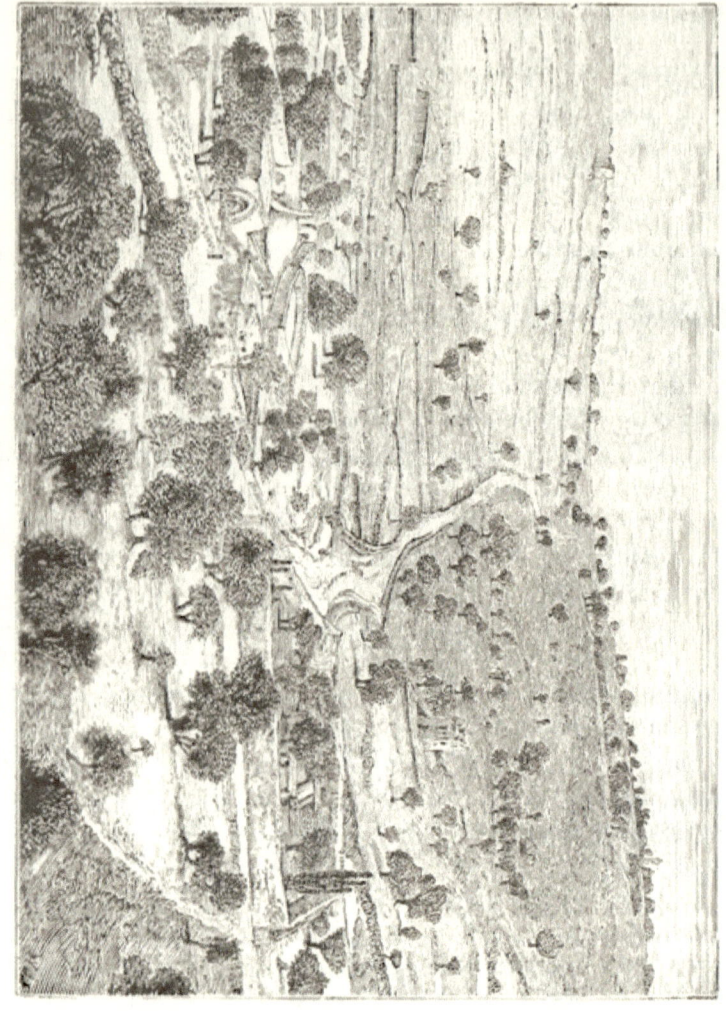

MOUNT OF OLIVES, AND GARDEN OF GETHSEMANE.

to train vines by the sides of the house (Ps. cxxviii. 3) or on trellises, and to plant fig-trees for shade in the court.

The Old-Testament allusions, so many and so various, to the vine and the fruit of the vine, — whether employed for poetic imagery or to convey divine truth to the mind, — are replete with human interest and spiritual force; but our Lord added to these a purely sacred association when he taught the direct "correspondence" of the vine and its branches to himself and his people: "I am the true vine, and my Father is the husbandman. Every branch in me that beareth not fruit, he taketh away: and every branch that beareth fruit, he purgeth" (pruneth) "it, that it may bring forth more fruit. . . . I am the vine, ye are the branches" (John xv. 1, 5). And when he sanctified the blood of the grape, for an everlasting memorial of himself, — to "shew the Lord's death till he come" (1 Cor. xi. 26).

Another most important industry among the Jews was the cultivation of the olive, if that can be called "cultivation" which appears to have been nothing more than the wholesome letting-alone of a tree that flourished best among the rocks, and continued fruitful to a great age. The invaluable oil was extracted, somewhat after the manner employed for grapes, by means of an oil-press, which commonly consisted of two large reservoirs hewn out of the rock. The berries, thrown into the perforated upper tank, were trodden with the feet, the oil flowing into the lower receptacle. The best was obtained from unripe fruit. Panniers or baskets were also used as presses. Egyptian olives were very inferior: hence the Hebrews sent their olive-oil as a gift to the Pharaohs. The olive-tree in its wild state is totally unfit for use: it must be subject to the process of grafting. This familiar fact furnishes St. Paul with one of his subtlest arguments, demonstrating the position held by the Gentile Church toward the Jewish: "For if thou wert cut out of the olive tree which is wild by nature, and wert graffed contrary to nature into a good olive tree; how much more shall these, which be the natural branches, be graffed into their own olive tree?" (Rom. xi. 24.)

XIV.

FLOCKS AND HERDS.

ABEL, that son of Adam whose innocent blood was shed by his brother's hand,—the earliest dim type of the Good Shepherd, who in after ages should give his life for the sheep,—was himself the first "keeper of sheep." The patriarchs and their descendants, prior to Israel's sojourn in Egypt, were employed in the same gentle industry, being almost exclusively shepherds and herdsmen; for when, in the fulfilment of the divine plan, Jacob and his sons were brought to the land of the Nile, Joseph instructed his brethren to explain this fact to Pharaoh: "Ye shall say, Thy servants' trade hath been about cattle from our youth even until now, both we, and also our fathers: that ye may dwell in the land of Goshen; for every shepherd is an abomination unto the Egyptians" (Gen. xlvi. 34). The wealth of the patriarchs consisted mainly of immense flocks and herds, in the care of which not only the sons but the daughters of the family bore their important part. David was sent for, from the field where he kept his father's sheep, to be anointed king of Israel by the saintly prophet (1 Sam. xvi. 11); Saul, "a choice young man and a goodly," son of Kish, "a mighty man of power," thought it not amiss to be sent to seek the lost asses of his father's herds (1 Sam. ix. 3); Rachel, Laban's daughter, came to the well at Haran "with her father's sheep: for she kept them" (Gen. xxix. 9); and the seven daughters of the priest of Midian "came and drew water, and filled the troughs to water their father's flock." What time Moses defended them against the rude shepherds, and so won Zipporah for his wife; while he himself, so soon to be the mighty leader and lawgiver of the people of God, "kept the flock of Jethro, his father-in-law" (Exod. ii. 16; iii. 1).

Thus it will be seen that the care of sheep, in patriarchal times, was considered a most honorable employment for Jewish men of mark; while the office of chief shepherd where there were many flocks, each with its trusty leader, was one of special dignity and responsibility, not derogatory even to royalty: for "Mesha king of Moab was a sheepmaster, and rendered unto the king of Israel a hundred thousand lambs, and a hundred thousand rams, with the wool" (2 Kings iii. 4).

The contempt in which shepherds were held by the Egyptians is accounted for by the indignities the nation had suffered at an early period in its history, at the hands of a powerful horde of sheep-breeders, who occupied the country for several centuries. The shrewd Hebrew vicegerent took advantage of this popular prejudice to settle his family in a region of rich pasture, and to preserve them as a peculiar people, isolated from idolaters.

The only right to the pasturage in Palestine seems to have consisted in taking possession, perhaps in some sligh cultivation, or in the ownership of an adjacent well, — a s tem of landholding possible only to a sparsely populated country, with a vast extent of virgin soil, permitting the removal of great flocks and herds from one place to another as fast as the herbage was exhausted. This nomadic life imposed great privations upon the shepherds, — exposure, possible lack of food, except what was afforded by the natural products of the land, and often extreme peril from wild beasts attracted by the proximity of the flocks to their native haunts. Jacob pathetically reminds Laban, his father-in-law, of his twenty years' experience in this service: "That which was torn of beasts I brought not unto thee; I bare the loss of it; of my hand didst thou require it, whether stolen

FLOCKS AND HERDS REPOSING.

by day, or stolen by night. Thus I was; in the day the drought consumed me, and the frost by night; and my sleep departed from mine eyes" (Gen. xxxi. 39, 40). David slew both the lion and the bear that "took a lamb out of the flock" he was keeping for his father Jesse (1 Sam. xvii. 34). And at least three of the prophets, Isaiah, Jeremiah, and Amos, have depicted spirited conflicts of this sort; to which our Lord has added his confirming praise: "The good shepherd giveth his life for the sheep. But he that is a hireling, and not the shepherd, whose own the sheep are not, seeth the wolf coming, and leaveth the sheep, and fleeth; and the wolf catcheth them, and scattereth the sheep" (John x. 11, 12). The necessity for care and courage on the part of the shepherd was naturally magnified by the fact, not without its profound spiritual application, that the sheep is the only animal, which, being lost or strayed ever so little, has no instinct to find its way home again: it must be sought for by the shepherd, and brought back, — in the beautiful words of the parable, "When he hath found it, he layeth it on his shoulders, rejoicing. And when he cometh home, he calleth together his friends and neighbours, saying unto them, Rejoice with me; for I have found my sheep which was lost" (Luke xv. 56).

The ancient shepherd was furnished with weapons of defence very insufficient in proportion to his possible danger, — the staff from four to six feet in length, with its crook, by which he managed his flock; and the sling, which to this day is used by the Bedouin Arabs. On his back he carried, and still carries, a "scrip," or bag of lambskin, suspended by straps, containing the simple meal of bread and cheese, with perhaps olives or onions for a relish. Job speaks contemptuously of men, "whom I would have disdained to have set with the dogs" of my flock (xxx. 1); showing, that, since an age of remote antiquity, this faithful animal has shared the shepherd's labor, and won his

SYRIAN SHEPHERD DOG.

friendship. A fine breed of shepherd-dog is found depicted on Babylonian sculptures. Both the Egyptians and the Assyrians used the apparently simple, but really formidable, "sling;" but none acquired such skill as the Hebrews, and of them the Benjamites were most famous (Judg. xx. 16). When David was a ruddy youth, and went out to meet the tremendous Goliath of Gath, the champion of the Philistines, he put on no armor but the simple equipment of a shepherd. "He took his staff in his hand, and chose him five smooth stones out of the brook, and put them in a shepherd's bag which he had, even in a scrip; and his sling was in his hand" (1 Sam. xvii. 40): but he returned to Jerusalem with the head of the Philistine. Relations of the utmost confidence and attachment have always existed between the Oriental shepherd and his sheep, — as true of to-day as of

FAT-TAILED SHEEP.

old. They are never driven, but led, by their faithful master, of whom it is literally true that "the sheep hear his voice; and he calleth his own sheep by name, and leadeth them out. And when he putteth forth his own sheep, he goeth before them, and the sheep follow him: for they know his voice. And a stranger will they not follow, but will flee from him; for they know not the voice of strangers" (John x. 3-5).

The curious breed of sheep peculiar to the East, known as the "broad-tailed," seems to have been the only species in existence in Palestine, Persia, and Egypt, in the Mosaic period. Its distinctive feature is the immense mass of delicate fat which accumulates on each side of the caudal spine, and is highly esteemed in the composition of Oriental dishes. This broad-tail is usually about twenty pounds in weight; but Van Lennep relates one instance in which that of a pampered pet sheep attained to one hundred and ten pounds (!) after having been accidentally diminished to some extent; and he had occasionally seen a pet sheep dragging about a toy ox-cart, on which some compassionate member of the family had fastened its tail, to relieve the poor animal of its excessive weight.

Herodotus describes this species of sheep, having tails "one cubit in width" (eighteen inches), as common in Arabia and Syria over two thousand years ago. Aristotle makes a similar record of them; and the bas-relief found among the ruins of Persepolis, the Persian capital, leaves no room for doubt as to their identity with the variety known to us. In the law for sacrifices of sheep and lambs, the Hebrew word translated "rump" is identical with the Arabic *liyeh*, which applies only to the sheep's-tail fat, — a zoölogical fact with which the English translators seem to have been unacquainted, or at least embarrassed (Lev. iii. 9).

With the Jews the sheep was pre-eminently the animal of sacrifice, and as a symbol of meekness and innocence was well adapted to that devout use. In recognition of the mission of the Messiah, especially in reference to his one "sacrifice of himself," is Christ called "the Lamb of God," "the Lamb slain from the foundation of the world."

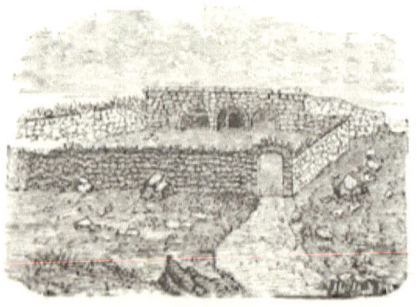

A SHEEPFOLD.

The sheepfolds of Eastern countries were not simple enclosures, but walled structures, having a low, narrow doorway, always carefully guarded against thieves or wild beasts: so Jesus warns his disciples,

"Verily, verily, I say unto you, He that entereth not by the door into the sheepfold, but climbeth up some other way, the same is a thief and a robber. But he that entereth in by the door is the shepherd of the sheep" (John x. 1, 2). Old customs are so permanent in the East, that it is probable that the ancient sheepfold, alluded to by our Lord, and even before his day, was like that of Syria in the present time, — a "low, flat building opening into a court, which is surrounded by a stone wall, protected on the top by layers of thorn-bushes. A door-way guards the entrance." In the yeaning season the shepherd leads his flock now, as in the remote past, to the fold at night, his own weary arms and rough cloak filled with the young lambs dropped by their dams during the day; wet, perhaps, and famished, "giving his life for the sheep," he is all unconscious of the exalted part he fills in one of the most touchingly beautiful of the inspired portraits of the Redeemer: "He shall feed his flock like a shepherd: he shall gather the lambs with his arm, and carry them in his bosom, and shall gently lead those that are with young" (Isa. xl. 11). As the sheep go in, one by one, through the low gateway, "passing under the rod," or the "hand" of the shepherd, he counts them, to know if any have been left out in the field or on the mountains. To "tithe" the flock, the rod was dipped in ochre, and every tenth sheep was touched, thus putting a mark upon it (Lev. xxvii. 32, and Jer. xxxii. 13). This expression, "passing under the rod," it will be seen, has no reference whatever to the wholesome chastisement of our heavenly Father, though it is so accounted in the popular sentiment. Natural caves in the earth were frequently used as folds, affording warmth and security. In remote and dangerous districts it was an ancient usage to erect towers for the protection of shepherds, as for the keepers of vineyards. It is recorded of Uzziah, king of Judah, that "he built towers in the desert, and digged many wells: for he had much cattle both in the low country and in the plains" (2 Chron. xxvi. 10).

Full of marvellous and tender interest for us is the "Tower

FLOCKS AND HERDS. 339

of Edar," beyond which Jacob "spread his tent," after he had buried the beloved Rachel in the way to Bethlehem (Gen. xxxv. 21), and which, some eight centuries later, we find alluded to by Micah as the "Tower of the Flock" (iv. 8). This watch-tower was near Bethlehem, on the road to Jerusalem, and was the station where the shepherds, bringing their flocks from afar for the service of the Temple sacrifices, watched them by night,

THE GOOD SHEPHERD.

and led them to the sanctuary as required. That this was a resting-place only for consecrated flocks, so to speak, is assured by an enactment of the Mishnah, which provided, that, " of all animals found as far from Jerusalem as *Migdal Eder*, and within that circuit on every side, the males were offered as burnt-offerings, the females as peace-offerings;" and the Rabbi Jehudah adds, " If suited for Paschal sacrifices, then they are Paschal sacrifices, provided it shall be not more than thirty days before the feast." Thus it appears that those humble shepherds, visited by the angel and a multitude of the heavenly host (Luke ii. 8), and appointed to be the heralds and witnesses of the Saviour's birth, — "the Lamb of God who taketh away the sin of the world," — were on that very night keeping watch at this station over "those sacrifices which they offered year by year continually, but which could never "take away sins" (Heb. x. 1, 4). It has been an objection to the traditional date of our

SYRIAN GOAT.

Lord's birth, that the rains of Palestine during the season corresponding to our December, would prevent the flocks from being "in the field" all night; but this argument avails little when it is considered that these sheep were on their way to Jerusalem, and therefore not in the usual conditions of pasturage at that time of year.

Goats were sometimes taken to pasture with flocks of sheep; but their characteristics and proclivities were so entirely different from those of the sheep, that it was frequently necessary for the shepherd to "**divide**" one from the other, — a familiar rustic practice that our Lord employs as an illustration of his solemn judgment of the world: "When the Son of man shall come in his glory, and all the holy angels with him, then shall he sit upon the throne of his glory: and before him shall be gathered all nations: and he shall separate them one from another, as a shepherd divideth his sheep from the goats" (Matt. xxv. 32).

THE ancient herdsman suffers by comparison with his gentler fellow-laborer, the shepherd; for we first hear of him in connection with quarrels about the possession of pasturage and wells, — an old and fruitful source of contention between owners of cattle: "A strife between the herdmen of Abram's cattle and the herdmen of Lot's cattle" (Gen. xiii. 7); and "the herdmen of Gerar did strive with Isaac's herdmen, say-

FOUR-HORNED RAM.

ing the water is ours" (Gen. xxvi. 20). In these days of the patriarchs the wealth of the Jewish nation consisted chiefly in cattle. It is recorded of Job, that "his substance also was seven thousand sheep, and three thousand camels, and five hundred yoke of oxen, and five hundred she asses, and a very great household" (i. 3). And when the Lord "turned the captivity" of the patriarch, he gave him "twice as much as he had before." Nabal had "three thousand sheep and a thousand goats" feeding on Carmel; and the merrymaking of shearing-time was going on when David sent his ten young men on a polite forage to the wealthy herd-owner's house (1 Sam. xxv. 4). Jacob, on his way from Padan-aram, with an immense stock of cattle, sent a costly present to propitiate his brother Esau, consisting of "two hundred she goats and twenty he goats, two hundred ewes and twenty rams, thirty milch camels with their colts, forty kine and ten bulls, twenty she asses and ten foals" (Gen. xxxii. 14, 15).

In a royal household the post of chief herdsman was one of dignity and distinction. Doeg, the faithful friend of the king, occupied this position in Saul's service (1 Sam. xxi. 7); and David's herdmasters, Shitrai and Shaphat, held a most responsible place among his functionaries of state (1 Chron. xxvii. 29).

In Solomon's charge to the possessor of these valuable domestic animals, he paints for our contemplation a charming little pastoral picture in the Book of Proverbs: "Be thou diligent to know the state of thy flocks, and look well to thy herds: for riches are not for ever: and doth the crown endure to every generation? The hay appeareth, and the tender grass sheweth itself, and herbs of the mountains are gathered. The lambs are for thy clothing, and the goats are the price of the field. And thou shalt have goats' milk enough for thy food, for the food of thy household, and for the maintenance of thy maidens" (xxvii. 23–27).

The ox was without doubt the most valuable possession of the ancient agriculturist and herdsman, whether we consider its uses as a beast of burden or in field-labor — ploughing, threshing, and treading out the grain; or in the household provision of milk, butter, and cheese, and finally in the conversion of its flesh into food. Oxen were also choice offerings for sacrifice, though it was common, both for the altar and the family table, to select the young animal, — the bullock, heifer, or calf.

The ancient monuments of Egypt represent the ox of that country as a superb animal of great beauty and strength. The people depended upon him in the tillage of their fields, and testified

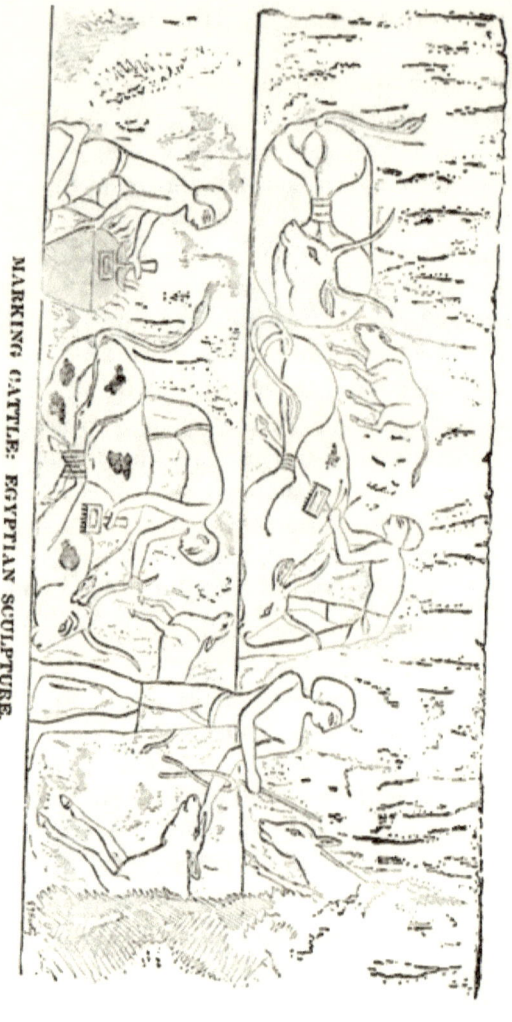

MARKING CATTLE: EGYPTIAN SCULPTURE.

their appreciation of his value by offering him worship under the name Apis. A special breed, preserved with the greatest care, was set apart, from which to select objects for this devotion; and at death these were embalmed and mourned with national honors. The Hebrews, during their two centuries' sojourn in Egypt, evidently became somewhat tainted with this idolatrous practice; for they were scarcely delivered from their cruel oppressors before they constrained Aaron to make them a golden calf, that they might offer it the Egyptian rites of worship. The Egyptian office of superintendent of the herds, says Wilkinson, was "a high and distinguished post, being held by persons of rank belonging to the priestly and military classes, who were called 'superintends of the cattle of the king,' or of 'some god.'"

East of the Jordan vast herds of cattle grazed through the entire year, driven from place to place as the pasture was exhausted. In Western Palestine this was not always possible, owing to variety of surface and climate. Cattle were fed with barley or with a mixture of chopped straw, barley, and beans, the "provender" or the torn "straw" left by the threshing-machine: "The oxen likewise and the young asses that ear the ground shall eat clean provender, which hath been winnowed with the shovel and with the fan" (Isa. xxx. 24). In more thickly populated districts the oxen were stall-fed for the table: "Better is a dinner of herbs where love is, than a stalled ox and hatred therewith" (Prov. xv. 17). And in the daily supply for Solomon's household a distinction is made between the "ten fat oxen" and the "twenty oxen out of the pastures" (1 Kings iv. 23). Among several enactments in the law for oxen and other cattle, there is one peculiarly interesting, in which the ox is apparently held accountable for his iniquity and punished with death: "If an ox gore a man or a woman, that they die: then the ox shall be surely stoned, and his flesh shall not be eaten; but the owner of the ox shall be quit" (Exod. xxi. 28). Among "the cattle on a thousand hills" David specifies the "strong bulls of Bashan" for our terrified admiration (Ps. xxii. 12), — in the words of the prophet, the "fatlings of Bashan" (Ezek. xxxix. 18). The unicorn, so frequently referred to in the Old Testament, is supposed to have been a very large and powerful wild ox, to which Pliny gave the name of urus, and Cæsar describes as "the gigantic ox of the Hercynian forest, in stature scarcely below an elephant, and of indomitable ferocity." The Assyrian sculptures represent this truly formidable animal as pursued by royal and noble hunters.

The camel and the ass have perhaps the earliest mention in the Bible as domesticated animals brought into complete subjection to the pleasures or necessities of man. The camel is commonly enumerated among the possessions of wealthy patriarchs and kings. We have seen, for instance, that Job had six thousand camels when the Lord blessed him after his great trial. Isaac, Jacob, David, all had a large number of these most useful burden-bearers, which were trained for the conveyance of merchandise on long caravan routes, or for personal convenience in making journeys of considerable distance. It was to a "company of Ishmaelites,"

CAMELS EQUIPPED FOR THE DESERT.

which "came from Gilead with their camels bearing spicery, and balm, and myrrh, going to carry it down to Egypt," that Joseph was sold by his brethren (Gen. xxxvii. 25, 28). Rebekah and Rachel travelled on camels (Gen. xxiv. 64; xxxi. 34); and the queen of Sheba, on her visit to Solomon, "came to Jerusalem with a very great train, with camels that bare spices, and very much gold, and precious stones" (1 Kings x. 2). It was customary for the wealthy to adorn their favorite camels with rich trappings, with bells and chains and collars, and pendent ornaments of gold or silver. When Gideon slew the two kings of Midian, he "took away the ornaments that were on their camels'

THE DESERT, FROM THE WELLS OF MOSES.

necks" (Judg. viii. 21). The flesh and milk of the camel were used for food, but not by the Hebrew, to whom it was prohibited: "The camel, because he cheweth the cud, but divideth not the hoof; he is unclean unto you" (Lev. xi. 4).

There is little doubt that the ass superseded the camel for daily use in Eastern households. It is mentioned as early as Abraham's time, and throughout the Bible appears as a most esteemed possession, equally essential to the wealthy, who owned large herds, as to the poor man, who looked, perhaps, to his one she-ass for the support, by her labor and her milk, of his family. In describing the desperately wicked, the wretched patriarch writes, "They drive away the ass of the fatherless, they take the widow's ox for a pledge" (Job xxiv. 3); while they themselves he compares to the "wild asses in the desert," swift and eager in their work of destruction. Besides the common animal, subsisting on the coarsest food, and subjected to the meanest drudgery, there were finer breeds of the ass monopolized by the wealthy for the saddle; while the milk of the female was highly esteemed as an article of diet, as well as for medicinal purposes. In ancient Palestine ladies preferred these finer asses for riding, whether in saddle or in the litters carried by them. When the Shunamite's son lay dead in the same "little chamber on the wall" she had made for Elisha, that he might "turn in thither,"

"she called unto her husband, and said, Send me, I pray thee, one of the young men, and one of the asses, that I may run to the man of God, and come again. . . . Then she saddled an ass, and said to her servant, Drive, and go forward; slack not thy riding for me, except I bid thee" (2 Kings iv. 22, 24). Abigail, wife of the churlish Nabal, "rode on the ass," as she carried her present to David (1 Sam. xxv. 20); Jair, one of the judges of Israel, had "thirty sons that rode on thirty ass-colts;" Abdon, another, had "forty sons and thirty nephews, that rode on three-score and ten ass-colts;" while Deborah sings of the high functionaries themselves as "ye that ride on white asses" (Judg. x. 4; xii. 14; v. 10). The silvery-white ass was especially esteemed; but the ordinary color of the animal, as mentioned in Scripture, is expressed by its Hebrew name, signifying *red*.

The wild ass was a beautiful, deer-like creature, marvellously fleet and spirited. Its flesh was "unclean" to the Jews, but much preferred by their Oriental neighbors, as well as by the Greeks and Romans. The Assyrian sculptures represent the ancient chase of this ass of the desert, which is described by Xenophon as pursued by relays of hounds, since no mounted horseman could hope to overtake it.

The mule is represented on the ancient monuments of Egypt, but seems not to have been known to the Israelites until the time of David. There is an early mention of this animal in the Bible, where Anah "found mules in the wilderness, as he fed the asses of Gibeon, his father" (Gen. xxxvi. 24); but the word rendered "mules" in this text is considered a gross mistranslation. It is certain that the mule had become fashionable for saddle-use in David's reign; for, after the murder of Amnon by order of his brother Absalom, it is recorded that "all the king's sons arose, and every man gat him up upon his mule, and fled" (2 Sam. xiii. 29). And the guilty "Absalom rode upon a mule," which was made the instrument of his death; for the mule went under the "thick boughs of a great oak, and his head caught hold of the oak, and he was taken up between the heaven and the earth; and the mule that was under him went

LASSOING WILD ASSES: ASSYRIAN SCULPTURE

away" (2 Sam. xviii. 9). Henceforward this valuable animal is often mentioned in connection with the horse. The greatly impoverished remnant of Israel that returned from their captivity in Babylon to the ruins of Jerusalem brought with them two hundred and forty-five mules (Neh. vii. 68). An Assyrian sculpture represents two women riding astride on a mule. The value of a white mule in the East at the present day is three or four times greater than that of an ordinary horse.

The horse, now so thoroughbred and so highly prized in the East, seems not to have been known in the history of the Jews before the reign of Solomon. Of this monarch, it is recorded that he had "twelve thousand horsemen;" also that "Solomon had horses brought out of Egypt."—"a horse for a hundred and fifty shekels of silver."—not only for himself, but for "the kings of the Hittites and for the kings of Syria" (1 Kings x. 26, 28, 29).

The first indirect allusion to the horse in the Bible is found in the prophetic benediction of the patriarch Jacob, dying in the land of Egypt: "Dan shall be a serpent by the way, an adder in the path, that biteth the horse heels, so that his rider shall fall backward" (Gen. xlix. 17). And, as this valuable creature begins to appear on Egyptian monuments only a short time previous to this date, it is certain that it was not very common even then; still, the imposing funeral procession, following the patriarch's remains to Canaan, consisted in part of "chariots and horsemen" (Gen. l. 9).

Allusions to the horse in the Scriptures are almost exclusively in connection with his participation in battles. The famous poem in the Book of Job is to the war-horse of that rude time: "Hast thou given the horse strength? hast thou clothed his neck with thunder? Canst thou make him afraid as a grasshopper? the glory of his nostrils is terrible. He paweth in the valley, and rejoiceth in his strength: he goeth on to meet the armed men. He mocketh at fear, and is not affrighted; neither turneth he back from the sword. The quiver rattleth against him, the glittering spear and the shield. He swalloweth the ground with fierceness and rage; neither believeth he that it is the sound of the trumpet. He saith among the trumpets, Ha, ha! and he smelleth the battle afar off, the thunder of the captains, and the shouting" (Job. xxxix. 19-25). Solomon speaks of the same

formidable foe as the horse "prepared against the day of battle" (Prov. xxi. 31); such the horses "swifter than eagles," and he that "rusheth into the battle," described by the prophet (Jer. iv. 13; viii. 16); and those "swifter than the leopards, and more fierce than the evening wolves" (Hab. i. 8).

That chariots drawn by horses formed an important part of the martial equipment of the Egyptians is learned from the record of the Exodus, where the Israelites were pursued by Pharaoh's "six hundred chosen chariots, and all the chariots of Egypt" (Exod. xiv. 7). The Assyrians and Babylonians, Syrians and Philistines, made use of chariots and cavalry in war. David was the first to introduce them into Hebrew warfare, contrary to the divine command to the king of the Jews, which was designed to prevent a renewal of national relations with the idolatrous race from which they had been delivered by a mighty Hand: "He shall not multiply horses to himself, nor cause the people to return to Egypt, to the end that he should multiply horses; forasmuch as the Lord hath said unto you, Ye shall henceforth return no more that way" (Deut. xvii. 16).

The sacred historian records that the heroic Josiah, king of Israel, in his effort thoroughly to purge the land of the idolatrous practices into which it had fallen, "took away the horses that the kings of Judah had given to the sun, . . . and burned the chariots of the sun with fire" (2 Kings xxiii. 11). This passage points to the ancient Persian custom of dedicating a chariot and horses to the sun, adopted by the backslidden Israelites. Representations of Italian women, riding sidewise upon horses, are to be seen on Etruscan vases, in the museum of Naples, older than the foundation of Rome (B.C. 752); showing that our extant fashion is by no means so modern as is generally believed. The ancient trappings of horses, as preserved in the sculptures of Nineveh and Egypt, appear to be almost identical with those of the present day; but the saddle varied in every country, and it seems never to have been the practice to shoe the horse. Isaiah says of the executors of God's judgments, "Their horses' hoofs shall be counted like flint" (v. 28).

THE foregoing consideration of the conditions of ancient agricultural and pastoral life in Bible lands, necessarily brief and condensed, must not be brought to a conclusion without some reference to one of the most important concerns of them that had the charge of large flocks and herds. A well of water, digged deep, and flowing perennially from the limestone-rock, was a possession absolutely priceless in a dry, hot country; and therefore it was a fruitful source of quarrels and even conflicts between rival shepherds and herdsmen. For this reason villages were built sufficiently near to a well or spring for the public convenience, but not so near as to be seriously annoyed by the dust consequent upon the daily gathering of the flocks to be watered, and the noisy bickering, not to say strife, of their masters. Wells were commonly approached by flights of steps, which the women descended to dip their pitchers into the water, and ascended to return to their homes; otherwise, when the well was deep, a rope was fastened to a leathern bucket or earthen jar, which was let down either by a simple pulley, or by merely sliding the rope over the stone curb of the well. The ancient wells of Beersheba on the southern borderland of Canaan, digged by Abraham (Gen. xxi. 31), still furnish water to the Arab herdsmen and women, who all day long draw and fill the troughs for their cattle, as in the patriarchal period of Bible history. "In four thousand years the ropes of these drawers of water have worn furrows in the face of the stones, some of them over four inches deep."

Jacob's Well, on which Jesus sat, "being wearied with his journey," and talked with the woman of Samaria, who asked him, perhaps in amazement, probably in scorn, because of the deep-rooted prejudice between Jew and Samaritan, "Art thou greater than our father Jacob, which gave us the well, and drank thereof himself, and his children, and his cattle? (John iv. 12) is one of the few localities positively identified by Orientals of whatever creed. It is situate a mile and a half from the ancient city of Shechem, where Jacob, after parting in peace from his brother Esau, "bought a parcel of a field where he had spread his tent" (Gen. xxxiii. 19).

It was customary to cover the mouths of wells with heavy stones to protect them from the shifting sands that would soon choke the water-supply. At morning and evening the women of all ranks in the primitive age went with their pitchers or jars to carry water for household use, while the shepherds and herdsmen brought their flocks for watering. These customs are admirably illustrated in the story of Eliezer, Abraham's servant, in search of a wife for his master's son Isaac. "He made his camels to kneel down without the city by a well of water at the time of the evening, even the time that women go out to draw water." And, when the fair Rebekah came "with her pitcher upon her shoulder," "she went down to the well, and filled her pitcher, and came up. And the servant ran to meet her, and said, Let me, I pray thee, drink a little water of thy pitcher. And she said, Drink, my lord: and she hasted, and let down her pitcher upon her hand, and gave him drink. And when she had done giving him drink, she said, I will draw water for thy camels also, until they have done drinking. And she hasted,

JACOB'S WELL.

and emptied her pitcher into the trough, and ran again unto the well to draw water, and drew for all his camels (Gen. xxxiv. 11, 16–20).

Another well of the Bible is responsible for a patriarchal love-match,— the well of Haran, where Jacob tarried to rest on his journey, and to inquire concerning his mother's kindred: "While he yet spake with them, Rachel came with her father's sheep, for she kept them." To water her flock, Jacob "rolled the stone from the well's mouth," kissed Rachel's, and "lifted up his voice and wept," telling her who he was,— a charming pastoral, that prepares us for the inevitable conclusion: " And Jacob served seven years for Rachel; and they seemed unto him but a few days, for the love he had to her" (Gen. xxiv. 9–11, 20).

Another means for providing a plentiful supply of water in a country where rain fell to excess in winter, and scarcely at all in summer, was the construction of cisterns. Palestine abounded in cisterns of all sorts long prior to the settlement of the Israelites in their promised land. The remains of these are found to-day, not only in towns and villages, but in remote wildernesses. Some were formed by merely excavating the earth, and lining it with wood or cement; others were large tanks or reservoirs, covered or roofed, into which the water was conducted. A door in the side of the structure opened upon a flight of steps that reached to the bottom of the tank, so that, however low the water, it was always accessible. Others were hewn in the rock with excessive labor, and even decorated elaborately.

When these pits became empty, except for the tenacious and noisome mire at the bottom, they were used as dungeons and places of cruel torture. It is supposed that Joseph was thrown into such a dry cistern by his brethren: "They took him and cast him into a pit; and the pit was empty, there was no water in it" (Gen. xxxvii. 24). Thus Jeremiah was cast into a pit " that was in the court of the prison; and they let down Jeremiah with cords. And in the dungeon there was no water, but mire; so Jeremiah sunk in the mire" (xxxviii. 6). This prophet is the author of that touching figure wherein the Almighty laments the backsliding of Israel: "My people have committed two evils; they have forsaken me the fountain of living waters, and hewed them out cisterns, broken cisterns, that can hold no water" (Jer. ii. 13). And Solomon, urging upon his "son" the exercise of both self-restraint and benevolence, employs a similar illustration: "Drink waters out of thine own cistern, and running waters out of thine own well. Let thy fountains be dispersed abroad, and rivers of water in the streets" (Prov. v. 15). Some of the Eastern cisterns are of immense size. One is described by a recent traveller as six hundred and sixty feet long by two hundred and seventy wide; and another, in Northern Syria, is over one hundred feet in depth and breadth. The cistern under the Temple platform in Jerusalem is very extensive, though not so deep as the one last mentioned. It is hewn from "the native rock, portions being left here and there, as rude pillars, to support the roof." A very ancient form of cistern was a circular shaft, tunnelled to the slanting depth of one hundred or one hundred and fifty feet, and enclosing a flight of steps. So generously was Jerusalem supplied with these wells and cisterns, that, during the many sieges she was called upon to endure, her citizens never suffered for lack of water.

It was very common in cities for private householders to have a cistern in the courtyard. When such cisterns become dry, they make excellent storerooms, or hiding-places for fugitives. The mouth being on a level with the ground, it was easy to cover it so as to hide it. In such a cistern the two servants of David were hidden in Bahurim, near Jerusalem, at the time of Absalom's rebellious conspiracy against the throne. "They went both of them away quickly, and came to a man's house in Bahurim, which had a well in his court; whither they went down. And the woman took and spread a covering over the well's mouth, and spread ground corn thereon; and the thing was not known" (2 Sam. xvii. 18, 19).

Palestine was also rich in perpetual springs or fountains, especially on either side of the Jordan, where there are now hundreds of such springs, many of them strongly impregnated with

SOLOMON'S POOLS.

medicinal properties. The Scriptures abound in spiritual allusions to these springs of living waters; to the "water brooks" and the "still waters;" to the "fountain opened to the house of David for sin and uncleanness," "a spring shut up, a fountain

"AS THE HART PANTETH AFTER THE WATER BROOKS."

sealed;" to a fountain that "shall come forth of the house of the Lord;" to the "living fountains of waters."

In view of all the illustrations and suggestions afforded to a devout mind by the phase of life we have been considering, it seems appropriate in closing to sum them up in the inspired words of the prophet Habakkuk: "Although the fig tree shall not blossom, neither shall fruit be in the vines; the labour of the olive shall fail, and the fields shall yield no meat; the flock shall be cut off from the fold, and there shall be no herd in the stalls: yet I will rejoice in the Lord, I will joy in the God of my salvation" (iii. 17, 18); and in the immortal song of the sweet Psalmist of Israel, expressing the same exalted spirit of an immutable confidence: "The Lord is my shepherd; I shall not want. He maketh me to lie down in green pastures: he leadeth me beside the still waters. He restoreth my soul: he leadeth me in the paths of righteousness for his name's sake. Yea, though I walk through the valley of the shadow of death, I will fear no evil: for thou art with me; thy rod and thy staff they comfort me. Thou preparest a table before me in the presence of mine enemies: thou anointest my head with oil; my cup runneth over. Surely goodness and mercy shall follow me all the days of my life: and I will dwell in the house of the Lord for ever" (Ps. xxiii. 1–6).

XV.

SICKNESS AND DEATH.

THE medical art is seldom alluded to in the early Biblical records of the Jewish nation, from which fact we may infer favorably for the general hygiene of that people, as well as from our knowledge of their Mosaic code, which provided as wisely for the physical as for the moral well-being of its faithful followers. Much also was due to their mode of life in the patriarchal period, simplicity of diet, scrupulous cleanliness, continual contact with the open air, complete exemption from all excesses and excitements. The climate of the Bible lands, moreover, is one of the most wholesome in the world, and most conducive to longevity; so that sickness and premature death came to be popularly regarded as a direct visitation of God in punishment of sin. The question of the disciples concerning the "man which was blind from his birth," "Master, who did sin, this man, or his parents, that he was born blind?" (John ix. 1, 2) is an

THE HEALED WATERS OF JERICHO.

extraordinary expression of this belief; for it admitted the possibility of pre-natal transgression. Health and long life were expected as blessings promised in reward to the faithful keeping of the law, as it was written: "I will take sickness away from

the midst of thee. . . . The number of thy days I will fulfil"
(Exod. xxiii. 25. 26). David expresses the sentiment and experience of his generation in the familiar words, "The days of our years are threescore years and ten; and if by reason of strength they be fourscore years, yet is their strength labour and sorrow; for it is soon cut off, and we fly away" (Ps. xc. 10). But we go back to the primeval age of his people for those wonderful instances of protracted years which we are scarcely disposed to accept as facts when tried by our present chronology,— the two hundred and five years of Terah, the one hundred and seventy-five years of his son Abraham, the one hundred and eighty of Isaac, and the one hundred and forty-seven of Jacob; while Moses died at one hundred and twenty years, "his eye not yet being dim with age, nor his natural force abated."

In the later days of the Rabbis, to die within fifty years of age was to be "cut off;" within fifty-two, to "die the death of Samuel the prophet;" at sixty, it was a "death at the hands of Heaven;" at seventy, as that "of an old man;" and at eighty, as that, in the words of the Psalmist, "of strength." The Rabbis, as demonstrators of the law, were keen observers of sanitary precautions; and no doubt the words of the son of Sirach worthily expressed their estimation of the blessing he extols: " Health and good estate of body are above all gold. . . . Death is better than a bitter life or continual sickness. . . . Excess of meats bringeth sickness, and surfeiting will turn into choler. By surfeiting have many perished; but he that taketh heed prolongeth his life" (Ecclus. xxx. 15. 17; xxxvii. 30. 31).

The art of healing, though not brought to any degree of perfection, was undoubtedly cultivated in Israel; but, as in every other human agency under the theocracy, the people were warned against putting their trust in an arm of flesh; thus the sin of Asa is rebuked for all time in sacred history, that "in his disease he sought not to the Lord, but to the physicians" (2 Chron. xvi. 12). It must be inferred that the Jews derived some knowledge of the practice of medicine from Egypt in that early epoch of their history, since one of their laws in Exodus pro-

SICKNESS AND DEATH. 367

vides that if one man hurt another, so that "he die not, but keepeth his bed" for a while, the offender shall be quit; "only he shall pay for the loss of his time, and cause him to be thor-

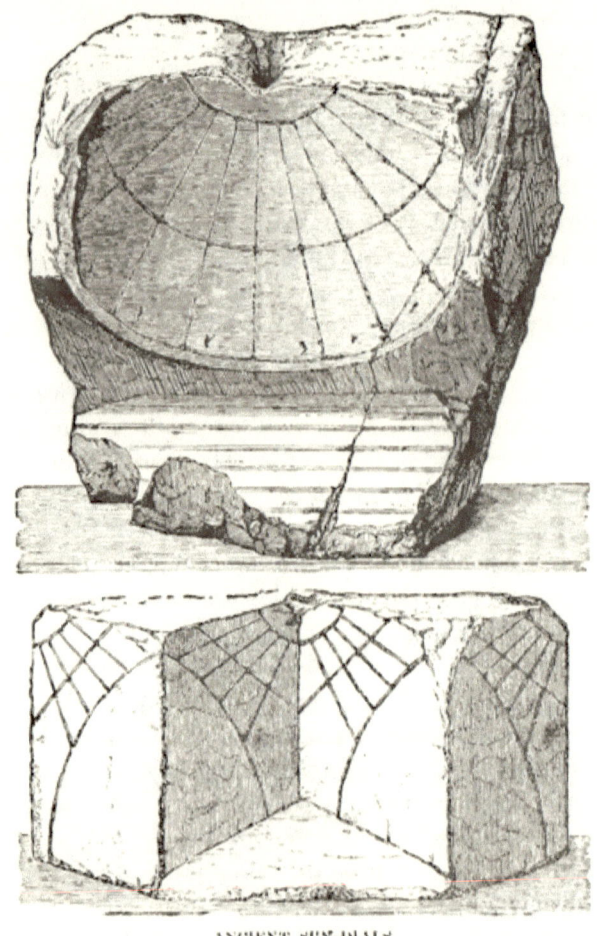

ANCIENT SUN-DIALS.

oughly healed" (xxi. 19). In the case of Hezekiah, the pious king of Judah, when he was "sick unto death," it seems that it was not unusual for a prophet to give medical advice: "Isaiah had said, Let them take a lump of figs, and lay it for a plaster upon the boil, and he shall recover" (Isa. xxxviii. 21). While in the exercise of his spiritual function, he procured a miraculous assurance of his royal patient's recovery: "This sign shalt thou have of the Lord, that the Lord will do the thing that he hath spoken: . . . and he brought the shadow ten degrees backward, by which it had gone down in the dial of Ahaz" (2 Kings xx. 9, 11).

The estimation in which a physician was held, as a mere instrument in God's hands for the public weal, is set forth in a curiously interesting homily in the Apocrypha: "Honor a physician with the honor due unto him for the uses which ye may have of him: for the Lord hath created him. For of the Most High cometh healing. The Lord hath created medicines out of the earth; and he that is wise will not abhor them. He hath given man skill that he might be honored in his marvellous works. My son, in thy sickness be not negligent; but pray unto the Lord, and he will make thee whole. Then give place to the physician, for the Lord hath created him: let him not go from thee, for thou hast need of him. There is a time when in their hands there is good success; for they shall also pray unto the Lord, that he would prosper that which they give for ease and remedy to prolong life. He that sinneth before his Maker, let him fall into the hand of the physician" (Ecclus. xxxviii.).

Among ancient nations Egypt was pre-eminently the seat of medical science. Its pursuit was encouraged and controlled by government, and a strict accountability required of practitioners, who were, almost without exception, specialists. Pliny informs us that *post-mortem* examinations were first made in Egypt in the prosecution of inquiry into the hidden causes of fatal disease, — an advantage that Hebrew students could not employ, on account of the ceremonial pollution of contact with a dead body. Herodotus declares that the great conquerors, Cyrus and Darius, depended for their court-physicians upon Egypt, the therapeutic skill of their own lands being altogether insignificant.

Jeremiah, prophesying the overthrow of Pharaoh's army at

the Euphrates, refers to the *materia medica* of Egypt: "Go up into Gilead, and take balm, O virgin, the daughter of Egypt: in vain shalt thou use many medicines; for thou shalt not be cured" (xlvi. 11); and again to one of the most esteemed of Oriental remedies, the famous balsam, that constituted so important an article of commerce among Eastern nations that Roman generals thought it worthy to form part of the spoils of their foreign conquests; and which, according to Josephus, was introduced to Judæa by the queen of Sheba among the precious gifts she brought to Solomon: "Is there no balm in Gilead? is there no physician there? why then is not the health of the daughter of my people recovered?" (viii. 22). Medical practice seems to have been mainly hygienic; though the ancients were disposed to bring to their aid the occult sciences in conjunction with their simple vegetable prescriptions, external ointments and lotions of oil and wine, and the careful diet imposed during the progress of disease. The Rabbis did not disdain to adopt the medical profession; and they ordained that every town should have its physician and surgeon; for all this, there were not wanting in that age caustic proverbs of a spirit not foreign to this: "Physician, heal thyself," is a genuine Jewish proverb, and "The best among doctors deserves Gehenna," the ungrateful sentiment of those patients, who, then as now, were exacting in proportion to their ignorance. Among the regular official staff on duty in the Temple was a physician to minister to the priesthood. In later days it was customary to have prayers offered in the synagogue for a person who was very ill, under the "new name," which by significant usage the sufferer assumed, thus making him "another man, a new creature, and like a child born to a good life and length of days." This extract from a Rabbinical prayer for the dying, is peculiarly suggestive to the Christian reader of the "new name" promised to "him that overcometh" (Rev. ii. 17). It was also customary to anoint the sick with a lotion of oil, wine, and water, which might be prepared even on the sabbath, as indicated by St. James: "Is any sick among you? Let him call for the elders of the Church, and let them pray over him, anointing him with oil in the name of the Lord" (v. 14).

Visits to the sick were accounted among the most sacred obligations. Maimonides, the great Jewish doctor, held that this act of charity takes precedence of all others; and the Talmud goes still farther when it asserts that "whoever visits

"GO, WASH IN THE POOL OF SILOAM."

the sick shall deliver his soul from Gehenna," while, on the part of the afflicted, we are assured that the visitor relieves him of "one-sixtieth part of his sufferings."

"All manner of sickness and all manner of disease" is freely spoken of in the New Testament in connection with the gracious ministry of our Lord, who "went about all Galilee," teaching, preaching, and healing. Everywhere we behold him, followed, crowded, with the sick and those who carried them, — the palsied, the dropsical, the blind, the lame, the deaf and dumb, the lepers, those consumed with fevers, the impotent, the possessed of devils, the paralyzed. Perhaps the majority of these sufferers were like the woman "which had spent all her living upon physicians, neither could be healed of any" (Luke viii. 43); and who might, with Job, have said to them, "Ye are all physicians of no value" (xiii. 4). How full of new hope to these, the news of this great Physician, visiting their towns and villages, who, with a word or a touch, restored to perfect health! "He cast out the spirits with his word, and healed all that were sick: that it might be fulfilled which was spoken by Esaias the prophet, saying, Himself took our infirmities, and bare our sicknesses" (Matt. viii. 16, 17). Nor would we forget his humble disciple, "Luke, the beloved physician," — as St. Paul calls him, writing to the Colossians, — who, as indicated by his writings, was educated among the polite and cultivated Greeks of Asia; but who, called of God to become a missionary of the cross, and a scribe "instructed to the kingdom," abandoned his profession for that exalted work.

THE Bible story of the death of the patriarch Jacob, brought into Egypt with all his family by his son Joseph, gives us with remarkable detail the customs surrounding the final scenes in the life of the head of a family. The assembling of the members of the immediate household about the deathbed; the laying of the paternal blessing upon each, beginning with the first-born; the "gathering up" of the feet into the bed at the last breath; the closing of the eyes, and the kiss; offices delegated to the nearest and dearest of kin, — all these compose an impressive picture of a great solemnity (Gen. xlix.). In the case of Jacob, it was the beloved and long-mourned Joseph who fell upon his dead "father's face, and wept upon him, and kissed him," even as the Lord had promised the patriarch "in the visions of the night" at Beersheba, when on his way to Egypt: "Joseph shall put his hand upon thine eyes" (Gen. xlvi. 4).

In the spirit of this remotely ancient custom, the Jew of Rabbinical times, finding himself near his end, invited at least ten persons to hear his general confession. He asked pardon of all whom he had offended, receiving the blessing of his own parents if living, and bestowing his benediction upon his children and dependents.

According to Rabbinical tradition, there were nine hundred and three different sorts of dying. The most painful of these was compared to "tearing out a thread from a piece of wool;" the sweet and almost imperceptible passing away of the spirit, compared to drawing a hair out of milk, was called "death by a kiss." Aaron and Moses are said to have died "according to the word,"— literally, "by the mouth of Jehovah." Certain superstitions prevailed as to the duration of the fatal illness, and as to the manner and posture of the dying. To die with a smile irradiating the countenance, or with the eyes looking upward, was a happy omen; while to look down, to be alarmed, or even to turn the face to the wall, was construed as a sign of evil. The actual dissolution of the sick person was followed by those extravagant demonstrations of grief common to the Orientals, the female members of the family announcing the death to the neighborhood by shrill and piercing cries rising above all the din of the city. It is to be supposed that in the early life of the Hebrew nation the funeral observances were characterized by great simplicity; but in a later day these partook of the prevailing luxuries of a higher civilization, and extended even to costly wrappings for the dead body. A reform in this particular was introduced by the Rabbi Gamaliel, at whose feet St. Paul sat as a pupil, who directed that he should be buried in plain linen garments. His grandson went even beyond this, and limited the number of garments to one, and that of the simplest and cheapest linen, poetically known as the "travelling-dress."

Reference is made in the New Testament to these details. At the miraculous raising of Lazarus, when Jesus "cried with a loud voice, Lazarus, come forth," it is written. "And he that was dead came forth, bound hand and foot with graveclothes; and his face was bound about with a napkin. Jesus saith unto them, Loose him, and let him go" (John xi. 44). It is supposed in this case that the grave-clothes consisted of separate wrappings of each limb, as was customary in Egypt. In the burial of Ananias mention is made of a less complicated form of this mode of dressing the corpse: "The young men arose, wound him up, and carried him out" (Acts v. 6). So unpretentious were the preparations for the funeral of Dorcas - the benevolent disciple in Joppa, whose extensive charities may justify us in the supposition that she was a woman of means — that it is simply said of her, "She was sick, and died: whom when they had washed, they laid in an upper chamber" (Acts ix. 37). Our Lord's funeral rites afford, perhaps, a better example of the "manner of the Jews to bury." Joseph, "a rich man of Arimathea," "took the body of Jesus. And there came also Nicodemus, (which at the first came to Jesus by night,) and brought a mixture of myrrh and aloes, about a hundred pound weight. Then took they the body of Jesus, and wound it in linen clothes with the spices" (John xix. 38-40).

In the other Gospel accounts of this precious death and burial, there is no mention of the use of spices at the hurried temporary sepulture; only that the body was "wrapped in linen," a "clean linen cloth," while the women "prepared spices and ointments" to be used as soon as the sabbath was past, and brought them to "anoint him" on the morning of the resurrection. St. Peter, it is written, "went into the sepulchre, and seeth the linen clothes lie, and the napkin, that was about his head, not lying with the linen clothes, but wrapped together in a place by itself" (John xx. 6, 7).

This must have been an ancient mode of burial in reference to the lavish use of spices, and one not altogether unworthy of a king. We read of Asa, king of Judah, nine centuries before Christ, that "they buried him in his own sepulchres, which he had made for himself in the city of David, and laid him in the bed which was filled with sweet odours and divers kinds of spices prepared by the apothecaries' art: and they made a very great burning for him" (2 Chron. xvi. 14).

Some commentators discover in this text, and others where "burnings" are mentioned, proof of the practice of cremation by the Jews. If this heathenish custom, as practised by the Greeks and Romans, ever did exist among them, it is certain that the national sentiment with regard to it underwent material change at different epochs of Jewish history. It is inferred from Judah's sentence upon Tamar — "Bring her forth, and let her be burnt" (Gen. xxxix. 24), — a punishment involving the greatest indignity — that the ancient Hebrews held the burning of a body in the utmost abhorrence; and we know that after the captivity they denounced the practice as contrary to the spirit and teaching of the law, the Rabbis explaining the texts wherein the "burning of odours" is mentioned as referring to the combustion of the aromatic substances only. It is positively asserted that all the "valiant men" of Israel "took the body of Saul and the bodies of his sons from the wall of Beth-shan, and came to Jabesh and burnt them there" (1 Sam. xxxi. 12); but this can easily be construed as an exigency of war, designed to protect the bodies of the royal family from further indignities at the hands of their conquerors.

There are other Oriental authorities who see in these burials with spices some remains or suggestions of the Egyptian embalming; but we have no evidence in the Bible of this remarkable disposition of dead bodies by the Jews, except in the case of Jacob and his son Joseph, who, dying in Egypt, were subject to the customs of the land, and for whom it was especially desirable, as their remains were to be removed to the Land of Promise. Immediately after the death of the patriarch Jacob, we are told that " Joseph commanded his servants the physicians to embalm his father; and the physicians embalmed Israel. And forty days were fulfilled for him; for so are fulfilled the days of those which are embalmed" (Gen. l. 2. 3).

"IN A PLEASANT LAND."

As the Egyptian physicians were invariably specialists, there were those of a subordinate class, but belonging to the sacerdotal order, who devoted themselves exclusively to this curious process, which was more or less elaborate according to the price paid,— for a single body, from fifteen hundred of our dollars to two or three hundred. The rarest aromatics were employed in filling the cavities of the head and abdomen, the whole body being steeped in a strong infusion of natron thirty, forty, or even seventy days. After this process the body, with every limb separately, was wrapped in narrow bandages of fine linen, smeared on one side with gum, hundreds of feet in length. Layers of dampened cloth plastered with lime were next adjusted to the body in sufficient thicknesses to constitute a case when dried and hardened. It was painted and ornamented, the "face" made to resemble, as nearly as possible, the features of the deceased. From the charred appearance of the bandages and bones of a mummy, it is conjectured that the next process was subjection to extreme heat. The whole was then put into another case of sycamore or cedar wood; and there might be even an additional outside coffin of wood or stone, which was covered with hieroglyphics; but this was not usual.

When Joseph died, it is recorded that "they embalmed him, and he was put in a coffin in Egypt" (Gen. l. 26). That this mummy was laid in a coffin is evidence of the exalted rank the "fruitful bough" of Jacob had attained in the land into which he had been brought and sold as a slave. Coffins were used by the Babylonians as well as the Egyptians, but not commonly by any Eastern people, except for convenience in transportation.

The final preparations having been made, the corpse was laid upon a bier, or sort of hand-barrow, with long poles projecting at the corners, by which it was borne aloft by four bearers. "King David himself followed the bier" of the lamented Abner (2 Sam. iii. 31). In this case the word "bier" is more correctly "bed," and in ancient times it was not unusual to carry a person of high rank or distinction to the grave on a bed prepared for the purpose. In the description of the funeral ceremonies of King Herod, conducted by his son Archelaus, Josephus says that "the body was placed on a gilded bed which was richly adorned with precious stones." In the time of the Rabbis babes less than a month old were carried to the grave by their mothers, while those under twelve months were borne on a little bed or stretcher. Miss Rogers, in her "Domestic Life in Palestine," describes a funeral bier that she saw as having a canopy "made of freshly gathered elastic palm-branches. They were bent like half-hoops, and then interlaced and secured lengthways with straight fronds."

THE BIRD OF THE TOMBS.

It was such a bier, perhaps, that Jesus, coming "nigh to the gate of the city" (Nain), "came and touched."

The Jews had a peculiar horror of being deprived of sepulture, — to them an ineffaceable disgrace. No more terrible judgment could have been pronounced upon the presumptuous Jehoiakim, king of Judah, than the word of the Lord at the mouth of Jeremiah: "His dead body shall be cast out, in the day to

"THAT I MAY DIE IN MINE OWN CITY."

the heat, and in the night to the frost" (xxxvi. 30); and it was a divinely ordained penalty for disobedience (Deut. xxviii. 26).

It is a curious fact, that, on the other hand, the ancient Magi exposed their dead to be consumed by birds, lest any other disposal of them should pollute one of the four elements, earth, air, fire, and water; but, deposited in living creatures, all such pollution is prevented. The fire-worshippers of the present day (Parsees), descendants of the ancient Persians, hold to this theory and practice. The Zendavesta contains particular directions for the construction of the dreadful "towers of silence" by which their purpose is accomplished.

The Hebrew's desire to be buried in his native land amounted to a passionate longing. In his last moments the dying Israel called his son Joseph, and said, "Deal kindly and truly with me; bury me not, I pray thee, in Egypt: but I will lie with my fathers, and thou shalt carry me out of Egypt, and bury me in their buryingplace. And he said, I will do as thou hast said. And he said, Swear unto me. And he sware unto him" (Gen. xlvii. 29–31). And in his turn "Joseph took an oath of the children of Israel, saying, God will surely visit you, and ye shall carry up my bones from hence" (Gen. l. 25). And when David wished to take the aged Barzillai with him to Jerusalem, he answered, "Let thy servant, I pray thee, turn back again, that I may die in mine own city, and be buried by the grave of my father and of my mother" (2 Sam. xix. 37). At a far later day this profound love of country was no less deeply rooted in the Jewish heart. The Talmud's exaggerated expression, "Whoever is buried in the land of Israel is as if he were buried under the altar," is supplemented by the argument of one of the most ancient Hebrew commentaries, that "those who lay there were to be the first to 'walk before the Lord in the land of the living' (Ps. cxvi. 9), the first to rise from the dead, and to enjoy the days of the Messiah." The promise in Ezekiel, "O my people, I will open your graves, and bring you into the land of Israel. . . . Ye shall live, and I shall place you in your own land" (xxxvii. 12–14), was explained to mean that "God would make subterranean roads into the Holy Land, and when their dust reached it the Spirit of the Lord would raise them to new life."

XVI.

BURIAL AND MOURNING.

THERE were various modes of burial common to the Jews, and changes from time to time in their mortuary fashions; but these related chiefly to the wealthy. The poor of all ages seem to have been consigned to the earth in fulfilment of the penalty attending the first transgression: "In the sweat of thy face shalt thou eat bread, till thou return unto the ground; for out of it wast thou taken; for dust thou art, and unto dust shalt thou return" (Gen. iii. 19). Cemeteries were always outside the city walls in retired situations; but

ROCK-TOMBS IN SYRIA.

kings and prophets, as a mark of high honor, were sometimes buried within the city: thus David and his royal son Solomon were both buried in "the city of David" (1 Kings ii. 10; xi. 43), a fact well known to the apostles, and referred to by St. Peter in his sermon on the day of Pentecost: "Men and brethren, let me freely speak unto you of the patriarch David, that he is both dead and buried, and his sepulchre is with us unto this day" (Acts ii. 29). Ahaz was buried in Jerusalem (2 Chron. xxviii. 27); and his son Hezekiah was laid there, "in the chiefest of the sepulchres of the sons of David"

(2 Chron. xxxii. 33); and Samuel was buried " in his house in Ramah " (1 Sam. xxv. 1).

Without question, the place of public burying fullest of awful interest for us is that known as Aceldama, " the field of blood," near Jerusalem. It was purchased, according to St. Matthew, by the chief priests with the thirty pieces of silver which they had paid to Judas Iscariot for the betrayal of his Master. Judas, dismayed at the results of his treachery, returned the money to the Sanhedrim the morning after the arrest of our Lord in the garden, and, in the words of the Gospel, " he cast down the pieces of silver in the temple, and departed, and went and hanged himself.

TOMB OF DAVID.

And the chief priests took the silver pieces, and said, It is not lawful for to put them into the treasury, because it is the price of blood. And they took counsel, and bought with them the potter's field, to bury strangers in. Wherefore that field was called, The field of blood, unto this day" (Matt. xxvii. 5-8). St. Peter refers to this place of burial as a " field " purchased by this man (Judas) " with the reward of iniquity," which became forthwith the scene of his ignominious death; the circumstances being " known unto all the dwellers at Jerusalem " (Acts i. 18, 19). The most remarkable fact connected with this cemetery is the fulfilment of a prophecy contained in the Book of Zechariah (B.C. 772), which strangely forecasts the details of the purchase-money, and its ultimate disposition: " And I said unto them, If ye think good, give me my price; and if not, forbear. So they weighed for my price thirty pieces of silver. And the Lord said unto me, Cast it unto the potter: a goodly price that I was prized at of them. And I took the thirty pieces of silver, and cast them to the potter in the house of the Lord" (Zech. xi. 12, 13). St. Matthew attributes the prophecy to Jeremiah, — the second part of the Book of Zechariah being supposed by some commentators to have been written by that more famous prophet.

Private tombs consisted usually of a small stone house, without door or window, erected in a garden situated perhaps just outside the city limits, for a family mausoleum. Manasseh "was buried in the garden of his own house, in the garden of Uzza; and Amon, his son, was buried in his sepulchre" in the same garden (2 Kings xxi. 18, 26). A more primitive grave than these was the natural cave, such as Abraham bought, within the field of Machpelah for a burying-place, now covered by the great Mosque of Hebron, in which he buried Sarah, his wife (Gen. xxiii.); and where the patriarch himself was laid to rest, with, in course of time, Isaac and Rebekah, and Jacob and Leah (Gen. xlix. 31).

In after ages very elaborate and costly sepulchres were hewn out of the solid rock, above or below the level of the natural surface, or in the sides of mountains, and of one or more chambers. Niches were made in either side of the tomb for the reception of the dead; otherwise the bodies rested on the rocky floor. The usual size of these family sepulchres was six feet in length, nine feet wide, and ten feet high. Some were single graves; others contained niches for eight bodies. A larger size was made for thirteen sepultures. Isaiah alludes to these graves in the following passage: "Thou hast hewed thee out a sepulchre here, as he that heweth him out a sepulchre on high, and that graveth a habitation for himself in a rock" (xxii. 16). It will readily be seen that in cases of great necessity or danger these rocky chambers could become places of shelter and refuge for those who would defy the ceremonial uncleanness contracted by such contact. When Jesus came into the country of the Gadarenes, we are told that "immediately there met him out of the tombs a man with an unclean spirit, who had his dwelling among the tombs; and no man could bind him, no, not with

BURIAL AND MOURNING.

chains: whom he mercifully delivered from his legion of tormentors" (Mark v. 2, 3, 8). Recent travellers have frequently found these old tombs used as shops and dwellings. Many of the ancient rock-tombs and catacombs, defying the ravages of time, are still to be seen in Palestine. Among the most famous are the "tombs of the judges," the "tombs of Petra," the "tombs of the kings," and the Holy Sepulchre at Jerusalem. The custom of whitening all graves or sepulchres with lime to make them conspicuous, and thus to protect the Jewish passer-by from ceremonial defilement by contact or too near approach, is alluded to in the simile the Lord Jesus makes use of in his scathing exposure of the religious teachers of his day: "Woe unto you, scribes and Pharisees, hypocrites! for ye are like unto whited sepulchres, which indeed appear beautiful outward, but are within full of dead men's bones, and of all uncleanness" (Matt. xxiii. 27). It is still the practice in Palestine, both of Jews and Mohammedans, to whitewash the tombs.

The entrances to rock-tombs were guarded with massive stones, or stone doors swinging on hinges, or rather sockets into which the doors fitted above and below. Thus Joseph of Arimathea took the body of Jesus, "and laid it in his own new tomb, which he had hewn out in the rock: and he rolled a great stone to the door of the sepulchre" (Matt. xxvii. 60). It was of this stone that the women talked "among themselves" as they "came unto the sepulchre at the rising of the sun:" "Who shall roll us away the stone from the door of the sepulchre? And when they looked, they saw that the stone was rolled way: for it was very great" (Mark xvi. 4). The recorded fact that this "very great" stone was officially sealed to prevent any tampering — not cemented, as some have thought — seems to imply a massive stone door, or disk, or slab, which could be rolled into the groove made for its reception. St. John says of this hallowed tomb, "In the place where he was crucified there was a garden; and in the garden a new sepulchre, wherein was never man yet laid. There laid they Jesus therefore because of the Jews' preparation day; for the sepulchre was nigh at hand" (John xix. 41, 42).

Several Hebrew words for an ordinary grave, whether dug in the earth or in the rock, are translated "pit;" so that "to go down to the pit" became an expression equivalent to the popular idea of burial. Thus David says, "I am counted with them that go down into the pit" (Ps. lxxxviii. 4); and Hezekiah sings in thanksgiving for recovery from sickness, "For the grave cannot

AT THE TOMBS.

praise thee, death cannot celebrate thee; they that go down into the pit cannot hope for thy truth" (Isa. xxxviii. 18). Single graves, especially if not in a cemetery, were often marked with memorial columns, or in early times with rude heaps of stones. When Rachel, the beloved wife of Jacob, died in giving birth to Benjamin, and "was buried in the way to Ephrath, which is Bethlehem," her husband "set a pillar upon her grave" (Gen. xxxv. 19, 20). Josiah, in the midst of destroying and defiling the heathen altars, "spied the sepulchres" in the mountain, and asked of one of them. "What title is that I see? And the men of the city told him, It is the sepulchre of the man of God, which came from Judah. and proclaimed these things that thou hast done against the altar of Beth-el. And he said, Let him alone; let no man move his bones" (2 Kings xxiii. 17, 18).

The word "title" is in another text rendered "sign," and without doubt refers to a memorial tombstone. The "heap of stones" was a very ancient mode of marking the ignominious grave of some noted criminal, devoting his memory to popular execration. Achan and the king of Ai were thus buried at the command of Joshua (Josh. vii. 26; viii. 29); and Absalom, slain by Joab's armor-bearers, was cast "into a great pit in the wood," where a "very great heap of stones" was laid upon him; and to this day the passers-by, both Jew and Gentile, express their abhorrence of this rebellious son by casting stones at the monument in the Valley of Jehoshaphat, known as "Absalom's Tomb," and supposed to be that which the prince "reared up for himself" in the "king's dale: for he said, I have no son to keep my mind in remembrance" (2 Sam. xviii. 17, 18). In the history of the Maccabees' revolt, about 167 B.C., contained in the Apocrypha, there is particular mention of sepulchral memorials. Simon, one of the Jewish leaders, "built a monument upon the sepulchre of his father and his brethren, and raised it aloft to the sight, with hewn stone behind and before. Moreover, he set up seven pyramids, one against another, for his father, and his mother, and his brethren; and in these he made cunning devices, about the which he set great pillars, and upon the pillars he made all their armor for a perpetual memory" (1 Macc. xiii. 27-29), — a curious suggestion of heraldry.

In the East burial followed as quickly as possible upon the decease, not only on account of the climate, and the absence of all the modern means of surmounting that difficulty, but because of the ceremonial uncleanness contracted by even conventional contact with the dead as declared in the law: "He that toucheth the dead body of any man shall be unclean seven days. . . . When a man dieth in a tent all that come into the tent, and all that is in the tent, shall be unclean seven days" (Num. xix. 11, 14). In Persia, we are told, it is still customary to bury the body the second or third hour after death. It was usual in Palestine to bury a corpse on the day of death. It is inferred from the account of his sickness and interment, that Lazarus had been thus hastily buried (John xi. 3, 17); while Ananias and his wife Sapphira were carried out to burial immediately after they had been stricken down for their perfidy (Acts v. 6, 10).

The most imposing funeral rites recorded in the Bible were those in honor of Jacob, who, having been embalmed in Egypt, was taken to Canaan for burial. When Joseph undertook this solemn journey in obedience to his father's command, it is said that "with him went up all the servants of Pharaoh, the elders of his house, and all the elders of the land of Egypt, and all the house of Joseph, and his brethren, and his father's house: and there went up with him both chariots and horsemen: and it was a very great company. And they came to the threshing-floor of Atad, which is beyond Jordan; and there they mourned with a great and very sore lamentation: and he made a mourning for his father seven days" (Gen. l. 7–10). In this funeral there was all the "pomp and circumstance" of the Egyptian observances,— the procession of nobles and the hired mourners, the seventy days of mourning (a royal honor) before leaving the country of his adoption, and the "grievous mourning" at the floor of Atad, on account of which its name was changed to Abel-Mizraim ("meadow of Egypt"). But the Hebrew element of extreme simplicity was strikingly exemplified in the tomb to which all this very great company repaired with the body of the dead Jacob,— the "double cave" of Machpelah, the burying-place of Abraham's purchase. That the mighty prime minister of Pharaoh should consign his father to so mean a resting-place must

BURIAL AND MOURNING.

have been matter of extreme astonishment to these builders of pyramids.

The touching Gospel account of the funeral procession that wound out of the gate of Nain, — probably down the steep road which now leads toward the ancient sepulchral caves west of the village, — as our Lord and his disciples came nigh, gives us probably the most familiar idea of the ordinary mode of commit-

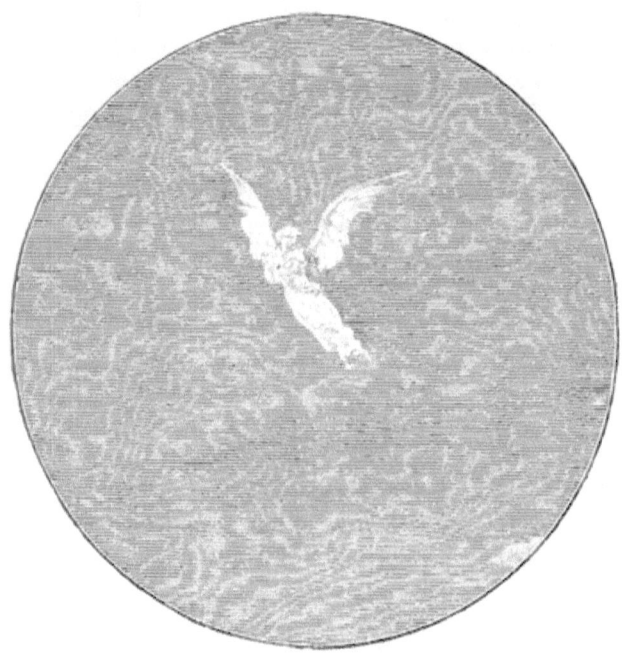

ting the dead to their "long homes" in that day. First in order came the women, according to an ancient commentary of the Jews, which explains, that, as "woman brought death into our world, she it is who ought to lead the way in a funeral procession." Among them, how easy for any one, much more the Lord, her Maker, to recognize the widow, about to hide away forever from her eyes an only son. Behind the bier followed "much people of the city," and last of all the hired mourners and the musicians, with their distracting and discordant wailing and piping. According to prevailing custom, our Lord and his companions should have joined the procession, and wept with them who wept, or shared in bearing the burden of the open bier on which lay the young man, "the only son of his mother, and she was a widow." The Apostle pauses in his record of this glorious miracle to emphasize the Saviour's compassion for this bereaved mother, whom he must comfort with a gentle "Weep not," though in a moment more he should place the dead son alive again in her arms. May he not at that moment have beheld, as in prophetic vision, the sorrows of that Virgin Mother for the death of her only Son, of which Simeon had testified, saying, "Yea, a sword shall pierce through thy own soul also"? (Luke ii. 35).

It was contrary to the law that a high priest should attend the funeral, or observe any of the customary rites of mourning for any relative, not even for his father or his mother; the priest might be "defiled" for his mother, father, son, daughter, brother, and unmarried sister, but for no other relation in life (Levit. xxi. 1–4, 10, 11).

In the time of Christ it was the custom, from the moment the body was carried out of the house, to reverse all chairs or couches, or seats of whatever sort. The mourners sat on the floor, except on the sabbath and on one hour of the Friday, the day of preparation, and on some feast-days in which "mourning" was prohibited. On the return of the family from the burial with their friends, they were served by their neighbors with a symbolical refreshment in earthen-ware, consisting of bread, hard-boiled eggs, and lentils. The friends and funeral guests, however, partook of a generous meal, but at which the supply of wine was limited to ten cups. These "cups" may have been a relic of the ancient custom referred to in Jeremiah: "Neither shall men give them" (the mourners) "the cup of consolation for their father or for their mother" (xvi. 6, 7). An allusion to funeral banquets is supposed to be found in the circumstance after Abner's death, as recorded in this text: "When all the people came to cause David to eat meat while it was yet day, David sware, saying, So do God to me, and more also, if I taste bread, or aught else, till the sun be down" (2 Sam. iii. 35); and Jeremy, in his Epistle, speaks of the priests in the temples of idols, who "roar and cry before their gods, as men do at the feast when one is dead" (Bar. vi. 32).

The Egyptians observed the custom of funeral feasts. They met at the house of the mourners, and ate the sacrifice or peace-offering,—a meal of meat, vegetables, bread, and drinks. The remains of this banquet were cast out to wild beasts: hence, on the tablets representing these scenes of sorrow, the jackal is styled, in hieroglyphics, "the devourer of what is set out for the dead." The ancient Greeks followed a similar custom. The friends of a bereaved family met, after the burial, at the house of mourning to eat together. The fragments of food that fell from the table were considered sacred, and were carried to the tomb, whence they would be taken by no one unless actually starving.

The son of Sirach, who brings much worldly philosophy to bear upon his admonitions of a higher wisdom, thus counsels in relation to these painful matters of human experience: "My son, let tears fall down over the dead, and begin to lament, as if thou hadst suffered great harm thyself; and then cover his body according to the custom, and neglect not his burial. Weep bitterly, and make great moan, and use lamentation, as he is worthy, and that a day or two, lest thou be evil spoken of: and then comfort thyself for thy heaviness. For . . . the heaviness of the heart breaketh strength" (Ecclus. xxxviii. 16–18).

WITH the return from the grave began the formal mourning, when the passionate expressions of grief, loud and demonstrative, before the burial, were, if possible, redoubled and intensified. The prescribed season for deep mourning was seven days, the first three of these being those

of "weeping," the others those of "lamentation." These being fulfilled, there followed a lighter mourning of thirty days or more, according to the nature of the bereavement. Under the Rabbis children mourned for their parents a whole year. The anniversary of the death of a relative was also to be kept; while, for a season, the Jewish "prayer for the dead" (not, however, intercessory in its character) was to be offered.

A recapitulation of the ceremonial of mourning during this period will indicate the elaborate character of these observances, as abundantly demonstrated in Scripture. Rending the clothes is perhaps the most ancient expression of grief, and the most frequently mentioned in the Bible: "Jacob rent his clothes, and put sackcloth upon his loins, and mourned for his son many days" (Gen. xxxvii. 34). "David took hold on his clothes, and rent them," and "mourned, and wept, and fasted until even, for Saul, and for Jonathan his son" (2 Sam. i. 11, 12).

And when tidings came to David that Absalom had slain all his royal brothers, "then the king arose, and tare his garments, and lay on the earth; and all his servants stood by with their clothes rent" (2 Sam. xiii. 31). Job, in his great bereavement of his sons and his daughters, "rent his mantle, and shaved his head, and fell down upon the ground, and worshipped" (i. 20). At the trial of Christ before Caiaphas, when the Lord asserted his divine sonship, "the high priest rent his clothes, saying, He hath spoken blasphemy; what further need have we of witnesses? behold, now ye have heard his blasphemy" (Matt. xxvi. 65). And at Lystra, when the people wished to sacrifice to St. Paul and St. Barnabas, the Apostles "rent their clothes," after the same ancient Jewish fashion.

In the politer period of the Rabbis the rending of the garments was a madness of grief no longer without method; for wife, son, daughter, brother, or sister, a bereaved Hebrew ripped his outer garment about four inches in a seam, which was sewed up again after the prescribed term of mourning. But, in the case of the loss of parents, this rent, with touching significance, was never closed.

The prophet Joel rebukes this custom of implied formality, when he exhorts Israel to repentance for national sins: "Now, saith the Lord, turn ye even to me with all your heart, and with fasting, and with weeping, and with mourning: and rend your heart, and not your garments, and turn unto the Lord your God · for he is gracious and merciful, slow to anger, and of great kindness" (Joel ii. 12, 13).

The wearing of sackcloth is often mentioned in connection with the rent clothes; as well as sprinkling the head and the person with ashes, dust, and earth, as Jeremiah eloquently exhorts: "O daughter of my people, gird thee with sackcloth, and wallow thyself in ashes: make thee mourning, as for an only son, most bitter lamentation" (vi. 26). The rejection of all fine clothing and of all ornaments; neglecting to bathe or anoint, or to pare the nails, or to eat any pleasant food, or to drink wine, are also mentioned.

A man shaved his head and his beard, sat on the ground, covered his head and his face, smote his breast and his thigh, put aside his phylacteries, refused to read the law or to engage in prayer, went barefoot. A woman, like Esther of the Apocrypha, "laid away her glorious apparel, and put on the garments of anguish and mourning; and, instead of precious ointments, she covered her head with ashes. . . . and all the places of her joy she filled with her torn hair;" or, if a widow, she would make, like Judith, "a tent upon the top of her house, and put on sackcloth upon her loins, and *would wear* her widow's apparel, fasting all the days of her widowhood. .

save the feasts and solemn days of the house of Israel" (Jud. viii. 5. 6).

The law — " Ye shall not cut yourselves, nor make any baldness between your eyes for the dead" (Deut. xiv. 1) — was, in later times, disobeyed by the Jews, who adopted this custom also from the heathen.

As if the bereaved could not be satisfied with their own expressions of sorrow, deeming them inadequate, the loud cries of the family were taken up, prolonged, and intensified by the shrill screams and artful wailing of the professional mourners, usually women, who constitute even yet a characteristic feature of Oriental mourning. To these Jeremiah alludes in his lamentation over the sin of his people : " Consider ye, and call for the mourning women, that they may come ; and send for cunning women, that they may come : and let them make haste, and take up a wailing for us, that our eyes may run down with tears, and our eyelids gush out with waters. . . . And teach your daughters wailing, and every one her neighbour lamentation " (ix. 17. 18. 20). And the preacher: " Man goeth to his long home, and the mourners go about the streets" (Eccles. xii. 5). Amos calls " such as are skilful of lamentation, to wailing" (v. 16); and when Jesus went to the house of Jairus, whose " little daughter" was " even now dead," he encountered these hired mourners, whom St. Matthew calls " the minstrels and the people making a noise" (ix. 23); and St. Mark describes their outcry as " the tumult, and them that wept and wailed greatly" (v. 38).

These women are described as having " their hair dishevelled, their clothes torn, their countenances daubed with paint and dirt ; as singing in a sort of chorus, mingled with shrill screams and loud wailing, distorting their limbs, swaying their bodies to and fro in a kind of melancholy dance to the thrumming music of tambourines." Their skill consists in the ingenuity with which they elicit increased cries of anguish from the family and friends ; recounting the virtues of the deceased, and lavishing upon him terms of tender endearment.

The "word of the Lord" to Jeremiah, prophesying grievous judgments upon the Jews, contains an admirable summary of these mortuary observances in the family: "Enter not into the house of mourning, neither go to lament nor bemoan them; both the great and the small shall die in this land; they shall not be buried, neither shall men lament for them, nor cut themselves, nor make themselves bald for them: neither shall men tear themselves for them in mourning, to comfort them for the dead; neither shall men give them the cup of consolation to drink for their father or for their mother" (Jer. xvi. 5-7).

And there is still another local picture of human mourning in the prophetical utterance, "A voice was heard in Ramah, lamentation, and bitter weeping; Rachel weeping for her children refused to be comforted for her children, because they were not" (Jer. xxxi. 15). Fulfilled some six centuries later by the massacre by Herod, wherein "all the children that were in Bethlehem, and in all the coasts thereof, from two years old and under," were slain (Matt. ii. 16). If Rachel was indeed buried at Ramah, as some authorities claim, with what additional and significant pathos is the familiar prophecy invested!

RACHEL'S TOMB.

The Bible affords no more pathetic example of parental bereavement than David's trial in the sickness and death of the beloved son of Bathsheba, accepted with humble submission to the will of God, whose law he had so recklessly broken: "The Lord struck the child that Uriah's wife bare unto David, and it was very sick. David therefore besought God for the child; and David fasted, and went in, and lay all night upon the earth. And the elders of his house arose, and went to him, to raise him up from the earth: but he would not, neither did he eat bread with them. And it came to pass on the seventh day, that the child died. And the servants of David feared to tell him that the child was dead; for they said, Behold, while the child was yet alive, we spake unto him, and he would not hearken unto our voice; how will he then vex himself, if we tell him that the child is dead? But when David saw that his servants whispered, David perceived that the child was dead: therefore David said unto his servants, Is the child dead? And they said, He is dead. Then David arose from the earth, and washed and anointed himself, and changed his apparel, and came into the house of the Lord, and worshipped: then he came to his own house, and when he required they set bread before him, and he did eat. Then said his servants unto him, What thing is this that thou hast done? thou didst fast and weep for the child, while it was alive; but when the child was dead, thou didst rise and eat bread. And he said, While the child was yet alive, I fasted and wept: for I said, Who can tell whether God will be gracious to me, that the child may live? But now he is dead, wherefore should I fast? can I bring him back again? I shall go to him, but he shall not return to me" (2 Sam. xii. 15–23).

Even sadder is the affliction of David in the death of his unworthy son Absalom; for shame, profound as his grief, added to the bitterness of natural sorrow. After a victorious battle with the rebels led by the young usurper, "the king said unto Cushi, Is the young man Absalom safe? And Cushi answered, The enemies of my lord the king, and all that rise against thee to do thee hurt, be as that young man is. And the king was much moved, and went up to the chamber over the gate, and wept: and as he went, thus he said, O my son Absalom! my son, my son Absalom! would God I had died for thee, O Absalom, my son, my son! . . . The king covered his face, and the king cried with a loud voice, O my son Absalom! O Absalom, my son, my son!" (2 Sam. xviii. 32, 33; xix. 4).

In view of all these recorded experiences of hopeless and

agonized grief for the dead, with what sublime simplicity of consolation are those words of the Apostle brought to the remembrance of the Christian mourner: "But I would not have you to be ignorant, brethren, concerning them which are asleep, that ye sorrow not, even as others which have no hope. For if we believe that Jesus died and rose again, even so them also which sleep in Jesus will God bring with him" (Thess. iv. 12, 14).

The antiquity of ceremonial mourning is shown in that which Abraham made for his wife who died in Hebron. In the words of the sacred history, "Abraham came to mourn for Sarah, and to weep for her" (Gen. xxiii. 2); indicating a formal manifestation of sorrow in her honor. Of this sort was the "grievous mourning," a "great and very sore lamentation," that Joseph made "for his father seven days," supplementary to the seventy days' mourning in Egypt, immediately following the death of Jacob. King David formally bewailed the murder of Abner. "He followed the bier, and they buried Abner in Hebron, and the king lifted up his voice and wept at the grave of Abner; and all the people wept, and the king lamented over Abner, and said, Died Abner as a fool dieth? Thy hands were not bound, nor thy feet put into fetters: as a man falleth before wicked men, so fellest thou. And all the people wept again over him" (2 Sam. iii. 31–35).

Thus the prophet honored the devout king of Judah at his funeral. "Jeremiah lamented for Josiah: and all the singing men and the singing women spake of Josiah in their lamentations to this day, and made them an ordinance in Israel" (2 Chron. xxv. 25). But the Lord forbade ceremonial burial to Jehoiakim, the reprobate son of Josiah: "They shall not lament for him, saying, Ah my brother! or, Ah sister! they shall not lament for him, saying, Ah lord! or, Ah his glory! He shall be buried with the burial of an ass, drawn and cast forth beyond the gates of Jerusalem" (Jer. xxii. 18, 19). To descend, however, from the mourning made for kings to that of affectionate hearts for a faithful servant, it is pleasant to recall, that, after carrying her mistress's grandchildren in her bosom, Deborah, Rebekah's nurse, was buried at Bethel under an oak, with so much grief that ever after the tree was called *Allon-backuth*, the "oak of weeping" (Gen. xxxv. 8).

The roof of the house was frequently made the scene of formal mourning: thus, in the "Burden of Moab," Isaiah declares of Kir, the fortified city, "in their streets they shall gird themselves with sackcloth: on the tops of their houses, and in their streets, every one shall howl, weeping abundantly" (Isa. xv. 3). In Persia it is even now the custom for a priest to declaim from the housetop in pathetic language the virtues of the deceased, and to depict the sorrow of the survivors, who, in their turn, respond by frantic demonstrations of anguish, beating the breast, and tearing their garments; the women plucking out their hair by handfuls, and throwing dust or ashes upon their heads. They even covered themselves with coarse brown sackcloth, the garb of slaves when offered for sale, which was also the Jewish mourning attire.

THE WAILING-PLACE WALL OF JERUSALEM.

Among the impressive sights of Jerusalem for the traveller, none perhaps is sadder than the Wailing-place of the Jews, which affords probably the only example of national ceremonial mourning in the world. The resident Hebrews assemble every Friday at the base of the wall of their ancient Temple in the Valley of the Tyropean, and with prayers and tears bewail before God the fallen glory of his chosen people. The formal lamentation consists of chanting certain appropriate portions of Scripture, such as the words of Isaiah: "Be not wroth very sore, O Lord, neither remember iniquity forever: behold, see, we beseech thee, we are all thy people. Thy holy cities are a wilderness, Zion is a wilderness, Jerusalem a desolation. Our holy and our beautiful house, where our fathers praised thee, is burned up with fire: and all our pleasant things are laid waste" (Isa. lxiv. 9–11); and those of the Psalmist: "O God, the heathen are come into thine inheritance; thy holy temple have they defiled; they have laid Jerusalem on heaps. Pour out thy wrath upon the heathen that have not known thee, and upon the kingdoms that have not called upon thy name. For they have devoured Jacob, and laid waste his dwellingplace. O remember not against us former iniquities; let thy tender mercies speedily prevent us; for we are brought very low" (Ps. lxxix. 1, 6–8). This touching custom is very old; and during periods of foreign oppression the Jews maintained it only by paying a heavy tax for the precious privilege of touching and kissing the stones of their once glorious sanctuary. In the reign of Constantine the expelled race were allowed to enter the city only once a year to wail over the ruined Temple.

TEAR-BOTTLES.

The once almost universal use of lachrymatories, or tear-bottles, by Oriental mourners of whatever nation, except perhaps the Jews, seems now to be confined to the Persians, who bottle up the tears of those who weep for the dead, not only as a mark of affection, but for certain superstitious notions as to their efficacy to revive the dying, and to drive off malign influences. The mode in which this curious collection of tears is made is described by Morier: "It is the custom for a priest to go about to each person at the height of his grief, with a piece of cotton in his hand, with which he carefully collects the falling tears, and which he then squeezes into a bottle, preserving them with the greatest caution." These tear-bottles were made of glass or earthenware, and of various shapes, though usually broad at the base, with long, funnel-shaped necks. They are found in almost all ancient tombs, having been buried with their dead as a token of sorrowing love.

It is easy to connect with this custom the words of the Psalmist: "Thou tellest my wanderings: put thou my tears into thy bottle" (lvi. 8); but there is no positive evidence of the use of lachrymatories by the Hebrews, and the allusion is supposed to be to their well-known practice of putting away articles of value in small bags or "bottles" of leather.

The royal Preacher expressed perfectly the popular sentiment of Jewry when he wrote, "It is better to go to the house of mourning, than to go to the house of feasting: for that is the end of all men; and the living will lay it to his heart" (Eccles. vii. 2); and we find its echo in apostolic days in the Epistle of St. James: "Pure religion and undefiled before God and the Father is this, To visit the fatherless and widows in their affliction, and to keep himself unspotted from the world" (i. 12); and again in St. Paul's injunction to "weep with them that weep" (Rom. xii. 15), at the same time exhorting the mourner to a lively faith in Christ and "the power of his resurrection," that they may "weep as though they wept not" (1 Cor. vii. 30). The utmost punctiliousness was observed by the Jews in the visits of condolence to a bereaved family during their period of mourning. The nearest relations accompanied them to the grave on the three "days of weeping," to be nearer to the beloved dead, in accordance with the rabbinical theory that the spirit did not finally leave the body until the completion of the third day after death.

In this connection there is a curious coincidence, if no more, in the prophetic words of the Psalmist: "My flesh also shall rest in hope. For thou wilt not leave my soul in hell; neither wilt thou suffer thine Holy One to see corruption" (xvi. 10); and the fulfilment of this Scripture, as announced by St. Peter on the day of Pentecost in his commentary on this text: "He" (David) "seeing this before, spake of the resurrection of Christ, that his soul was not left in hell, neither his flesh did see corruption" (Acts ii. 31). "He suffered and was buried; on the third day he rose from the dead." The fourth day was one of peculiar lamentation, multiplied by the dramatic arts of the professional mourners and musicians.

It was on the fourth day after the death of Lazarus, that the Jewish friends and relations "which were with her in the house, and comforted her, when they saw Mary, that she rose up hastily and went out, followed her, saying, She goeth unto the grave to weep there." And on the same day at the grave Martha ventured indirectly to oppose the Lord's command, "Take ye away the stone," by the significant reminder, "For he hath been dead four days" (John xi. 31, 39). Going "to the grave to weep there" is a very common indulgence of grief among Orientals at this day. It is especially observed by the women, who do not take part in the funeral procession, only setting up the *tahlil*, or death-cry, as it leaves the house, but who afterward visit the grave to mourn over it in funeral dance and mournful wailing.

The Rabbis, who brought even the ministrations of sympathy and love to a very fine point of formalism, were not necessarily lacking in either delicacy or shrewdness, as many of their prescriptions prove. In dictating rules for visits of condolence, they came boldly to the relief, one might almost say rescue, of those mourners to whom the injudicious tongue of some loquacious visitor would be as salt applied to a fresh wound. It was ordered that the recently bereaved were not to be tormented by talk; more than this, it was an obligation of the etiquette of sorrow upon a visitor not to speak until addressed by the immediate objects of sympathy. Lest the silence should become oppressive, — and this supposes a period succeeding the excited ceremonial demonstrations, — a "fixed formula of comfort" was spoken by a leader of devotions, or some experienced friend. Tradition holds that there was a special gate in the Temple by which mourners passed in to their devotions, not without a word of consolation from a Levite official.

There is much to compel our admiration in these practices of a religious faith, so perverted and distorted that it is difficult to recognize in its teachers the seed of Abraham, the father of the faithful; but alas for the blessedness of them that mourned, if they looked for comfort to the "doctrines of men" as promulgated by the Rabbis before and after the coming of our Redeemer! "Never," says Edersheim, "are the voices of the Rabbis more discordant, and their utterances more contradictory or unsatisfying, than in view of the great problems of humanity, — sin, sickness, death, and the hereafter."

The final conclusions at which Rabbinism arrived were not the pardon and peace of the gospel, but labor, with the dreadful "perhaps" of reward. To sum up the message of the synagogue: "Work, righteousness, and study of the law are the surest key to heaven. There is a kind of purgation after death; or, according to some, the annihilation of the wicked. All Israel have share in the world to come: the pious among the Gentiles also have part in it. Only the perfectly just enter at once into paradise: all the rest pass through a period of purification and perfection, variously lasting, up to one year. But notorious breakers of the law, and especially apostates from the Jewish faith, and heretics, have no hope whatever, either here or hereafter."

We can conceive with what triumphant joy in the reception of the truth St. Paul — learned hitherto only in these traditions and inconsistent theories of the fathers — hastened to declare the good tidings to all who, like him, had "sat in darkness;" to make known to Jew and Gentile the "appearing of our Saviour Jesus Christ, who hath abolished death, and hath brought life and immortality to light through the gospel" (1 Tim. i. 10); and to "deliver them, who through fear of death were all their lifetime subject to bondage" (Heb. ii. 15).

It is necessary to dwell upon this perverted state of religious things in Palestine during the ministry of our Lord, to comprehend the fierce indignation of the false, bigoted, self-righteous teachers of the synagogue at the presentation of the Truth, pure from its Divine Source; while, on the contrary, the fathers and mothers and children of the land, "the common people," perishing for the "words of eternal life," "heard him gladly" (Mark xii. 37).

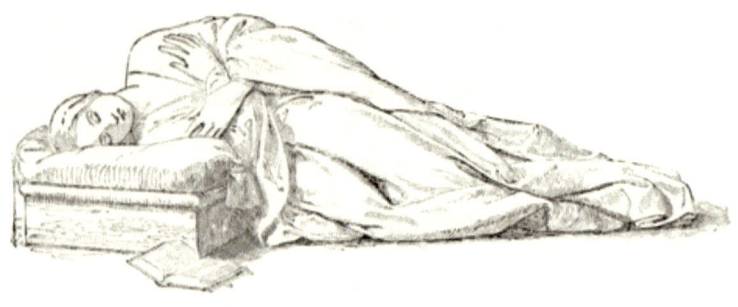

Index.

INDEX.

ABEL, first keeper of sheep, killed by his brother Cain, 332.
Abraham, "sat in the tent-door, in the heat of the day," when the Lord appeared to him in the plains of Mamre, 12.
Absalom, fate of, 350.
Academies, established for lads of sixteen or eighteen, 129.
Aceldama, field of blood, 381.
"A day's journey," generally about twenty miles, 271.
"A sabbath day's journey," about three-fourths of a mile, 271.
Ahab, house of ivory made by, 15.
Ahasuerus, king, description of feast given by, 23; court of, 248; purification of maidens destined for the harem of, 248.
Ahaziah, King of Samaria, 26, 36, 37.
Alabaster, a kind of soft white marble, easily carved, and susceptible of a high polish, — so called from Alabastron, an Egyptian town. 237.
Aleppo, an entire village of houses, near, with the conical roof, 18.
Alexandria, synagogue of, gorgeous in displays of architecture, 287.
Allon-backuth, "oak of weeping," 396.
Almsdeeds, enjoined by the law, and inculcated by parental exhortation; a prominent feature in the Jewish religion, 300; Christ's instruction to the people concerning, 304, certain rules upon receiving, 311; the law and gospel of, 311.
Amos, speaks of dwellings of unusual luxury built of hewn stone, 15; of ivory, 15; sycamore fruit gathered by, 196.
Animals, palace of Herod Antipas destroyed because decorated with representations of, 33.
Anointing, a common practice, but formerly used only on religious occasions, 235; act of, symbolical of luxury, of joy; omission of, denoted mourning, 236; omission to anoint guests construed as an insult, 237.
Apparel, festal robes presented to guests on all occasions of magnificent entertainment, especially at marriage-feasts; to reject one of these considered an insult, 76.
Apple, what fruit meant by, not known; in Hebrew signifies "breathing forth;" rare in the Holy Land, 200.
Ark, taken by the Philistines, 40; a strong box or coffer, 391.
Armenia, original birthplace of the Eastern grape-vine, 325.
Ass, superseded camel for daily use; most esteemed possession; milk used as a diet and for medicinal purposes; used for riding by ladies, 349; the wild, a deer-like creature, very spirited; flesh unclean to Jews; Assyrian sculptures represent the chase of the wild, described by Xenophon, 350.
Athaliah, 36.
Avims, cities dwelt in by, 2.

BABEL, tower of, three ruins present equal claims to; one an oblong mass, one hundred and ten feet high, 13.
Babylon, built by Nebuchadnezzar, 19.
Balaam, Spirit of God came upon, in beholding "Israel abiding in his tents, according to their tribes," 12.

Balm, a universal medicine, "Is there no balm in Gilead?" 369.

Balsam, one of the most esteemed of Oriental remedies, 369.

Baskets, of common use, made of wicker or rushes, and of various shapes and colors; white, mentioned in history of Joseph, 48; sometimes made of metal and rope; of dignified interest to us, 49.

Bathing, frequent, a necessity, owing to heat, costume, and custom; running water preferred for, 241; favorite mode of Eastern; frequent washing of the hands essential, at meals for example, 242; method of washing the hands, 246.

Baths, public, erected at great cost, favorite lounging-places, similar to the modern clubs; distinctive feature of Mosaic code; rendered symbolical, 241.

Beans, very unlike those known to us by the same name, 182.

Beard, care of the, an object of special veneration to the Jew, 227; absence of, denoted grief; Egyptian custom of, a decided contrast to Jewish, 228.

Beds, simple mats or padded quilts, 36; description of Solomon's, 38; of an Oriental, 38; "beds of gold and silver" in Book of Esther, 38; "dinner-beds," 159.

Bedstead, mentioned only once in the Bible, 37; of wood and metal, common among the Egyptians, as their sculptures testify, 38.

Beggars form a large part of the community in Oriental lands, 310.

Belts, their use, 209.

Bethany, "house of dates," 196.

Bethphage, "house of green figs," 196.

Boaz, 166, 195, 300, 322.

Bonnets and hoods, simple adornments for the head, 210.

Books, earliest, were written on linen or cotton cloth, on skins, or on leaves made of the papyrus, description of, 130; modern, made of sheets bound together at the back, description of, 131; valuable cases for, as in the Koran, 131; description of Rabbinical, 137.

Bottles, used in great variety, and made of metal, earthenware, or wood; the more primitive made of skins; shape of animal distinguishable in, 47; simile of our Lord concerning, 48; skin still used throughout the East for, and in some parts of Spain, 48.

Bread, principal food of an Oriental, 43; process of baking, 43.

Bread-making, 165.

Bricks, Egyptian, made of clay, moistened with water, 14; used for ordinary buildings, but stone for large public works, as reservoirs and quays, 14; stamped with name of reigning sovereign, 14; manufacture of, a fatiguing task; a penance, 14; depicted in an ancient fresco from Thebes, 14.

Brides, adornment of, 78; appearance before husband, imaged to him heretofore only in dreams, 78; one-tenth of the dowry of, appropriated to perfumes, 78.

British Museum, the Rosetta Stone in a famous example of writing on stone, 134.

Burial, various modes of; changes in from time to time, relating chiefly to the wealthy, 380; followed quickly after death, 385.

Butter, 182; unlike modern, 182; churning of, 183; combined with honey,—a favorite combination, 183.

Butter and milk, 182.

CAIN, builded a city, 2.

Calamus, or reed pen, introduced, 139.

Camel, earliest mention of as a domesticated animal, commonly enumerated among possessions of wealthy patriarchs, 346; trained for conveyance of merchandise, or for personal convenience; examples of its use, 346; not used for food, 349.

Cana, marriage feast at, 47, 77.

Canaan, land of, 5.

Canaanites, cities of; great and goodly, 5.

Candlestick, or lamp-stand, of various forms, often very beautiful in design and workmanship; of brass, silver, bronze, or even gold; wood for common people, 40; that familiar to us as an illustration in the Sermon on the Mount, 41.

Captivity, time of, 68, 126.

Capua, noted for the effeminate manners of its people, 230.

Carts, Egyptian, 314.

Caves, earliest dwellings known to man, 9; used for temporary refuge, 10; found in the calcareous ledges, or artificially made, 10.

Cereals, various preparations of, 165; corn, in Bible, a general name for all kinds of; no grain in Palestine to correspond to our Indian corn; parched corn, 166.

Chairs, very general among early Hebrews, who were slow to adopt the effeminate custom of reclining on cushions, 40.

Chambers, 24; those over the gate projected beyond the original structure, and were supplied with windows, 25.

Chariots, drawn by horses, formed an important part of martial equipments of the Egyptians; David first to introduce into Hebrew warfare, 354.

Cheese, common article of food; imported for epicures; mentioned but three times in Bible, 184.

Children, training and schooling of; the expectation with which Israel waited for the promised Messiah made a numerous offspring a coveted blessing; no greater misfortune to a Hebrew than to die childless; nine words for, expressive of successive states of development, besides the general terms *ben* and *bath* (son and daughter), demonstrating parental affection, 92, 93; first-born son of every Jewish family regarded with peculiar homage and affection, 93; in the absence or death of father, the male officiated as priest of the family, until priesthood was delegated exclusively to tribe of Levi; blessing an important feature of birthright of; sons inherited father's property to exclusion of daughters, 94; matters of family inheritance fixed by law; no wills, on account of inborn reverence for law, 95; name-days for, optional among different nations, 102; sports of, are the same the world over, 110; only mention in Bible of, is made by Christ to exemplify perverseness of Jews, 110; instances of, 111; training and schooling of; religious discipline before scholastic; testimony of Josephus; law very emphatic in its commands to parents to teach the commandments of the Lord to; course of study required at the age of six or seven, 121; the habit of early instruction in religion, 121, 122; a simple rudimentary education considered sufficient for girls; means of teaching, 126; position occupied by teacher and pupil; provision for the poor, 128.

Chimneys, in allusion to, the same Hebrew word is used that in other parts of Scripture is translated "window," 31.

Christ, preaching of, 289; restoring the temple to its proper use, 310.

Christian, emancipation of the, 163.

Chronology, wonderful instances of protracted years, 366.

Circumcision, 101.

Cisterns, Palestine abounded in; remains of still exist; description of; used as dungeons, 359; of immense size; used as hiding-places, 360.

Cities, collections of tents or huts, 2; temporary abiding-places, 5; walled, taken by the Israelites, 5; not always of stone, but built of combustible materials, 5.

Cithern, 206.

City gates, places of popular meeting, 6; supplied with tower, 9; little door in, for admission of belated travellers, referred to by the Saviour in the passage, "It is harder for a camel," etc., 9; narrow and difficult to pass through; "Enter ye in at the strait gate," 9.

Climate of the Holy Land, one of the most wholesome in the world, 365.

Clothing, perfumed, universal, 235.

Cnidus, women of, 132.

Columns, memorial, 384, 385.

Concubines, differed from wives, 54; rights of, carefully protected by law, 57.

Conical roofs, houses with, 18.

Corn, a general name in the Bible for all kinds of cereals, 166.

Cosmetics, use of, prevailed in connection with the bath, 248.

Courts, places of living and recreation, paved with rare marbles, or laid out in gardens, 22; places of entertainment, 23; in which are erected altars, 23.

Cow, held sacred by Egyptians, 168; fatted calf esteemed the choicest dish by the Hebrew, 168.

Crisping-pins, 222.

Crown of King Solomon, presented to him

by his mother, on day of his espousals, 78; another, called the dodos, 80.
Culture, grape, commenced by Noah, 324; table-lands and mountain-slopes selected as choice sites for, 325; an ancient method of, 325.
Cummin and fitches, plants raised for their small seeds; threshed with a rod or flail, 322.
Customs of women, 147-149; Persian, 355; funeral, 388.
Cuttle-fish, sepia made from, 140.
Cymbals, instruments of percussion, as the cistrum and timbrel; St. Paul refers to the clanging accompaniment of, 297.

Damascus, the oldest city in the world, 2; a wealthy city, 22.
Dancing, act of triumphant worship; had no part in festivities, except in their connection with religious feasts, 284; of damsels at Feast of Harvest, and close of Day of Atonement; sometimes participated in by men only, as in Feast of Tabernacles, 286; formed a prominent feature in religious ceremonies of Egyptians, 286.
Daniel, the pious Israelite, worshipped on the housetop, 19.
Dates, the fruit of the palm-tree; a rich source of profit, 199; some eaten fresh, and others saved for household stores, 199; yield a rich sirup, 200.
David, his preparation for the temple; sings of "the ivory palaces," 15; at eventide walked on the roof, 19; devout asseveration of, 36; apt simile of, 48; honey described by, 184; player on the harp, sent for from court to soothe the melancholy of the king, 293; triumph of, 335, 336; his pathetic example of parental bereavement, 393, 394; affliction of, in the death of his unworthy son Absalom, 394.
Day of rest, seventh, its early institution, 256; description of, 257; keeping it holy, 258; Rabbinical rules for, 258, 259.
Dead, the, preparation of, 375, 376; contact with, declared unclean, 386.
Death, of the head of the family, 371; according to tradition, 368; sorts of, 372.
Devotion, ceremonial, the period succeeding, 399, 400.

Dibs, a sirup obtained by boiling down the juice of grapes, 192.
Divination, methods of, 261, 262; all these practices prohibited to the Hebrews in the words of the law, 262.
Divorce, formed a subject of special inquiry to the Great Teacher, showing its popularity, 85; obtained on very trivial grounds; Mosaic law of, 86; St. Paul's advice on, a knowledge of pagan society to appreciate, 87; no case of, recorded in Old Testament, notwithstanding the facility of, 88; inspired religious feeling on the subject of, 88.
Doors, street, of heavy wood or stone, and kept locked in charge of a porter; peculiarity of opening; porter of, summoned with a "knocker;" description of porch connected with street; secured by locks, frequently depicted in Egyptian sculptures, 28; portal inscriptions in use among ancient Egyptians and Jews, 30.
Doors, gates of, made low to prevent horsemen from entering through porch to court-yard, and unattractive to divert attention of covetous, 29; proverb of Solomon in regard to, 29.
Dress, veil, distinguishing feature, and its signification; every-day attire of both sexes described; description of the "coat," 203; use of cloak, 204; description of the cloak and its borders, 204, 205; excesses indulged in; warning to women converts on, 218; fashionable men subject to rebuke concerning, 219.
Dulcimer, a sort of bagpipe, 297.
Dwellings, caves in the earth or mud huts, 9; inhabited by the Horites (dwellers in caves of the earth), 9; usually used as temporary habitations, 10; superior to common hut or tent, 10; places of refuge, 10; private, of Oriental cities, external appearance very plain, 17, 18; flat roof predominant in, 18; houses of the better class built in form of cloister, those of wealthy with several, 22; description of the verandas of, 23, 24.
Dyeing, art of, 206; Phœnicians excelled in, 207; instances of the result of, 207.

Edar, Tower of, Tower of the Flock, near Bethlehem, station for shepherds,

resting-place only for consecrated flocks, 338, 339.
Eden, first home mentioned in the Bible, 1; too beautiful to be pictured, 1.
Edna, 71.
Egypt, pictorial monuments of, a royal monopoly, represent the process of the manufacture of bricks, 14.
Eli, 40.
Elisha, entertainment to, 40; pot of oil miraculously multiplied by, for the destitute widow, 47.
Elijah, message of, to the guilty Ahaziah, 36; "little cake" begged by, from the widow woman of Zarephath, 43.
Esaias, 132.
Examinations, *post-mortem*, first made in Egypt, 368.
Exchange, city gates general place of, 6.
Exhortation by the wise men of Israel, 84.
Eyelids and eyebrows, painting the, with kohl, an ancient fashion, 249; of great popularity as early as the time of Job, 250.

FARMING, chief occupation from Adam to Noah, 312, 313.
Feasts, marriage, and those made on other occasions; times of rejoicing, and magnificent demonstrations, 74-76; governor of, necessary, 76; duties of governor of, 77; given by the bridegroom, 77; the three great, commanded to be celebrated, 267, 273; modes of travelling to the, 267; luxury of chariot enjoyed only by rich in travelling to the, 268; Tabernacles, 277-279; Purim and Dedication, 280, 281; only, of Mosaic obligation was the great Day of Atonement, commanded as a statute forever, 281-283; funeral, 389.
Feet, covering of the, of the rudest sort; description of sandals, 214; slippers of costly fabric, 217; to go barefoot, a token of mourning or humiliation, 217; customs in regard to the, 218.
Fenced city, enclosed by ditch or wall, 2; built by Cain, 2; character of, 5.
Figs, a staple product; two kinds only named; description of; esteemed for medicinal properties, 196.
Filicaja, Italian poet, lines of, 106.
Fish, favorite article of food, 174, 177; a watchword, 178.

Fishing, an important industry, owing to the abundance of fish; how pursued, 174; whole subject of, interesting to Bible-lovers, 177.
Fitches and cummin, plants raised for their small seeds; threshed with a rod or flail, 322.
Flagon, means cake of compressed raisins, 192.
Food, 163-169.
Fountains, perpetual and abounding, many contain medicinal properties; spiritual allusions to, abound, 363.
Fruits, Holy Land abounded in; varieties of; grape the principal kind of; soil and climate adapted to culture of the grape, 184; figs, dates, and pomegranates among the most important, 195.
Fowl, only mention of, 169; introduced by the Romans into Judæa, 169.
Furniture, 34; coarse carpet, thin mattresses and pillows, low stand for dinner-table, the universal hand-mill, rude pottery and wooden spoons for the poor, 35; the inventory of the rich scarcely surpassed, except in value, 35; Egyptian carpenters skilful in manufacture of, especially veneering, 39.

GAD and Reuben, tribes of, 2; cities of, 5.
Games, unlike the young Greek and Roman, the Jewish youth had no public; opposed to religious bias of Hebrew character; theatres considered disreputable, 112.
Garments, description of outer; changeable suits of apparel; wimples, 208, 209; fine linen, 210; rending of, no longer without method, 391.
Gates, imposing structures, very strong, 6; places of popular concourse, judgment-seats, halls of debate, and general trading exchanges, 6; city, supplied with one tower, often with two, 9.
Gaza, Samson's exploit at, 3.
Gethsemane, garden of, kind of lamps used in, 42.
Gideon, mighty man of valor, 58.
Gilead, cities of, 5.
Goats, sometimes pastured with sheep; characteristics different from sheep; necessary to divide them, 340.
Grain, receptacles for, 323.

Grain-harvest, 320.
Grape, cultivated extensively, 184; red and black fruit only, produced, except the white grape of Sorek; juice of, called blood, translated "red wine," 187; prized in Egypt, 191.
Grape-vine, first found in Armenia, 325.
Grave, several Hebrew words for an ordinary grave are translated "pit," 384.
Guitar, known to us as the cittern, of Greek origin, 296.
Gymnasium, a place for training, 114.

Habakkuk, inspired words of, 364.
Hair-dressing, elaborate, a common practice; expensive wigs common; also the plaiting of the hair, 229; scented pomades and oils a great favorite; no less than ten varieties used, 229; *coiffeur* excelled that of to-day, 230.
Hand-mills, universally found in an Eastern kitchen, 44; consisted of two circular stones, the "upper" and "nether" millstones; method of working, 45; cessation of sound of mill-stones, a general ruin, 45; Egypt employed the mortar and pestle only, 45; worked by women; process very tedious and laborious, 45; imposed as a punishment on prisoners of war, 45.
Harp, description of the, 295, 296.
Harvest, the feast of, 277.
Hazerim, meaning of, 2.
Head-dresses, horned, 209.
Healing, the art of, cultivated in Israel, 366.
Hearths, first mention made by Abraham on the plains of Mamre; in this case the hot stones on which bread was baked; generally a portable furnace, used in Eastern apartments to this day; such was the one into which King Jehoiakim threw the leaves of Jeremiah's prophecy, 31; an oven, 43.
Hebrews, adopted at an early period the flat roof, in accordance with their protective code, 18; the last desire of the, 379.
Henna, a plant from which dye is made, 249.
Herdsman, suffers by comparison with his gentler fellow-laborer the shepherd; first hear of him in connection with quarrels about the possession of pasturage, 341;

in a royal household the position one of dignity; Solomon's charge, 342.
Herod Antipas, the palace of, destroyed because decorated with representations of animals, 33.
Herod the Great, erected theatres in Jerusalem, 112; funeral ceremonies of, 376.
Herodotus, description of sheep by, 337.
History of earrings, bracelets, and anklets, 220; instances of their use, 221.
Holofernes, the chief captain of the Assyrian hosts, 38; bed of, 38; bidding of, in regard to Judith, 163.
Home, first mention of, 2.
Home discipline, did not err on side of weak indulgence; profound reverence for parental authority enforced both by law and family rule; relation between parents and children typical of that between the Almighty Father and his chosen people, 115; no crime regarded with more horror than any breach of the "commandment with promise;" crimes against parents unknown; terrible duty exacted from parents on account of a rebellious son, 116; son his own master from the time he could support himself, 116; daughter subject to father until marriage, 117; forbidden to chastise a grown-up child, on pain of excommunication; decided amelioration of the rigor exercised in the more orthodox period; severe examples of, 119.
Honey, how partaken of, 183, 184.
Hoods and bonnets, 210, 213.
Horites, cave-dwellers, 9.
Horse, now so prized in the East, was not known before the reign of Solomon; allusions to, in Scripture, are in battle, 353; description of the, 353, 354; trappings almost identical with the present; never shod, 355.
Houses, description of dedication of, 32; woodwork of various materials in, 32; elaborate carving in, 32; profuse veneering of ivory in, in the reign of Solomon, 33; no reproduction of any living creature permitted in the Jewish, 33; reception-rooms in, on ground floor, opening into court, 35.
Hunter and fowler, arts of, studied at first for food, but afterwards for recreation,

INDEX. 411

170; spoils of, in great demand, 173; consisted of wild goats, gazelles, hares, wild geese and ducks, teal, quails, partridges, etc., 173.

Hygiene, favorable; due to mode of life, 365.

IMPLEMENTS, necessarily simple; description of; symbolic, 317; sickle like modern; scythe unknown, 319.

Inkhorn, spoken of but once in the Bible; receptacle for writing-materials; description of, 140.

Inks, for brilliancy and durability have never been equalled; commonest made of pulverized charcoal, or ivory or lamp black mixed with gum and water; Greeks used ink similar to our India ink; kind of, used by the Romans; colored; invisible; use of red and green, mentioned frequently in New Testament; black, 140.

Instruments, musical, classed under three heads, — wind, stringed, and those of percussion; organ, pipe, and flute earliest and simplest of; pipe especially appropriate for occasions of merrymaking; the horn and cornet, 294; trumpets; harps regarded of first importance, 295; decree of Nebuchadnezzar, 297.

Invitations, double; of very ancient origin, frequent allusions to, in Scripture narrative; to rich and poor, friends and strangers, in name of charity, 74; made by women; a similar custom of, in Egypt; in days of Christ, made by men, 75.

Irrigation, methods of artificial, 314.

Isaac, prototype of Saviour, 120.

Isaiah apostrophizes the doomed city, 45; prophecy of, 183.

Israel, Psalmist of; immortal song of, 364; children of, take possession of Canaan, 5; dwelt in tents or booths during their forty-years' wandering in the wilderness, 13.

Israelites, favorite dish with, 181.

Ivory, houses built of, 15.

JABAL, father of such as dwell in tents, 9.

Jacob, imposing funeral rites of; death of, 386; resting-place of, 386.

Jael, wife of Heber the Kenite, smote Sisera; blessed above women, as sung by Deborah and Barak, 11; kind of butter given by, to Sisera, 182.

Jehoiakim, 131.

Jehosheba, 37.

Jeremiah describes, by inference, "a wide house and large chambers," with windows, "ceiled with cedar and painted with vermilion," 15; ceiled houses described in, 33; basket alluded to by, 48; ornaments alluded to by, 78, 92, 139; cast into a pit, 359; refers to the *materia medica* of Egypt, 369; words of the Lord to, 393.

Jericho, the house of Rahab in, the hiding-place of the Hebrew spies, 20; the city of palm-trees, 196.

Jerusalem, the Lord's love for, expressed in an allegory, 79; abominations of, 99; description of books in, 131; charitable women in, 188; victorious entry of our Lord into, 196; hospitality of, 272.

Jews, fond of names with significations; doubtful if any pure Hebrew name is lacking in that distinctive feature of, 102; instances from Bible of names of, 102, 103; sacred custom of, 105.

Joachim, husband of the chaste Susanna, and Uriah the Hittite, places of the bath, 23.

Joash, 37.

Job refers to clay walls; describes creation of the sea, by a metaphor, 100; allusion found in, to three ancient methods of preserving records, 132; gave his daughters "inheritance among their brethren;" speaks of "an iron pen," 139; property of, 341.

Joel, a prophet, 391.

Joppa, vision of Peter from house-top in, 164.

Joram, 37.

Joshua, 133.

Journey, a day's, 271; a sabbath day's, 271.

Judah, sin of, 225.

Judas, 42.

Judith, toilet of, 251; Holofernes slain by, 38; story of, 163.

KEYS, large and clumsy, ordinarily of wood, 29; very ancient, shaped like a sickle, and carried on shoulder, 29; symbol of official authority, 29.

Kneading-trough, indispensable article for domestic use, 46; for the poor, simply a wooden basin; for the rich, of copper or iron, 46.
Kohl, a black powder; how made, 249; how kept and applied, 249.
Koran, case of, very valuable; over four hundred gems in embroidered wrapper of, 131; the spirit of the, in regard to morning prayer, the same as Talmud, 253.

LAMECH confessed himself a murderer to his wives, 58.
Lamps, shallow oval vessels, made of baked clay, terra-cotta, bronze, and sometimes of precious metals, 41; specimens of, recovered and preserved in all important museums, 41; most ancient representations of, on Egyptian monuments, 41; some date before, or soon after, the birth of our Lord, 41; suspended from ceiling, or fixed on wall, 42; torches called, 42.
Lamp-wicks, 42.
Lares and penates, household gods, signified the same as teraphim; small figures in terra-cotta, wax, bronze, or silver, 260.
Law, Mosaic, a remarkable requirement of, 313.
Leah, the despised, 96.
Leben, sour milk, 183.
Letters, writing, formal and delegated to a public scribe; ancient, written on parchment; tablets for writing, in common use among Greeks and Romans, as well as Hebrews, 139; first one recorded in Bible, 141; to what use they are put, 141, 142; description of, 142.
Locks, description of, 28; inner chambers furnished with, 29.
Looking-glasses, important adjunct to the toilet; highly ornamented.

MANDRAKES, love-plants, particularly esteemed for their strong odors, 182.
Mamre, three angels appear to Abraham in the plains of, 165.
Manna, the "bread from heaven," 166.
Marriage, the patriarchal system; a feature in Eastern households strange to us, 53; a plurality of wives up to time of captivity opposed by Mosaic law, but not prohibited; polygamy not revolting as among pagan nations; rights of chief wife never disputed; those of inferior ones likewise well established; children of wives proper preferred in cases of inheritance, but all considered legitimate, 54; first instance of polygamy recorded in Bible found in family of descendant of the accursed Cain; law admonished kings especially not to multiply wives; David and Solomon distinguished examples of offenders against this restriction; polygamy unknown in Egypt; Hebrew practice, 58; between relatives preferred, 66; St. Paul's admonition, 66; proposal of, from family of bridegroom, 67; primitive idea for bride to be purchased, 67; no written contract of, required until after captivity; of Rebekah, 68; espousal as binding as the married state, 72; in Cana of Galilee, 77.
Materials, building, first described in Bible by Moses, 13; brick for stone, and slime for mortar, 13; earliest sun-dried bricks, 14; more lasting than marble or granite for, 14; superb palaces of kings of Nineveh, and the Nimrod pyramid, composed of this crude brick, 14; Babylonian edifices, faced with bricks, burned or highly glazed, 14; limestone and irregularly broken stone used for, 15.
Measures, the one in daily use in the kitchen was the one familiar to us in the parable of the leaven, 50; Roman bushel corresponded to our peck, 50; list of liquid and dry, 50, 51.
Meat, food in general terms, 44; offering of, always a vegetable sacrifice, 44; preparation of, 167; locust, especially interesting, 173; lessons drawn from subject of, and drinks, 201.
Medicine, art of, seldom alluded to; Mosaic code provided as wisely for physical as moral well-being, 365.
Mephibosheth, owed his life to the devotion of his nurse, 155.
Mesha, king of Moab, was a sheep-master, 333.
"Mesusah," description of the, 30; believed to avert disease, and forbid entrance of evil spirits, 30.
Metals and stones, precious, description

and enumeration of, 223, 224; superstitions in regard to, 224, 225; held in high esteem, 225; art of polishing, cutting, and mounting, 226; art of imitating true gems, 226.

Michal, deceit of, 37.

Mishnah, one of the Rabbinical law books, 145.

Moabitess maidens, 63.

Money, places for storing, and valuable articles, 308.

Mourning, of what it consisted, 389-392; ceremonial, 395; national ceremonial, 396.

Mortars, made of metal, earthenware, wood, or stone, mostly of stone, 46.

Mosaic law, a remarkable requirement of, 313.

Moses describes the bedstead of Og, king of Bashan, 37.

Mothers, Eastern, praise due, 106.

Mount of Olives, 196.

Mule, not known till time of David; fashionable for saddle use, 350; value of a white, in the East, at present day, is three or four times greater than that of an ordinary horse, 353.

Museum, British, the famous Rosetta Stone in, 134.

Music, both instrumental and vocal, filled an exalted office, 291; David endowed with remarkable musical gifts, and personally proficient on one instrument, 292; Babylonians extremely fond of; very meagre notice of in New Testament; allusion of Paul to, 298, 299.

Mujdeh, "good news," 95.

NAMES, always significant, 102; bestowed on daughters, expressive of personal charms or qualities, 103; Tamar, a favorite with the ancients, 104.

Nain, widow of, 64.

Naomi, took leave of daughters-in-law, 63; as a nurse, 155.

Necklaces, worn by both sexes, 219.

Nehemiah, report of, 174.

New Testament, sickness in the, 370, 371.

Nimrod, the "mighty hunter before the Lord," 170.

Nineveh and Babylon, many valuable books of stone found in, as well as bricks and tiles with inscriptions, 134.

Nitre, or *natron*, a salt, 247.

Nominalia, "name-days," 102.

Nose-jewels, peculiar to Oriental women, 219.

Nurse, an important personage in an Eastern family; repeated examples in Bible of her superiority and devotion; of Rebekah; in times of rebellion entire trust placed in, for safety of child, 109; position of, of great dignity and importance; authority inferior only to that of a parent; duties of, 155; notable examples of devotion of, 155, 156.

Nuts and almonds, 200; gifts of, sent by Jacob to Joseph in Egypt, 200.

OFFERINGS, according to Mosaic law, the mother brought prescribed, to the priest (forty days after birth of son, and eighty days after birth of daughter), 104; kind of, 105.

Og, king of Bashan, 37; alone remained of the remnant of giants, 37.

Oil, that from the olive-tree, 41; an indispensable element in cookery, 181; extracted by means of an oil-press; best obtained from unripe fruit, 331.

Ointments and perfumes, first mentioned in connection with the service of the tabernacle; Moses commanded to compound the sweet incense and holy anointing oil; into these compositions entered the precious spices; incense regarded as symbol of prayer, 232; this mode of worship by appeals to blind and deaf, 233; not used for medicinal purposes, 234; necessary to counteract offensive odors by, caused by defects of a sanitary character, 234.

Old Testament, allusions to vine and fruit of vine, in; replete with human interest; simile of our Lord in, 331.

Olive, culture of, only second to that of the vine; emblem of beauty; leaf of, symbol of peace, 181; description of; argument of Paul concerning, 331.

Orientals, water a luxury esteemed by, 22; large consumers of fish, 174; addicted to highly seasoned food, 178.

Ornamentation, 39; heads, legs, and even the entire bodies, of animals were favorite devices of, 39.

Ovens, houses in the cities provided with portable, of metal, earthenware, and stone, which were heated with grass, 44.

Ox, the most valuable possession of the herdsman; choice offerings for sacrifice; represented of great beauty and strength, 342; mourned with national honors; food of the, 345.

PALESTINE, contained costly residences other than royal, 15; mud hovels in, for poor, 15; vegetables of, 181; famous for grape-culture, 184; agricultural year of, divided into dry and rainy seasons, 319; best adapted to the cultivation of the grape; only right to pasturage in, 333.

Palm-tree, no branches of, properly speaking; immense leaves of; fruit of, 199.

Papyrus, used by Greeks and Romans for manuscripts; good for a great variety of purposes, 134.

Paranymph, 71; signification of, 73.

Passover, description of the, 273–276.

Paul, *dictum* of, to the church at Corinth, 164.

Pens, several varieties of; in early times common to paint letters with a hair-pencil, 139.

Performances, outward, substitution of, for the symbolical worship of the temple; showed a spiritual decline; studied informality of, afforded the best opportunities to preach gospel to common people, 288.

Persian king, the palace of the, upheld by "pillars of marble," 15.

Persians, introduced the extraordinary fashion of "dinner-beds," 150.

Phœnicians, excelled in art of dyeing, 207.

Phylacteries, use of, 205; instance of, in Deuteronomy, 205; of two sorts, 206; not worn by women, 206.

Physicians, highly esteemed, 368; ordained for every town, 369; Egyptian, invariably specialists, 375.

Pillows, ordinary, made of a goat's skin, and stuffed with wool, 37; that of the Saviour, rough cushion, on which rowers sat, 37.

Plague, the first sent upon Egypt a great calamity, 177.

Polygamy, Hebrew practice of, 58.

Pomegranate, admired for beauty of flowering-bush and agreeable fruit; color of flowers of; size of fruit of; its juice made into wine; used for decoration on account of its gracefulness, 200.

Processions, wedding, a peculiar feature of Oriental customs, 80; description of wedding, 81, 82; order in funeral, women first, 387, 388.

Prophets, sons of the, selected among young men of intellectual promise, who had completed a prescribed course of study; installed in sacred office of expounders of holy things to the people; few allusions to, 120.

QUEEN ESTHER, "banquet of wine" given to King Ahasuerus by, 30.

Queen of Sheba, 369.

RABBINICAL books, description of; common for private families to possess at least a portion of the, 137.

Raguel, 71.

Raisins, dried, important provision for domestic use, 192.

Records, many stone, invaluable as confirming Biblical facts; the famous Moabite Stone as an example of, discovered in 1868, 134.

Rhoda, the porter at gate of Mary's house, 27.

Rosetta stone, 134.

Romans, skilled in manufacture of colored inks; of invisible inks, 140.

Rome, book found in, made entirely of lead, 32.

Roofs, hemispherical, comparatively recent invention, adopted by the Saracens for their mosques and other public buildings, 18; conical, the precedent, 18; construction and description of flat, 18; places of conference and of recreation, 19; for sight-seeing, as windows were sparingly introduced, 19; places of safety, and used for domestic purposes, 20; places of mourning, as in case of Judith, 21; construction of, 21; growth of grass retarded on, 21; rudely constructed, 22.

Rooms, 35; reception-rooms on ground-floor, furnished at one end with a platform, covered with carpets and cushions, the corner being the seat of honor; here master of house received guests; converted into dormitories on cold nights, 35; connected with, were closets for storing bedding used at night, 36.

SACRED WRITINGS, the, abound in touching expressions of reverence for gray hairs, 230.

Salt, invested with peculiar significance; symbol of purity, 178; pledge of friendship, 181.

Samson, when taken captive by the Philistines, ground in the prison-house, 45; marriage of, 75.

Samuel, "communed with Saul upon the top of the house;" established theological seminaries in an heroic effort to restore purity of priesthood; through his influence schools were opened in Bethel, Jericho, Gilgal, and other cities, 129.

Sara, 71.

Sarah, joy of, 96.

Sardis, seat of one of the seven churches in Asia, celebrated for manufacture of children's toys, 111.

Saul, king, 37; David played to, 293.

Saviour, the, his parable of the two house-builders, 17; at the passover, 162; passion of, 188.

"Schools of the Prophets," theological seminaries, 129.

Science, medical; Egypt, seat of; its pursuit encouraged by government, 368.

Scribes, calling of, of acknowledged importance; occupied no mean position among their brethren; secular, military, and sacred, 134; multiplied to repair losses; pretentious, 138.

Seals, 142; devices preferred for, 143; scarabæus, a favorite design for, 143; used for other purposes than letters, 143.

Seats, appointment of, at feasts, 77.

Seir, cave-dwellings of, still to be seen, 9; used for shelter by shepherds, 9.

Sepia, a black secretion of the cuttle-fish, 140.

Servants, a numerous retinue of menial, 156; their duties, 156, 157.

Sheepfolds, walled structures, doorways of, carefully guarded, 337; like those of the present day, 338.

Sheep, as food, an abomination to the Egyptians, 168; care of, a most honorable employment; description of broad-tailed, 336, 337; animal of sacrifice, 337; symbol of meekness, 337.

Shekel (weight), subdivided for convenience, 49, 50.

Shell-fish, prohibited to Jews, 174.

"Shema," a sort of creed, composed of certain texts of Scripture, 289.

Shepherd-dog, a fine breed of, is found depicted on Babylonian sculptures, 335.

Shepherds, held in contempt by Egyptians, 333; privations of, 334; duty of, magnified, 335; weapons of; great attachment existing between, and sheep, 336.

Shibta, an evil spirit, 246.

Shushan, feast of, 159.

Sisera, killed by Jael, wife of Heber, 11.

Sistrum, sacred instrument of Egyptians, description of the, 298.

Slavery, found in Israel, in earliest records of the nation, but, like polygamy, humane and protective, 150; could last by law only six years, shorter for debt, 153; a peculiar feature of, exemplified in history of Joseph and in the elevation of Abraham's steward Eliezer, 154; in edifying contrast to that of heathen communities, 157.

Sling, apparently simple, but really formidable; Hebrews very skilful in use of, 335.

Soap, described, 246; soft, 247; nitre used for cleansing, 247.

Solomon, King, proverb of, 29; throne of, 30; sings of the fairest among women, "Thy stature is like to a palm-tree," 30; crown of, 78.

Son, given freedom, 116.

Sons of the Prophets, selected among young men of intellectual promise who had completed a prescribed course of study; installed in sacred office of expounders of holy things to the people; few allusions to, 129.

Sowing and reaping, the processes of, have furnished methods of instruction to sacred writers, 319.

Stadium (a ground for running), 114.

Steward, honorable office of, very ancient; what the office consisted of; special guardianship over son and heir of master, 154.

Stones, heap of, ancient mode of marking the ignominious grave, 385.
Stools, very general among early Hebrews, who were slow to adopt the effeminate custom of reclining on cushions, 40.
St. Paul, limiting the bishopric or deaconship in early Christian Church to the husband of one wife, 58, 59, 120; calling upon the Church to honor widows that are widows indeed, 64; familiarity of, with amusements, 114; words in reference to his active participation in Greek games, 114, 115.
St. Peter, in porch of palace of High Priest, 28.
Streets, crooked and narrow, as in Alexandria, Cairo, Jerusalem, and Damascus, 9.
Stylus, how employed, 139.
Synagogue, origin of the, is wrapped in obscurity; beginnings of the, discovered in the days of Ezra and Nehemiah; found in every town, while large cities had several, 286; highest ground selected for site; a meritorious act of devotion to build a, 287; earliest church edifices constructed on model of a, 288; main object of service of, was teaching, which included the reading of a portion of the law, 288, 289.
Syrian persecutions; monthly search of the Scriptures, a feature of, 137.

TABERNACLES, memorial feast of, a religious observance, 12; establishment of, 263; feast of, 277-279.
Table, reclining at, 160; ancient example of, 160.
Talith, "fringed garment," 125; description of, 204, 205.
Talmud, description of a bride in, 78; records the words of a celebrated Rabbi, in regard to theatres, 112, 113; parchment rolls for use of children, recorded in, 125; Jewish Bible, 253.
Tamar (palm-tree), a favorite name with the ancients, owing to the grace and beauty of the, 104; in the Old Testament are three notable instances of women who bore the name of, 104.
Tear-bottles, 397; usually buried with the dead, 398.
Tents, those familiar to us, more agreeable, 10; formed first of skins, then of cloth, 10; referred to, in Song of Solomon, 10; edges of covers of, furnished with leather loops fastened to ground by iron or wooden pins, 11; various shapes and sizes, 11; divided into separate apartments, 11; floors of, covered with mats or skins, 11; doors of, curtains of cloth, 12; doors of, served as places of worship, 12; solid foundations of, the common opinion, 16.
Teraphim, or images identical with *lares* and *penates* of Romans, a remarkable element in household worship, 259; rude representations of the human form, of various sizes, 259; rather consulted as oracles than worshipped as idols, 260.
Thanks, offering of, at the beginning of each meal, 162.
Theatres, erected in Jerusalem by Herod the Great, 112.
Thebes, ancient fresco from, depicts Hebrews making bricks as a punishment, 14.
Threshing-floors, always out of doors; the most famous is that of Ornan, serving the purpose of an entire village, 321; description of, 321, 322.
Timbrel, or tabret, identical with the familiar tambourine of our street-singers; very popular; examples of its use, 298.
Timothy, religious education of, 122, 125.
Title (sign) refers to a memorial tombstone, 385.
Tobias, 71.
Tobit, story of, 307.
Tombs, description of, 382, 383.
Tower of Babel, 13.
Toys, examples of, 111, 112.
Trades, a striking feature in education of Jewish children; considered vulgar by Greeks and Romans, honored by Jewish, 144; prejudice to tanners, dyers, and miners; engaged in, by scholars; that of Paul, 145; those of women, 146, 147; of perfumer and barber held in disrepute, 233; the fuller compelled to work outside the city, 247.
Travelling, usually in company, for safety, and to beguile the time; exemplified in the account of the Holy Family, 268; monotony of, relieved by music, 268; accommodations, the rudest, 271.

Treacle, a sort of, is obtained by boiling down the juice of grapes, 192.

Tribulum, a Roman threshing-sledge, heavy and sharply grinding, having given us the expressive word "tribulation," 322, 323.

Tyrian purple obtained from certain shell-fish; the imperial color, 207.

Tyropœon Valley, valley of cheesemongers, 184.

Unicorn, a powerful wild ox, to which Pliny gave the name of urus; stature scarcely below an elephant; represented in Assyrian sculptures, 346.

Utensils, exceedingly simple, 43; the hand-mill universally found in an Eastern kitchen, whether of the rich Dives or the destitute Lazarus, 44, 45; kneading-troughs, indispensable articles, 46; caldrons, pans and frying-pans, earthen vessels and brazen pots, bowls, cups, and spoons, and lordly dishes made of pure gold, 46, 47.

Veil, an important feature of Jewish bridal costume, 80; of Rebekah, 80; antiquity of; its use, 80.

Vellum, made of the inner side of the sheepskin; used for the Rabbinical books in preference to the papyrus, 137.

Verandas, description of, 23, 24.

Vinegar, or sour wine, several kinds of, were used as a beverage, or stimulating sauce, 195; offered by Boaz; description of, offered the Saviour, 195.

Vineyards, first planted by Noah, 324; extensively cultivated, 325; enclosed by stone walls, 326; privilege of poor in, 328.

Virgil, refers to "watering with the foot," 314.

Visits to the sick accounted a sacred obligation; held that this act of charity takes precedence of all others, 370.

Wailing-place of the Jews, 396.

Walled cities, 2.

Water-pots, 34; insignificant, except in royal houses, 34; characteristic feature of a Hebrew home, 47; used when large quantities of water were needed, as on festive occasions, 47.

Weights and measures, only those associated with the lessons of the New Testament are here considered; Hebrews required to be punctiliously just in matter of; inspectors of, required, 49; shekel, common in Mosaic period, 49; mineh and talent used, 50.

Wells, description of, 355, 356, 359.

Widow, the poor, 308.

Wilkinson, speaks of the high office of superintendent of the herds, 345.

Windows, description of, 26.

Wine, various sorts of, produced; that of Helbon and Lebanon particularly choice; accounted one of the great blessings; Noah, first cultivator of; used to great excess by succeeding generations, 187; words of Solomon in regard to; its beneficial qualities; mixed wine is diluted with water by Greeks and Romans, with spices and opiates by Hebrews, 188; custom of straining, 192; common, to cool, 192; an inexhaustible theme, 195.

Wine-presses, hewn out of ledges of rock; consisted of two parts, 327; some very ancient still remain, 328.

Wine-strainer, a very elegant, found in the ruins of Herculaneum, is described by Winckelmann, 192.

Wives, plurality of, 54.

Woman, occupy an important part in the sacred story, 59; Hebrew, not secluded after manner of other Orientals; rights of wives corresponded to those of husbands; position of a widow, or unmarried, especially in ancient times, unhappy and insecure; a husband's house only sure refuge of, from insult or neglect, and hence it was called by the Hebrews the woman's *menuchah* (rest); farewell of Naomi; Mosaic law provided for immediate protection of young widows; privilege of widows; Ruth, 63; the poor widow in the temple; expected to marry at seventeen or eighteen, twenty extreme limit, 64; wives chosen by parents, without interference of young people interested, 65.

Woods, principal, for furniture, were the date or the Theban palm, acacia and sycamore, the fir, ebony, and cedar being reserved for the finest cabinet-work, 39.

Worship, domestic and public; great stress laid on observances connected with devotion; he who prays in his house surrounds it with a wall of iron; custom of lights and prayers, 252; superior efficacy of morning prayer insisted upon, 253; the posture not arbitrarily described; attitude of Solomon, 254; places for, 255, 256; rebuke of Christ, 256; images an element in household, 259; divine institution of the tabernacle, 263.

Wrestlers, their feats, 113.

XENOPHON, represented as pursued by hounds, 350; wild ass described by, 350.

YOKE, passing under the, 317; "take my yoke upon you," 318.

ZACCHEUS, 307.
Zacharias naming his son, 139.
Zadok, 235.
Zendavesta, the, 379.
Zion, 321.

Citations from Scripture.

Citations from Scripture.

OLD TESTAMENT.

Reference	Page	Reference	Page	Reference	Page
Genesis ii. 3	257	Genesis xxiii.	382	Genesis xxxi. 27	291
ii. 8, 15	312	xxiii. 2	395	xxxi. 34	259, 346
ii. 22	88	xxiv. 4	66	xxxi. 39, 40	334
iii. 19	380	xxiv. 9–11, 20	359	xxxii. 14, 15	342
iii. 20	104	xxiv. 13, 15	147	xxxiii. 19	356
iii. 21	208, 304	xxiv. 22	221	xxxiv. 3, 4	65
iv. 17	2	xxiv. 45	47	xxxiv. 11, 12	68
iv. 19	58	xxiv. 58–67	68	xxxiv. 11, 16–20	359
iv. 21	291	xxiv. 61	267	xxxv. 4	220
v. 29	313	xxiv. 64	346	xxxv. 8	155, 306
ix. 20	313	xxiv. 65	80	xxxv. 19, 20	385
ix. 21	187	xxiv. 67	54	xxxv. 21	339
x. 9	170	xxv. 11	304	xxxvi. 24	350
xi. 2–4	13	xxv. 31	94	xxxvii. 5, 6	320
xiii. 7	341	xxv. 59	155	xxxvii. 18	221
xiv. 6	9	xxvi. 20	341	xxxvii. 24	350
xiv. 20	300	xxvi. 23	162	xxxvii. 25, 28	346
xvi. 3	57	xxvi. 35	65	xxxvii. 34	300
xvii. 5, 15	101	xxvii. 14	178	xxxviii. 6	65
xvii. 12	101	xxvii. 26, 27	235	xxxviii. 14	80
xviii. 1	12, 304	xxvii. 46	65	xxxix. 24	374
xviii. 6	31, 147, 165	xxviii. 22	300	xl. 11	326
xviii. 7	167	xxix. 9	148, 333	xl. 16	48
xviii. 8	182	xxix. 19	66	xlii. 42	142, 219
xix. 30	10	xxix. 26	67	xlii. 43	268
xxi. 6, 7	99	xxix. 32–35	102	xlii. 48	324
xxi. 8	106	xxx. 1	92	xliii. 17	271
xxi. 14	48	xxx. 1, 4	57	xliii. 38	231
xxi. 21	65	xxx. 14–16	182	xliii. 11	200
xxi. 31	356	xxx. 21	104	xliii. 21	271
xxii. 3	268	xxxi. 14, 15	95	xliii. 32–34	161

CITATIONS FROM SCRIPTURE.

Reference	Page
GENESIS xliv. 2, 5	262
xlvi. 4	372
xlvi. 34	392
xlvii. 29–31	379
xlix.	371
xlix. 17	353
xlix. 31	382
l. 2, 3	375
l. 7–10	386
l. 9	353
l. 25	379
l. 26	276
EXODUS ii. 5	242
ii. 16	148, 333
ii. 21	67
iii. 1	333
iii. 7, 8	313
iii. 8	184
xii. 11	274
xii. 19	274
xii. 26, 27	274
xii. 29	273
xii. 34	46
xiii. 1–10	204
xiii. 11–16	204
xiv. 7	354
xv. 1, 20	291
xv. 20	285
xvi. 4, 13–15, 31	166
xvi. 23, 26	257
xvi. 32	51
xvii. 6	278
xix. 17	73
xx. 8–12	257
xxi. 5, 6	153
xxi. 9	150
xxi. 15	116
xxi. 19	367
xxi. 28	345
xxii. 26, 27	208
xxiii. 14, 17	261
xxiii. 25, 26	366
xxiv. 10	225
xxv. 4, 5	204
xxv. 8	263
xxv. 16	263
xxvii. 20	41
xxviii. 11	143
xxviii. 11	223
xxviii. 33, 34	200
xxx. 13	50
xxx. 23, 34	232
EXODUS xxx. 32, 37	233
xxxiii. 10, 11	11
xxxv. 2, 3	257
xxxv. 25, 26	146
xxxvi. 6	149
xxxviii. 8	222
xl. 15	235
LEVITICUS iii. 9	337
vi. 28	46
xi. 4	349
xi. 23, 43	192
xi. 35	44
xii. 8	108
xiv. 13	51
xiv. 34	31
xvi. 21, 22	283
xvi. 29, 30	282
xviii. 6–18	66
xix. 9, 10	300
xix. 10	328
xix. 27	227
xix. 32	230
xix. 35, 36	49
xx. 9	116
xxi. 1–4, 10, 11	388
xxiii. 5	273
xxiii. 40, 42	278
xxiii. 40–43	13
xxv. 4	313
xxv. 23	313
xxv. 39–41	150
xxvii. 32	338
NUMBERS iii. 13	94
vi. 23–26	289
xi. 5	177, 181
xi. 8	46
xi. 12	110
xv. 38, 39	204
xviii. 21	300
xix. 11, 14	386
xx. 5	200
xxii. 24	326
xxiv. 5, 6	11
xxvii. 8	95
xxxii. 16, 17, 26	5
DEUTERONOMY ii. 23	2
vi. 4–9	204
vi. 6, 7	121
vi. 10, 11	5
vi. 11	313
viii. 8, 9	167
xi. 10, 11	314
DEUTERONOMY xi. 13–21	204
xi. 18, 20	30
xiv. 1	250, 392
xiv. 7	354
xiv. 28, 29	306
xv. 11	303
xv. 14	153
xvii. 17	58
xviii. 9, 14	262
xviii. 18	92
xx. 5	32
xx. 7	83
xxi. 10–14	57
xxi. 15–17	58
xxi. 18–21	116
xxii. 8	18
xxii. 10	92
xxiii. 25	166, 328
xxiv. 1	86
xxiv. 5	83
xxiv. 6	46
xxiv. 13	208
xxiv. 20	181
xxv. 5, 6	63
xxv. 9	218
xxv. 9, 10	63
xxv. 13–15	49
xxvi. 2	277
xxvii. 16	116
xxviii. 5	48
xxviii. 26	378
xxxiii. 19	177
xxxiv. 3	196
xxxiv. 6	304
JOSHUA i. 23	222
ii. 6	20
vii. 21	210
vii. 26	385
viii. 29	385
viii. 30, 32	133
xv. 19, 17	67
JUDGES iii. 20	24
iii. 23, 25	29
iii. 31	317
v.	292
v. 10	350
v. 24–27	11
v. 25	183
v. 28–31	27
vi. 2	10
vi. 11	322

CITATIONS FROM SCRIPTURE. 423

Reference	Page	Reference	Page	Reference	Page
Judges vi. 19	49	1 Samuel xxv. 18.	166, 168, 192, 196	1 Kings xvii. 19.	24
vii. 16	42	xxv. 20	350	xviii. 33	47
viii. 21	349	xxvi. 12	37	xix. 6	37, 43
ix. 27	228	xxviii. 24	167	xxi. 8	141
x. 4	350	xxxi. 12	374	xxii. 39	15
xi. 34	208	2 Samuel i. 10	221	2 Kings i. 2	26
xii. 14	350	i. 11, 12	390	i. 4	36
xiii. 7	232	i. 24	208	ii. 3, 5, 7	129
xiv. 1, 2	65	ii. 14, 16	113	iii.	134
xiv. 10, 11	76	iii. 31	376	iii. 4	339
xvi. 3	6	iii. 31-35	395	iv. 1, 2. 3, 43	129
xvi. 21	45	iii. 35	389	iv. 2	47
xx. 16	114, 335	vi. 5	296	iv. 10	40
xxi. 21	285	vi. 14, 16	286	iv. 22, 24	350
Ruth i. 9	63	xi. 2	19, 23	v. 5	142
ii. 7	320	xi. 14, 15	141	v. 9	208
ii. 8, 9	148	xii. 15-23	394	v. 23	223
ii. 14	162, 166	xii. 20	296	vi. 1, 2	129
ii. 15, 16	303	xiii. 18	210	vi. 25	51
ii. 17	322	xiii. 29	350	vii. 1	6
iii. 3	236	xiii. 31	390	ix. 30	250
iii. 7	322	xiv. 26	232	ix. 30, 32, 33	26
iii. 15	204	xv. 30	214, 217	xi. 2	37
iv. 1, 2	9	xvi. 1	192	xx. 9, 11	308
iv. 7	218	xvii. 18, 19	300	xxi. 18, 26	382
iv. 16	155	xvii. 28	183	xxiii. 11	355
1 Samuel i. 3	207	xvii. 29	183, 184	xxiii. 17, 18	385
i. 9	40	xviii. 9	353	xxiii. 24	260
i. 24	166	xviii. 17, 18	385	xxv. 12	326
ii. 1	96	xviii. 27	113	1 Chronicles ii. 34, 35,	154
ii. 19	207	xviii. 32, 33	394	xii. 2	114
iii. 1	109	xviii. 33	25	xiii. 8	292
iv. 12	113	xix. 4	25, 394	xv. 28	292
iv. 18	40	xix. 37	379	xxi. 18-25	321
viii. 13	233	1 Kings i. 9	168	xxiii. 5	293
ix. 3	333	i. 39	235	xxvii. 25	324
ix. 11	147	i. 40	294	xxvii. 28	181
x. 5, 10	129	ii. 10	380	xxvii. 29	342
xvi. 11	333	iv. 23	168, 345	xxix. 2	15
xvi. 16	293	iv. 25	328	2 Chronicles ii. 10	51
xvii. 18	184	vii. 26	242	iv. 2	242
xvii. 34	334	viii. 22	255	v. 13	294
xvii. 40	336	x. 2	346	vi. 13	254
xviii. 27	67	x. 18-20	40	ix. 11	296
xix. 13	37	x. 21	47	xi. 11	181
xix. 13, 16	260	x. 26, 28, 29	353	xvi. 12	306
xix. 19, 20	129	xi. 1, 3	58	xvi. 14	374
xix. 24	203	xi. 43	380	xxii. 12	156
xx. 36	92	xiv. 6	221	xxv. 25	395
xxi. 7	342	xvii. 12	47	xxvi. 10	328
xxv. 1	381	xvii. 13	43	xxviii. 27	380
xxv. 4	342			xxxii. 33	381

CITATIONS FROM SCRIPTURE.

	Page		Page		Page
EZRA vi. 15, 16, 17	32	PSALMS xli. 9	272	PROVERBS vii. 16	38
NEHEMIAH iii. 3	174	xliv. 11	168	ix. 2, 3	74
v. 18	168	xlv. 7, 8	234	x. 26	195
vi. 5	142	xlv. 8	15	xi. 1	52
vii. 68	353	xlv. 13, 14	210	xl. 22	220
viii. 15, 16	278	xlviii. 1, 2	264	xii. 27	170
xii. 27	32	xlix. 9	310	xv. 17	168, 345
xiii. 16	174	l. 4	322	xvi. 11	52
xiii. 24	286	li. 2, 7, 10	242	xvi. 31	230
ESTHER i. 5, 6	23	lii. 8	181	xvii. 19	29
i. 6	15, 206	lv. 17	252	xix. 18	119
i. 7	47	lvi. 8	308	xx. 13	21
ii. 8, 12	248	lxii. 9	52	xxi. 20	230
iii. 10–12	142	lxv. 9–13	317	xxi. 31	354
vi. 12	214	lxviii. 35	208	xxii. 6	121
vii. 8	30	lxix. 21	195	xxii. 15	119
viii. 15	207	lxix. 22	161	xxiii. 13, 14	119
ix. 22, 28	280	lxxi. 18	231	xxiii. 29–32	188
xv. 6	207	lxxix. 1, 6–8	397	xxiv. 31	326
JOB i. 3	341	lxxx. 12, 13	326	xxv. 13	192
i. 20	390	lxxxi. 2	206	xxv. 16, 27	184
iv. 19	16	lxxxi. 16	184	xxv. 20	195
v. 24	84	lxxxviii. 4	384	xxvii. 15	21
vi. 2	51	lxxxviii. 13	253	xxvii. 23–27	342
vi. 6	178	xc. 10	366	xxx. 33	183
viii. 5	51	xci. 3	170	xxxi. 4–7	188
x. 10	184	xcii. 10	236	xxxi. 10–31	60
xii. 7	51	xcviii. 6	295	xxxi. 13, 19	146
xiii. 4	371	civ. 15	187, 319	xxxi. 18	40
xx. 17	183	cvii. 16	6	xxxi. 24	208
xxi. 12	208	cviii. 2	206	ECCLESIASTES i. 9	206
xxiv. 3	349	cix. 19	303	ii. 4	33
xxiv. 16	16	cxvi. 9	379	ii. 6	314
xxix. 11–16	307	cxix. 62	252	vii. 2	308
xxx. 1	335	cxix. 83	48	vii. 6	44
xxx. 6	9	cxix. 148	252	ix. 9	84
xxxi. 6	51	cxxi. 8	30	ix. 11	114
xxxi. 17	272	cxxiii. 2	157	xii. 5	201, 392
xxxvii. 18	222	cxxvi. 6	320	SONG OF SOLOMON i. 2,	195
xxxviii. 6, 16	225	cxxvii.	84	i. 5,	10
xxxviii. 9	100	cxxviii. 2, 3	35	i. 10	223
xxxviii. 14	143	cxxviii. 3	331	ii. 12, 14	24
xxxix. 10	319	cxxix. 6, 7	22	ii. 13	196
xxxix. 19–25	354	cxxxii. 3	30	iii. 6	235
xlii. 15	95	cxxxiii. 2	236	iii. 9	38
PSALMS v. 3	253	cxxxvii. 1–6	290	iv. 1	228
xvi. 10	308	cxlix. 3	286	iv. 2	235
xix. 5	114	cl. 4	286	iv. 11	183
xxii. 12	345	PROVERBS v. 15	360	v. 1	184
xxiii. 1–6	364	v. 18, 19	84	v. 2	27, 225
xxxiii. 2	286	v. 25	251	v. 4	28
xxxiv. 20	274	vii. 3	206	v. 11	229

CITATIONS FROM SCRIPTURE.

	Page		Page		Page
Song of Solomon, vi. 7,	200	Jeremiah vi. 9	48	Hosea iii. 4	260
vi. 11	200	vi. 26	391	iv. 12	261
vii. 13	182	vii. 17, 18	261	vii. 1	196
viii. 2	200	vii. 34	81	vii. 4, 6	165
xxv. 16, 27	184	viii. 16	354	vii. 9	231
Isaiah i. 8	321	viii. 22	369	xiii. 3	31
iii. 21	219	ix. 17, 18, 20	392	xiv. 7	187
iii. 24	229	xvi. 6, 7	388	Joel ii. 12, 13	391
v. 5	327	xvi. 5–7	393	Amos i. 7, 10, 12, 14	6
v. 11, 22	187	xvii. 1	139, 225	ii. 13	321
v. 28	355	xx. 15	95	iii. 12	38
vii. 14	93	xxi. 4	208	iii. 15	15
vii. 15	183	xxii. 14	15, 33	v. 16	392
ix. 3	320	xxii. 18, 19	395	v. 11	15
ix. 6	29	xxxi. 15	393	vi. 4	38
xv. 3	396	xxxii. 13	338	vi. 6	236
xvi. 10	328	xxxvi. 22, 23	31	vii. 14	196
xix. 7	134	xxxvi. 23	131, 139	ix. 9	323
xix. 8, 10	177	xxxvi. 30	378	Micah iv. 4	196, 328
xix. 9	146	xxxvii. 21	165	iv. 8	339
xx. 3	217	xxxviii. 6	359	vi. 11	52
xxii. 1, 2	20	xli. 8	324	xl. 12	52
xxii. 16	382	xlvi. 11	369	Nahum iii. 14	14
xxii. 22	29	Lamentations iv. 4	92	Habakkuk i. 8	354
xxii. 24	102	Ezekiel i. 26	225	iii. 17, 18	364
xxvii. 2	187	iv. 9	182	Zechariah viii. 5	111
xxviii. 1, 7	187	v. 1	228	ix. 9	268
xxviii. 4	196	ix. 2	140	xi. 12, 23	382
xxviii. 24, 25	310	xiii. 10, 11	16	xlii. 6	273
xxviii. 27, 28	322	xvi. 4	99	Malachi ii. 14–16	91
xxx. 24	322, 345	xvi. 8–13	79	iii. 2	246
xxx. 29	208	xvi. 9	236	Tobit ii. 11, 12	147
xxxii. 20	319	xvi. 13	210	iv. 8, 11, 16	307
xxxiv. 4	132	xxi. 21	261	iv. 12	66
xxxviii. 18	384	xxiii. 12, 15	207	vi., vii., x.	71
xxxviii. 21	368	xxiii. 40	250	xi.	54
xl. 11	338	xxiii. 41	39	Judith viii. 5	21
xl. 15	40	xxiv. 17	217	viii. 5, 6	392
xl. 22	10	xxvii. 7, 16, 24	207	x. 3, 4	251
xli. 15	321	xxvii. 18	187	xii. 1, 2	163
xlii. 3	43	xxviii. 13	223	xii. 15	11
xlv. 2	6	xxxvii. 12–14	379	xvi. 9	217
xlvii. 2	46	xxxix. 18	345	xvi. 19	38
xlix. 23	100	xliv. 20	227	Ecclesiasticus vii. 24,	119
liii. 5, 6	284	Daniel i. 5, 8	163	xxx. 1, 2, 9–12	119
lx. 4	110	iii. 4	297	xxx. 15, 17	306
lxiii. 2, 3	328	iii. 21	213	xxxi. 27–29	188
lxiv. 9–11	397	iv. 30	19	xxxii. 5, 6	291
Jeremiah ii. 13	360	v. 27	52	xxxvii. 30, 31	306
ii. 22	246	vi. 10	255	xxxviii.	368
iv. 13	354	vi. 17	143	xxxviii. 16–18	398
iv. 30	250	vii. 9	231	xlii. 9	119

Baruch vi. 32 . . . 389	History of Susanna i. 17 246	1 Maccabees iv. . . 280
History of Susanna i. 15 23	1 Maccabees i. 56, 57, 137	xiii. 27–29 . . . 385
		2 Maccabees iv. 12 . 213

NEW TESTAMENT.

Matthew i. 18, 19 . . 72	Matthew xxii. 2–4 . . 74	Mark xiv. 3 237
ii. 16 303	xxii. 4 168	xiv. 7 303
iii. 4 173	xxii. 11 76	xiv. 8 150
iii. 11 157	xxii. 41 255	xiv. 20 162
iii. 12 322	xxiii. 5 204	xiv. 26 275
v. 1, 2 128	xxiii. 6 . . . 77, 288	xiv. 52 204
v. 13 178	xxiii. 23 178	xv. 23 188
v. 15 . . . . 41, 50	xxiii. 24 192	xv. 42 257
v. 36 231	xxiii. 27 383	xvi. 4 383
vi. 1–4 307	xxiii. 37 169	Luke i. 46–55 . . . 99
vi. 6 255	xxiv. 319	i. 58 99
vi. 17, 18 237	xxiv. 17 20	i. 59–63 102
vi. 19 16	xxiv. 41 . . . 35, 45	i. 62, 63 139
vi. 25, 33 201	xxv. 81	ii. 7 . . . . 99, 271
vi. 28, 29 289	xxv. 32 341	ii. 8 340
vi. 30 44	xxv. 35–40 311	ii. 12 99
vii. 13, 14 9	xxvi. 17 276	ii. 21 101
vii. 46 289	xxvi. 27, 28, 29 . . . 195	ii. 22, 24 105
viii. 16, 17 371	xxvi. 30 255	ii. 35 388
ix. 6 36	xxvi. 55 128	ii. 41 267
ix. 15 73	xxvi. 65 390	ii. 43, 44 271
ix. 17 48	xxvii. 5–8 381	ii. 49 146
ix. 23 392	xxvii. 34 195	ii. 51, 52 120
x. 30 231	xxvii. 46, 50 . . . 277	iii. 11 303
xi. 29, 30 318	xxvii. 60 383	iv. 16–19 132
xii. 5 258	xxvii. 66 143	iv. 20 128
xiii. 3 319	Mark i. 7 157	iv. 22 289
xiii. 30 324	ii. 3, 4 22	iv. 32 289
xiii. 35 289	ii. 4 36	v. 6 177
xiii. 45 225	ii. 16 163	v. 18 36
xiii. 54 289	iii. 6 259	vi. 1 166
xiv. 20 49	iv. 38 37	vi. 6 170
xv. 6 116	v. 2, 3, 8, ... 383	vi. 11 259
xv. 34 177	v. 38 392	vi. 47–49 17
xv. 37 49	vii. 3, 4 245	vii. 4, 5 287
xvi. 19 29	ix. 3 248	vii. 15 64
xix. 3–8 86	x. 10 86	vii. 31, 32 111
xix. 10 86	x. 12 86	vii. 32 294
xix. 13 106	x. 14, 16 106	vii. 34 163
xix. 24 9	xi. 25 255	vii. 38 160
xxi. 4 368	xii. 1 327	vii. 41 . . . 214, 232
xxi. 13 310	xii. 37 401	vii. 44–46 237
xxi. 15, 16 279	xii. 43, 44 64	viii. 43 371

CITATIONS FROM SCRIPTURE. 427

	Page		Page		Page
Luke x. 34	238	John ix. 1, 2	365	Acts xvi. 13	290
x. 35	271	ix. 8	310	xviii. 3	145
x. 39	128	ix. 44	373	xix. 24, 35	260
x. 41, 42	150	x. 3–5	336	xx. 8	25
xi. 7	35	x. 11, 12	335	xx. 24	114
xi. 12	170	x. 12	338	xxii. 3	128
xii. 18	324	x. 22, 23	280	xxvi. 14	317
xii. 33	308	xi. 3, 17	386	Romans vii. 2	88
xii. 35	208	xi. 31, 39	390	xi. 24	331
xiii. 6	328	xi. 55	267	xii. 15	398
xiii. 14	259	xii. 24	320	xiv. 17	200
xiii. 21	50	xiii. 4	204	xv. 26	308
xiii. 25	82	xiii. 18	272	1 Corinthians iv. 11,	
xiv. 8–10	77	xiii. 23	160	12	145
xiv. 14	304	xiii. 26	162	v. 7	276
xiv. 16, 17	74	xv. 1, 5	331	vii. 10–16	86
xiv. 20	83	xv. 15	158	vii. 22	158
xiv. 28	327	xvii. 1	255	vii. 30	308
xv. 23	168	xviii. 3	42	vii. 39	66
xv. 56	335	xix. 23	203	viii. 13	202
xvi. 5–7	50	xix. 36	274	x. 16	162
xvi. 20	311	xix. 38–40	373	x. 25, 31, 32	165
xvii. 11	170	xix. 41, 42	383	x. 31	202
xix. 8	307	xx. 6, 7	374	xi. 15	228
xx. 29–33	64	xxi. 5	44	xi. 26	331
xx. 35, 36	64	xxi. 6	177	xiii. 1	297
xx. 46, 47	138	xxi. 7	203	xiii. 3	311
xxi. 1–4	308	xxi. 9, 13	177	2 Corinthians iii. 18	222
xxi. 5	309	Acts i. 5	277	v. 21	284
xxii. 21	162	i. 12	271	vi. 14	86
xxii. 31	323	i. 12, 13, 14	26	xi. 2	73
xxiii. 54	257	i. 18, 19	381	xvi. 15	308
xxiv. 30, 31	162	ii. 5	272	xvi. 19	288
xxiv. 42	178	ii. 15	254	Galatians iii. 24	125
John ii. 6	47, 51	ii. 17	277	iv. 1, 2	155
ii. 8	77, 157	ii. 29	380	v. 1	318
ii. 14–16	310	ii. 31	399	vi. 11	143
iii. 29	73	ii. 40	288	Ephesians iii. 14	255
iv. 7	147	iii. 2	311	v. 19	290
iv. 9	163	v. 6	373	v. 33	84
iv. 12	356	v. 6, 10	386	vi. 1–14	120
iv. 28	47	v. 15	36	vi. 5, 9	158
iv. 31, 32, 34	200	viii. 27	208	vi. 14	208
v. 9	36	ix. 36	308	Colossians iii. 16	290
vi.	177	ix. 36, 43	174	iv. 15	288
vi. 11	162	ix. 37	25, 373	iv. 18	143
vi. 27	200	x. 9	19, 256	1 Thessalonians iv.	
vi. 51, 55	200	x. 12	164	13, 14	395
vi. 59	287	x. 28	164	2 Thessalonians iii.	
vii. 32	289	x. 31	308	17	143
vii. 37	279	xii. 10	6	1 Timothy i. 10	400
viii. 2	128	xii. 13, 14	27	ii. 8	255

	Page		Page		Page
1 Timothy ii. 10	149	Philemon 2	288	Revelation ii. 1	41
iii. 2, 12	59	Hebrews ii. 15	400	ii. 17	369
iii. 4, 5	120	x. 1, 4	340	iii. 20	27
iii. 12	120	xi. 37	208	vii. 9, 14	248
v. 3, 11	64	xi. 38	10	viii. 3	232
v. 5, 10, 11, 14	149	James i. 12	398	xiii. 8	276
2 Timothy ii. 26	170	i. 23	222	xiv. 2, 3	299
iii. 14, 15	125	v. 14	211, 370	xv. 3	299
iv. 7, 8	114	1 Peter iii. 4	104, 149	xvii. 4	225
iv. 13	131	iii. 5, 6	59	xix. 7	88
Titus ii. 3–5	149	Revelation i. 13	208	xxi. 19, 20	224

www.ingramcontent.com/pod-product-compliance
Lightning Source LLC
Chambersburg PA
CBHW022143300426
44115CB00006B/327